Financial Management

(TEXT CUM SUGGESTED ANSWERS)

Financial Management

(TEXT CUM SUGGESTED ANSWERS)

CA C Rama Gopal
Fellow of ICA (I), ICS (I)
&
Associate Member of Indian Institute of Bankers

NEW AGE MANAGEMENT

An Imprint of

NEW AGE INTERNATIONAL (P) LIMITED, PUBLISHERS
LONDON • NEW DELHI • NAIROBI
Bangalore • Chennai • Cochin • Guwahati • Hyderabad • Kolkata • Lucknow • Mumbai
Visit us at www.newagepublishers.com

Published by New Age International (P) Ltd., Publishers
Fourth Edition: 2008
Reprint: 2017

GLOBAL OFFICES

- **New Delhi** **NEW AGE INTERNATIONAL (P) LIMITED, PUBLISHERS**
7/30 A, Daryaganj, New Delhi-110002, (INDIA)
Tel.: (011) 23253771, 23253472, **Telefax:** 23267437, 43551305
E-mail: contactus@newagepublishers.com • Visit us at www.newagepublishers.com
- **London** **NEW AGE INTERNATIONAL (UK) LTD.**
27 Old Gloucester Street, London, WC1N 3AX, UK
E-mail: info@newacademicscience.co.uk • Visit us at www.newacademicscience.co.uk
- **Nairobi** **NEW AGE GOLDEN (EAST AFRICA) LTD.**
Ground Floor, Westlands Arcade, Chiromo Road (Next to Naivas Supermarket)
Westlands, Nairobi, KENYA, **Tel.:** 00-254-713848772, 00-254-725700286
E-mail: kenya@newagepublishers.com

BRANCHES

- **Bangalore** 37/10, 8th Cross (Near Hanuman Temple), Azad Nagar, Chamarajpet, Bangalore- 560 018
Tel.: (080) 26756823, **Telefax:** 26756820, **E-mail: bangalore@newagepublishers.com**
- **Chennai** 26, Damodaran Street, T. Nagar, Chennai-600 017, **Tel.:** (044) 24353401, **Telefax:** 24351463
E-mail: chennai@newagepublishers.com
- **Cochin** CC-39/1016, Carrier Station Road, Ernakulam South, Cochin-682 016, **Tel.:** (0484) 2377303, **Telefax:** 4051304
E-mail: cochin@newagepublishers.com
- **Guwahati** Hemsen Complex, Mohd. Shah Road, Paltan Bazar, Near Starline Hotel, Guwahati-781 008,
Tel.: (0361) 2513881, **Telefax:** 2543669, **E-mail: guwahati@newagepublishers.com**
- **Hyderabad** 105, 1st Floor, Madhiray Kaveri Tower, 3-2-19, Azam Jahi Road, Near Kumar Theater, Nimboliadda Kachiguda, Hyderabad-500 027, **Tel.:** (040) 24652456, **Telefax:** 24652457
E-mail: hyderabad@newagepublishers.com
- **Kolkata** RDB Chambers (Formerly Lotus Cinema) 106A, 1st Floor, S N Banerjee Road, Kolkata-700 014
Tel.: (033) 22273773, **Telefax:** 22275247, **E-mail: kolkata@newagepublishers.com**
- **Lucknow** 16-A, Jopling Road, Lucknow-226 001, **Tel.:** (0522) 2209578, 4045297, **Telefax:** 2204098
E-mail: lucknow@newagepublishers.com
- **Mumbai** 142C, Victor House, Ground Floor, N.M. Joshi Marg, Lower Parel, Mumbai-400 013
Tel.: (022) 24927869, **Telefax:** 24915415, **E-mail: mumbai@newagepublishers.com**
- **New Delhi** 22, Golden House, Daryaganj, New Delhi-110 002, **Tel.:** (011) 23262368, 23262370, **Telefax:** 43551305
E-mail: sales@newagepublishers.com

ISBN: 978-81-224-2206-1

C-16-10-9691

Printed in India at Saras Graphics, Rai, Haryana.
Typeset at In-house

NEW AGE INTERNATIONAL (P) LIMITED, PUBLISHERS
7/30 A, Daryaganj, New Delhi-110002
Visit us at **www.newagepublishers.com**
(CIN: U74899DL1966PTC004618)

DEDICATED TO

LORD VENKATESWARA

PREFACE —SHARING MY THOUGHTS

I did not wish to write a bulky book on 'Financial Management'. Many books are, already available, belonging to that category. My wish is to present a simple book to my students, straight to the point, with emphasis on the concepts' clarity, to meet the needs for examination and creation of interest on the subject.

When so many books on the subject are available, some by renowned authors, I had a haunting feeling what I can contribute, additionally, by writing a book, again. Answer to this pertinent question has been found from the behaviour of my students. They experience difficulty in understanding the subject and, equally, failures in the subject are more compared to other subjects, in MBA. This is a paradox, when books on the subject are plenty.

A detailed interaction with my students has revealed that they want a student-friendly book, simple and straight in language, easy to remember the concepts with total clarity. The non-commerce students, a recent upsurge in admissions to MBA, have been more vocal in explaining their difficulties to understand the subject. More so, the book should not be bulky to create fear before they begin to read! Many universities have begun to give more importance, in examinations, in allocating good number of marks to objective questions and existing books have not given exhaustive coverage for this new area, from the view point of examination. My students have desired to have a book, filling these gaps. I have found an answer, why I have to write a book!

My trip to U.S.A. with a long vacation of six months has given me the required time to satisfy me and the need of my students -THE BOOK THEY WANT- is before them, now.

This book totally covers the UGC syllabus of MBA students, comprehensively. In this process, many university students' requirements are covered, to a large extent, as a greater number of institutions have, involuntarily, chosen same topics in their syllabus too.

During my inter action and long observation, **majority of students and, in particular, working executives, busy with their employment, start preparing, a couple of weeks before the commencement of examinations.** To facilitate them for quick and easy understanding, **Review Questions provide the necessary clues (reference to paragraphs, broadly) for finding answers, quickly, and also serving as a ready suggested answer book**. This also helps serious students too, for a quick revision, just before exams.

My Director Shri P.K.Chopra has inspired me to do **"RAMDEV YOGA"**. In fact, he has been after me till I made a beginning of YOGA as I have been showing excuses, initially, to start with. He has not left me until I made a beginning. I owe and show my gratitude, recording this, to him for inspiring and showing the doors of good health. I have attended yoga classes, earlier, elsewhere, too, and attempted to do, but the results have always been not comfortable, resulting in exhaustion and occasional fever. The focus of this yoga is to do in a natural manner, at one's own pace. I have secured health and peace of mind, not only in my life, but my wife and children too have been benefited, whom I have motivated to do. This has helped my family, greatly, to keep depression, at a distance. I make this specific mention and appeal my students to do Yoga to achieve better concentration and memory.

What more is needed in life than health, peace of mind and occasional writing a few books to satisfy the eagerly waiting students? Incidentally, to satisfy me, personally, my brother **Dr. C. Srinivasulu**, a great admirer of mine to see me as an author in the family, puts it?

I record my affection and respects to my father Late C. Kameswara Rao, mother Rajeswari and Ammumma for what I am today.

I have been inspired to write this book with the overwhelming success of my previous book, in the last year, by the present publishers. My book- "EXPORT-IMPORT PROCEDURES, DOCUMENTATION AND LOGISTICS" has been well received by my students, complimenting me for the student-friendly concise presentation of book. I thank them for making the book to go for reprint, within six months of its first appearance.

I have read the following statement from the career of an NRI who has turned into a global awe inspiring person, with his achievement and his simple belief has inspired me and, may be my students too.

"Many obstacles can come on the road from the first inner conception of an idea to its actual material realisation. But a resolute purpose, faith, hope, and a calm steady effort can enable even seemingly ordinary people to accomplish extraordinary feats. But, you must never consider yourself to be just ordinary."

The best thing that has happened in my life is to marry Sandhya as my partner. What I can give, in return, except expressing my mute love to her for her affection, care, balancing the whole family, and above all meticulous planning, behind me, for reaching the heights in my life with which I am happy.

I have my family members Radhi, Kalyan, Dheera and Kish, and my lovely little American grandsons – Theer and Tarkh- who have extended their support in one way or other, not preventing me to write, to steer the book to a happy ending.

My typed script of this book has been ready and is eager for a good

proof reader, before it goes for print. Luckily, my second daughter- Dheera, a double masters in finance in India and CPA from America-has returned after my return to spend vacation for a couple of months. She has given the necessary treatment for this book in proof reading.

I give credit to Mr. Pankaj Kalmegh, of M/s New Age International Private Ltd. for his coordination and excellent follow up in getting it printed, at the earliest.

Prof. C. Rama Gopal

Contents

1

AIMS AND FUNCTIONS OF FINANCE

1.1 INTRODUCTION

Financial Management is nothing but management of the limited financial resources the organisation has, to its utmost advantage. Resources are always limited, compared to its demands or needs.

This is the case with every type of organisation. Proprietorship or limited company, be it public or private, profit oriented or even non-profitable organisation.

1.2 FINANCE FUNCTION– IMPORTANCE

In general, the term "Finance" is understood as provision of funds as and when needed. Finance is the essential requirement *–sine qua non–* of every organisation.

Required Everywhere: All activities, be it production, marketing, human resources development, purchases and even research and development, depend on the adequate and timely availability of finance both for commencement and their smooth continuation to completion. Finance is regarded as the life-blood of every business enterprise.

Efficient Utilisation More Important: Finance function is the most important function of all business activities. The efficient management of business enterprise is closely linked with the efficient management of its finances. The need of finance starts with the setting up of business. Its growth and expansion require more funds. The funds have to be raised from various sources. The sources have to be selected keeping in relation to the implications, in particular, risk attached. Raising of money, alone, is not important. Terms and conditions while raising money are more important. Cost of funds is an important element. Its utilisation is rather more important. If funds are utilised properly, repayment would be possible and easier, too. Care has to be exercised to match the inflow and outflow of funds. Needless to say, profitability of any firm is dependent on its cost as well as its efficient utilisation.

1.3 CONCEPT OF FINANCIAL MANAGEMENT

As already discussed, the general meaning of finance refers to providing funds, as and when needed. However, as management function, the term 'Financial Management' has a distinct meaning. **Financial management deals with the study of procuring funds and its effective and judicious utilisation, in terms of the overall objectives of the firm, and expectations of the providers of funds.** The basic objective is to maximise the value of the firm. **The purpose is to achieve maximisation of share value to the owners i.e. equity shareholders.**

The term financial management has been defined, differently, by various authors. Some of the authoritative definitions are given below:

1. "Financial Management is concerned with the efficient use of an important economic resource, namely, Capital Funds" **—Solomon**
2. "Financial Management is concerned with the managerial decisions that result in the acquisition and financing of short-term and long-term credits for the firm" **—Phillioppatus**
3. "Business finance is that business activity which is concerned with the conservation and acquisition of capital funds in meeting financial needs and overall objectives of a business enterprise" **—Wheeler**

4. "Financial Management deals with procurement of funds and their effective utilisation in the business" **—S.C. Kuchhal**

The definition provided by Kuchhal is most acceptable as it focuses, clearly, the **Basic requirements of financial management**. From his definition, two basic aspects emerge:

(A) Procurement of funds.

(B) Effective and judicious utilisation of funds.

Financial management has become so important that it has given birth to Financial Management as a separate subject.

1.4 NATURE OF FINANCIAL MANAGEMENT

Financial management refers to that part of management activity, which is concerned with the planning and controlling of firm's financial resources. Financial management is a part of overall management. All business decisions involve finance. Where finance is needed, role of finance manager is inevitable. **Financial management deals with raising of funds from various sources, dependant on availability and existing capital structure of the organisation.** The sources must be suitable and economical to the organisation. Emphasis of financial management is more on its efficient utilisation, rather than raising of funds, alone.

The scope and complexity of financial management has been widening, with the growth of business in different diverse directions. As business competition has been increasing, with a greater pace, support of financial management is more needed, in a more innovative way, to make the business grow, ahead of others.

1.5 SCOPE OF FINANCIAL MANAGEMENT

Financial management is concerned with optimum utilisation of resources. Resources are limited, particularly in developing countries like India. So, the focus, everywhere, is to take maximum benefit, in the form of output, from the limited inputs.

Financial management is needed in every type of organisation, be it public or private sector. Equally, its importance exists in both profit oriented and non-profit organisations. In fact, need of financial management is more in loss-making organisations to turn them to profitable enterprises. Study reveals many organisations have sustained losses, due to absence of professional financial management.

Financial management has undergone significant changes, over the years in its scope and coverage.

Approaches: Broadly, it has two approaches:

Traditional Approach-Procurement of Funds

Modern Approach-Effective Utilisation of Funds

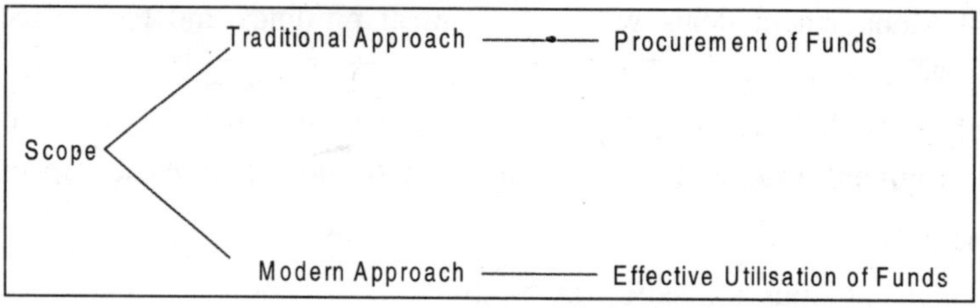

Scope of Financial Management

Traditional Approach

The scope of finance function was treated, in the narrow sense of procurement or arrangement of funds. The finance manager was treated as just provider of funds, when organisation was in need of them. **The utilisation or administering resources was considered outside the purview of the finance function. It was felt that the finance manager had no role to play in decision-making for its utilisation.** Others used to take decisions regarding its application in the organisation, without the involvement of finance personnel. Finance manager had been treated, in fact, as an outsider with a very specific and limited function, supplier of funds, to perform when the need of funds was felt by the organisation.

As per this approach, the following aspects only were included in the scope of financial management:

(i) Estimation of requirements of finance,

(ii) Arrangement of funds from financial institutions,

(iii) Arrangement of funds through financial instruments such as shares, debentures, bonds and loans, and

(iv) Looking after the accounting and legal work connected with the raising of funds.

Limitations

The traditional approach was evolved during the 1920s and 1930s period and continued till 1950. The approach had been discarded due to the following limitations:

(i) No Involvement in Application of Funds: The finance manager had not been involved in decision-making in allocation of funds. He had been treated as an outsider. He had been ignored in internal decision making process and considered as an outsider.

(ii) No Involvement in day to day Management: The focus was on providing long-term funds from a combination of sources. This process was more of one time happening. The finance manager was not involved in day to day administration of working capital management. Smooth functioning depends on working capital management, where the finance manager was not involved and allowed to play any role.

(iii) Not Associated in Decision-Making Allocation of Funds: The issue of allocation of funds was kept outside his functioning. He had not been involved in decision- making for its judicious utilisation.

Raising finance was an infrequent event. Its natural implication was that the issues involved in working capital management were not in the purview of the finance function. In a nutshell, during the traditional phase, the finance manager was called upon, in particular, when his speciality was required to locate new sources of funds and as and when the requirement of funds was felt.

The following issues, as pointed by Solomon, were ignored in the scope of financial management, under this approach:

(A) Should an enterprise commit capital funds to a certain purpose?

(B) Do the expected returns meet financial standards of performance?

(C) How does the cost vary with the mixture of financing methods used?

The traditional approach has outlived its utility in the changed business situation. The scope of finance function has undergone a sea change with the emergence of different capital instruments.

Modern Approach

Since 1950s, the approach and utility of financial management has started changing in a revolutionary manner. Financial management is considered as vital and an integral part of overall management. **The emphasis of Financial Management has been shifted from raising of funds to the effective and judicious utilisation of funds. The modern approach is analytical way of looking into the financial problems of the firm.** Advice of finance manager is required at every moment, whenever any decision with involvement of funds is taken. Hardly, there is an activity that does not involve funds.

In the words of Solomon **"The central issue of financial policy is the use of funds. It is helpful in achieving the broad financial goals which an enterprise sets for itself".**

Nowadays, the finance manger is required to look into the financial implications of every decision to be taken by the firm. **His Involvement of finance manager has been before taking the decision, during its review and, finally, when the final outcome is judged.** In other words, his association has been continuous in every decision-making process from the inception till its end.

1.6 AIMS OF FINANCE FUNCTION

The following are the aims of finance function:

1. **Acquiring Sufficient and Suitable Funds:** The primary aim of finance function is to assess the needs of the enterprise, properly, and procure funds, in time. Time is also an important element in meeting the needs of the organisation. If the funds are not available as and when required, the firm may become sick or, at least, the profitability of the firm would be, definitely, affected.

   It is necessary that the funds should be, reasonably, adequate to the demands of the firm. The funds should be raised from different sources, commensurate to the nature of business and risk profile of the organisation. When the nature of business is such that the production does not commence, immediately, and requires long gestation period, it is necessary to have the long-term sources like share capital, debentures and long term loan etc. A concern with longer gestation period does not have profits for some years. So, the firm should rely more on the permanent capital like share capital to avoid interest burden on the borrowing component.

2. **Proper Utilisation of Funds:** Raising funds is important, more than that is its proper utilisation. If proper utilisation of funds were not made, there would be no revenue generation. Benefits should always exceed cost of funds so that the organisation can be profitable. Beneficial projects only are to be undertaken. So, it is all the more necessary that careful planning and cost-benefit analysis should be made before the actual commencement of projects.
3. **Increasing Profitability:** Profitability is necessary for every organisation. The planning and control functions of finance aim at increasing profitability of the firm. To achieve profitability, the cost of funds should be low. Idle funds do not yield any return, but incur cost. So, the organisation should avoid idle funds. Finance function also requires matching of cost and returns of funds. If funds are used efficiently, profitability gets a boost.
4. **Maximising Firm's Value:** The ultimate aim of finance function is maximising the value of the firm, which is reflected in wealth maximisation of shareholders. The market value of the equity shares is an indicator of the wealth maximisation.

1.7 FUNCTIONS OF FINANCE

Finance function is the most important function of a business. Finance is, closely, connected with production, marketing and other activities. In the absence of finance, all these activities come to a halt. In fact, only with finance, a business activity can be commenced, continued and expanded. Finance exists everywhere, be it production, marketing, human resource development or undertaking research activity. **Understanding the universality and importance of finance, finance manager is associated, in modern business, in all activities as no activity can exist without funds.**

Financial Decisions or Finance Functions are closely inter-connected. All decisions mostly involve finance. When a decision involves finance, it is a financial decision in a business firm. In all the following financial areas of decision-making, the role of finance manager is vital. We can classify the finance functions or financial decisions into four major groups:

(A) Investment Decision or Long-term Asset mix decision
(B) Finance Decision or Capital mix decision
(C) Liquidity Decision or Short-term asset mix decision
(D) Dividend Decision or Profit allocation decision

(A) Investment Decision

Investment decisions relate to selection of assets in which funds are to be invested by the firm. Investment alternatives are numerous. Resources are scarce and limited. They have to be rationed and discretely used. Investment decisions allocate and ration the resources among the competing investment alternatives or opportunities. The effort is to find out the projects, which are acceptable.

Investment decisions relate to the total amount of assets to be held and their composition in the form of fixed and current assets. Both the factors influence the risk the organisation is exposed to. The more important aspect is how the investors perceive the risk.

The investment decisions result in purchase of assets. Assets can be classified, under two broad categories:

(i) Long-term investment decisions – Long-term assets

(ii) Short-term investment decisions – Short-term assets

Long-term Investment Decisions: The long-term capital decisions are referred to as capital budgeting decisions, which relate to fixed assets. The fixed assets are long term, in nature. Basically, fixed assets create earnings to the firm. They give benefit in future. It is difficult to measure the benefits as future is uncertain.

The investment decision is important not only for setting up new units but also for expansion of existing units. Decisions related to them are, generally, irreversible. Often, reversal of decisions results in substantial loss. When a brand new car is sold, even after a day of its purchase, still, buyer treats the vehicle as a second-hand car. The transaction, invariably, results in heavy loss for a short period of owning. So, the finance manager has to evaluate profitability of every investment proposal, carefully, before funds are committed to them.

Short-term Investment Decisions: The short-term investment decisions are, generally, referred as working capital management. The finance manger has to allocate among cash and cash equivalents, receivables and inventories. Though these current assets do not, directly, contribute to the earnings, their existence is necessary for proper, efficient and optimum utilisation of fixed assets.

(B) Finance Decision

Once investment decision is made, the next step is how to raise finance for the concerned investment. **Finance decision is concerned with the mix or composition of the sources of raising the funds required by the firm. In other words, it is related to the pattern of financing.** In finance decision, the finance manager is required to determine the proportion of equity and debt, which is known as capital structure. There are two main sources of funds, shareholders' funds (variable in the form of dividend) and borrowed funds (fixed interest-bearing). These sources have their own peculiar characteristics. The key distinction lies in the fixed commitment. Borrowed funds are to be paid interest, irrespective of the profitability of the firm. Interest has to be paid, even if the firm incurs loss and this permanent obligation is not there with the funds raised from the shareholders. **The borrowed funds are relatively cheaper compared to shareholders' funds, however they carry risk.** This risk is known as financial risk i.e. Risk of insolvency due to non-payment of interest or non-repayment of borrowed capital.

On the other hand, the shareholders' funds are permanent source to the firm. The shareholders' funds could be from equity shareholders or preference shareholders. Equity share capital is not repayable and does not have fixed commitment in the form of dividend. However, preference share capital has a fixed commitment, in the form of dividend and is redeemable, if they are redeemable preference shares.

Barring a few exceptions, every firm tries to employ both borrowed funds and shareholders' funds to finance its activities. The employment of these funds, in combination, is known as financial leverage. Financial leverage provides profitability, but carries risk. Without risk, there is no return. This is the case in every walk of life!

When the return on capital employed (equity and borrowed funds) is greater than the rate of interest paid on the debt, shareholders' return get magnified or increased. In period of inflation, this would be advantageous while it is a disadvantage or curse in times of recession.

Example:

Total investment:	Rs.	1,00,000
Return		15%.
Composition of investment:		
Equity	Rs.	60,000
Debt @ 7% interest	Rs.	40,000
Return on investment		
@ 15%	Rs.	15,000
Interest on Debt	Rs.	2,800
7% on Rs.40,000		
Earnings available to		
Equity shareholders	Rs.	12,200

Return on equity (ignoring tax) is 20%, which is at the expense of debt as they get 7% interest only.

In the normal course, equity would get a return of 15%. But they are enjoying 20% due to financing by a combination of debt and equity.

This area would be discussed in detail while dealing with Leverages, in the later chapter.

The finance manager follows that combination of raising funds which is optimal mix of debt and equity. The optimal mix minimises the risk and maximises the wealth of shareholders.

(C) Liquidity Decision

Liquidity decision is concerned with the management of current assets. Basically, this is Working Capital Management. Working Capital Management is concerned with the management of current assets. It is concerned with short-term survival. Short term-survival is a prerequisite for long-term survival.

When more funds are tied up in current assets, the firm would enjoy greater liquidity. In consequence, the firm would not experience any difficulty in making payment of debts, as and when they fall due. With excess liquidity, there would be no default in payments. So, there would be no threat of insolvency for failure of payments. However, funds have economic cost. Idle current assets do not earn anything. Higher liquidity is at the cost of profitability. Profitability would suffer with more idle funds. Investment in current assets affects the profitability, liquidity and risk. **A proper balance must be maintained between liquidity and profitability of the firm. This is the key area where finance manager has to play significant role. The strategy is in ensuring a trade-off between liquidity and profitability.** This is, indeed, a balancing act and continuous process. It is a continuous process as the conditions and requirements of business change, time to time. In accordance with the requirements of the firm, the liquidity has to vary and in consequence, the profitability changes. This is the major dimension of liquidity decision-working capital management. Working capital management is day to day problem to the finance manager. His skills of financial management are put to test, daily.

(D) Dividend Decision

Dividend decision is concerned with the amount of profits to be distributed and retained in the firm.

Dividend: The term 'dividend' relates to the portion of profit, which is distributed to shareholders of the company. It is a reward or compensation to them for their investment made in the firm. The dividend can be declared from the current profits or accumulated profits.

Which course should be followed – dividend or retention? Normally, companies distribute certain amount in the form of dividend, in a stable manner, to meet the expectations of shareholders and balance is retained within the organisation for expansion. If dividend is not distributed, there would be great dissatisfaction to the shareholders. Non-declaration of dividend affects the market price of equity shares, severely. One significant element in the dividend decision is, therefore, the dividend payout ratio i.e. what proportion of dividend is to be paid to the shareholders. The dividend decision depends on the preference of the equity shareholders and investment opportunities, available within the firm. A higher rate of dividend, beyond the market expectations, increases the market price of shares. However, it leaves a small amount in the form of retained earnings for expansion. The business that reinvests less will tend to grow slower. The other alternative is to raise funds in the market for expansion. It is not a desirable decision to retain all the profits for expansion, without distributing any amount in the form of dividend.

There is no ready-made answer, how much is to be distributed and what portion is to be retained. Retention of profit is related to

- Reinvestment opportunities available to the firm.
- Alternative rate of return available to equity shareholders, if they invest themselves.

1.8 INTER-RELATIONSHIP OF FINANCE FUNCTIONS OR DECISIONS

All the major functions or decisions – Investment function, Finance function, Liquidity function and Dividend function, are inter-related and inter-connected. They are inter-related because the goal of all the functions is one and the same. Their ultimate objective is only one – achievement of maximisation of shareholders' wealth or maximising the market value of the shares.

All the decisions are also inter-connected or inter-dependent also. Let us illustrate, both these aspects with an example.

Example: If a firm wants to undertake a project requiring funds, this investment decision can not be taken, in isolation, without considering the availability of finances, which is a finance decision. Both the decisions are inter-connected.

If the firm allocates more funds for fixed assets, lesser amount would be available for current assets. So, financing decision and liquidity decision are inter-connected.

The firm has two options to finance the project, either from internal resources or raising funds, externally, from the market. If the firm decides to meet the total project cost only from internal resources, the profits, otherwise available for distribution in the form of dividend, have to be retained to meet the project cost. Here, the finance decision has influenced the dividend decision.

So, an efficient financial management takes the optimal decision by considering the implications or impact of all the decisions, together, on the market value of the company's shares. The decision has to be taken considering all the angles, simultaneously.

No Function is Superior: All the functions are important. Importance of the function depends on the situation of the firm. If a firm has adequate investment opportunities but experiences difficulty to raise funds, then the finance function is superior to the firm, at that juncture. It does not mean that investment decision is less important compared to finance decision, always.

The essence is no financial function or decision is superior to others.

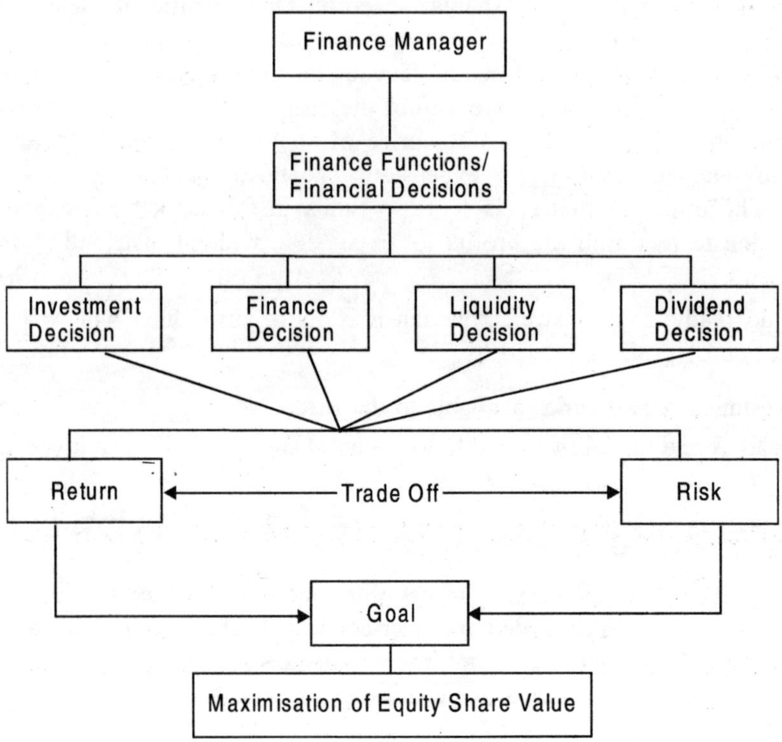

Goal of Financial Management

1.9 LIQUIDITY VS PROFITABILITY (RISK–RETURN TRADE-OFF)

In the course of performance of duties, a finance manager has to take various types of financial decisions – Investment Decision, Finance Decision, Liquidity Decision and Dividend Decision, as detailed above, from time to time. In every area of financial management, the finance manger is always faced with the dilemma of liquidity vs. profitability. He has to strike a balance between the two.

Liquidity means that the firm has:

(A) Adequate cash to pay bills as and when they fall due, and

(B) Sufficient cash reserves to meet emergencies and unforeseen demands, at all time.

Profitability goal, on the other hand, requires that the funds of the firm be so utilised as to yield the highest return.

Liquidity and profitability are conflicting decisions. When one increases, the other decreases. More liquidity results in less profitability and vice versa. This conflict finance manager has to face as all the financial decisions involve both liquidity and profitability.

Example: Firm may borrow more, beyond the risk-free limit, to take the advantage of cheap interest rate. This decision increases the liquidity to meet the requirements of firm. Firm has to pay committed fixed rate of interest, at fixed time, irrespective of the return the liquidity (funds) gives. Profitability suffers, in this process of decision, if the expected return does not materialise. This is the risk the organisation faces by this financial decision.

Risk: Risk is defined as the variability of the expected return from the investment.

Return: Return is measured as a gain or profit expected to be made, over a period, at the time of making the investment.

Example: If an investor makes a deposit in a nationalised bank, carrying an interest of 7% p.a., virtually, the investment is risk free for repayment, both principal and interest. However, if a similar amount is invested in the equity shares, there is no certainty for the amount of dividend or even for getting back initial investment as market price may fall, subsequently, at the time of sale. The expected dividend may or may not materialise. In other words, the dividend amount may vary or the company may not declare dividend, at all. A bank deposit is a safe investment, while equity shares are not so. So, **risk is associated with the quality of investment.**

The relationship between risk and return can be expressed as follows:

Return = Risk free rate + Risk premium

Risk free rate is a compensation or reward for time and risk premium for risk. Risk and return go hand in hand. Higher the risk, higher the required return expected. It is only an expectation, at the time of investment. There is no guarantee that the return would be, definitely, higher. If one wants to make an investment, without risk, the return is always lower. For this reason only, deposit in a bank and post office carry lower returns, compared to equity shares.

So, every financial decision involves liquidity and profitability implications, which carries risk as well as return. However, the quantum of risk differs from one decision to another. Equally, the return from all the decisions is not uniform and also varies, even from time to time.

Relationship between Liquidity & Profitability and Risk & Return:

Example: If higher inventories are built, in anticipation of an increase in price, more funds are locked in inventories. So, organisation may experience problems in making other payments, in time. If the expected price increase materialises, firm enjoys a boost in profits due to the windfall return the decision yields. The expected increase in price is a contingent event. In other words, the increase in price may or may not happen. But, firm suffers liquidity problems, immediately. This is the price firm has to pay, which otherwise is the risk the firm carries.

It may be emphasised risk and return always go together, hand in hand. More risk, chances of higher return exist. One thing must be remembered, there is no guarantee of higher returns, with higher risk. The classical example is lottery. There is a great risk, if one invests amount in a lottery. There is no guarantee that you would win the lottery. **However, liquidity and profitability are conflicting decisions.** There is a direct relationship between higher risk and higher return. In the above example, building higher inventories, more than required, is a higher risk decision. This higher risk has created liquidity problem. But, the benefit of higher return is also available. Higher risk, on the one hand, endangers liquidity and higher returns, on the other hand, increases profitability.

Liquidity and Profitability are conflicting while Risk and Return go together. The pictorial presentation is as under:

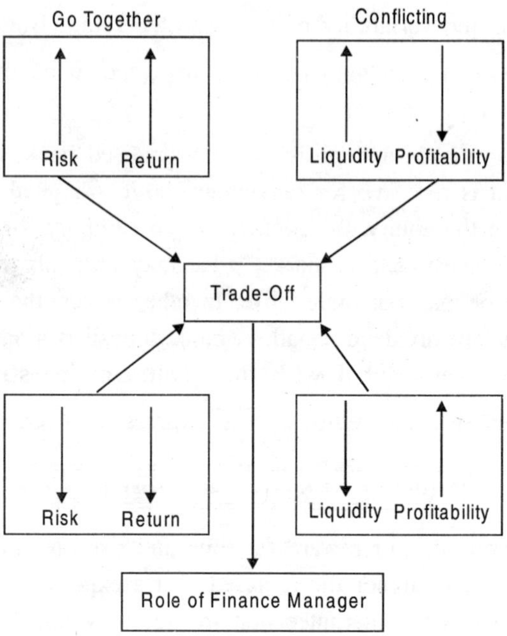

Role of Finance Manager Relationship between Risk-Return and Liquidity Vs. Profitability

Balanced Approach: A finance manager can not avoid the risk, altogether, in his decision-making. At the same time, he should not take decisions, considering the returns aspect only. At the time of taking any financial decision, the finance manger has to weigh both the risks and returns in the proposed decision and optimise the risk and returns, at the same time. A proper balance between risk and return should be maintained by the finance manager to maximise the market value of shares. **A particular combination where both risk and return are optimised is known as Risk–Return Trade-off.**

Basic objective of Finance Manager: An efficient finance manager fixes that level of operations, where he can achieve maximisation of the shareholders' wealth. Such a level is termed as risk-return trade off. **Every finance manager attempts to achieve that trade-off in every finance decision.** At this level, the market value of the company's shares would be maximum. To achieve maximum return, funds flowing in and out of the firm are to be constantly monitored to ensure their safety and proper utilisation.

1.10 ROLE OF FINANCE MANAGER

The finance manager handles finance. The role of finance manager is pivotal. He can change the fortunes of the organisation with proper planning, monitoring and timely guidance. Equally, if the manager is not competent, even a profitable organisation may dwindle or even sink. The finance manger is, now, responsible in shaping the fortunes of the enterprise. The role of finance manager, in a modern business, is pervasive in all the activities of business firm, including production and marketing.

It has been rightly said, money begets money. Business needs money to make more money. However, business can make money, when it is properly managed. The financial history is replete with stories how even the profitable organisations were wound up, when the management of finance had turned bad due to mismanagement of financial affairs.

It is misunderstood, in some corners, that the role of finance manager is important only in private organisations. It is not so. His role is important, both in private and public sector. He has a positive role to play in every type of organisation. Even in non-profit making organisations, his role exists as long as there is involvement of funds.

Influences Fortunes of Firm: The history of failures of organisations is interesting. **Many firms have failed, not because of inefficiency of production, inability in marketing or non-availability of funds but due to the absence of competent finance manager.** In many public sector undertakings, in particular, state government undertakings, importance is given to the appointment of peons, more than adequately, but not to the appointment of competent professional manager in finance, even after lapse of several years. That is the real secret of numerous loss-making organisations, in public sector! Over the years, the picture has been changing, but only after the real damage has already occurred in those public sector undertakings, due to the non-appointment of professional finance managers, at the time of formation of those undertakings.

In several public sector undertakings, the presence of competent finance manager is often found inconvenient. A finance manager can not play any significant role in the public sector, unless he is allowed to play.

Exists Everywhere: The role of finance manager, in modern times, can be well said, universal and pervasive. Hardly, we find any activity, which does not involve finance. Even entertainment in a firm requires financial management due to financial implications. In modern business, no decision is taken without the consultation of finance. Even in recruitment, the presence of finance representative has been a normal feature manager. Only the level of finance representative changes, dependant upon the status of position for which recruitment is held. At times, people working in other departments feel that the finance manager has been interfering in all matters, unconnected to him. It is due to inadequate understanding of the role and expectations expected of him in modern business. The finance manager can, definitely, contribute to the overall development of the organisation provided he is competent and allowed to perform his functions, independently.

In his new role, the finance manager must find answers for the following three questions, again in the words of Solomon:

- How large should an enterprise be, and how fast should it grow?
- How should the funds be raised?
- In what form, should the firm hold its assets?

To sum up, finance functions or decisions include the following important areas, where the finance manager has to contribute:

- Investment decision or long term asset-mix decision
- Finance decision or capital-mix decision
- Liquidity decision or short-term asset mix decision
- Dividend decision or profit allocation decision

The main objective of all the above decisions is to increase the value of the shares, held by the equity shareholders. **The finance manager has to strive for shareholders' wealth maximisation.**

While discharging the functions, the finance manager has to focus his attention on the following aspects to maximise the shareholders' wealth:

1. Procuring the funds as and when necessary, at the lowest cost,
2. Investing the funds in those assets, which are more profitable, and
3. Distributing the dividends to the shareholders to meet their expectations and facilitate expansion to achieve the long-term goals of organisation.

Check Your Understanding

(A) State whether the following statements are TRUE or FALSE.

1. Finance function is limited to supply of funds to the requirements of the organisation.
2. Finance function involves procurement of funds, at economic cost, and their effective utilisation in business.
3. Financial Management involves receipt and disbursement of cash.
4. Finance function is concerned with all aspects of business operations, where money is involved.
5. The financial management decisions can be classified into four basic kinds¾ Investment Decisions, Financing Decisions, Liquidity Decisions and Dividend Decisions.
6. Investment decision is concerned with allocating limited resources among the competing investment alternatives.
7. Cash flows, at different times, carry different values.
8. The finance manager is required to look into the financial implications of every decision in the firm.
9. It is not the function of finance manager to look to the optimal mix of debt and equity to finance the investment needs.
10. It is not the job of finance manager to get involved with the change in distribution channel decision.
11. Finance manager creates problems in decision-making process where money is involved.
12. Market prices of shares in the stock market fall when expectations of shareholders in respect of dividend declaration are not fulfilled.
13. Board of Directors is the owners of Joint Stock Company.
14. Dividend can be declared by the company in the form of cash or bonus shares.
15. Board of Directors is the final authority to decide the quantum of dividend.
16. Dividend can be declared from the current as well as cumulative profits of an organisation.
17. It is not wise to borrow when interest rate is lower than the return on capital employed.
18. Bonus shares are issued by the company, capitalising profits.
19. Working Capital Management is concerned with management of fixed assets.

Answers

1. False 2. True 3. False 4. True 5. True
6. True 7. True 8. True 9. False
10. False (decision involves financial implication)
11. False 12. True 13. False 14. True 15. False
16. True 17. False 18. True 19. False

(B) Select the most appropriate answer from the following statements:

1. Financial management is mainly concerned with
   - (A) Efficient management of every activity of business
   - (B) Arrangement of funds required to the firm
   - (C) Obtaining required funds in the appropriate mix and utilising them, efficiently
2. Financial decisions involve
   - (A) Investment, sales and dividend decisions
   - (B) Finance, investment and dividend decisions
   - (C) Finance, investment and cash decisions
3. Financial management helps in
   - (A) Short-term planning of company's activities
   - (B) Estimating the total funds' requirement and their proper utilisation in fixed assets and working capital
   - (C) Profit planning of the firm

Answers

1. C 2. B 3. B

(C) Fill in the Blanks

1. One who takes financial risks is called the ________________.
2. The finance function provides the _____________ required by the Business enterprises.
3. Ownership is divorced from the ___________ in a limited company

Answers

1. Entrepreneur 2. Funds 3. Management

Review Questions

1. The horizons of Financial Management have changed substantially in scope and complexity over the years. Justify the statement? **(1.1 to 1.5)**
2. Explain the scope of financial management. Describe the role of finance manager in a modern business? **(1.5 and 1.10)**
3. Detail the aims of finance function? **(1.6)**
4. The role of Finance Manager has remained as it had been. Discuss? **(1.7, 1.9 and 1.10)**
5. Detail the basic finance functions? How trade-off is possible between return and risk? **(1.7, 1.8 and 1.9)**
6. In addition to raising funds, financial management is directly concerned with production, marketing and all other functions within an organisation. Explain with suitable examples the inter-relationship with other functions? **(1.7, 1.8 and 1.9)**

7. "An optimal combination of decisions relating to investment, financing and dividends will maximise the value of the firm to its shareholders", Examine? **(1.7, 1.8 and 1.9)**
8. What role should the finance manager play in the modern enterprise? **(1.7, 1.9 and 1.10)**
9. Examine inter-relationship among the investment, financing and dividend decisions with an example and analyse the superiority amongst the different decisions? **(1.7 and 1.8)**
10. The financial manager plays a pivotal role in the multifarious facets of a business enterprise. Do you advocate his role as interference or contribution? **(1.7, 1.8, 1.9 and 1.10)**
11. Describe the prominent areas of financial decision-making? **(1.7)**
12. "Liquidity and profitability are competing goals of the finance manager"- Comment? **(1.9)**
13. Write Short Notes on the following:
    (A) Finance **(1.2)**
    (B) Risk-return trade-off **(1.9)**

2

OBJECTIVES OF FINANCIAL MANAGEMENT

2.1 INTRODUCTION

Financial management is concerned with the procurement and judicious use of funds. Its main aim is to maximise the earnings and value of the equity share, in the best interests of the firm.

Every firm should have a goal or objective to achieve. In the context of that objective, the finance manager evaluates the decisions to be taken. A goal of the firm may be defined as 'a target against which its performance can be measured'. Several goals of financial management have been cited. The goals are maximisation of sales revenue, net profit, return on investment, size of the firm, percentage of market share etc. The problem is to identify one of these several goals. **It is, generally, agreed that the financial goal of the firm should be the maximisation of owners' economic welfare. Owners' economic welfare can be maximised with the Shareholders' Wealth Maximisation (SWM) as reflected in the market value of the equity shares.**

The above objective of financial management can be achieved, by the following widely accepted approaches:

(A) Profit maximisation

(B) Wealth maximisation

2.2 CHARACTERISTICS OF A GOOD OPERATIONAL DECISION CRITERION

An appropriate operational (financial) decision criterion should

(a) **Precision Concept** – Be precise and exact.

(b) **Time Concept** – Recognise the Time value of Money

(c) **Quantity Concept** – Be based on 'Bigger the Better' principle.

(d) **Quality Concept** – Consider both Quantity and Quality dimensions.

Now, let us examine which approach, profit maximisation or wealth maximisation, would comply with all the characteristics of a good operational decision criterion.

2.3 OBJECTIVES OF FINANCIAL MANAGEMENT

Profit Maximisation

Profit earning is the main aim of every economic activity. Business is also an economic activity. So, every business seeks profit. Profit earning is the real barometer to measure the efficiency of business firm.

The term 'profit' refers to the amount of income, which is due to the owners of business, whether distributed in the form of dividend or not. Profitability is an operational concept. In other words, profitability refers to a situation where output exceeds input i.e. the value created by the use of resources is more than the total of input resources. Profitability refers to Earnings Before Interest and Taxes (E.B.I.T).

Arguments in Support

1. **Aim of Business:** According to this approach, actions that increase profit should be undertaken and those that decrease profit are to be avoided. The approach is, indeed,

simple. It implies that all the financial management decisions, the investment, finance and dividend decisions – should be oriented towards maximisation of profits.

2. **Barometer for Measuring Efficiency:** Real test for measuring comparative performance of firms is profit. So, this is the ground of rationality.
3. **Economic Conditions Change:** Business may undergo recession, depression and severe competition, as economic conditions do not remain the same, always. When conditions are favourable, firm has to make more profits to withstand the unfavourable situations, later. Firm can rely on the past earnings, if it sustains loss. So, every firm has to concentrate to make more money, when the going is good.
4. **Growth:** Firm can accumulate profits, which could be a supporting or main source of finance for expansion and growth, in future years.
5. **Social Goals:** Personal objectives are primary to every-one. If profits are high, a business firm can meet its personal objectives and also can help the society for socio-economic welfare. If profits are small, who allocates funds for social benefits? So, profitability is essential for fulfilling social goals.

In view of the above, it is argued that every firm should be guided by the aim of profit maximisation.

Criticism:

The arguments against profit maximisation and main technical flaws of this criterion are as follows:

(A) **Ambiguity-Vague:** The term 'profit' is vague and has different interpretations. It means different things to different people. It can be pre-tax or post-tax profit. It is not clear whether it is short-term profit or long-term profit. Does it mean operating profit or profit available for shareholders? The other equivalent term, often used, is 'Return'. Return can be on total capital employed or total assets or shareholders equity and so on.

Further, it is also possible that the net profits may increase, but earning per share may decline. To illustrate, a firm has issued 1,000 equity shares and has made a net profit of Rs. 10,000. So, the earnings per share (EPS) are Rs.10 per share. Later, the firm has increased the number of equity shares, further by 2,000. After increase of share capital, the net profit of the firm has been Rs. 15,000. The net profit has increased by 50% from Rs. 10,000 to Rs. 15,000 but EPS has declined from Rs. 10 to Rs. 5. In such a situation, the market value of the share does not increase, despite more profits. In fact, there would be a fall in market price of equity share, due to reduction in EPS.

The above explains maximising profits does not maximise economic welfare of the owners.

Profit maximisation concept is neither precise nor exact. A loose expression like profit can not be the basis for operational financial management.

(B) **Timing and Value of Money - Ignored:** The concept of profit maximisation does not help in making a choice between projects, giving different benefits, spread over a period of time. It ignores the difference in time in respect of benefits arising from the similar amount of investment. The fact that a rupee received today is more valuable than the rupee received later is ignored in this concept.

The following illustration explains how time value of money is ignored.

Time pattern of Benefits (Profits)		
	Alternative A (Rs.)	Alternative B (Rs.)
First Year	5,000	Nil
Second year	10,000	10,000
Third year	5,000	10,000
Total	20,000	20,000

If profit maximisation were the decision criterion, both the alternatives would be ranked, equally, as the amount of profit is same in both the alternatives.

'A' provides higher returns in earlier years. In case of 'B', the returns are in later years. The returns, arising in the earlier years, can always be reinvested to earn extra returns. **The basic dictum in financial planning is "The Earlier-The Better".** This is referred to as time value of money.

Profit maximisation criterion does not differentiate the returns received at different periods. Costs and benefits, received over a period, are treated alike, irrespective of their timings.

The second and third characteristics of a good operational decision criterion – Recognition of time value of money and 'Bigger the Better' principle are not complied by profit maximisation concept.

(C) **Quality (Certainty) of Benefits:** The term 'Quality' refers to certainty, with which benefit can be expected to materialise. Profit maximisation gives weight to the size of returns, but not to the certainty of the returns. Basically, investors are risk averse i.e. they want to avoid or at least minimise risk. So, the investors give preference to those returns, which are certain even with small variations, over the years.

This concept can be understood well with the following example:

Uncertainty about Expected Benefits (Profits)		
State of Economy	**Alternative A (Rs.)**	**Alternative B (Rs.)**
RECESSION (Period I)	900	NIL
NORMAL (Period II)	1,000	1,000
BOOM (Period III)	1,100	2,000
Total	3,000	3,000

Returns are identical in the normal situation, in both the cases. However, the returns vary, widely, during recession and boom, in both the alternatives, and fluctuate depending on the state of economy.

To put it differently, earnings associated with alternative 'B' are more uncertain and risky, with no returns during the recession period and highest returns in the boom period. In recession period, it is difficult to make money and every firm can make profits during boom.

Obviously, alternative 'A' is better from the point of risk and certainty.

Profit maximisation criterion is inappropriate and unsustainable as operational objective in the financial management decisions of different kinds – investment, finance and dividend decisions of a firm. It ignores two important dimensions, namely, (i) risk and (ii) time value of money.

So, the last characteristic of a good operational decision criterion, 'quantity and quality' is also ignored by profit maximisation theory.

(D) **Change in Organisation Structure:** Principle of profit maximisation was, earlier, accepted when the structure of the business was sole proprietorship. In this type of structure, sole proprietor managed the business, individually, and was the recipient of total profits. As total profit belonged to him, his wealth maximised. This was the picture in 19th century, when the business was, totally, self-managed.

Over a period, the sole proprietorship concept has changed to Joint stock company. In this changed structure, there is divorcee between ownership and management. Shareholders own the company while professional managers manage the business. There are several stakeholders in the joint stock company-shareholders, customers, employees, Government and society. Due to varied stakeholders, their interests are diverse and so finance manager has to reconcile their divergent and conflicting interests.

In the changed scenario, the concept of 'Profit Maximisation' is unrealistic and inappropriate.

(E) **Social Welfare may be Ignored:** Due to profit maximisation objective, business may produce goods and services, which may not be necessary and beneficial to the society. So, it is, indeed, doubtful how far the profit maximisation objective serves or promotes social welfare, let alone optimises social welfare.

(F) **Ignores Financing and Dividend Aspects:** The profit maximisation concept concentrates on profitability aspect alone and impact of financing and dividend decisions on the market value of shares are, totally, ignored.

Let us explain the point further. A firm may borrow, beyond its capacity, to finance the projects on hand. The firm's main concern is to maximise the profit alone, ignoring the financial risk- risk of insolvency due to non-payment of interest and repayment of principal. Totally ignoring risks associated with the huge borrowing is not in the interests of organisation. So, it can not be said that such type of borrowing is to promote economic welfare of shareholders as risk aspect has been ignored. More so, this heavy risk is likely to dampen the market price of shares.

Normally, dividend decision influences market price of equity shares. Even if the firm declares a higher rate of dividend than the preceding year, still, market price of the equity share may decline if the market expectations are not fulfilled. In such a situation, even if the firm makes more profit and ignores the expectations of shareholders in respect of dividend, it is unlikely the market value of share would improve. The logic is simple. The real owners, equity shareholders may not appreciate this type of working.

So, profit maximisation is not a proper objective of financial management.

Let us examine whether wealth maximisation is a better objective of Financial Management, compared to Profit Maximisation.

2.4 WEALTH MAXIMISATION

Wealth maximisation of the firm is the most appropriate objective of the enterprise. The wealth maximisation principle implies to maximise the value of its equity shares. The wealth created by a company is reflected in the market value of the company's equity shares. This situation indicates efficiency of management.

When this objective is achieved, the net worth of the firm would be high. When net worth is high, earnings per share (EPS) would be at its peak. When EPS is high, market price of the share would also be high. The shareholders' wealth would be maximum as the wealth of the shareholder is a product of number of shares held and its market price.

Shareholders' current wealth in a firm = Number of equity shares owned × Current market price

Presence of All Characteristics of a Good Operational Decision Criterion

The wealth maximisation criterion is based on the concept of cash flows. Cash flows refer to the firm's future cash flows. In case of profit maximisation criterion, the accounting profit is the basis of the measurement of benefits.

Cash Flow is a Better Concept: The concept of cash flows is better than the accounting profit, for the following reasons:

1. **Precision Concept:** Cash flow is a precise concept, with a definite connotation.
2. **Quality Concept:** The more certain the cash flows are, the better the quality of benefits and higher the value. Conversely, the less certain the flows are, the lower the quality and, therefore, value of benefits is also lower. So, quality dimension is complied with.
3. **Time Concept:** Cash flows are discounted (taking the opportunity cost of capital) to arrive at the present value, which reflects the recognition of time value of money.
4. **Quantity Concept:** Bigger cash flows, after discounting, would result in bigger value. So, quantity aspect is also complied with. All financial decisions should be based on cost-benefit analysis. Financial action has to be undertaken, only when benefit exceeds cost. Conversely, if cost is more than benefit, the decision will not serve the purpose of maximising the wealth. So, those actions should be rejected. 'The bigger, The better' principle is recognised.

So, wealth maximisation complies with all the characteristics of a good operational decision criterion.

Maximisation of Market Price in Long Run: Here, market price refers to market price, in the long run. The long run means a period long enough so that a normalised price can be worked out. Market price, over a long term, serves as a performance index of the company's progress.

At times, in some firms, management may make decisions to get the short-term advantage, at the expense of the long run. For instance, a company may cut its research and development expenses, significantly, in order to increase current earnings. This action increases the current earnings, immediately. This may result in the increase of current market price. However, the firm is likely to suffer, without significant research and development and the result will be a sharp drop in market price, in the long run.

The market price of a share is linked to the three basis functions of finance:

Investment Decision: Expansion news - once expansion news appears market price flares, anticipating faster development, in short-run.

Finance Decision: Raising a big loan, at a cheap rate of interest in the international market - once the news appears, market price goes up.

Dividend Decision: If a company declares a dividend, beyond the expectations of market, the market price takes a jump. Market price is also dependent on other factors like market sentiments about the proposed investment, economic and political issues.

Maximising Economic Welfare of Shareholders

The objective of maximisation of wealth is the primary goal of financial decision- making. Any financial action which creates wealth or which has a net present worth, above zero, is desirable one and should be undertaken. If two desirable courses of action are mutually exclusive (only one of the two projects can be undertaken, which is the most suitable or economical), then the decision should be to do that action, which shows the highest amount of net present value.

Finance Manager Should Concentrate on Maximising Earnings Per Share: The value of the share, largely, depends on earnings per share. Earnings per share (EPS) depend on the net worth of the firm. This objective is also consistent with the objective of maximising the economic welfare of the shareholders.

Formula for Shareholders' Wealth Maximisation: Net present value concept can be used to measure the shareholders' wealth maximisation. The net present value or worth can be defined, explicitly, in the following way:

$$W = \frac{A_1}{(1+k)} + \frac{A_2}{(1+k)^2} + \ldots \frac{A_n}{(1+k)^n} - C_0$$

$$= \sum_{t=k}^{n} \frac{A_t}{(1+k)^t} - C_0$$

Σ = Sigma (sum)

A = Stream of benefits expected to occur to the firm

k = Appropriate discount rate (cost of capital)

W = Wealth

t assumes values from 1 to η

C_0 = Cost of action

Assumption: The underlying assumption is that the shares are traded in an efficient capital market. In practice, the share price is subject to the influence of several extra forces/factors. The overall economic and political scenario in the country influences the market price of a share. More often than not, the market price of a share may fluctuate on account of speculative activities. All the factors are assumed to be given and constant in this objective.

Profit maximisation can be considered as a part of the wealth maximisation strategy, but should never be permitted to overshadow the latter.

2.5 CRITICISM OF WEALTH MAXIMISATION

Wealth maximisation is criticised by certain financial theorists on the following grounds:

1. The objective of wealth maximisation is not, necessarily, socially desirable.
2. There is some controversy whether the objective of maximisation of wealth is of the firm or stockholders. If wealth of firm were maximised, it would be benefiting the interests of debenture holders and preference shareholders too.
3. In corporate sector, ownership and management are separate unlike in a sole proprietorship. Management acts as the agents of real owners i.e. shareholders. However, there is always a possibility of conflict of interest between the shareholders' interests and managerial interests. The managers may act to maximise their managerial utility but not the wealth of stockholders of the firm. A particular decision may be taken to exhibit their managerial utility and that decision may not be in the exclusive interests of the firm. Many a time, individuals place their personal preferences and selfish interests, ahead of the institutional interests.

2.6 SUPERIORITY OF WEALTH MAXIMISATION COMPARED TO PROFIT MAXIMISATION

Wealth maximisation is superior to profit maximisation for the following reasons:

1. Profit maximisation objective measures the performance of firm, in terms of total profits only. This objective does not consider the risk the firm may undertake in maximising the profits. This objective ignores the effect of earnings per share, dividends paid or any other return to the shareholders.

   The wealth maximisation objective considers all future cash flows, dividend, earning per share and impact of risk decisions. The objective of wealth maximisation is operational and objective in its approach.

2. A firm that wishes profit maximisation may opt not to declare any dividend, at all, and invest the amount of retained earnings for expansion. The objective of wealth maximisation allows the firm to pay regular dividend. Shareholders, certainly, prefer dividend declaration.

   The profit maximisation can be considered as a part of wealth maximisation strategy.

It can be said wealth maximisation is considered to be the main objective of financial management, in comparison to profit maximisation.

2.7 OTHER OBJECTIVES OF FINANCIAL MANAGEMENT

Besides the above basic objectives, the following are the other objectives of financial management:

1. Ensuring a fair return to shareholders.
2. Ensuring maximum operational efficiency by efficient and effective utilisation of finances.
3. Building up reserves for expansion and growth, and
4. Ensuring financial discipline in the organisation.

2.8 CONFLICT OF GOALS

Conflict between departmental goal and firm goal: There are several departments in a firm such as sales department, purchase department, production department and marketing department etc. There may be conflicts among the goals of these departments. Moreover, the internal operative goal of the department may conflict with the goal of the firm. At times, the departmental head may fail to visualise the ultimate corporate goal, which is more important to achieve. It is necessary to resolve these conflicts to achieve the goal of the firm.

Diverse Interests of Stakeholders: Company is a complex organisation. There are various stakeholders in a company, other than the shareholders. They are creditors, debenture holders, employees, customers and society who have their own interest in the organisation.

The interests of stakeholders are different. Every group wants to evaluate the performance of management from its own objective viewpoint. Each group recognises the efficiency of management only when their interests are satisfied. So, management has to satisfy all the groups. By achieving wealth maximisation, management can satisfy all stakeholders. Shareholders are benefited with the maximisation of their equity share prices in the market. Market is defined as the place where the shares are quoted e.g. Bombay stock exchange or National stock exchange. Creditors are more secured about refund of their principal as well as interest amount. Employees get better salaries and can have better career, with improved working conditions.

The real focus of wealth maximisation is on the satisfaction of customers through production of goods and services, with better quality. Unless the customers are satisfied, there would be no survival for the organisation. Even the Government can secure higher revenue through higher tax collection, due to increase in profits. Society, in general, gets the gain in the long run.

Concentration on easily attainable goals: In case of corporate firms, the ownership is held by the shareholders while the management is in the hands of Board of Directors and senior management who work as functional directors or heads. The owners set the goals for management to achieve. Certain goals are easy while others may be difficult to achieve. In a company, the decision-making authority lies in the hands of management. The management may concentrate on easily attainable goals like achievement of production and ignore the effect of the other variables on the market price of the share.

Differing Viewpoints: Usually, the shareholders are scattered and ill organised to control the Board of Directors. Board of Directors may tend to develop their own goals on account of their functional autonomy. More so, now, the professionals hold the senior management positions. This may result in differing viewpoints between the shareholders and management. The professional management may alienate from the viewpoint of the shareholders. This situation has not been there, earlier, when sole proprietorship firms conduct the business.

Survival of Management: The survival of management will be threatened if any objective of the stakeholders remains unfulfilled. It is certain that the management wants to survive, satisfying the interests of all stakeholders, over a long run. So, the management can not pursue its own personal goals because of the continuous supervision by the company's owners, employees, creditors, customers and Government. The responsibility of the management is to maintain a balance between the goals of various groups.

The objective of wealth maximisation may be in general harmony with the interests of the various groups such as owners, employees, creditors and society.

2.9 ORGANISATION OF FINANCE FUNCTION IN A MUTI-DIVISIONAL INDIAN COMPANY

Structure not standardised: The finance function is very vital for every business firm. A firm should give proper attention to the structure and organisation of its finance department. However, the structure of the finance department is not standardised. The structure depends upon the nature, size of the business and requirements and, in particular, expectations of the top management. When sole proprietor conducts the business, he performs even the finance function. With the increase in size of business, joint stock companies have been formed. As there is a divorce in ownership and management, professionals handle this important function.

Freedom with accountability: Due to development of corporate functioning, the finance function is centralised due to its importance. Organisation of the finance function differs from company to company, dependent upon their respective needs and financial philosophy. More so, the role of finance has been increasing as the realisation has been gaining ground, gradually, that the survival and growth of business are more dependent on the finance function. The finance function is delegated to a top management executive who is designated as General Manager (Finance), Executive Director (Finance), Chief Financial Officer (CFO) or even Vice-President (Finance). The finance chief is a member of top management and closely associated with the formulation of policy and decision- making. Below the top head, various functions are described and responsibilities assigned to avoid overlapping and at the same time given freedom of functioning, with the necessary accountability.

Structure Chart: Basically, there are two most important functions – the accounting and finance functions. **The accounting functions are performed by Controller while the Treasurer performs the finance functions.** Both these functionaries work under the close supervision of vice-president (Finance).

An illustrative organisation chart of finance function of management in a large, multi-divisional Indian company is shown, diagrammatically, below:

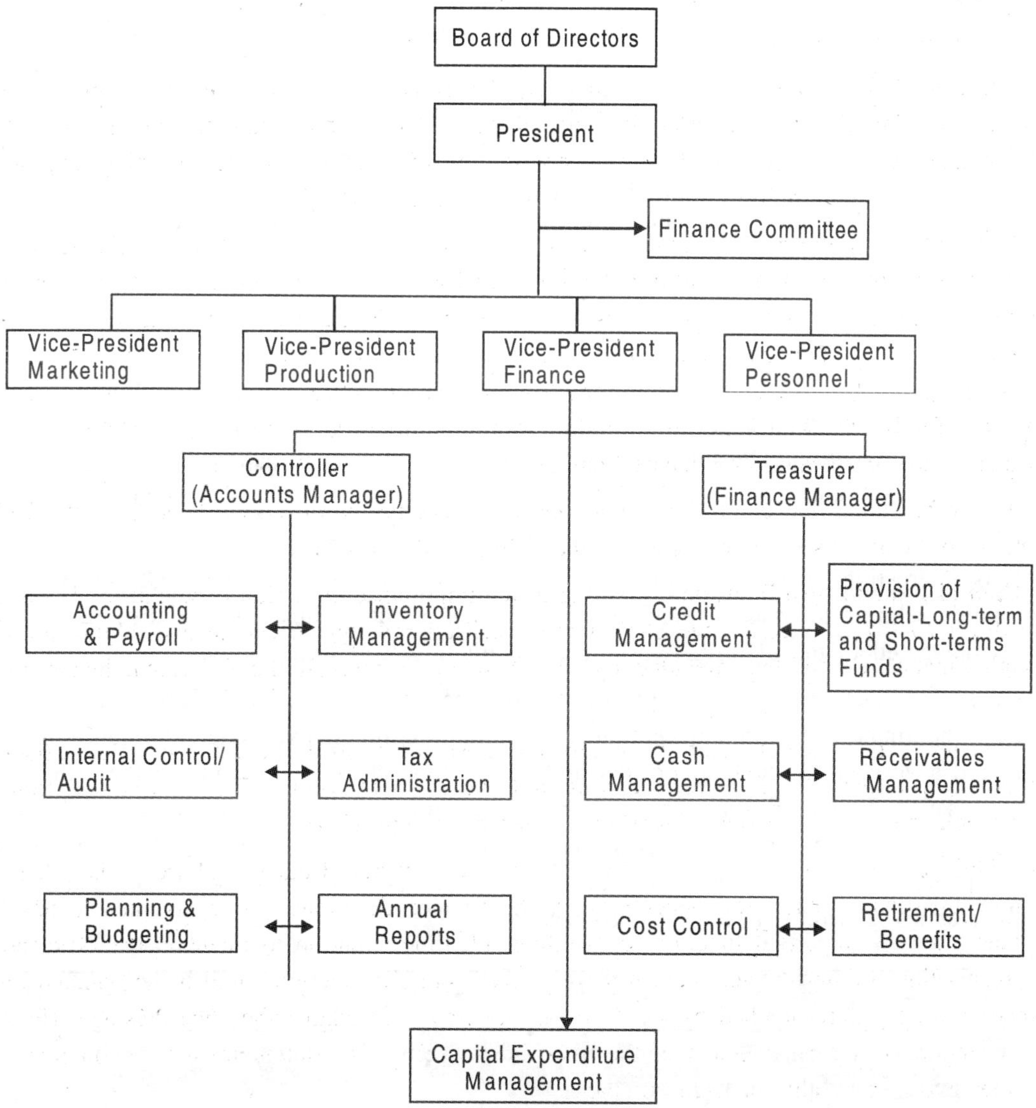

Organisation of Finance Function in a Multi-Division Indian Company

The organisation chart shows that the Vice-President (Finance) is supported by two deputies known as:

1. Controller or Comptroller (Accounts Manager)
2. Treasurer (Finance Manager)

Controller's Functions: Controller's functions, basically, include accounting function, inventory management, planning and budgeting, payroll, all types of tax administration, statutory and internal audit, preparation of annual and financial reports, economic appraisal and reporting and internal control. In some organisations, he is designated as Accounts Manager.

Treasurer's Functions: The major duties of Treasurer include forecasting of financial needs, present and future, both long-term and short-term and arranging required funds, at economic cost, in time. The main function of treasurer is to plan, provide the needed capital and working capital funds and their management. Additionally, he assumes responsibility for cash management and administering the flow of cash, management of receivables, retirement benefits, cost control and protecting funds and securities. He is to coordinate with banks and financial institutions. The treasurer is also designated as Finance Manager.

It may be stated that controller's functions are concerned with the assets side of the balance sheet, while treasurer's functions relate to the liability side in a firm.

Capital Expenditure Decisions: Looking to the importance of capital expenditure, the function is in direct control of Vice-President (Finance). Decisions relating to capital expenditure are taken through Finance Committee, presided by the President, where all the functional heads are the members.

It is interesting to note that the controller does not control the finances. He utilises the information relating to finance for planning and management control. The routine functions are always delegated to the officers, working under their supervision.

Additional functions may be assigned to the finance division. But, the culture, of late, has been to allow the finance chief to concentrate on the finance functions, alone, as finance has been considered a very important function, demanding full time attention to maintain the efficiency of the organisation. Earlier, Government reporting and insurance functions used to be handled by the finance. Now, they are handled by the Company Secretary to enable the Vice-President (Finance) to concentrate on the management of the financial resources. His duties are not compounded with the other duties, generally, in large companies.

Treasurer	Controller
1. Provision of capital (Both long-term and short-term funds)	1. Accounting function
2. Maintaining relationship with banks and financial institutions	2. Preparation of Annual Report and financial reports

3. Credit Management	3. Planning and Budgetary control
4. Cash Management	4. Statutory Audit and Internal Audit
5. Receivables Management	5. Tax Administration
6. Protection of funds and securities	6. Internal Control
7. Cost Control	7. Economic Appraisal

Controller Vs. Treasurer: Both the terms 'Controller' and 'Treasurer' are used in the United States of America, where the total finance functions are divided between them. Many a time, their functions overlap with each other. Both these designations have not become popular in India and these functions are performed by the Manager (Accounts) and Manager (Finance). However, in private sector, with modern management, there is always a trend to give the designations, in a phasionable manner.

The functions of finance depend, largely, on the size of the organisation and the competence and professional background of the person who handles the functions.

Check your Understanding

A. State whether the following statements are True or False:

1. The objective of every company is to maximise value of the equity shares held by its shareholders.
2. A company has drastically reduced the expenditure on R & D to increase current earnings, significantly, which is termed as a good long-term decision as it, maximises profits, immediately.
3. The market price of a share depends on the current and prospective earnings per share.
4. The proper goal of financial management is wealth maximisation, not profit maximisation.
5. When the organisation carries excessive liquidity, profitability does not suffer.
6. It is function of finance manager to bring trade off between liquidity and profitability.
7. Decisions that increase profits are to be undertaken and those that decrease profits are to be avoided.
8. Profit maximisation criterion does not differentiate the returns received at different periods and treats them, alike, irrespective of their timing.
9. Profit maximisation criterion does not recognise time value of money.
10. Wealth maximisation concept is based on the concept of cash flows generated by the organisation.
11. Wealth maximisation is the primary goal of financial decision-making.
12. The traditional objective of financial management is maximisation of profitability of the organisation.
13. Financial management is nothing but cash management.
14. Controller performs the accounting functions while the Treasurer performs the finance functions.
15. The basic dictum in financial planning is "The Earlier-The Better", also referred as time value of money.

Answers

1. True	2. False	3. True	4. True	5. False
6. True	7. True	8. True	9. True	10. True
11. True	12 True	13. False	14. True	15. True

B. Select the most appropriate answer

1. The appropriate objective of an enterprise is
   (A) Maximisation of owner's wealth
   (B) Maximisation of net profits
   (C) Maximisation of sales
2. Basic objective of financial management is
   (A) Maximisation of profits
   (B) Maximisation of shareholders' wealth
   (C) Ensuring financial discipline in the firm

Answers

1. A 2. B

C. Fill in the blanks with the most appropriate word

1. The ______ side of the balance sheet is managed by the Comptroller.
2. Amongst the functions of __________, rising of finance is a primary function.

Answers

1. assets 2. treasurer

Review Questions

1. "The Profit Maximisation is not an operationally feasible criterion". Illustrate your views with suitable examples? **(2.1 to 2.3)**
2. "Goal of wealth maximisation is a better operational criterion than profit maximisation" – Illustrate? **(2.1 to 2.4)**
3. Of the two objectives of financial management viz.profit maximisation and wealth maximisation, which one do you think is a better operational guide for a finance manager and justify with reasoning? **(2.1 to 2.4)**
4. In what ways is the wealth maximisation objective superior to the profit maximisation objective. Explain? **(2.1 to 2.6)**
5. Explain the two goals of financial management (a) Maximisation of profits and (b) Maximisation of wealth and show which one you think to be better and why? **(2.1 to 2.6)**
6. Describe the objectives of Financial Management? **(2.1 to 2.7)**

7. When can there be conflicts between owners and management's goals? How wealth maximisation can take care of this? **(2.8)**
8. Draw an illustrative chart of a multi-divisional Indian Company showing the finance functions? What functions do the financial officers perform? **(2.9)**
9. How should the finance function of a large enterprise be organised? What functions are performed by the finance division? Do you advocate additional functions to them? **(2.9)**
10. Write short notes on
    (A) Interests of stakeholders in Wealth maximisation **(2.8)**
    (B) Functions of Controller and Treasurer **(2.9)**

3

FINANCIAL RATIO ANALYSIS

- Introduction
  - Meaning
  - Scope
- Users of Financial Analysis
- Types of Financial Analysis
  - Internal Analysis
  - External Analysis
  - Horizontal Analysis
  - Vertical Analysis
- Standards of Companions
- Types of Ratios
  - Liquidity Ratios
    - Problem of Window Dressing
  - Leverage Ratios
  - Activity Ratios
  - Profitability Ratios
    - Trading on Equity
- Different Terms in Ratios Analysis
- Liquids Ratios
  - Current Ratios
- Leverage Ratios
- Activity Ratios
- Limitations of Ratio Analysis
- Common-size statement
- Summary of Ratios and their Purpose
- Illustrations
- Review Questions
- Check Your Understanding

3.1 INTRODUCTION

Ratio analysis is an important and powerful technique or method, generally, used for financial analysis. **The term 'Financial Analysis' is also known as analysis and interpretation of financial statements.** The purpose of financial analysis is to diagnose the information content in financial statements so as to judge the profitability, financial soundness of the firm and chalk out the way to improve existing performance. Every management is interested in knowing the financial strengths to make their better use and spot out the weaknesses of the firm to take suitable corrective action, in time.

A ratio or financial ratio is a relationship between two accounting figures, expressed mathematically. It helps to ascertain the financial condition of the firm. In financial analysis, a ratio is compared against a benchmark for evaluating the financial position and performance of a firm. Ratios help to summarise large quantities of financial data to make qualitative judgement about the firm's financial performance.

Meaning: Financial analysis is the process of identifying the financial strengths and weaknesses of the firm, by properly establishing the relationships between the items contained in balance sheet and profit and loss account.

Scope: Ratios are the symptoms of health of an organisation like blood pressure, pulse or temperature of an individual. **Ratios are the indicators for further investigation**. With a single ratio, no conclusion is to be arrived at. The ratios are to be studied in relation to each other, in comparison of the past ratios of the firm as well as ratios of the industry, better with its immediate competitors to understand their relative significance and impact.

3.2 USERS OF FINANCIAL ANALYSIS

Financial analysis can be undertaken by the management of the firm, or by the interested parties, outside the firm. The outsiders of the firm are owners (shareholders), creditors, investors and others, in particular potential lenders. The nature of the analysis depends upon their purpose or requirement. They make the necessary analysis and take the decision, based on their assessment of the results obtained.

Trade creditors are those who have supplied goods and services to the firm. They are interested in their timely repayment. So, before they supply or render service, they want to be sure that the firm would be in a position to pay their dues, in a short period. They analyse their evaluation of the firm to the firm's short-term liquidity position. The term 'liquidity' refers to the ability to pay, as and when the debts fall due for payment.

Suppliers of long-term debt are those who provide loans for a long period. They are concerned with the firm's **long-term solvency and survival**, which depends on profitability and cash generation. Before they lend, they want to assure themselves that the organisation would be able to generate adequate liquid funds to pay the loan instalment and interest. They are more concerned with the future outlook, rather than the past, based on the projections of the firm. They analyse the historical data, based on the financial statements, to determine the basis and reasonableness of the projections to decide the future financial standing of the firm.

Shareholders and investors invest their money in the firm's shares to earn dividend and appreciation of share value. They are concerned with the firm's **present and future profitability**. The ability of the company to pay dividends depends on the future prospects and earning capacity of the organisation. They would have more confidence in those firms, which show steady growth in earnings. They are also interested in the firm's financial structure to the extent it influences the firm's earning ability.

Employees and Management: The importance of trust and harmonious relationship between the employees and management requires no more emphasis for accelerated growth of the firm. If the employees feel confident of more salaries, retirement benefits and fast track career growth, in future, their loyalty would be assured. Employees look for stability and profitability in financial statements.

Management of the firm would be interested in **every aspect of financial analysis**. Management is concerned with the effective and efficient utilisation of resources, analysing the financial statements and other information available to them.

Government regulates the functioning of all organisations for the benefit of public. It has to generate adequate revenue for this purpose. Collection of taxes and information for deciding future policies are based on the financial statements of the firms.

It is clear that the different users need the financial statements for different purposes. The aim of the financial statements is to provide the information required for divergent needs.

3.3 TYPES OF FINANCIAL ANALYSIS

Financial analysis can be classified into two categories depending upon

(i) Material used and

(ii) Method of operation followed (modus operandi analysis)

(i) On the basis of Material used: According to this category, financial analysis can be of two types. They are:

(A) External Analysis: Those people who do not have access to the internal records of the firm do this analysis. Basically, they are creditors, present and potential investors, Government agencies, credit agencies and the general public. Normally, except select employees in the firm, all others do not have access to the internal records. There is always a time lag, after the publication of accounts. So, updated or recent information is not available for analysis. Due to this inherent limitation, this type of analysis serves a limited purpose as the analysis is based on the published financial accounts, audited or not audited. However, of late, the position has, significantly, improved due to government regulations to make the published accounts more frequent, transparent and detailed.

(B) Internal Analysis: This analysis is done by those persons who have the access to the books of accounts, financial and other records, of the firm. Basically, this analysis can be done by the employees and executives of the firm who have access to the records. Even the Government agencies also can do when they have the statutory powers to access the records. This analysis would be more meaningful and useful as the analysis is made on the basis of full records and with a specific objective. The management of the firm would, invariably, adopt internal analysis for managerial purposes.

(ii) **On the basis of Method of Operation:** Financial analysis can be of two types, based on this method. They are of two types, viz. Horizontal analysis and Vertical Analysis.

(C) Horizontal Analysis: When financial statements of a number of years of the same firm are compared and reviewed, it is known as Horizontal Analysis. Horizontal analysis helps to observe the changes in the financial variables, across the years. For this analysis, first base or standard year is chosen as a starting point. Any year may be taken as the base year, but, generally, the starting or initial year is taken as the base year. All the financial figures are presented in a horizontal manner.— The figures of the various years are compared to the base or standard year. Keeping the data of base year in the beginning, the data of the different years are kept in separate columns. — Base year figures are taken as 100 for the purpose of comparison. The attention of the management would be focussed on those items, which have changed significantly. The purpose of the analysis is to identify the strengths and weaknesses of the firm. Comparison of the item, over several years, shows the development of trend. The management would be able to get insight of the strength or problem for necessary action, in time. Since this analysis is based on the data from year to year rather than on one year data, this analysis is also termed as **Dynamic analysis**.

(D) Vertical Analysis: Vertical analysis refers to the study of relationship of the various items contained in the financial statement of one accounting period. For example, the ratios of different items of cost for a particular period are calculated with the sales for that period. So, sales are taken as 100 and each expense is taken as a percentage of sales, i.e. 100. Such analysis is useful in comparing the performance of several companies in the same group or industry, or divisions or departments in the same company.

Common–size financial statements and financial ratios are the two tools employed in vertical analysis. Vertical analysis is also known as **'Static Analysis'**.

Combined use of Horizontal and Vertical Analysis: Both analyses can be used, simultaneously. Vertical analysis can be used along with horizontal analysis to make it more effective and meaningful.

A simple sample of vertical analyses and its comparison with the industry and its immediate competitor would be like this:

Vertical Analysis for X Ltd

Item	2003 (Base year)	2004	2005	2006
Sales	100	100	100	100
Cost of sales	70	69	68	67
Selling and administrative expenses	7	7	7	7
Financial expenses	13	14	15	16
Profit	10	10	10	10

Vertical Analysis for X Ltd in comparison with Industry and its immediate Competitor (Year 2006)

Item	X Ltd	Industry Average	Immediate Competitor (Z Ltd)
Sales	100	100	100
Cost of sales	67	72	71
Selling and administrative expenses	7	7	7
Financial expenses	16	13	12
Profit	10	8	10

The position reveals that the financial expenses of X Ltd have been increasing from year to year, compared to the base year 2003. The same is confirmed that the firm's percentage of financial expenses for the year 2006 is more than the industry as well as its immediate competitor. On other hand, production and purchase departments have been improving their performance year after year, reducing cost of production. Even their cost of sales is lower than the industry and its immediate competitor for the year 2006. The efficiency of production and purchase departments is neutralised, greately, by the inefficiency of finance division in X Ltd that requires further investigation to improve its profitability. Despite the inefficiency of finance division, still profitability of X Ltd is higher than the industry and equal to its immediate competitor. The profit margin to sales has been stagnant during the period 2003-06. If finance division's performance is improved, X Ltd can improve its profitability, further. This analysis indicates the area, where focus of action and improvement is immediately essential to show better results.

3.4 STANDARDS OF COMPARISON

A single ratio is not meaningful. For proper interpretation and understanding, ratios are to be compared. Comparison can be with

- **Past ratios** i.e. ratios from previous years' financial statements of the same firm.
- **Competitors' ratios** i.e. similar ratios of the nearest successful competitors.
- **Industry ratios** i.e. ratios of the industry to which the firm belongs to.
- **Projected ratios** i.e. ratios developed by the firm which were prepared, earlier, and projected to achieve.

3.5 TYPES OF RATIOS

Several ratios can be grouped into various classes, according to the activity or function they perform. We have, already, discussed there are several groups of persons—creditors, investors, lenders, management and public—interested in interpretation of the ratios. Each group wishes to interpret ratios for those purposes, they are interested in, to take appropriate decisions to serve their own individual interests. In view of the requirements of the various users of the ratios, the ratios can be classified into four categories:

A. Liquidity Ratios: They measure the firm's ability to meet current obligations.

B. Leverage Ratios: These ratios show the proportion of debt and equity in financing the firm's assets.

C. Activity Ratios: They reflect the firm's efficiency in utilising the assets.

D. Profitability Ratios: These ratios measure overall performance and effectiveness of the firm.

3.5.1 Analysis of ratios without interpretation is meaningless and interpretation without analysis is impossible.

Here, a distinction is to be drawn between analysis and interpretation. Analysis means methodical classification of data and presented in a simplified form for easy understanding. Interpretation means assigning reasons for the behaviour in respect of the data, presented in the simplified form. Once analysis is made, interpretation should follow. Only analysis does not serve any purpose, without interpretation. Interpretation is not possible without making the analysis. Careful analysis and meaningful interpretation, both are important. Analysis and interpretation are complementary to each other. Both are essential. They are not independent, but they go hand in hand.

To have meaningful utilisation of analysis, it is necessary to be clear to whom the analysis is made and their purpose or requirement for analysis. **Once the purpose is clear, the required ratios can be identified**. There are different formulae available for different ratios. For calculation of debt-equity ratio, some authors take total liabilities while others take only long-term liabilities for computation. Different reasoning is given for the treatment adopted. Similarly, while calculating current ratio, current liabilities are calculated, differently. Some authors include short-term bank borrowing while some do not include in current liabilities, again for different interpretations. **What is important and necessary is consistent approach**. The same formulae and similar treatment have to be used for all the years of comparison. Equally, the approach should be uniform for all the firms for which comparison is made. Otherwise, distorted results would emerge and the interpretation based on the results would be meaningless. This situation is to be avoided. Once the results are calculated, interpretation is necessary to understand and arrived some indications or signals. The results are not the end, but they are the beginning for further investigation. After calculating one ratio, no conclusion is to be arrived at. Ratios are to be studied together, not in isolation.

3.6 DIFFERENT TERMS IN RATIO ANALYSIS

To have understanding of ratios, it is required to know how the required information can be calculated from:

Statement of Cost of Goods Sold

Raw Materials	xxx
Direct Labour	xxx
Depreciation	xxx
Other manufacturing expenses	xxx
	xxx
Add: Opening stock in process	xxx
	xxx
Less: Closing stock in process	xxx
Cost of Production	**xxx**
Add: Opening Stock of Finished goods	xxx
	xxx
Less: Closing stock of finished goods	xxx
Cost of Goods Sold	**xxx**

Break up of Profit and Loss Account for the year ending ......

A.	Net Sales	xxx
B.	Cost of Goods sold	xxx
C.	Gross Profit (A-B)	xxx
D.	Less: Selling & Administrative expenses	xxx
E.	Operating income (C-D)	xxx
F.	Add: Other income	xxx
G.	Earning before interest and tax (EBIT) (E+F)	xxx
H.	Less: Interest	xxx
I.	Profit before tax (PBT) (G-H)	xxx
J.	Provision for tax	xxx
K.	Profit after tax (PAT) (I-J)	xxx
L.	Dividend distributed	xxx
M.	Retained earnings	xxx

Break up of Balance Sheet as on...

A. Net Worth			
Equity Share capital	xxx		
Preference Share capital	xxx		
Reserves	xxx		
Net worth			xxx
B. Long-Term Borrowings			
Long–term: Debentures	xxx		
Others	xxx		
Long–term debt	xxx		
Long–term borrowings			xxx
C. Capital Employed (A+B)			**xxx**
D. Fixed Assets			
Gross block	xxx		
Less: depreciation	xxx		
Net block		xxx	
Other non-current assets	xxx		
Net fixed assets			xxx
E. Current Assets			
Inventories:			
Raw material	xxx		
Stock in process	xxx		
Finished goods	xxx		
Inventories		xxx	
Debtors		xxx	
Cash and bank balance		xxx	
Others		xxx	
Current assets			xxx
F. Less: Current Liabilities			
Trade creditors		xxx	
Bank overdraft/cash credit		xxx	
Provision and others		xxx	
Current liabilities			xxx

G. **Net Current Assets (E-F)** xxx

H. **Net Assets (D+G)** xxx

The above statement shows

Net Assets = Capital Employed

3.7 LIQUIDITY RATIOS

Liquidity ratios are highly useful to creditors and commercial banks that provide short-term credit. Short-term refers to a period not exceeding one year. Liquidity ratios measure the firm's ability to meet current obligations, as and when they fall due. **A firm should ensure that it does not suffer from lack of liquidity, and also does not have excess liquidity**. In the absence of adequate liquidity, the firm would not be able to pay creditors who have supplied goods and services, on the due date promised. Firm's goodwill suffers, in case of default in payment. In fact, dissatisfied suppliers, normally, refuse to supply, further. Who can finance, indefinitely? Loss of creditworthiness may result in legal problems, finally, culminating in the closure of business of a company, even. If the firm maintains more liquidity, it will not experience any difficulty in making payments. However, a higher degree of liquidity is bad, as idle assets earn nothing while there is cost for the funds. The firm's funds will be, unnecessarily, tied up in liquid assets.

So, both inadequate and excess liquidity are not desirable. Therefore, it is necessary for the firm to strike a proper balance between high liquidity and lack of liquidity.

3.7.1. Current Ratio

Current ratio is defined as the relationship between current assets and current liabilities. It is also known as working capital ratio. This is calculated by dividing total current assets by total current liabilities.

$$\text{Current ratio} = \frac{\text{Current assets}}{\text{Current liabilities}}$$

The two basic components of the ratio are current assets and current liabilities. Current assets are those which can be realised within a short period of time, generally one year. Similarly, current liabilities are those which are to be paid, within a period of one year. The components of current assets and current liabilities are shown hereunder. It is significant to note, even, prepaid expenses are included in current assets as they have been paid, in advance, and will not have to be paid, in near future.

Similarly, **current liabilities include bank overdraft or cash credit account as they are, normally, sanctioned by the bank for a period of one year**. Technically, they are sanctioned for one year, but banks renew them unless there are significant adverse reasons or firm does not require renewal. **Reason for inclusion in current liability category is the written sanction of bank is available for one year, only.**

Treatment of Bank Overdraft/Cash Credit: There is a difference of opinion about the treatment of bank overdraft/cash credit. Some authors treat them as current liabilities while others treat as part of long-term liabilities. Bank sanctions overdraft/cash credit limits for a period of one year, only. In the normal course, after the expiry of one year, the firm has to repay the borrowing. Firms do not, normally, repay as the banks renew the limit, at the request of the firm. However, the written sanction of the borrowing is, invariably, for one year only. **Unless bank renews the limit, technically, firm can not avail the limit, further. We have treated Bank overdraft/ cash credit as current liabilities, through out the book**. Some authors treat them as long-term borrowings. The reason is firms continue to enjoy the borrowings, indefinitely, as banks renew the sanction, without much difficulty. Normally, banks give renewal sanction, at the request of the firm, after submission of the required data, unless there are adverse features in the conduct of the account. **Students are advised to give specific mention of their treatment and give the reasoning for the treatment given either as current liabilities or long-term liabilities**. Whatever approach is followed, the treatment is to be consistently followed.

Components of Current Ratio

	Current Assets		Current Liabilities
1.	Cash in hand	1.	Sundry Creditors
2.	Cash at Bank	2.	Bills Payable
3.	Marketable Securities (short-term)	3.	Bank Overdraft/Cash credit
4.	Short-term investments	4.	Short-term Advances
5.	Sundry Debtors	5.	Outstanding Expenses
6.	Bills Receivable	6.	Income-Tax Payable
7.	Inventory-Raw Materials	7.	Dividend Payable
8.	Inventory-Work in Process		
9.	Inventory-Finished Goods		
10.	Prepaid Expenses		
11.	Advance Tax paid		
12.	Accrued Income		

Interpretation of Current Ratio: As a conventional rule, current ratio of 2:1 is considered satisfactory. The rule is based on the logic that in the worst situation, even if the value of current assets becomes half, the firm will be able to meet its obligations, fully. A 'two to one ratio' is referred to as 'Rule of thumb' or arbitrary standard of the liquidity of the firm. This current ratio represents a margin of safety for creditors. Realisation of assets may decline, but, all the liabilities have to be paid, in full.

However, the arbitrary ratio of 2:1 should not be, blindly, followed. Firms with less than 2:1 ratio may be meeting the liabilities, without difficulty, though firms with a ratio of more than 2:1 may be struggling to meet their obligations to pay. A current ratio of 1.33: 1 is considered as the minimum acceptable level by banks for providing working capital finance. Looking at the mere ratio in figures, no conclusion is to be arrived at. This is because the **current ratio is a test of quantity, not test of quality. It is essential to verify the composition and quality of assets before, finally, taking a decision about the adequacy of the ratio**. The current ratio is a crude-and-quick measure of the firm's liquidity.

A high current ratio, due to the following causes, may not be favourable for the following reasons:

1. Slow-moving or dead stock/s piled up due to poor sales.
2. Figure of debtors may be high as debtors are not capable of paying or debt collection system of the firm is not satisfactory.
3. Cash or bank balances may be high, due to idle funds.

On the other hand, a low current ratio may be due to the following reasons:

1. Insufficiency of funds to pay creditors
2. Firm may be trading beyond resources and the resources are inadequate to the high volume of trade.

Illustration No.1: To explain composition and quality of Current Assets is more important to comment on adequacy of current ratio, not merely basing on crude figures of current ratio:

Balance sheet as at 31st March, 2006
(Rs. in thousands)

	X	Z		X	Z
Liabilities			Assets		
Share Capital	400	600	Fixed Assets	100	100
Sundry Creditors	600	400	Cash	50	10
			Stock	150	700
			Debtors	700	190
	1,000	1,000		1,000	1,000

Let us analyse the current ratio of both the companies X and Z.

$$\text{Current Ratio} = \frac{\text{Current Assets}}{\text{Current Liabilities}}$$

$$= \frac{\text{Cash} + \text{Stock} + \text{Debtors}}{\text{Creditors}}$$

$$\text{Current Ratio of X} = \frac{10 + 700 + 190}{400} = 1.5$$

$$\text{Current Ratio of Z} = \frac{50+150+700}{400}$$

$$= 2.25$$

The current ratio of Z is 2.25, which appears better as it exceeds the standard ratio of 2 while the ratio of X is 1.5, low compared to the standard. So, one may conclude that the current ratio of Z is better than X.

But, once we analyse the composition of quality of current assets, after collecting further information and the relevant ratios, of both X and Z, it is ascertained:

	Standard	X	Z
Stock holding	2 months' turnover	2 months	7 months
Debtors' collection Period	30 days	20 days	100 days
Creditors' payment Period	30 days	30 days	90 days

This situation points out with a single ratio, immediately; conclusions are not to be drawn.

It is desirable, further, to seek confirmation that X has not been missing business opportunities due to limited holding of stocks and quick realisation of debtors. The above analysis indicates X has been collecting its debtors, more speedily, and managing the inventory, efficiently. For these reasons, X is able to meet the current obligations, even though its current ratio is lower than the standard ratio. Unless we analyse the composition and quality of current assets, and analyzing the other ratios, one should not conclude, merely, based on one ratio.

Problem of Window Dressing : When current assets and current liabilities are manipulated to show a better picture than what is real, it is known as Window Dressing. Current assets and current liabilities are manipulated in such a way that the current ratio loses its significance. Assume current assets are 90,000 and current liabilities are also 60,000, in the normal times. Here, the current ratio is 1.5, not totally satisfactory. Firm makes special efforts, just before the end of the year, to realize 30,000 from debtors and pay off the creditors to that extent. In consequence, current assets become 60,000 and current liabilities 30,000. Now, the current ratio is 2. This ratio is considered, now, satisfactory. The position of current assets and current liabilities is not the true picture as they do not appear in the normal times. With effort, the firm has managed to realize the debts and paid the creditors, deliberately, to show a rosy picture, at the end of the year.

Window dressing can be created in the following ways:

(i) Over valuation of closing stock

(ii) Treating a short-term liability as long-term liability

(iii) Omission of a liability

(iv) Including obsolete inventory in the closing stock, instead of writing off

(v) Not treating debtors as bad even though not recoverable and continuing to exhibit as if they are still recoverable, and

(vi) Clearing creditors at the end of the year, bringing pressure on debtors for collection, only at the end of the year, to show a better picture.

The purpose of window dressing is to show a rosy picture of the firm, which is not in reality. The inference drawn on such a ratio will be faulty and deceptive.

Limitations of Current Ratio: Though current ratio is one of the important ratios to measure liquidity, it suffers from the following limitations:

1. It is a crude measurement of liquidity. It measures only the quantity, not quality of current assets.
2. Ratio is calculated from the balance sheet figures at the end of the year. This can be manipulated to show a better position than what is actually at the end of the year.
3. Even though the ratio may be good, the firm may be in financial problem with heavy stocks not able to convert into cash and debtors not being realized, within the standard period of credit allowed.

3.7.2. Liquid / Quick /Acid Test Ratio / Near Money Ratio

Liquid ratio establishes the relationship between liquid assets and current liabilities. Liquid assets are those that can be converted into cash quickly, without loss of value. Cash and balance in current account with bank are the most liquid assets. Other assets that are considered, relatively, liquid are debtors, bills receivable and marketable securities (temporary, quoted investments purchased, instead of holding idle cash). Inventories and prepaid expenses are excluded from this category. Inventories are considered less liquid as they require time for realising into cash and have a tendency to fluctuate, in value, at the time of realisation. Prepaid expenses cannot be recovered in cash, normally, hence they are excluded.

$$\text{Quick ration} = \frac{\text{Liquid assets*}}{\text{Current liabilities}}$$

*inventories and prepaid expenses are excluded

Interpretation of Liquid Ratio: Liquid ratio of 1:1 is, normally, considered satisfactory. However, firms with the ratio of more than 1:1 need not be liquid and those having less than the standard need not, necessarily, be illiquid. It depends more on the composition of liquid assets. Debtors, normally, constitute a major part in liquid assets. If the debtors are slow paying, doubtful and long outstanding, they may not be totally liquid. So, firms even with high liquid ratio, containing such type of debtors, may experience the problem in meeting current obligations, as and when they fall due. On the other hand, inventories may not be, totally, non-liquid. To a certain extent, they may be available to meet current obligations. So, firms not having the liquid ratio of 1:1 may not experience difficulty in meeting the current obligations, depending on the efficient realisation of inventories. On the other hand, firms with a better ratio (more than 1:1) may still struggle, if their debtors are not realised as per the schedule.

3.7.3. Cash Ratio or Absolute Liquid Ratio

Cash is the most liquid asset. Although receivables (debtors) and bills receivable are, generally, better realisable than inventories, still, there are doubts regarding their realisation, more so, in time. So, they are not considered, immediately, available for making payments and so excluded for the calculation of cash ratio.

$$\text{Cash ratio} = \frac{\text{Cash \& Bank + Short-Term Securities}}{\text{Current Liabilities}}$$

Cash ratio of 1:2 is considered acceptable. It means Rs. 1 liquid assets are considered adequate to pay Rs. 2 of current liabilities as all the creditors are not expected to demand cash, at the same time, and cash may be realised, at least something, from debtors and inventories too. More so, sanctioned working capital limits of the bank are not always, fully, utilised and the balance drawing power is available to the firm for immediate withdrawal of cash.

Illustration No.2:

Current Ratio = 2.8

Acid-test Ratio = 1.5

Working Capital = Rs. 1,62,000

Find out

(A) Current Assets

(B) Current Liabilities

(C) Liquid Assets

(B.U. - MBA June, 2004)

Solution:

$$\text{Current Ratio} = 2.8$$

It means if current assets are 280, current liabilities are 100.

$$\text{Current Ratio} = \frac{\text{Current Assets}}{\text{Current liabilities}}$$

$$= \frac{280}{100} = 2.8$$

Working Capital = Current Assets – Current Liabilities

= 2.8 – 1

= 1.8

Working Capital = 1,62,000

In such a case, if 1.8 is Rs. 1,62,000, current Assets (2.8) would be 2,52,000 and current liabilities (1) would be Rs. 90,000.

The correctness can be checked with the current ratio.

$$\text{Current Ratio} = \frac{2,52,000}{90,000}$$

$$= 2.8$$

$$\text{Acid Test Ratio or Liquid Ratio} = \frac{\text{Liquid Assets}}{\text{Current Liabilities}}$$

Liquid assets = Current Assets – Stock

Liquid ratio is 1.5. It means if current liabilities are 1, liquid assets are 1.5.

Current liabilities are Rs. 90,000, so liquid assets are Rs. 1,35,000.

$$\text{Acid Test Ratio or Liquid Ratio} = \frac{1,35,000}{90,000}$$

$$= 1.5$$

(A) Current Assets = Rs. 2,52,000

(B) Current Liabilities = Rs. 90,000

(C) Liquid Assets = Rs. 1,35,000

Illustration No.3:

(A) The only current assets possessed by a firm are – cash Rs. 1,05,000, inventories Rs. 5,60,000 and debtors Rs. 4,20,000. If the current ratio for the firm is 2:1, determine its current liabilities.

(B) At the close of the year, a company has an inventory of Rs. 1,50,000 and cost of goods sold Rs. 9,75,000. If the company's turnover ratio is 5, determine the opening balance of inventory.

(B.U. -MBA -2004)

Solution:

(A) **Current Assets**	**Rs.**
Cash	1,05,000
Inventories	5,60,000
Debtors	4,20,000
Total current Assets	10,85,000

Current ratio of the firm is 2:1. If current assets are 2, Current liabilities are 1.

$$\text{Current Ratio} = \frac{\text{Current Assets}}{\text{Current liabilities}} = 2$$

$$= \frac{10{,}85{,}000}{\text{Current liabilities}} = 2$$

$$\text{Current liabilities} = \frac{10{,}85{,}000}{2}$$

$$= 5{,}42{,}500$$

(B) Stock Turnover Ratio $= \dfrac{\text{Cost of goods sold}}{(\text{Opening stock} + \text{Closing stock})/2}$

$$\frac{9{,}75{,}000}{(\text{Opening stock} + 1{,}50{,}000)} = 5$$

$$\frac{19{,}50{,}000}{(\text{Opening stock} + 1{,}50{,}000)} = 5$$

$$5(\text{Opening stock} + 1{,}50{,}000) = 19{,}50{,}000$$

$$5 \times \text{Opening stock} + 7{,}50{,}000 = 19{,}50{,}000$$

$$\text{Opening stock} = \frac{19{,}50{,}000 - 7{,}50{,}000}{5}$$

$$= \frac{12{,}00{,}000}{5}$$

$$= 2{,}40{,}000$$

The correctness can be checked with the calculation of average stock, (2,40,000+1,50,000)/2 which works out to 1,95,000.

$$\frac{9,75,000}{1,95,000} = 5$$

So, opening stock = 2,40,000

Tutorial Note: In the examinations, students are advised to check the correctness of their answer with the formulae, once the required information is found out.

3.8. LEVERAGE RATIOS

Leverage ratios indicate the long-term solvency of the firm. Leverage ratios indicate the mix of debt and owners' equity in financing the assets of the firm. These ratios measure the extent of debt financing in a firm.

To whom these ratios are important? : Short-term creditors like suppliers of raw materials and banks that provide working capital are concerned with short-term solvency of the firm. On the other hand, long term-creditors like debenture holders, financial institutions that provide long-term capital are concerned with long-term solvency. In fact, it is necessary for the firm to have short-term as well as long-term solvency for financial strength. Long-term solvency relate to the firm's ability to meet

(i) Interest on the debt and

(ii) Instalment on the principal amount, on the due date.

3.8.1. Debt-Equity Ratio

Debt-Equity Ratio is also known as External-Internal Equity Ratio. **This ratio is calculated to measure the relative claims of outsiders and owners against the firm's assets.** The ratio shows the relationship between the external equities (outsiders' funds) and internal equities (shareholders' funds).

This ratio can be calculated in two ways. The numerator can only be long-term debt such as debentures, mortgages or long-term loans. Alternatively, it can be total debt that includes both long-term and short-term liabilities. **We are of the opinion that current liabilities (short-term liabilities) should be included in the total debt for calculating debt equity ratio.**

$$\text{Debt-Equity Ration} = \frac{\text{Total Debt}}{\text{Net Worth*}}$$

or

$$\frac{\text{Long-term Debt}}{\text{Net Worth*}}$$

* Net Worth = Equity Share Capital + Preference Share Capital + Reserves and Surplus

The accumulated losses and deferred expenses, if any, should be deducted to arrive at net worth.

Treatment of Preference Share Capital: There is a difference of opinion on the inclusion of preference share capital in outsiders' funds (numerator) or shareholders' funds (denominator). The reason for including in numerator (Total debt) is that the funds bear a fixed rate of dividend as commitment to the firm, similar to interest on debentures. If preference share capital is treated as borrowing, it is to be included in the numerator. It may be noted though the preference share capital bears the obligation of fixed dividend, yet, is not in the nature of debt, a basic aspect to be remembered. **The preference share capital does not bring any financial risk to the firm, in the absence of profit and non-payment of dividend, which is the basic character of debt. We are of the opinion to treat the preference share capital as shareholders' funds and be included in the net worth (denominator). Students are advised to give specific mention of the treatment and substantiate with reasoning.**

Interpretation of Debt-Equity Ratio: This ratio indicates the extent to which debt financing has been used in business. The purpose is to get an idea about the cushion available to outsiders, in the event of liquidation. As a general rule, there should be a mix of debt and equity. The owners want to conduct business, with maximum outsiders' funds to take less risk for their investment. At the same time, they want to maximise their earnings, at the cost and risk of outsiders' funds. The outsiders (lenders and creditors) want the owners to invest their share, on a higher side, in the business and assume the incidental risk.

Total debt to Net worth of 1:1 is considered satisfactory, although there is no rule of thumb. In some businesses, a high ratio 2:1 or even more may be considered satisfactory, say, for example in the case of contractor's business. It all depends upon the financial policy of the firm and nature of business. Generally speaking, the long-term creditors welcome a low ratio as owners' funds provide the necessary cushion to them, in the event of liquidation. It is a better approach to compare the DE ratio of the firm with that of the industry to which it belongs to for proper comparison. Every industry has its own peculiar characteristics relating to capital requirements. For example, in case of basic and heavy industries, the DE ratio is always higher compared to manufacturing concerns.

Impact of High Ratio: A high debt-Equity Ratio may be unfavourable as the firm may not be able to raise further borrowing, without paying higher interest, and accepting stringent conditions. This situation creates undue pressures and unfavourable conditions to the firm from the creditors.

3.8.2. Total Debt Ratio (TD Ratio)

Total Debt Ratio compares the total debts (long-term as well as short-term) with total assets.

$$\text{Total Debt Ratio} = \frac{\text{Total Debt}}{\text{Total Assets}}$$

$$= \frac{\text{Long Term Debts} + \text{Current liabilities}}{\text{Total Debts} + \text{Net Worth}}$$

Interpretation of Total Debt Ratio: This ratio depicts the proportion of total assets, financed by total liabilities. Impliedly, the remaining assets are financed by the shareholders.

A higher DE ratio or TD ratio shows the firm is trading on equity. In case, the rate of return of the firm is more than the cost of debt, it implies higher return to the shareholders. On the other hand, a lower ratio implies low risk to lenders and creditors of the firm and non-existence of trading on equity. So, neither the higher nor the lower ratio is desirable from the point of view of the shareholders. A higher ratio is a threat to the solvency of the firm. A lower ratio is an indication that the firm may be missing the available opportunities to improve profitability. What is required a balanced proportion of debt and equity so as to take care of the interests of lenders, the shareholders and the firm, as a whole.

The degree of financial leverage and the return to shareholders will be analysed, in detail, in the chapter dealing with leverages, later.

3.8.3 Coverage Ratios

Debt ratios are static and fail to indicate the ability of the firm to meet interest obligations. The interest coverage ratio is used to test the firm's debt-servicing capacity. The interest coverage ratio shows the number of times the interest charges are covered by funds that are ordinarily available to pay interest charges.

As taxes are computed on earnings after deducting interest, earnings before taxes are taken. Depreciation is a non-cash item. Therefore, funds equal to depreciation are also available for payment of interest charges. So, the interest coverage ratio is computed by dividing the earnings before depreciation interest and taxes (EBDIT) by interest charges.

$$\text{Interest Coverage} = \frac{\text{EBDIT}}{\text{Interest}}$$

Interpretation of Coverage Ratio: This ratio indicates the extent to which earnings can fall, without causing any embarrassment to the firm, regarding the payment of interest charges. The higher the IC ratio, better it is both for the firm and lenders. For the firm, the probability of default in payment of interest is reduced and for the lenders, the firm is considered to be less risky. However, too high a ratio indicates the firm is very conservative in not using the debt to its best advantage of the shareholders. On the other hand, a lower coverage ratio indicates the excessive use of debt. When the firm is having excessive coverage ratio, it should improve its operational efficiency or retire the debt, early, to have a comfortable coverage ratio.

Limitations

1. IC ratio is based on the accrual concept of accounting. In practice, the interest is to be paid in cash. Therefore, it is better to compare the interest liability with the cash profits (based on cash inflows and outflows, both for incomes and expenses) of the firm.
2. This ratio also ignores the repayment of installment liability of the firm.

3.9 ACTIVITY RATIOS

Firm invests funds of outsiders (lenders and creditors) and shareholders in various assets in business to make sales and profits. The better the management of assets, more would be sales and higher would be the profit. **Activity ratios reflect the management of assets and their effective utilisation**. If assets are converted into sales, with speed, profits would be more. **Activity ratios bring out the relationship between the assets and sales**. These ratios are called Turnover Ratios. For example, funds invested in inventories are converted or turned over into sales. Activity ratios are employed to evaluate the efficiency with which the firm manages and utilises the assets, in particular, debtors and stock.

Importance of Activity Ratios: Both current ratio and acid test ratio may give misleading results. If current assets include high volume of debtors due to slow credit collections, current assets would be high, resulting in a high current and acid test ratio. These ratios fail to show the movement of debtors, as they do not exhibit the quality of debtors. Similarly, if inventories are non-moving or obsolete and not written off, current ratio would be high. It is important to calculate the turnover of these assets to ascertain their quality and how efficiently these assets are used in the business.

3.9.1 Inventory Turnover Ratio/Inventory Velocity

Inventory turnover ratio is also known as stock turnover ratio. This is calculated by dividing cost of goods sold by average inventory.

$$\text{Inventory Turnover Ratio} = \frac{\text{Cost of goods sold}}{\text{Average inventory at cost}}$$

$$\text{Average inventory} = \frac{\text{Opening Stock} + \text{Closing stock}}{2}$$

$$\text{Cost of goods sold} = \text{Opening stock} + \text{Purchases} - \text{Closing stock}$$

$$= \text{Net Sales} - \text{Gross profit}$$

Interpretation: Inventory turnover ratio shows the velocity of stocks. A higher ratio is an indication that the firm is moving the stocks better so profitability, in such a situation, would be more. However, a very high ratio may show that the firm has been maintaining only fast moving stocks. The firm may not be maintaining the total range and so may be missing business opportunities, which may otherwise be available. So, it is better to compare the turnover ratio, with the industry or its immediate competitor.

In the ratio analysis, readers would have observed, by now, standards are difficult to decide and the ratios of industry and other firms, in competition, are best for comparison.

Points for Consideration: Two points are worth noting in the formula, which are as follows:

(a) Instead of sales, cost of goods sold is to be taken, as inventory is valued at cost so that both numerator and denominator are on the same basis. If there is no possibility to calculate cost of sales, sales may be taken for calculating the ratio.

(b) It is the normal practice to liquidate the stocks at the end of the year. So, it is often advocated to take the average of opening stock and closing stock for a better picture. The situation does not, really, improve. Reason is simple. Last year closing stock is the opening stock of the current year. At the end of last year too, liquidation of stocks would have occurred to bring out a better picture. So, by adding opening stock to closing stock at the end of the year, alone, may not show a real picture, if the firm has the tendency of liquidating the stocks, at the end of the year, to improve the ratio. Better ratio and picture would be available if the opening and closing inventory, at the end of every month, are taken and average is arrived at.

However, in questions, the stock figures at the end of every month are not available, so average of opening and closing inventory at the end of the year is to be taken. In case, cost of goods sold is not available, sales are to be taken in their place. But, the ratio, in such a case, may not give satisfactory findings.

Days of Inventory holdings: If we want to know the holding of inventory in the form of number of days, the following formula helps us.

$$\text{No. of days inventory holding} = \frac{360}{\text{Inventory turnover ratio}}$$

Ideal Standard: There is no standard ratio. **Ratio is a test of inventory management**. The ratio depends upon the nature of business. The ratio has to be compared with the ratio of the industry, other firms or past ratio of the same firm. Every firm has to maintain certain level of inventory, be it raw materials or finished goods, to carry on the business, smoothly. This level of inventory should be neither too high nor too low. If the level is too high, the result would be:

(i) Blocks unnecessary funds that can be utilised somewhere else, more profitably.

(ii) Unnecessary payment for extra godown space for piled stocks

(iii) Chances of obsolescence and pilferage are more

(iv) Likely deterioration in quality, and

(v) Above all, slow movement of stocks means slow recovery of cash, tied in stocks

On the other hand, if stocks are too low:

(i) Stoppage of production, in the absence of continuous availability of raw materials ,and

(ii) Loss of business opportunities as range of finished goods is not available, at all times.

To avoid the situation, the firm should know the position, periodically, whether it is carrying excessive or inadequate stocks for necessary corrective action, in time.

3.9.2. Debtors' (Receivables) Turnover Ratio / Debtors' Velocity

Firms sell goods on cash and credit. As and when goods are sold on credit, debtors (receivables) appear in accounts. Debtors are expected to be converted into cash, over a short period, and they are included in current assets. To judge the quality or liquidity of debtors, financial analysts apply three ratios, which are:

(a) debtors turnover ratio
(b) collection period
(c) aging schedule of debtors

Debtors' Turnover Ratio: Debtors turnover is found out by dividing credit sales by average debtors.

$$\text{Debtors Turnover Ratio} = \frac{\text{Credit sales}}{\text{Average debtors}}$$

Debtors' turnover ratio indicates the number of times debtors are turned over, each year. The higher the debtors' turnover, more efficient is the management of credit. If Bills Receivable is outstanding, they are to be added to the debtors as bills receivable have come into balance sheet, in place of debtors and they are, still, outstanding for payment.

Collection Period: The collection period is calculated by

$$\text{Collection Period} = \frac{360}{\text{Debtors's Turnover Ratio}}$$

Signals of Collection Period: This ratio indicates the speed of their collection. The shorter the period of collection, the better is the quality of debtors. A short collection period indicates the efficiency of credit management. The average collection period should be compared with the credit terms and policy of the firm to judge the quality of collection efficiency. Suppose, the firm's credit policy is to extend 45 days credit and on calculation, the actual collection period is 60 days. This shows the laxity in collection. An excessively long collection period implies an inefficient credit and collection policy. On the other hand, too low a collection period is also not a favourable signal. The firm may be insisting to extend credit sales only to those customers whose creditworthiness is beyond doubt so that there would be total certainty of payment, with no bad debts. The firm may succeed with no bad debts. But, in the process of rigid credit standards to have no bad debts, the firm may be missing sales opportunities and, equally, possible improved profitability. If credit period is relaxed more, the firm may be gaining with more sales and improved profitability, even after providing for the losses towards bad debts. The best way is to compare the collection period of the firm with the industry's average collection period and decide whether the firm has to make any change in credit policy.

Aging Schedule: The average collection period measures the quality of debtors, in the aggregate way. The aging schedule gives the detailed break up of debtors, according to the length of time, they have been outstanding. The aging schedule gives more information than the collection period as it spots the slow-paying debtors. Through this process, the firm can focus on those debtors, where attention is required to improve the collection efforts.

The different debtors, classified according to the age, are as under:

Aging schedule of debtors as on

Outstanding	Debtors	% of Total
Period (Days)	(Rs.)	
0—30	2,00,000	20
31—35	1,80,000	18
36—40	1,20,000	12
41—50	1,00,000	10
51 and above	4,00,000	40
	10,00,000	100

Assumed, the firm has a policy of allowing credit for 35 days. Out of the above total debtors, 62% are overdue. In other words, almost two-thirds— a very big proportion- of the debtors have not been paying, in time. Indeed, a serious situation it is. This requires an immediate and thorough review of the credit administration and in particular, selection of customers to whom goods are to be sold on credit, in future. Otherwise, shortly, the firm would be facing a grave problem with major debtors remaining unpaid, affecting liquidity as well as profitability, seriously. So, it may be necessary to initiate legal action, if necessary, in respect of 40% of debtors, the last category in the above schedule, as they are likely to cause serious damage to the business. The chunk is high and age-wise, it is anxiety causing. As the period is above 51 days, a further detailed analysis is essential about the age of the debtors, on a case to case basis.

3.9.3. Total Assets Turnover Ratio

Assets are used to generate sales. If the firm manages the assets more efficiently, sales would be more and equally profits would be up. This ratio is calculated by dividing sales by total assets.

$$\text{Total Assets Turnover Ratio} = \frac{\text{Sales}}{\text{Total Assets}}$$

Importance: A firm's ability to make sales indicates its operating performance.

Caution: This ratio should be interpreted, carefully. Between two firms, a firm having old assets, with lower depreciated book value of fixed assets, may generate more sales compared with a firm, with new fixed assets purchased, recently. The firm, with old assets, may generate a misleading impression of high turnover, without any actual improvement in sales.

3.9.4. Working Capital Turnover Ratio

The WCT Ratio indicates the velocity of utilisation of working capital of the firm, during the year. The working capital refers to net working capital, which is equal to total current assets less current liabilities. The ratio is calculated as follows:

$$\text{Working Capital Ratio} = \frac{\text{Cost of Sales or Sales}}{\text{Average Working Capital}}$$

Working capital average can be calculated from working capital, at the beginning and end of the year.

Importance: This ratio measures the efficiency of working capital management. A higher ratio indicates efficient utilisation of working capital and a low ratio shows otherwise. A high working capital ratio indicates a lower investment in working capital has generated more volume of sales. Higher ratio improves the profitability of the firm. But, a very high ratio is also not desirable for any firm. This may also imply overtrading, as there may be inadequacy of working capital to support the increasing volume of sales. This may be a risky proposition to the firm. The ratio is to be compared with the trend of the other firms in the industry for different periods to understand the right working capital ratio, without resulting overtrading.

3.9.5 Creditors/Payable Turnover Ratio

In the course of business operations of the firm, a firm has to make credit purchases and incurs short-term liabilities. Before supply of goods, suppliers can check up the ratio to understand the normal period of payment, firm has been making, for the goods supplied. The ratio is calculated, similar to Debtors' turnover ratio. In the place of debtors, creditors are to be substituted and credit purchases in place of credit sales. The ratio can be calculated

$$\text{Creditors' Turnover Ratio} = \frac{\text{Credit Purchases}}{\text{Average Trade Creditors} + \text{Average Bills Payable}}$$

Similarly, to understand the number of days the creditors are outstanding, the ratio is

$$\text{Payment Period} = \frac{360}{\text{Creditors' Turnover Ratio}}$$

Interpretation of Payment Period: This indicates the number of days the creditors are outstanding for payment. If the number of days is lower than the assured period of payment, it indicates liquidity of the firm. This would be good news to the suppliers as they can expect the payment, within the assured period. If the period is more, it indicates the firm is defaulting in payments and enjoying longer period of credit from the suppliers. This position may improve, in the short run, the profitability of the firm. But, the firm may be missing discounts and paying more prices for the goods purchased. To make proper interpretation, a comparative comparison of the period of credit with the other firms is needed.

3.10 PROFITABILITY RATIOS

The last group of financial ratios, more often used, is Profitability Ratios. Profit is the difference between revenue and expenses over a period, usually, one year. Profitability ratios are to measure the operating efficiency of the company. Besides management, lenders and owners of the company are interested in the analysis of the profitability of the firm. If profits are adequate, there would be no difficulty for lenders to get payment of interest and repayment of principal. Owners want to get required rate of return on investment. The finance manager should evaluate the efficiency of the company, in terms of profits. So, profit is important to everyone associated with the firm.

Generally, two major types of profitability ratios can be calculated:

- Profitability ratios based on sales
- Profitability ratios based on investment

3.10.1 Profitability Ratios Based on Sales

Profit is a factor of sales. Profit is earned, after meeting all expenses, as and when sales are made. These ratios can be further divided into

- Gross profit ratio
- Expenses ratios
- Net profit margin ratio

(A) Gross Profit Ratio: The first ratio in relation to sales is gross profit ratio or gross margin ratio. The ratio can be calculated by

$$\text{Gross Profit Ratio} = \frac{\text{Sales} - \text{Cost of Goods} \times 100}{\text{Sales}}$$

$$= \frac{\text{Gross Profit} \times 100}{\text{Sales}}$$

Importance: The ratio reflects the efficiency with which a firm produces its different products. This ratio indicates the spread between the cost of goods sold and revenue. Analysis gives the clues to the management how to improve the depressed profit margins. The ratio indicates the extent to which the selling price can decline, without resulting in losses on operations of a firm.

Reasons for high gross profit ratio: High gross profit ratio is a sign of good management. Reasons could be:

- High sales price, cost of goods remaining constant
- Lower cost of goods sold, sales price remaining constant
- A combination of factors in sales price and costs of different products, widening the margin and

- An increase in proportion of volume of sales of those products that carry a higher margin
- A misleading factor due to overvaluation of closing stock

Reasons for fall in gross profit ratio: Reasons may be:

- Purchase of raw materials, at unfavourable rates
- Over investment and/ or inefficient utilisation of plant and machinery, resulting in higher cost of production
- Excessive competition, compelling to sell at reduced prices

The finance manger has to analyse the reasons for the fall and initiate the action, necessary to improve the situation.

(B) Net Profit Ratio: Net profit is obtained, after deducting operating expenses, interest and taxes from gross profit. The net profit ratio is calculated by

$$\text{Net Profit Ratio} = \frac{\text{Profit after tax}}{\text{Sales}} \times 100$$

Net profit includes non-operating income so the later may be deducted to arrive at profitability arising, directly, from operations.

Interpretation: Net Profit ratio indicates the overall efficiency of the management in manufacturing, administering and selling the products. Net profit has a direct relationship with the return on investment. If net profit is high, with no change in investment, return on investment would be high. If there is fall in profits, return on investment would also go down.

For a meaningful understanding, both the ratios – gross profit ratio and net profit ratio—have to be interpreted together. If gross margin increases but net margin declines, this indicates operating expenses have gone up. Further analysis has to be made which operating expense has contributed to the declining position, for control. Reverse situation is also possible with gross margin declining with net margin going up. This could be due to increase of cost of production, without any change in selling price, and operating expenses reducing more to compensate the change. The crux is both the ratios are to be analysed together to find out the causes of increase/decline for control and corrective action.

(C) Operating Expenses Ratios: To identify the cause of fall or rise in net profit, each operating expense ratio is to be calculated. This can be calculated by

$$\text{Operating Expenses Ratio} = \frac{\text{Operating Expense}}{\text{Sales}}$$

The behaviour of specific expenditure is to be seen, in comparison to the earlier years, in the same firm. This throws the light on the managerial policies and actions. For example, advertisement expenditure may be going up, from year to year, with no significant increase in sales. This may be due to ineffective sales promotional expenditure in not bringing increased sales, despite more expenditure on advertisement. A general rise in advertisement expenses, throughout the industry, or inefficiency of marketing / advertisement department of the firm, alone, may be the contributing factor. The real reason can be better understood, once the comparative ratios of the same expenditure in the other firms of the same industry are known for suitable action.

3.10.2 Profitability ratios based on investment

Equity shareholders are the owners of the company. Profits belong to the owners of the firm who have invested their funds, in anticipation of return. If preference shares exist, then profits, after tax and after deducting the dividend due to preference shareholders, are to be considered for calculation of the return to equity shareholders. It is not important, whether the profits are distributed to the equity shareholders or left in the firm as retained profits. The profitability of a firm can be analysed from the point of view of owners in different perspectives, as follows:

(A) Return on Investment: It is the primary ratio and is most popularly used to measure the overall profitability and efficiency of business.

The term investment may refer to Total Assets or Net Assets.

(i) **Return on Total Assets:** 'Total assets' is the total amount appearing on the assets side of the balance sheet. However, in calculating total assets, fictitious assets like preliminary expenses, accumulated losses and discount on issue of shares are to be excluded. However, intangible assets like goodwill, patents and trademarks are to be included. Reason is these intangible assets contribute for the development of sales and business while the fictitious assets do not add anything for the growth in business.

When return on investment is calculated on total assets, it is called ROTA. Total assets are related to operating profit. Operating profit is EBIT. EBIT is arrived at by adding financial charges (interest etc) and taxes to net operating profit. By this, we are separating financing effect from the operating effect.

$$\text{ROI} = \text{ROTA} = \frac{\text{EBIT}}{\text{Total Assets}}$$

The above formula for ROTA ratio is commonly followed. Different authors discuss different formulae in their books, in particular, in ratio analysis and use them to different problems, even when there is no change in situations. This causes confusion to students to understand. To avoid confusion, the formulae that are discussed only are used in the problems. The above formula is preferred as by some authors taxes are not controllable by the management. More so, firm's opportunities for availing tax incentives also differ, depending on the location, which is one of the many factors. So, it may be more prudent to use before-tax measure to calculate ROI.

Another alternative way to calculate ROTA is:

$$\text{ROI} = \text{ROTA} = \frac{\text{Profit after tax, before interest}}{\text{Total Assets}}$$

All said and done, what is left to the shareholders is the final amount of profit, after tax. Tax Management also is necessary and a significant part of management. So, some firms advocate the alternative formula. When we have different formulae, it is necessary to use the right formula, understanding the requirement of the situation.

(ii) Return on Capital Employed: Another way to calculate return on investment is through capital employed or net assets. Net assets are equal to net fixed assets plus current assets minus current liabilities. **Net assets are equal to capital employed. So, net assets and capital employed convey the same meaning, though called differently**. Capital employed can be calculated in two ways:

Capital Employed = Net worth + Long term Borrowings

OR

= Net Fixed Assets + Current Assets – Current Liabilities

Net worth includes preference share capital too, as already stated.

Return on net assets is called RONA. **As net assets are equal to capital employed, the terms RONA and ROCE indicate the same**. The following ratio indicates the overall efficiency of business, before tax. The formula for calculation is

$$\text{ROI} = \begin{matrix}\text{RONA} \\ \text{OR} \\ \text{ROCE}\end{matrix} = \frac{\text{EBIT}}{\text{Capital Employed}}$$

Adjustments: Firm may be having some investments, not connected to the business. The investments and income on those investments are not related to the business. So, both require adjustment. Investments are to be excluded from capital employed and income from investments is to be deducted from EBIT. This treatment is necessary for proper matching.

Another interesting point is interest. Interest on long-term loans only is to be added to arrive at EBIT, but not interest on short-term loans. The reason is short-term loans are not included in capital employed.

Both the numerator and denominator should always match with each other, otherwise distorted results appear.

Another alternative way is:

$$ROI = \begin{matrix} RONA \\ OR \\ ROCE \end{matrix} = \frac{\text{Profit after tax, before interest}}{\text{Capital Employed}}$$

Tax also is an outgo to the company, Profit after tax, but before interest is considered to have uniformity in both the numerator and denominator.

Capital employed consists of debentures too. Both the numerator and denominator should be at the same length, otherwise there would be imbalance. For this reason, interest is included in numerator.

Interpretation

1. **ROI (ROTA and RONA) measure the overall efficiency of business.**
2. The owners are interested in knowing the profitability of the firm, in relation to the total assets and amount invested in the firm. A higher percentage of return on capital employed will satisfy the owners that their funds are profitably utilised.
3. It indicates the efficiency of the management of various departments as funds are kept at its disposal for making investment in assets.
4. If the firm increases its size, but is unable to increase its profits proportionately, then ROI (both ROTA and RONA) decreases. In such a case, increasing the size of the firm does not advance the welfare of the owners.
5. Inter-firm comparison would be useful. Both the ratios of a particular firm should be compared with the industry average or its immediate competitor to understand the efficiency of the management in managing the assets, profitably. So, a higher rate of return on capital employed, without comparison, does not imply that the firm is managed efficiently. Once a comparison is made with other firms, having similar characteristics, in the same industry, a fair conclusion is possible.
6. The ratios help in formulating the borrowing policy of the firm. The rate of interest on the borrowings should always be lower than the return on capital employed. Then only, funds are to be borrowed.
7. With both the ratios, the outsiders like bankers, financial institutions and creditors know the viability of the firm so that they can lend funds, comfortably.

Tutorial Note: There are several types of formulae for calculation of ROI, followed by different authors. Students are advised to give their assumption regarding computation.

(B) Return on Equity: In the real sense, equity shareholders are the real owners of the company. They assume the risk in the firm. Preference shareholders enjoy fixed dividend and preference for payment of dividend, before dividend is distributed to equity shareholders. Similarly, in the event of the liquidation of the company, preference share capital has to be repaid first, before refunding to equity shareholders. Net profits after tax, after dividend is paid to preference shareholders, entirely belong to the equity shareholders. Equity shareholders would be interested to know what their real return is on the funds invested.

This ratio for return on equity is calculated as under:

$$\text{Return on Equity} = \frac{\text{Profit after Tax} - \text{Preference Dividend}}{\text{Equity Shareholders' funds}}$$

Equity shareholders' funds are equity share capital, accumulated reserves (both general reserves and capital reserves), share premium and balance in profit and loss account less accumulated losses, if any. **Preference shareholders are not to be included as the dividend due to them has already been deducted from profits, after tax.**

Interpretation:

1. ROE indicates how well the firm has used the resources of owners.
2. Earnings a satisfactory return is the most desirable objective of a business. **This ratio is of greatest interest** to the **management as it is their responsibility to maximise the owners' welfare.**
3. This ratio is more meaningful to equity shareholders as they are interested to know their return. Interpretation of this ratio is similar to return on investments. The higher the ratio, the better it is to equity shareholders.

(C) Earnings per Share: The profitability of the equity shareholders can be measured, in other ways. One such measure is to calculate the earnings per equity share. The earnings per equity share is calculated by

$$\text{Earnings per equity share} = \frac{\text{Net Profit after tax Preference dividend}}{\text{Number of equity shares outstanding}}$$

Interpretation

1. EPS simply shows the profitability of the firm per equity share basis.
2. EPS calculation, over the years, indicates how the firm's earning power, per share basis, has changed over the years.
3. EPS of the firm is to be compared with the industry and its immediate competing firm to understand the relative performance of the firm.
4. As a profitability index, it is widely used ratio.

Bonus issue Adjustment: Adjustments for bonus issue should be made while comparing EPS, over a period of time. Bonus shares are additional free shares issued to the existing shareholders, out of the profits of the company. Reserves and surplus profit is utilised for issue of bonus shares, by transferring the amount to the equity share capital account. In the process of issue of bonus shares, there is no inflow or outflow of cash to the firm. If bonus shares 1:3 are issued, a shareholder holding 3 shares gets extra 1 share, freely. Suppose, the market price of the share, before bonus issue, is Rs.100, his total wealth was Rs.300.Immediate to the issue of bonus shares, there is no increase in the wealth of the shareholders, even though additional shares are received. Existing earning is to be distributed amongst more shares. This is the real reason for the fall in prices of shares, after bonus issue. The share price gets diluted to Rs.75, after issue, and so his total wealth remains the same Rs.300 (75×4). **The total wealth of a shareholder, before and after bonus issue, immediately, remains the same**. EPS calculated, after the issue of bonus shares, requires adjustment for proper comparison. For example, if a bonus issue in the proportion of 1:3 is made, then the adjustment factor 4/3 should be applied to adjust EPS of the year in which the bonus is made as well as the subsequent years. After the issue of bonus shares, If EPS is 9 for the subsequent year, then adjusted EPS would be 12 (9×4/3) for comparison to the EPS of previous year. EPS has to be adjusted to reflect the correct earning position, in view of the increased number of equity shares.

(D) Dividends per Share (DPS): After payment of dividend to preference shareholders, balance net profit belongs to equity shareholders, whether distributed in the form of dividend or retained in business. However, equity shareholders are interested in the amount of dividend, distributed to them. Dividend per share is calculated as under:

$$\text{DPS} = \frac{\text{Total Dividend distributed to equity shareholders}}{\text{Number of equity shares outstanding}}$$

Investors, both existing and potential, are interested in DPS rather than EPS.

(E) Dividend Pay out Ratio or Pay out Ratio: Dividend pay out ratio is calculated to find out the proportion of dividend distributed out of earnings per share. For example, if the firm has an EPS and DPS of Rs. 5 and Rs. 3 respectively, DP ratio is 3/5 i.e. 60%. So, the firm has distributed 60% of PAT (profits after tax) as dividend among its shareholders. So, the ratio is calculated by

$$\text{Pay-Out Ratio} = \frac{\text{Dividend per equity share}}{\text{Earnings per equity share}}$$

Earnings not distributed are impliedly retained in the business for the purpose of expansion and growth of the firm. The proportion of retained earnings is equal to 1 – DP ratio. So, in the above case, the retained earnings ratio is 40%.

(F) Dividend Yield Ratio: Shareholders are the true owners, interested in the earnings distributed and paid to them as dividend. Therefore, dividend yield ratio is calculated to evaluate the relationship between the dividend paid per share and the market value of the share.

$$\text{Dividend yield ratio} = \frac{\text{Dividend per equity share}}{\text{Market value per equity share}}$$

(G) **Price Earnings Ratio:** This is the ratio that establishes the relationship between the market price of a share and its EPS. **This ratio indicates the number of times the earnings per share is covered by its market price**. The ratio is calculated as per the following formula:

$$\text{Price Earnings Ratio} = \frac{\text{Market price per equity share}}{\text{Earning per equity share}}$$

The price earnings ratio indicates investors' judgement or expectations about the firm's future performance. It signifies the number of years, in which the earnings can equal to market price of share. This ratio is widely used by the security analysts and investors to decide whether to buy or not to buy the shares, in a particular company, at that price.

Generally, higher the price-earnings ratio, the better it is for the management of that firm. If the P/E ratio falls, it is a cause of anxiety to the management of the firm as the investor's perception about the future performance of the company is not expected to be good. So, the management has to look into the causes for the fall of the ratio.

For those who want to buy equity shares in that firm, if the P/E ratio of a company is low, compared to its competing firms, the equity shares of that company is a 'good buy', provided they anticipate the future performance of the company would be brighter. For example, if the market price of X Ltd is Rs. 80 and its EPS is 4, its P/E ratio is 20. Equally good performing company Z Ltd, its competitor in the industry, is quoted Rs. 200 with EPS 8. So, its P/E ratio is 25. By calculating the P/E ratio, investor can decide that the share of X Ltd is undervalued and worth buying.

Significance: Price-earning ratio helps the investor in deciding whether to buy the shares of a company, at a particular market price, or book profit by selling at that rate. The decision depends on the investor's perception about the future market.

(H) **Capital Gearing Ratio:** Capital gearing ratio refers to the proportion between fixed interest/dividend bearing funds and non-fixed interest or dividend bearing funds, in the total capital employed in the business.

The fixed interest or dividend-bearing funds include funds provided by the debenture holders and preference shareholders. Funds provided by equity shareholders do not bear fixed commitment, unlike preference shareholders and debenture holders.

In case, the total amount of preference share capital and other fixed interest bearing loans exceed the equity shareholders' funds, the firm is said to be "high geared". In other words, if the capital gearing ratio is more than one, it is said to be high geared. On the other hand, if preference share capital and other fixed interest bearing loans are less than equity shareholders' funds, capital gearing ratio is less than one, the firm is said to be "low geared". In case the two are equal, the capital structure is said to be "even geared".

For computation of capital gearing ratio, funds that belong to equity shareholders such as equity share capital, share premium and other reserves are to be considered. The capital gearing ratio can be ascertained as under:

Capital Gearing Ratio = (Preference share capital + Debentures + Long Term Loan)/(Equity share capital + Reserves and surplus)

Interpretation: If the capital gearing ratio is high, the profits available to equity shareholders would be subject to wider fluctuations compared to a company that has a low gearing ratio.

3.11 TRADING ON EQUITY

Normally, assets of the firm are financed by debt and equity. Suppliers of the debt would look to the equity as margin of safety. The use of debt in financing the assets has a number of implications:

Implications of Debt: Firstly, debt is more **risky to the firm**, compared to equity. Whether the firm makes profit or not, interest on debt has to be paid. If interest and instalment are not paid, there may be a threat of insolvency, even. Secondly, debt is **advantageous to the equity shareholders.** The equity shareholders can retain control, with a limited stake. They can find a way to magnify their earnings. When the firm is able to earn on borrowed funds higher than the interest rate paid, the return to owners would be magnified. **The process of magnifying the earnings of equity shareholders through the process of debt is called "financial leverage" or "financial gearing" or "Trading on Equity".** It is important to note that if the interest rate is higher than the rate of return on the project, it is not desirable to borrow, as the return on equity would get reduced. Thirdly, if the firm is burdened with more debt, it **experiences greater difficulty in raising funds,** at the normal rate of interest. If the firm's equity is thin, the creditors' financial risk is high and so they demand higher interest rate and also impose stringent conditions, even though they lend.

Relationship between ROCE and Cost of Debt and impact on ROE: When the return on capital employed is greater than the cost of debt, it is advantageous to borrow as the return on equity goes up. At the expense of debt, the beneficiaries are the equity shareholders. The risk the firm would experience on long-term borrowings is in the form of cost of debt- **interest burden is permanent.** Additionally, when the earnings fall, the ROCE also falls but, the equity shareholders are the real sufferers. With the fall of ROCE, the return on equity goes down. In other words, debt can prove to be either beneficial or detrimental to the interests of equity shareholders. This may happen to the advantage and also to the disadvantage of the equity shareholders. This is called trading on equity, which is a double edged sword. The key is the relationship between the ROCE and cost of debt.

The pictorial presentation is as under:

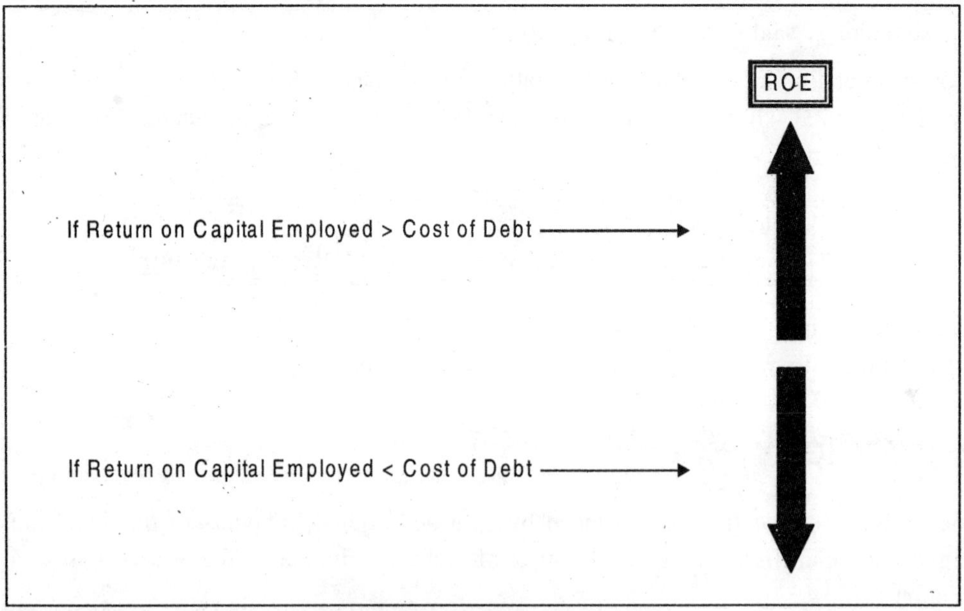

Relationship between ROCE and Cost of Debt and impact on ROE

Impact of Capital Gearing Ratio: The capital gearing ratio influences the return to equity shareholders. Higher the capital gearing ratio, the impact on equity shareholders would be greater. If the rate of return on total capital employed is more than the average cost of fixed charge bearing funds, the residue goes to the benefit of equity shareholders. As a result, the return on equity would be more than the return on total capital employed. The process of magnifying the earnings, through the use of debt, is beneficial to equity shareholders. However, the leverage can also work in the opposite direction too. When the return on capital employed falls below the cost of debt, the fall in return on equity would be higher. The equity shareholders suffer more. **So, a higher gearing ratio can prove to its advantage as well as disadvantage**.

A change in EBIT results in a corresponding similar change, either increase or fall, in Return on capital employed. However, the corresponding change in ROE would be greater. When the capital gearing ratio is high, an increase of EBIT would result in a higher increase of ROE. If the EBIT increases, say, by 25%, the increase of ROCE would be 25%. But, ROE would increase more than 25%. Similarly, if EBIT falls by 25%, the fall in ROCE would be 25%. But, the decrease in ROE would be more than 25%. A proper balance between the two funds (fixed charge and non-fixed charge bearing funds) is necessary in order to keep the cost of capital and risk at the minimum.

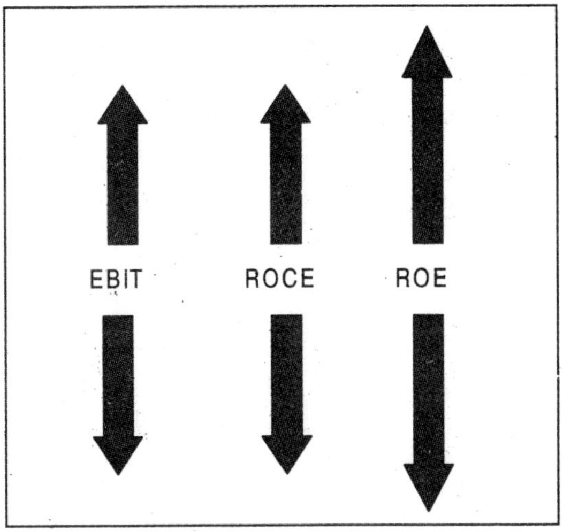

Impact of EBIT on ROCE and ROE in a Highly Geared Firm

The concept of 'Trading on Equity' can be explained with the following example.

Illustration No. 4

Calculate the capital gearing from the following information:

	Rs.
Equity Share Capital	3,00,000
Reserves	2,00,000
5% Debentures	4,00,000
6% Preference Share Capital	3,00,000
10% Long Term Loan	1,00,000
	13,00,000

The firm earns a profit of Rs. 4,00,000 before interest and tax. Calculate the capital gearing ratio and test it for 'Trading on Equity'. Tax rate may be taken at 50%.

Solution:

The Capital Gearing Ratio has been calculated as follows:

Capital Gearing Ratio = (Preference share capital + Debentures + Long Term Loan) / (Equity share capital + Reserves and surplus)

(3,00,000+4,00,000+1,00,000)/((3,00,000+2,00,000) = 8,00,000/5,00,000

= 1.6

Since the Capital Gearing Ratio is more than one, the firm is said to be high geared.

As the firm is high geared, there should be 'Trading on Equity'. This can be verified as follows:

	Rs.
Profit as given	4,00,000
Less Interest (20,000+10,000)	30,000
	3,70,000
Less Tax (at 50%)	1,85,000
Profit after tax	1,85,000
Less Preference Dividend	18,000
Profit available to equity shareholders	1,67,000

$$\text{Return on Equity to shareholders} = \frac{\text{Profits after tax} - \text{Preference Dividend}}{\text{Equity Shareholders' funds}}$$

$$= \frac{\text{Profits available to equity shareholders}}{\text{Equity Shareholders' funds}}$$

$$= \frac{1{,}67{,}000 \times 100}{5{,}00{,}000}$$

$$= 33.4\%$$

$$\text{Return on capital employed} = \frac{\text{EBIT}}{\text{Capital Employed}}$$

Capital Employed = Net worth + Long term Borrowings

$$= (3{,}00{,}000 + 2{,}00{,}000 + 3{,}00{,}000) + (4{,}00{,}000 + 1{,}00{,}000)$$

$$= \frac{4{,}00{,}000 \times 100}{13{,}00{,}000}$$

$$= 30.76\%$$

The return on capital employed is only 30.76% while the return on equity shareholders' funds is 33.4%. The equity shareholders have been benefited, at the expense of fixed charge bearing funds. So, there is 'Trading on Equity'.

Tutorial Note: Equity Shareholders' funds do not include preference share capital while net worth includes Preference share capital.

Illustration No.5

The capital employed in a business has been financed, as below:

	Rs.
Equity Share Capital	6,00,000
7% Preference Share Capital	4,00,000
6% Debentures	8,00,000
Reserves and Surplus	2,00,000
	20,00,000

The company earns a profit of Rs. 4,00,000 before interest. Tax rate may be taken 50%.

You are required to:

(A) Explain the principles of "Trading on Equity" and Test the data for the principle.

(B) Elaborate the impact of changes in EBIT, both increase and decrease, on Return on capital Employed (ROCE) and Return on Equity (ROE) with suitable examples, making the required valid assumption. **(B.U. (MBA) - 2003)**

Solution:

(A) The process of using the debt in capital employed to magnify the return of equity shareholders is called "Trading on Equity".

The extent of benefit of debt depends on capital gearing ratio. If capital gearing of the company is more than one, with the increase of EBIT, there would be a similar corresponding increase in ROCE. Similarly, ROE also increases. But, the important point is the % increase of ROE would be more than % increase of EBIT. The reverse also is true. To explain further, if EBIT increases by 10%, ROCE increases by 10%. But, ROE increases more than by 10%. If EBIT falls by 10%, the ROCE also falls, similarly, by 10%. But, ROE falls more than 10%. For this reason, "trading on equity" is said to be double-edged sword.

The capital gearing ratio can be ascertained as under:

$$\text{Capital Gearing Ratio} = \frac{\text{(Preference Share Capital + Debentures)}}{\text{(Equity Share Capital + Reserves and Surplus)}}$$

$$= \frac{4,00,000 + 8,00,000}{6,00,000 + 2,00,000}$$

$$= \frac{12,00,000}{8,00,000} = 1.5$$

As the capital-gearing ratio of the company is more than one, the company is said to be 'high geared'.

(B) Impact of change in EBIT on ROCE and ROE

Capital employed = Equity share capital + Reserves + Preference share capital + Debentures + Long-term loan

$$= 6{,}00{,}000+2{,}00{,}000+4{,}00{,}000+8{,}00{,}000$$

$$= 20{,}00{,}000$$

$$\text{Return on capital employed} = \frac{\text{EBIT}}{\text{Capital Employed}}$$

$$\text{Return on capital employed} = \frac{40{,}00{,}000 \times 100}{20{,}00{,}000}$$

$$= 20\%$$

$$\text{Return on Equity} = \frac{\text{Profits after tax} - \text{Preference Devidend}}{\text{Equity Shareholders' funds}}$$

Profits available to Equity shareholders:

EBIT	4,00,000
Less Interest on debentures	
6% on Rs. 8,00,000	48,000
	3,52,000
Tax @ 50%	1,76,000
Profit after tax	1,76,000
7% Preference Dividend	
on Rs. 4,00,000	28,000
Profits available to equity shareholders	1,48,000

$$\text{Return on Equity} = \frac{\text{Profits after tax} - \text{Preference Devidend}}{\text{Equity Shareholders' funds}}$$

$$= \frac{1{,}48{,}000 \times 100}{8{,}00{,}000} = 18.5\%$$

Let us presume that there is a change of EBIT by 50%.

If EBIT increases by 50%:

EBIT becomes Rs. 6,00,000.

$$\text{Return on capital employed} = \frac{6{,}00{,}000}{20{,}00{,}000} \times 100$$

$$= 30\%$$

Profits available to Equity shareholders:

EBIT	6,00,000
Less Interest on debentures	
6% on Rs. 8,00,000	48,000
	5,52,000
Tax @ 50%	2,76,000
Profit after tax	2,76,000
7% Preference Dividend	
on Rs. 4,00,000	28,000
Profits available to equity shareholders	2,48,000

Return on Equity to shareholders $= \dfrac{\text{Profits after tax} - \text{Preference Dividend}}{\text{Equity Shareholders' funds}}$

$= \dfrac{2{,}48{,}00 \times 100}{8{,}00{,}000} = 31\%$

So, if EBIT increases by 50%, ROCE also has increased by similar 50% (from 20% to 30%).

But ROE has increased by 67.57% (increased from 18.5% to 31% *i.e.* $\dfrac{12.5}{18.5} \times 100$)

If EBIT falls by 50%:

EBIT becomes Rs. 2,00,000.

Return on capital employed $= \dfrac{2{,}00{,}000 \times 100}{20{,}00{,}000}$

$= 10\%$

Profits available to Equity shareholders:

EBIT	2,00,000
Less Interest on debentures	
6% on Rs. 8,00,000	48,000
	1,52,000
Tax @ 50%	76,000
Profit after tax	76,000
7% Preference Dividend	
on Rs. 4,00,000	28,000
Profits available to equity shareholders	48,000

$$\text{Return on Equity} = \frac{\text{Profits after tax} - \text{Preference Dividend}}{\text{Equity Shareholders' funds}}$$

$$= \frac{48{,}000 \times 100}{8{,}00{,}000} = 6\%$$

So, if EBIT falls by 50%, ROCE also has fallen by similar 50% (from 20% to 10%). But ROE has fallen by 67.57 % (fell from 18.5% to 6% *i.e.* $\frac{12.5}{18.5} \times 100$)

This impact can be presented in pictorial presentation for quick understanding:

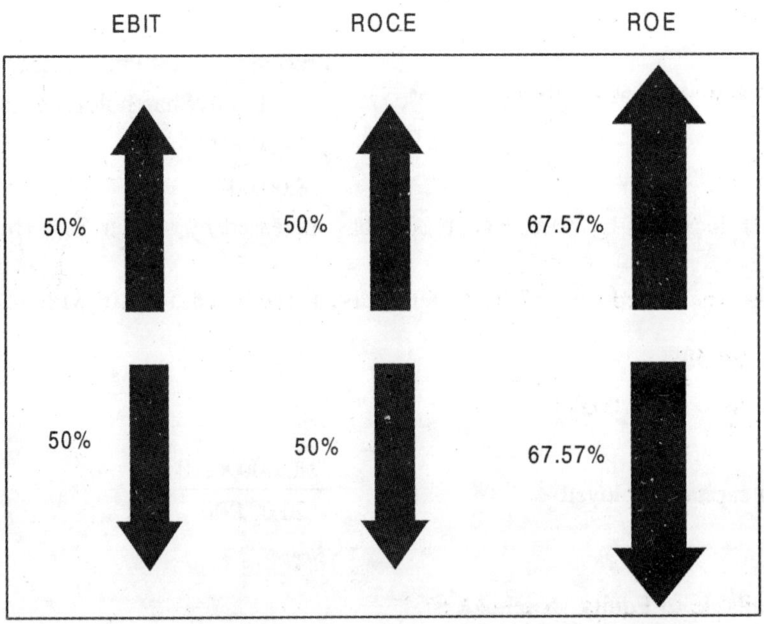

Relationship between EBIT, ROCE and ROE

Illustration No. 6

From the following information of Cherry & Cherry Company Ltd, prepare the balance sheet and compute the Return on Capital Employed (ROCE), return on total Assets (ROTA) and Return on Equity (ROE):

	Rs.
Current assets	1,00,000
Investments in Treasury Bonds	1,00,000
Fixed Assets	5,00,000
Sales	5,00,000
Cost of goods sold	3,00,000
10% Debentures	1,00,000
Income from Treasury bonds	10,000
Interest on Debentures	10,000
10% Preference share capital	1,00,000
Equity share capital	2,00,000
Capital Reserve	1,00,000

Provision for tax at 30% of net profits

Solution:

Cherry & Cherry Company Ltd
Profit and Loss Account for the year ended 31st March, 2005

	Rs.		Rs.
To cost of goods sold	3,00,000	By Sales	5,00,000
To interest on Debentures	10,000	By income from	
To Provision for taxation	60,000	Treasury bonds	10,000
To Net Profit after tax	1,40,000		
	5,10,000		5,10,000

Balance Sheet as on 31st March, 2005

Liabilities	Rs	Assets	Rs
Equity Share Capital	2,00,000	Fixed assets	5,00,000
10% Pref. share capital	1,00,000	Investments in Treasury Bonds	1,00,000
Capital Reserve	1,00,000	Current Assets	1,00,000
Profit and Loss account	1,40,000		
10% Debentures	1,00,000		
Provision for Taxation *	60,000		
	7,00,000		7,00,000

$$\text{Return on Capital Employed (ROCE)} = \frac{\text{EBIT}}{\text{Capital Employed}}$$

EBIT** = Net Profits + Interest + Tax – Non operating income

= 1,40,000 + 10,000 + 60,000 – 10,000

= 2,00,000

Capital Employed = Net Fixed assets + Current assets – Current liabilities (provision for taxation)

= 5,00,000 + 1,00,000 – 60,000

= 5,40,000

$$\text{ROCE} = \frac{2,00,000 \times 100}{5,40,000} = 37.03$$

$$\text{ROTA} = \frac{\text{EBIT}}{\text{Total Assets}}$$

$$= \frac{2,00,000 \times 100}{6,00,000} = 33.33\%$$

$$\text{Return on Equity} = \frac{\text{Net Profit after tax – Preference Dividend}}{\text{Equity Shareholders' funds}}$$

$$= \frac{1,40,000 - 10,000}{2,00,000 + 1,00,000 + 1,40,000}$$

$$= \frac{1,30,000 \times 100}{4,40,000} = 29.55\%$$

* Provision for tax is calculated as under:

Profits before tax = 5,00,000 + 10,000 – (3,00,000 + 10,000)

= 2,00,000

Tax @ 30% = 60,000

* * EBIT does not include income from Treasury Bonds as it is non-operating income. So, total assets, also, should not include the relevant assets – Treasury Bonds. When income is excluded, relevant assets of that income are also to be excluded for proper matching.

Illustration No. 7

From the following details available, prepare balance sheet of Dimpy & Co as on 31st March, 2006 and compute proprietary funds.

(a) Net Worth turnover ratio (on cost of sales) = 2

(b) Fixed assets turnover ratio (on cost of sales) = 4

(c) Gross profits turnover ratio = 20%

(d) Creditors velocity = 73 days

(e) Debtors velocity = 2 months

(f) Stock velocity = 6

Reserves and surplus amount to Rs. 10,000. Closing stock was Rs. 5,000 in excess of opening stock. Gross profit was Rs. 60,000.

You can make the necessary assumption, where required.

Solution:

Total Sales:

Gross profit was Rs. 60,000 and Gross profits turnover ratio = 20%

$$\text{Gross Profit Ratio} = \frac{\text{Gross Profit}}{\text{Total sales}}$$

$$20\% = \frac{60{,}000}{\text{Total sales}}$$

$$\text{Total Sales} = \frac{60{,}000}{20\%}$$

$$\text{Total sales} = 60{,}000 \times \frac{100}{20}$$

$$= 3{,}00{,}000$$

Debtors

Debtors velocity = 2 months. Debtors are turning over 6 times in a year

$$\frac{\text{Sales}}{\text{Debtors}} = 6$$

$$\text{Debtors} = \frac{\text{Sales}}{6}$$

$$= \frac{3{,}00{,}000}{6}$$

$$= 50{,}000$$

Cost of sales:

$$\text{Cost of sales} = \text{Sales} - \text{Gross profit}$$

$$= 3{,}00{,}000 - 60{,}000$$

$$= 2{,}40{,}000$$

Net worth:

Net worth turnover ratio (on cost of sales) = 2

$$\frac{\text{Cost of Sales}}{\text{Net worth}} = 2$$

$$\text{Net worth} = \frac{\text{Cost of Sales}}{2}$$

$$= \frac{2,40,000}{2}$$

$$= 1,20,000$$

Net worth = Capital + Reserves

Capital = Net worth – Reserves

$$= 1,20,000 - 10,000$$

$$= 1,10,000$$

Fixed Assets:

Fixed assets turnover ratio (on cost of sales) = 4

$$\frac{\text{Cost of sales}}{\text{Fixed Assets}} = 4$$

$$\text{Fixed Assets} = \frac{\text{Cost of sales}}{4}$$

$$= \frac{2,40,000}{4} = 60,000$$

Stock:

$$\text{Stock velocity} = 6$$

$$\frac{\text{Cost of sales}}{\text{Average stock}} = 6$$

$$\text{Average stock} = \frac{\text{Cost of sales}}{6}$$

$$= \frac{2,40,000}{6} = 40,000$$

$$\text{Closing stock} = 40,000 + 5,000/2$$

$$= 42,500$$

Opening stock was lower than closing stock by 5,000.

Opening stock = 42,500-5,000

= 37,500

Purchases:

To arrive at purchases, let us prepare Trading Account to get the balancing figure.

Trading Account			
	Rs.		Rs.
To opening stock	37,500	By sales	3,00,000
Purchases*	2,45,000	closing stock	42,500
Gross profit	60,000		
Total	3,42,500	Total	3,42,500

*** Balancing figure -Purchases**

Alternative way

Cost of sales	=	2,40,000
Increase in closing stock	=	5,000
Purchases		2,45,000

Creditors:

Creditors velocity = 73 days. In other words, creditors have turned over 5 times in a year.

$$\text{Creditors turnover ratio} = \frac{\text{Purchases}}{\text{Creditors}}$$

$$\frac{\text{Purchases}}{\text{Creditors}} = 5$$

$$\text{Creditors} = \frac{\text{Purchases}}{5}$$

$$= \frac{2{,}45{,}000}{5}$$

$$= 49{,}000$$

Balance Sheet of Dimpy & Co as on 31st March, 2006			
Liabilities	**Rs.**	**Assets**	**Rs.**
Capital	1,10,000	Fixed Assets	60,000
Reserves & Surplus	10,000	Cash*	16,500
		Debtors	50,000
Creditors	49,000	Stock	42,500
	1,69,000		1,69,000

* *Balancing figure*

Proprietary funds:

Capital	1,10,000
Reserves & Surplus	10,000
Total	1,20,000

Tutorial Note: Both the terms Debtors Turnover Ratio and Velocity convey the same meaning. However, the problem has stated the velocity in months, so the meaning is different.

3.12 LIMITATIONS OF RATIO ANALYSIS

No doubt, Ratio analysis is one of the most powerful tools of financial management. They are simple and easy to understand.

Ratio analysis is a useful tool to raise relevant questions on a number of managerial issues. It provides clues to investigate those issues, in detail, further. They must always be compared with:

- Previous ratios in order to assess trends
- Ratios achieved in other comparable companies

Ratios by themselves mean nothing as they have serious limitations. While using the ratios, caution has to be exercised in respect of the following. The following are some of the limitations:

1. **Absence of identical situations:** Ratios are useful in judging the efficiency of business, only when they are compared with the past results of the firm, with identical circumstances, or with the results of similar businesses. It is difficult to obtain identical situations for different firms. Circumstances do not remain the same, even, for the same firm between two different periods. Comparison becomes difficult due to lack of uniformity of situation between two companies.
2. **Change in accounting policies:** Management has a choice about the accounting policies. The management of different companies may adopt different accounting policies regarding valuation of inventories, depreciation, research and development expenditure and treatment of deferred revenue expenditure etc. The differences between the definitions of items in the balance sheet and profit and loss statement make the interpretation of the ratios difficult. Comparison would be meaningful and valuable if their base is similar. All companies may not be following the same method. For example, one may calculate depreciation on straight-line method while the other may be following written down value method. Different companies may be following different methods of valuation of closing stock (e.g. FIFO or LIFO etc).
3. **Based on historical data:** The ratios are calculated from past financial statements, and thus no indicators of future. Such ratios may provide information about the past. But, for forecasting the future, there are many factors that may change, in future. Market conditions and management policies may not remain the same, as they were earlier.
4. **Qualitative factors are ignored:** Ratios are expressed in quantitative form only. Qualitative factors are ignored. A high current ratio may not guarantee liquidity, as current assets may be high due to inclusion of obsolete inventory and non-paying debtors.

5. **Ratios alone are not adequate:** Ratios are means of financial analysis and they are not end in themselves. They are indicators. They cannot be taken as final regarding good or bad financial position of the business.
6. **Over use could be dangerous:** Over use of ratios as controls on managers could be dangerous. If too much reliance is placed on ratios, management may concentrate in improving the ratios, rather than dealing with significant issues. For example, reducing assets rather than increasing profits can improve the return on capital employed.
7. **Window Dressing:** The term 'window dressing' means manipulation of accounts in a way so as to conceal the actual facts and present the financial statements, in a way, to show better position than what actually it is. For example, a high current ratio is considered as an indicator of satisfactory liquidity position. To show an impressive current ratio, firm may postpone credit purchases. A company may have current assets of Rs. 4,000 and current liabilities of Rs.2,000. So, its current ratio is 2:1 that is normally considered satisfactory. The firm may postpone credit purchases, though needed, just to maintain the ratio, in a satisfactory manner. If it makes credit purchases of Rs.2,000 for meeting its normal requirements, current assets increase to Rs.6,000 and current liabilities also increase to Rs.4,000. Then, its current ratio declines to 1.5. The firm has concealed the true picture, just by postponing credit purchases, at the end of the year, though very much needed to its requirements. Similarly, firms may make payments at the end of the year to improve the depressed ratio. In the above situation, if the firm pays Rs.1,000 to creditors, its current ratio becomes 3.
8. **Problems of Price level Changes:** Financial analysis based on accounting ratios will give misleading results, if effects of change in price level are not taken into account. For example, two companies that have set up plant and machinery in two different periods, with a long gap, may give misleading results. Firm that has purchased the plant and machinery, very earlier, would have lower amount towards depreciation when compared with the firm that has set up the machinery, quite later. So, the operating results of both the firms vary substantially. The financial statements of the two firms cannot be compared, without making suitable changes to the price level changes.
9. **No fixed Standards:** No fixed standards can be laid down for ratios. Though current ratio 2:1 is normally required, firms those enjoy adequate arrangements with banks to provide additional credit, as and when needed, may be able to manage with lesser current ratio. It is, therefore, necessary to avoid any rule of thumb.

   Ratios are only a post-mortem of what has happened between two balance sheet dates. The interim position is not revealed by the ratio analysis. They can be used as trigger points for further investigation.

3.12.1 RATIOS MAY BECOME MEANINGLESS

Ratios are only indicators, not end in themselves: They identify the trends, shift in trends or other factors. They are not to be accepted on their face value. They are helpful in identifying the problem areas of a firm. They lead the way for further investigation and meaningful conclusion. They are only the means to achieve a particular end. By themselves, they do not give final results.

Ratios are meaningless, if detached from the details from which they are derived. Ratios are based on the data of the company concerned. So, ratios are relevant to that particular company only, which are based on the circumstances and policies of that company. If those ratios are compared to any other company, where the circumstances and policies adopted are totally different, conclusions drawn based on the divergent data would be meaningless. It may, therefore, be concluded that the ratio analysis, if done mechanically, is not only misleading but, equally, dangerous.

The analyst must have practical knowledge as well as experience for calculating the ratios and interpreting the results, carefully. Unless the analyst is able to correlate the ratios, he would not be able to arrive at meaningful clues. Remember, ratios are only indicators or signals for the direction to investigate, further, and conclude with specific conclusions. Conclusions can be drawn only after careful analysis of all the relevant ratios and gathering detailed information, the inquiries may, further, require.

Ratios, like statistics, have a set of principles and finality about them, at times, may be misleading. It has been said that "a man who has his head in the oven and his head in the oven and his feet in the ice-box is on the average, comfortable"! To say a final word on ratio analysis, conclusions on study of single ratios, in isolation, are dangerous.

3.13 RELEVANCE OF RATIO ANALYSIS FOR PREDICTING FUTURE

The basis to calculate ratio analysis is historical financial statements. Historical financial statements indicate what has happened in the past. The financial analyst is interested to know what would happen, in future. Management of the company has the information about the company's future plans and policies. Using the historical data and equipped with the knowledge of future plans and constraints to achieve, management is in a better position to predict future happening to a certain reasonable extent. But, outside analyst has his own limitation and the analysis based on past ratios may not, necessarily, reflect the financial position and performance in the future.

Illustration No. 8

Complete the following Balance Sheet, assuming that only the Equity Capital and Retained Earning figures are given.

Liabilities	Rs.	Assets	Rs.
Equity Capital	1,20,000	Fixed Assets	?
Retained Earnings	1,20,000	Stock	?
Creditors	?	Debtors	?
		Cash	?
Total (Rs.)	?	Total (Rs.)	?

Total debt is Two-Third of Net Worth. Turnover of Total Assets is 1.8; 30 days sales are in the form of Debtors; Turnover of inventory is 5; cost of goods sold in the year is Rs.3,60,000; and the acid test is 1:1.

(B.U. (MBA), 2003)

Solution:

Total debt is Two-Third of Net Worth.

Net Worth = Equity share capital + Retained earnings

= 1,20,000+1,20,000

= 2,40,000

$$\text{Therefore, Total debts, creditors} = 2{,}40{,}000 \times \frac{2}{3} = 1{,}60{,}000$$

Total Liabilities = Equity capital + Retained earnings + Creditors

= 1,20,000+1,20,000+1,60,000

= 4,00,000

Total Liabilities = Total Assets = 4,00,000

Inventory Turnover Ratio = 5

$$\frac{\text{Cost of goods sold}}{\text{stock}} = 5$$

$$\frac{3{,}60{,}000}{\text{Stock}} = 5$$

$$\text{Stock} = \frac{3{,}60{,}000}{5} = 72{,}000$$

Turnover of Total Assets is 1.8

Total assets have turned over 1.8 times. It implies the firm has generated a sale of Rs.1.8 for every rupee invested in total assets.

$$\text{Assets turnover ratio} = \frac{\text{Sales}}{\text{Total Assets}} = 1.8$$

Sales = Total Assets × 1.8

= 4,00,000 × 1.8

= 7,20,000

30 days sales are in the form of debtors. In other words, debtors have turned over 12 times in a year.

$$\text{Debtors Turnover} = \frac{\text{Sales}}{\text{Debtors}} = 12$$

$$\text{Debtors} = \frac{\text{Sales}}{12}$$

$$= \frac{7,20,000}{12} = 60,000$$

Acid test is 1:1

$$\text{Acid Test Ratio} = \frac{\text{Current Assets} - \text{Inventory}}{\text{Current Liabilities}}$$

There are only cash and debtors other than stock in current assets.

So, total cash and debtors are equal to current liabilities (creditors) i.e. 1,60,000.

$$\text{Cash} + \text{Debtors} = 1,60,000$$

$$\text{Cash} = 1,60,000 - \text{Debtors}$$

$$= 1,60,000 - 60,000$$

$$= 1,00,000$$

Now, let us fill the figures in the balance sheet.

Balance Sheet

Liabilities	Rs.	Assets	Rs.
Equity Capital	1,20,000	Fixed Assets *	1,68,000
Retained Earnings	1,20,000	Stock	72,000
Creditors	1,60,000	Debtors	60,000
		Cash	1,00,000
Total	4,00,000	Total	4,00,000

* *Balancing figure*

3.14 COMMON-SIZE STATEMENT (CSS)

The common-size statements, balance sheet and income statement are shown in analytical percentages. The CSS represents the relationship of different items of a financial statement with some common item by expressing each item as a percentage of the common item. The common-size statements may be prepared in the following ways:

(1) The totals of assets and liabilities in the balance sheet are taken as 100.

(2) The individual assets are expressed as a percentage of total assets. i.e. 100. Different liabilities are calculated in relation to total liabilities. For example, if total assets are Rs. 10 lakhs and debtors value is Rs. 1,00,000. Debtors will be 10% of total assets.

$$\frac{(1,00,000 \times 100)}{10,00,000}$$

(3) Similarly, in Common Size Income Statement, each item is stated as percentage of the Net Sales. The percentages for different items are computed by dividing the absolute amount of that item by the Common base (i.e. Net Sales) and then multiplying by 100. The percentages, so calculated, can be easily compared with the corresponding percentages, in some other period.

Purpose: Impact of increase or decrease is immediately known as every item is compared to a common standard base of a fixed value i.e.100. The CSS is useful not only in intra-firm comparisons over a series of different years but also in making inter-firm comparisons for the same year or several years.

Illustration No.9

Following are the Income Statement and Balance Sheet of Theer & Co. for the year 2005 and 2006. Prepare the CBS and CIS for these two years.

Income Statements for the year 2005 – 2006
(Figures in Rs.)

	2005	2006		2005	2006
To cost of goods sold	5,00,000	3,75,000	By Net Sales	6,00,000	5,00,000
To General Expenses	10,000	10,000			
To Selling Expenses	15,000	20,000			
To Net Profit	75,000	95,000			
	6,00,000	5,00,000		6,00,000	5,00,000

Balance Sheets as on 31st December, 2005 and 2006

(Figures in Rs.)

Liabilities	2005	2006	Assets	2005	2006
Capital	3,00,000	4,00,000	Land	50,000	50,000
Reserves	1,50,000	72,500	Building	1,50,000	1,35,000
Secured Loans	50,000	75,000	Plant	1,50,000	1,35,000
Creditors	1,00,000	1,37,500	Furniture	50,000	70,000
Outstanding Expenses	50,000	75,000	Cash	80,000	90,000
			Debtors	70,000	1,30,000
			Finished stock	1,00,000	1,50,000
	6,50,000	7,60,000		6,50,000	7,60,000

Solution:

Common Size Income Statement

	Amount (Rs.)		Percentages	
	2005	2006	2005	2006
Net Sales	6,00,000	5,00,000	100.00	100.00
Less : Cost of goods sold	5,00,000	3,75,000	83.33	75.00
Gross : Profit (1)	1,00,000	1,25,000	16.67	25.00
Less : General Expenses	10,000	10,000	1.67	2.00
Selling Expenses	15,000	20,000	2.50	4.00
Total Operating Expenses (2)	25,000	30,000	4.17	6.00
Net Profit (1 – 2)	75,000	95,000	12.50	19.00

Common Size Balance Sheet

	Amount (Rs.)		Percentages	
	2005	2006	2005	2006
Land	50,000	50,000	7.70	6.58
Building	1,50,000	1,35,000	23.07	17.76
Plant	1,50,000	1,35,000	23.07	17.76

Furniture	50,000	70,000	7.70	9.21
Total Fixed Assets (1)	4,00,000	3,90,000	61.54	51.31
Cash	80,000	90,000	12.31	11.84
Debtors	70,000	1,30,000	10.76	17.10
Finished Stock	1,00,000	1,50,000	15.39	1049.75
Total Current Assets (2)	2,50,000	3,70,000	38.46	48.69
Total Assets (1+2)	6,50,000	7,60,000	100	100
Capital	3,00,000	4,00,0.000	46.15	52.63
Reserves	1,50,000	72,500	23.08	9.54
Net Worth (3)	4,50,000	4,72,500	69.23	62.17
Secured Loans	50,000	75,000	7.70	9.87
Creditors	1,00,000	1,37,500	15.37	18.09
Outstanding Expenses	50,000	1,50,000	15.39	1049.75
Total Liabilities (4)	2,00,000	2,87,000	30.77	37.83
Total Capitals + Liabilities (3+4)	6,50,000	7,60,000	100	100

3.15 SUMMARY OF RATIOS AND THEIR PURPOSE

(1)	(2) Ratio	(3) Computation Formula	(4) Purpose
1	Current Ratio	$\frac{\text{Current Assets}}{\text{Current Liabilities}}$	Measures short-term debt paying ability.
2	Quick (AcidTest) Ratio	$\frac{\text{Quick Assets}}{\text{Current Liabilities}}$	A refined measure of the short-term debt-paying ability of the firm. Measures short-term solvency.
3	Gross Profit Ratio	$\frac{\text{Gross Profit}}{\text{Net Sales}} \times 100$	Measures efficiency of company's operations, production and trading activities.!
4	Net Profit Ratio	$\frac{\text{Net Profit}}{\text{Net Sales}} \times 100$	Shows net margin on sales, final indicator for management's efficiency.
5	Operating Ratio	$\frac{\text{Operating Costs}}{\text{Net Sales}} \times 100$	A yardstick to measure Expenses operating efficiency of management's ability to keep contain operating expenses for level of sales achieved.
6	Return on Equity	$\frac{\text{Net profit (after tax)} - \text{Profit to Preference}}{\text{Equity Shareholders' Funds}} \times 100$	Measures earning power of equity shareholders' funds.
7	Earning per Equity Share	$\frac{\text{Profits available for Equity shareholders}}{\text{No. of Equity shares}} \times 100$	Sh ows the amount of earnings available foreach equity share.

8	Dividend Yield	$\frac{\text{Dividend per equity share}}{\text{Market price share}} \times 100$	Shows the rate of return to equity share-holders, in the form of dividends, based on the market price of the share.
9	Price Earning Ratio	$\frac{\text{Market price of equity share}}{\text{Earning per equity share}} \times 100$	A guide to buy /sell at that price. May also indicate rate of return expected by investors.
10	Interest Coverage	$\frac{\text{EBDIT}}{\text{Interest}}$	A test for firm's debt servicing capacity. Useful to long-term lenders.
11	Debt Equity Ratio	$\frac{\text{Total Debt}}{\text{Net worth}}$	Depicts extent of total debt financing in business.
12	Total Debt Ratio	$\frac{\text{Total Debt}}{\text{Total Assets}}$	Shows the proportion of total assets financed by total liabilities.
13	Inventory Turnover Ratio	$\frac{\text{Cost of goods sold}}{\text{Average Inventory, at cost}}$	Evaluation of efficiency in producing and selling goods and adequacy of controls on inventory holding.
14	No. of days inventory holding	$\frac{360}{\text{Inventory Turnover Ratio}}$	Shows the inventory holding, in days, and control on inventory management.
15	Accounts Receivable (Debtors) Turnover	$\frac{\text{Credi sales}}{\text{Average debtors}}$	Measures liquidity of debtors and effectiveness of the credit policy.

16	Debtors Collection Period	$\frac{360}{\text{Debors' Turnover Ratio}}$	Shows period of holding of debtors and indicates effectiveness of collection department.
17	Working Capital Ratio	$\frac{\text{Cost of Sales or Sales}}{\text{Average Working Capital}}$	Shows velocity of utilisation of working capital.
18	Return on Investment, before tax (i) ROCE (ii) ROTA	(i) $\frac{\text{EBIT}}{\text{Capital Employed}}$ (ii) $\frac{\text{EBIT}}{\text{Total Assets}}$	Measures the overall efficiency of business, before tax
19	Return on investment, after tax (ROCE, ROTA)	$\frac{\text{Profit after tax, before interest}}{\text{Capital employed or Total Assets}}$	Shows overall efficiency of business, after tax.
20	Pay –Out Ratio	$\frac{\text{Dividend Per Equity Share}}{\text{Earnings per equity share}}$	Shows proportion of payment of dividend out of earnings and stability of dividend policy.
21	Capital Gearing Ratio	(Preference share capital + Debentures + Long–Term Loan) / (Equity share capital + Reserves and surplus)	Refers to the proportion between fixed interest or dividend bearing funds and non-fixed interest or dividend bearing funds in the total capital employed in the business that influences the variability of profits.

Review Questions

1. What is meant by 'Financial Analysis'? Discuss the utility and significance of the ratios to the management and others, interested in the business? **(3.1 and 3.2)**
2. "Ratios are the symptoms of health of an organisation like blood pressure, the pulse or temperature of an individual" Explain and state their uses? **(3.1 and 3.2)**
3. Detail and describe the different types of financial analysis? **(3.3)**
4. Describe the types of Financial Analysis? Explain 'Analysis without interpretation is meaningless and interpretation without analysis is impossible'? **(3.3 to 3.5.1)**
5. Is it possible for a firm to have a high current ratio and still experience difficulties in paying its current debt? Explain with illustration? **(3.7.1)**
6. Explain composition and quality of Current Assets is more important than mere adequacy of current ratio, with an illustration? **(3.7.1)**
7. Describe different types of Ratios and standards of comparison for evaluating the performance of the firm? **(3.5, 3.4)**
8. Describe the different types of ratios? Explain any two ratios in each category with their significance? **(3.5, 3.7, 3.8, 3.9 and 3.10)**
9. What are the important profitability ratios? How they are worked out? Explain and illustrate? **(3.10)**
10. Describe the concept 'Trading on Equity'? Explain the relationship between Return on capital employed and Return on equity, with a suitable illustration? **(3.11)**
11. What is meant by Capital Gearing? Elaborate the consequences of significant changes in EBIT, when the firm is highly geared? **(3.10 and 3.11 and 3.12.1)**
12. Explain the limitations of the ratio analysis? **(3.12 and 3.12.1)**
13. "Ratios are meaningless if detached from the details from which they are derived." Comment and bring out the limitations of ratio analysis. **(3.12)**
14. Explain common-size statements? Explain the technique of preparing the common size balance sheet? **(3.14)**
15. Write short notes on:
    (A) Window Dressing **(3.7.1)**
    (B) Cost of goods sold **(3.6)**
    (C) EBIT **(3.6)**
    (D) Trading on Equity **(3.11)**
    (E) Relevance of Ratio Analysis for predicting future **(3.13)**

Check your Understanding

A. State whether the following statements are TRUE or False

1. Current Ratio represents margin of safety.
2. A very high degree of liquidity is good for the firm as it does not experience any difficulty in making payments.

3. Activity Ratios are also called Turnover Ratios because they indicate the speed of converting assets into sales.
4. Aging Schedule does not show the period debtors are outstanding in a firm.
5. Working Capital gap is met by Bank Borrowings alone.
6. Gross Profit Ratio shows the spread between sales revenue and cost of goods sold.
7. Net Profit after Tax to sales indicates Net Profit Margin.
8. The term 'financial analysis' includes both 'analyses and interpretation'.
9. If price earnings ratio of a company is more than the industry's average, it is better to buy the scrip at that market price.
10. On the basis of modus operandi, financial analysis can be classified as external analysis and internal analysis.
11. A large number of potential and present investors would be interested in DPS rather than EPS.
12. Common–size financial statements and financial ratios are the two tools employed in Vertical analysis.
13. If Net Profit margin is inadequate, return on shareholder's funds would be low.
14. If EBIT increases, percentage increase of ROE depends on the capital gearing of the firm.
15. EBIT and ROCE do not increase in the same percentage.
16. Liquidity ratios measure long-term solvency of a concern.
17. Horizontal analysis refers to the study of relationship of the various items in the financial statements of one accounting period.
18. While analysing ratios, investors concentrate on the firm's present and future profitability.
19. Horizontal analysis is also known as 'static analysis'.
20. An arbitrary Current Ratio of 2:1 should not be blindly followed.
21. Inventory is part of liquid assets.
22. A firm should ensure neither excess liquidity nor inadequate liquidity.
23. Rule of thumb for acid–test ratio is 1:1.
24. Current ratio measures quality of assets.
25. A decreased Stock Turnover Ratio usually indicates expanding business.

Answers

1. True	2. False	3. True	4. False	5. False
6. True	7. True	8. True	9. False	10. False
11. True	12. True	13. True	14. True	15. False
16. False	17. False	18. True	19. False	20. True
21. False	22. True	23. True	24. False	25. False

B. Pick up the most appropriate answer

1. Financial analysis is the process for
   a. Identifying strength of firm.
   b. Identifying weakness of firm.
   c. Identifying strengths and weaknesses of firm.

2. Financial Analysis can be made from
   a. Profit and Loss Account.
   b. Balance Sheet.
   c. Items in Profit and Loss Account and Balance Sheet by establishing relationship.
3. Financial Analysis is meant for the following category.
   a. Trade creditors.
   b. Trade creditors and suppliers of long-term debt.
   c. Investors.
   d. Management.
   e. All above categories specified in A, B, C and D.
4 Which statement is wrong?
   a. Liquidity Ratio – Measures firm's ability to meet current obligations.
   b. Activity Ratio – Reflects efficiency in utilising assets of the firm.
   c. Management is not interested in valuing every aspect of firm's performance.
   d. Accounting data is taken from financial statements.
5. Calculate current ratio from the following data:
   Bank OD: 20,000; Cash: 15,000; Outstanding expenses: 10,000
   Accrued income: 5,000; Stock: 5,000; Prepaid expenses: 5,000
   a. 2:1. b. 1:1.
   c. 1.5:1. d. 1:1.5.
6. Find out the missing figure if current ratio is 2:1.

Work in progress	:	20,000.
Bank cash credit	:	5,000.
Raw Materials	:	10,000.
Creditors	:	4,000.
Bills payable	:	?

   a. 10,000. b. 9,000.
   c. 12,000. d. 6,000.
7. Calculate Quick Ratio from the following.

Debentures	:	10,000
Long Term Loan	:	20,000
Cash	:	15,000
Raw Materials	:	6,000
Debtors	:	5,000
Creditors	:	5,000
Prepaid expenses	:	5,000

   a. 3:1 b. 4:1
   c. 2:1 d. 1:1

8. This ratio is a 'Test of Quantity but not Quality'.
   a. Quick Ratio.
   b. Debt-Equity Ratio.
   c. Current Ratio
   d. Dividend payout Ratio
9. A company can meet its financial obligations as and when they fall due if
   a. Current Ratio is 2:1.
   b. Current Ratio is less than 2:1
   c. More depends on composition of current assets rather than current ratio alone.
   d. Current assets just cover current liabilities.

10 Calculate Net Working Capital
Cash: 5,000 ; Finished Goods: 12,000
Debtors: 20,000; Prepaid expenses: 3,000
Debentures: 4,000; Long-term loan: 5,000 and
Bank Cash credit: 6,000;
Creditors = 10,000
   a. 24,000.
   b. 26,000.
   c. 21,000.
   d. 15,000.
   e. 20,000.

11. Capital employed means
   a. Net Worth
   b. Net Worth + Long term loans.
   c. Current Assets + Current Liabilities
   d. Net Current Assets.
12. Cost of goods sold includes
   a. Depreciation
   b. Gross Profit
   c. Administrative expenses
   d. Interest
   e. None.
13. Debt Equity Ratio is a
   a. Liquidity Ratio
   b. Solvency Ratio
   c. Profitability Ratio
   d. Activity Ratio
14. Calculate the inventory holding, in terms of days:
Opening stock: 10,000;
Closing stock: 20,000;
Sales: 40,000; Gross Profit: 10%
   a. 150
   b. 30
   c. 60
   d. 120
15. For calculating inventory ratio, the following information is more appropriate.
   a. Opening Stocks
   b. Closing Stock

c. Sales d. Gross Profit

e. Average Stock

Answers

1. c	2. c	3. e	4. c	5. b
6. d	7. b	8. c	9. c	10. a
11. b	12. a	13. b	14. a	15. e

(C) Check your ability in Fast Calculations:

1. Calculate Return on Equity with the following information:

   EBIT : 50,000; 6% Debentures : 5,00,000
   Tax rate : 50%; Equity share capital : 1,00,000 (Face value Rs.10)

   General Reserves: 3,00,000

   a. 10% b. 2.5% c. 20% d. 15% e. 30%

Ans. 1.d

$$\frac{\underline{\text{Profit after tax}}}{\text{Equity Shareholders' funds}} \quad \frac{50{,}000-30{,}000-50\%\,(50{,}000-30{,}000)}{1{,}00{,}000+3{,}00{,}000}$$

2. Share price, before bonus issue is Rs.100. Bonus issue 1:4 is made. What would be the ex-bonus price of a share, if other factors are constant?

   a. 60 b. 70 c. 80 d. 100 e. 20

Ans. **(c) (For every 4 shares held, one bonus share is issued)** $\frac{100 \times 4}{5}$

4. Earnings per share are Rs.80. Bonus shares are issued in the ratio of 1:4 during the year. What is the adjusted earning per share of the year in which bonus is made?

   a. 60 b. 70 c. 80 d. 100 e. 20

Ans.(d) $\left(\frac{80 \times 5}{4}\right)$

(D) Find out impact of Decisions taken

The current ratio of Kishore & Co is 2:1. Which of the following decisions would improve the ratio, which would reduce it and which one would not change it?

1. To pay substantial amount of creditors from the available cash balance?
2. To sell a vehicle, used for carrying staff from their residences to office, for cash at a slight loss.
3. To borrow money for a short period, with a nominal interest rate, executing a promissory note.

4. To purchase marketable investments for cash.
5. To give an interest bearing promissory note to a creditor to whom money was owed on current account.
6. Purchase of a fixed asset
7. Bills receivable dishonoured
8. Issue of Preference shares

Answers

1. Improves the ratio	2. Improves the ratio	3. Reduces the ratio
4. No change in the ratio	5. No change in the ratio	6. Reduces the ratio
7. No change	8. Improves the ratio	

E. State whether the following statements are TRUE or False

1. Liabilities are not subject to fall, as they have to be paid.
2. Creditors turnover ratio is a 'Solvency Ratio'.
3. Current Ratio is a crude and quick measure of firm's liquidity.
4. Rate of return on capital employed is a turnover ratio.
5. Quick ratio establishes a relationship between liquid assets and current liabilities.
6. Low gearing is preferable to high gearing from the viewpoint of creditors.
7. Generally, a Quick ratio is not better than current ratio in a test of liquidity.
8. A firm's ability to meet the interest charges and repayment dues on long-term obligations is referred to as its short-term solvency.
9. Leverage Ratio indicates proportion of debt and equity in financing firm's assets.
10. 'Acid Test' denotes liquidity.
11. The process of magnifying the equity shareholder's earnings through the use of debt is called 'Financial Leverage' or 'Trading on Equity'.
12. Ratio analysis is a technique of planning and control.
13. If cost of debt is lower than the firm's overall rate of return, the earnings of shareholders will be reduced.
14. A high debt company can borrow on favourable terms and conditions.
15. The term 'Investment' may refer to total assets or net assets.
16. A low debt equity ratio indicates a greater claim of owners than creditors.
17. An appropriate debt - equity combination involves a trade-off between return and risk.
18. Profit is not a factor of sales.

Answers

1. True	2. False	3. True	4. False	5. True
6. True	7. False	8. False	9. True	10. True
11. True	12. True	13. False	14. False	15. True
16. True	17. True	18. False		

4

SOURCES AND APPLICATION OF FUNDS

- *Need of Funds Flow Statement*
- *Concept of Funds*
- *Meaning of Flow of Funds*
- *Objectives of Funds Flow Statement*
- *Utility of Funds Flow Statement to Different Parties*
- *Sources of Funds*
- *Depreciation as a Source of Funds*
- *Application or Uses of Funds*
- *Procedure for knowing Whether a Transaction Finds a Place in Funds Flow Statement*
- *Preparation of Funds Flow Statement*
    - *Statement of Changes in Working Capital*
    - *Calculation of Funds from Operations*
    - *Finding out Hidden Information*
- *Funds Flow Statement, Income Statement and Balance Sheet*
- *Limitations of Funds Flow Statement*
- *Objective Questions*
- *Check Your Understanding*

The most commonly used forms of the Statement of Changes in Financial Position are Sources and Application of Funds (Funds Flow Statement) and Cash Flow Statement.

4.1 NEED OF FUNDS FLOW STATEMENT

Profit and Loss Account and Balance Sheet are the two basic financial statements, which are of immense importance to owners, management and investors. When Profit and Loss Account and Balance Sheet are prepared, what is the need of preparing this separate Funds Flow Statement, again? Balance Sheet shows the summary of assets and liabilities of a firm. The assets side of the balance sheet shows the deployment of funds while the liabilities side shows how the resources have been raised. In other words, balance sheet shows sources and uses of finance too. It indicates the financial position of a firm on a particular date. However, **Balance Sheet is a static statement and does not show the causes for the changes in assets and liabilities or movement of finances, between two periods.** Balance Sheet does not show the changes that take place during the period. If loan has been raised and repaid during the same period, balance sheet, at the end of the period, does not show both the transactions. Similarly, Profit and loss account shows the expenses and revenues realised for an accounting period. **Profit and Loss Account also reflects the operational results of a business for a particular period, which causes changes in owners' equity, partially.** Capital raised and funds withdrawn resulting in change in owner's equity does not appear. In other words, Profit and loss account explains only partial story in respect of owner's equity. Profit and Loss Account and Balance Sheet provide the basic essential information about the business activities of the firm. **However, both these two statements do not explain the causes for changes in assets, liabilities and owner's equity.** Moreover, usefulness of both balance sheet and profit and loss account is limited and fail to serve the purposes of financial analysis and planning.

It is clear, from the above, that Profit and Loss Account and Balance Sheet do not provide sufficiently wide range of information to make assessment of the organisation by the end user for the purpose of analysis and planning. **So, there is a need to prepare a separate statement that explains the changes in assets and liabilities, from one period of time to the end of another period. The statement is called "Funds Flow Statement".**

Purposes: Both Profit and Loss Account and Balance Sheet do not explain the changes in assets, liabilities and owners' equity between two dates. So, an additional statement is needed to serve this purpose. Funds Flow Statement serves this purpose. Funds Flow Statement, broadly, serves the following purposes. The Funds Flow Statement shows:

(i) Changes in assets and liabilities, including working capital, between two periods and

(ii) Utilisation of financial resources during the period such as acquisition of assets, payment of debts and distribution of dividends to shareholders etc.

4.2 CONCEPT OF FUNDS

The term 'Funds' has been defined in a number of ways. They are:

(A) **In the Narrow sense:** Here, the term 'funds' refer to cash only. Transactions that involve cash only are taken. **Cash Flow Statement is prepared, in this approach,** where only cash receipts and disbursements are included. It is a summary of cash transactions.

(B) **In the Popular sense:** 'Funds' refer to working capital, the excess of current assets over current liabilities. Total resources of a business are invested in fixed assets and working capital, the later is partly in the liquid form .**This is the most popular form of 'Statement of Changes in Financial Position'. Sources and Application of Funds is prepared on this basis.**

(C) **In the Broader sense:** The term 'Funds' refer to financial resources, in whatever form, they may exist. **Statement of Total Financial Resources is prepared as per this approach.** This is a comprehensive statement involving cash and non-cash transactions. Transactions involving money, materials, machinery and others are included. When machinery or building is purchased, in exchange of shares, it is not reported both in cash flow statement and Sources and Application of Funds. However, this type of transaction involves financial resources and so finds place in the Statement of Total Financial Resources. All types of transactions involving financial resources are included in this statement.

The working capital concept of funds is the most popular one, as already stated, amongst the different ways of defining the term 'Funds'. **In this chapter, when we discuss Sources and Application of funds, the term 'funds' refer to working capital only.**

4.3 MEANING OF FLOW OF FUNDS

The term 'Flow' refers to movement of funds. The movement can be in the form of increase or decrease of funds i.e. working capital. If a transaction creates a change in the quantum of working capital, 'flow' of funds takes place. The transaction may increase or decrease the existing amount of working capital. Every transaction has two sides. Let us take some examples to explain the concept of flow of funds. Issue of shares for cash results in increase of working capital, it is a transaction of 'Source'. The transaction has resulted in 'inflow' of funds. Purchase of furniture on credit reduces the amount of working capital; it is 'Application' of funds. There is outflow of funds with the transaction. **There would be change in working capital if one of the items were related to current assets or current liabilities.** If the transaction creates a change in working capital, the transaction would find a place in the Sources and Application of Funds Statement.

If the transaction does not change the amount of working capital, it is said to be non-fund transaction and does not appear in the Sources and Uses of Funds Statement. In a non-fund transaction, both the items are non-current or current items. We are referring to current assets and current liabilities. When machinery has been purchased and in consideration debentures are issued, the transaction has not changed the working capital, both the items are non-current, it is non-fund transaction. If cash is realised from debtors, there is no increase in working capital as both the items are current items. These types of transactions do not appear in the sources and application of funds statement.

Simple Rule: The simple rule is "Ask the transaction, whether it changes working capital, if it is 'YES', the transaction finds a place in Sources and Application of Funds. If the answer is 'NO', no place for the transaction in the Statement.

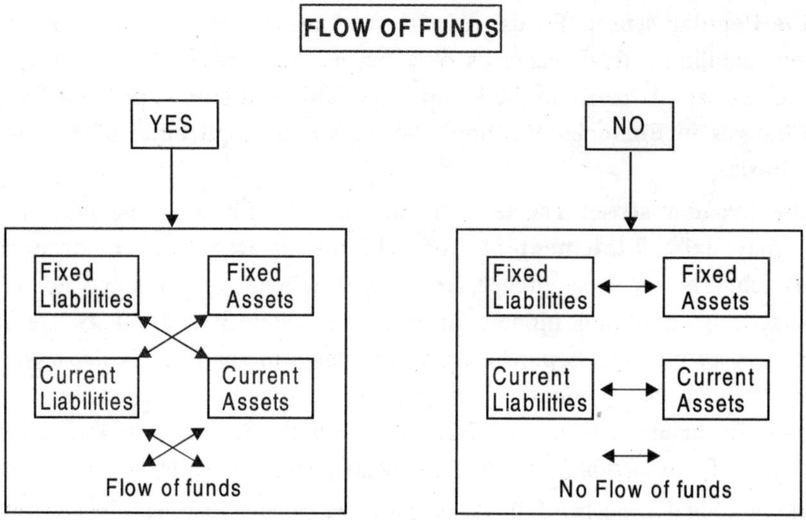

Flow of Funds

4.4 OBJECTIVES OF FUNDS FLOW STATEMENT

Meaning and Definition: Funds Flow Statement is a device that indicates the various means through which funds have been obtained, during a specified period and the ways they have been used. Simply, it shows the different sources of procuring funds and their varied application during that period. It shows the inflow and outflow of funds. **The term 'funds' refer to working capital.** Funds Flow Statement shows the change in financial position of a firm between beginning and ending financial statement dates.

Foulke defines this statement as:

> *"A statement of sources and application of funds is a device designed to analyse the changes in financial condition of a business enterprise between two dates".*
>
> *The statement has two sides, the left side shows the sources and the right side presents their uses.*
>
> *The statement is an important tool for financial analysis for the management, bankers and investors who are interested in knowing the changes in the financial position of the firm. It is a supplement to the financial statements. Banks insist on this statement as and when loan application is submitted for financial assistance. Now, Funds Flow Statement is a mandatory requirement of reporting in India for limited companies.*

Funds Flow Statement is called by various names such as:

(i) Statement of Sources and Uses of Funds

(ii) Where got, where gone Statement

(iii) Statement of Inflow and Outflow of Funds

(iv) Funds Received and Funds Disbursed Statement

(v) Statement of Sources and Applications of Funds

As observed rightly, the key word is 'Funds'.

Importance and Objectives of Funds Flow Statement: This statement is widely used by the financial institutions, banks and credit rating agencies. By preparing the statement, the management can know well, in advance, about the adequacy or otherwise of working capital position for proper planning.

1. **Analysis of Financial Position and Profits:** Balance sheet is a static statement about the financial position, on a particular date. It shows the net effect of various transactions on the operational and financial position of a concern. It does not explain the causes for the change in assets and liabilities, between two different dates. The fund's flow statement explains its effect on the liquidity position of the organisation. At times, even after the firm is profitable, still, it experiences difficulty in meeting normal payments. Firm does not understand reasons for such a situation. Sources and Application of Funds gives the answers for these questions.
2. **Throws light on perplex questions:** Questions of general interest but answers not available elsewhere are found from this statement such as:
   (i) Why firm is not able to declare higher dividend despite increase in profits?
   (ii) Where the proceeds of shares and debentures have gone?
   (iii) In what manner, the sale proceeds of fixed assets have been used?
   (iv) What are the sources of repayment of long-term debts?
   (v) How the increase in working capital requirement was financed and how further requirements would be met?
3. **Information of Profit from operations and non-operations:** Profit and Loss Account shows the summary or net effect of operating and non-operating expenses, in the form of net profit. In other words, operating and non-operating profit is not calculated and shown separately. Firm may be in net profit, due to non-operation profit, even after offsetting the operating losses. This alarming picture is not known from the profit and loss account for timely action. Funds Flow Statement shows the operating and non-operating profit, separately, that helps timely managerial action.
4. **Management of Working Capital:** Statement of changes in working capital reveals to management the ways in which working capital was obtained and used in the past. Projections are always prepared by the management to achieve future plans. A projected statement of working capital may reveal the need of large amount of working capital. In case, the firm is not able to meet the future working capital needs from internal resources, it can plan, in advance, to procure to meet its needs.

5. **Helps in Borrowing Decision:** Nowadays, banks and other financial institutions insist on the submission of Funds Flow Statement along with loan application. This helps the bank to assess the working capital needs of the firm. Based on this statement, banks consider whether to sanction working capital limits or not and if so to what extent the limit is to be sanctioned. This statement also facilitates the long-term institutions to appreciate the means of the firm for repaying the installment on long-term debt. This is a necessary statement both for commercial banks and long-term institutions while assessing the borrowing needs of the firm.
6. **Knowledge of Sources and Uses:** Sources in the Funds Flow Statement provide knowledge in respect of the various ways funds have been raised. In a similar manner, information in respect of Applications or uses gives knowledge about the different ways in which the funds of the firm have been used. Firm may be able to plan future course of action with the information.
7. **Other Information:** Funds Flow Statement provides that information that is not precisely available in the financial statements. If the firm purchases building and sells the same in the same accounting year for loss, the transaction does not appear in the Balance Sheet hence it would not be known. For this reason, Funds Flow Statement is always needed as a supplementary statement.

4.5 UTILITY OF FUNDS FLOW STATEMENT TO DIFFERENT PARTIES

The versatile utility of Funds Flow Statement to different parties can be summarised as follows:

1. **Management:** The historical Funds Flow Statement (Statements of the earlier years) provides the information how the funds were available and their use in the past. They provide the means to understand why the targets of the earlier years were not achieved. That would be useful information to avoid recurrence, in future. Funds Flow Statements can be prepared for future too. Planning can be more effective with their help. **They provide the necessary hints to the management whether it is necessary for them to review and recast their plans, in a more realistic way, in case the future inflows are not adequate to meet the anticipated outflows.**
2. **Financial Institutions:** Commercial banks require them to assess the working capital needs of the firm. Term-lending institutions want to satisfy the repayment capacity of the firm. Funds Flow Statement provides the information how the firm used the funds, earlier. Instances of diversion of sanctioned working capital for acquisition of fixed assets, contrary to the terms of sanction, would be known. The lenders would know firm's style of functioning. The borrowings may be secured by the assets, but the financial institutions want to satisfy with the financial integrity of the borrower too. **Financial institutions would know the ways the funds were used, earlier, and future ways of use to judge their repaying ability.**
3. **Debenture holders:** Debenture holders too are long-term creditors of the firm. Their stake is similar to financial institutions. They would get back their money after several

years, dependant on the maturity period of the debentures. Debenture holders look for redemption and projected Funds— **Flow Statement shows the position of availability of funds when the debentures fall due for repayment.** To continue to hold the debentures till such time or not, Funds Flow Statement is useful for them to take a suitable decision.

4. **Trade Creditors:** They are the suppliers of goods and services and look for short-term liquidity for payment. Liquidity of the firm and operating profits assure the repayment schedule. **Statement of Working Capital Position indicates how far the firm is liquid to meet the promised payment schedule to review their credit policy.**
5. **Shareholders:** Shareholders are basically interested about the financial position of the firm and their future investment plans that generate operating profits. This holds well to the existing as well as potential shareholders. **Future investment plans and the operating profits that are likely to generate would be known from the Funds Flow Statement.**

4.6 SOURCES OF FUNDS

These are the sources through which funds come into the business of the firm.

1. **Funds from operations:** Profits from business is the main source of funds. Profit does not mean the amount that is shown in the profit and loss account. When profit and loss account is prepared, several operating and non-operating expenses are debited. Similarly, operating and non-operating incomes are also credited. Non-operating item is one, which is not connected with the conduct of the business such as loss on sale of assets; preliminary expenses written off and rent from building, not connected to the business. Adjustment is necessary to arrive at the correct profit from business operations. To arrive at operating income, non-operating expenses are to be added and non-operating income is to be deducted from the amount of profit shown in profit and loss account. Profit from operations is the source as funds are received into the business.
2. **Sale of Fixed Assets:** If any fixed asset such as land, building, plant and machinery is sold, the total sale proceeds are a source. Sale of fixed assets increases the working capital. However, if one non-current asset (Fixed asset) is exchanged for another non-current asset, it does not constitute inflow of funds, as there is no change in working capital.
3. **Issue of Shares and Debentures:** When shares and debentures are issued to be public and cash is received, the amount of cash received is a source. The important point is if cash is received then only it is a source. In the following instances, it is not to be treated as source:

   (A) Issue of shares and debentures for consideration other than current assets

   (B) Conversion of debentures and loans into shares

   (C) Issue of bonus shares or making partly paid shares as fully paid shares out of the accumulated profits.

The reason is simple. Such above instances do not increase the working capital.

4. **Increase in Long-term Loans:** Long-term loans from financial institutions and banks are a source as the amount increases the availability of funds.
5. **Decrease in Working Capital:** If the working capital at the end of the period is decreased compared to the amount at the beginning of the period, it is a source. This can happen due to reduction of current assets or increase of current liabilities. If stock Rs.60,000 is reduced to Rs.40,000, working capital is decreased by Rs.20,000 and the decrease is a source. Similarly, creditors may increase from Rs.10,000 to Rs. 15,000 and the effect is reduction of working capital by Rs.5,000. Decrease of working capital is a source of funds.
6. **Non-Trading Receipts:** Non-trading receipts like dividend and rent are also credited to profit and loss account. These items are deducted from the net profit to arrive at profit from business operations. So, these items are to be shown, separately, in the Funds Flow Statement, as they are also sources of funds, not included in the funds from operations.

4.7 IS DEPRECIATION A SOURCE OF FUNDS?

Depreciation means decrease in the value of an asset due to wear and tear, passage of time, obsolescence, exhaustion and accident. It is a part of capital cost of fixed asset spread over the life of the asset. Depreciation is taken as an operating expense while arriving at true profits of a business. Depreciation is, simply, a book entry to arrive at book profits. Depreciation is a non-cash item.

It is myth depreciation is a source. People misunderstand depreciation as a source as it is added to net profits to calculate funds from operations. Funds (Working capital or cash) are provided by revenues, but not by depreciation. Depreciation does not affect current assets or current liabilities. Preliminary expenses and goodwill written off are also added to net profits as these transactions do not result in any outflow of cash with them. The same treatment is extended to depreciation, while adding back to net profits to arrive at funds from operations.

Depreciation is neither a direct source nor application of funds. **To quality to be a source, depreciation should increase quantum of working capital.** This is not happening. As depreciation is not decreasing working capital, it is also not an application of funds.

Another dimension is depreciation does not generate funds, but it saves funds. For example, if the firm takes the assets on hire, it has to pay rent for them. Payment of rent is avoided by owning assets, which would have otherwise gone in the outflow of funds. So, ownership of assets has only saved funds but not generated any new funds.

Depreciation is not a direct source of funds. Then, is it an indirect source of funds? The answer is both YES and NO. When it is an indirect source? If so, to what extent? These are the questions to be answered. Depreciation can be taken as an indirect source of funds — in a limited sense. It depends upon circumstances. If the firm is in profits, depreciation acts as a tax shield in helping the firm for reducing tax liability. Income tax permits depreciation as an admissible expenditure to the extent it is provided as per its rules. As a result, taxable profits are reduced and tax liability is reduced. So, to that extent, depreciation is a source. **In consequence, depreciation is a source to the extent tax liability is reduced.** Due to depreciation, profits available for distribution of dividend get reduced. But, more funds would be available to the business for expansion. In these circumstances, depreciation is a source. But, when the firm is in loss, question of tax payment does not rise. In those circumstances, depreciation is not a source. **It can be said, with certainty, that depreciation is not a source of funds, directly. Depreciation is only an indirect source to a limited extent, under certain circumstances.**

The above point can be understood with a simple example:

	Case I (Rs.)	Case II (Rs.)
Income before depreciation	80,000	80,000
Depreciation provided (A)	- - -	20,000
Taxable income	80,000	60,000
Income Tax Rate, say 50%	40,000	30,000
Net income after tax (B)	40,000	30,000
Net flow of funds after tax (A+B)	40,000	50,000

In case of II, funds from operations are Rs.50,000 while they are only Rs.40,000 in case of I. In case of II, depreciation is a source to the extent of Rs. 10,000 and these funds are, additionally, available to the firm for future expansion.

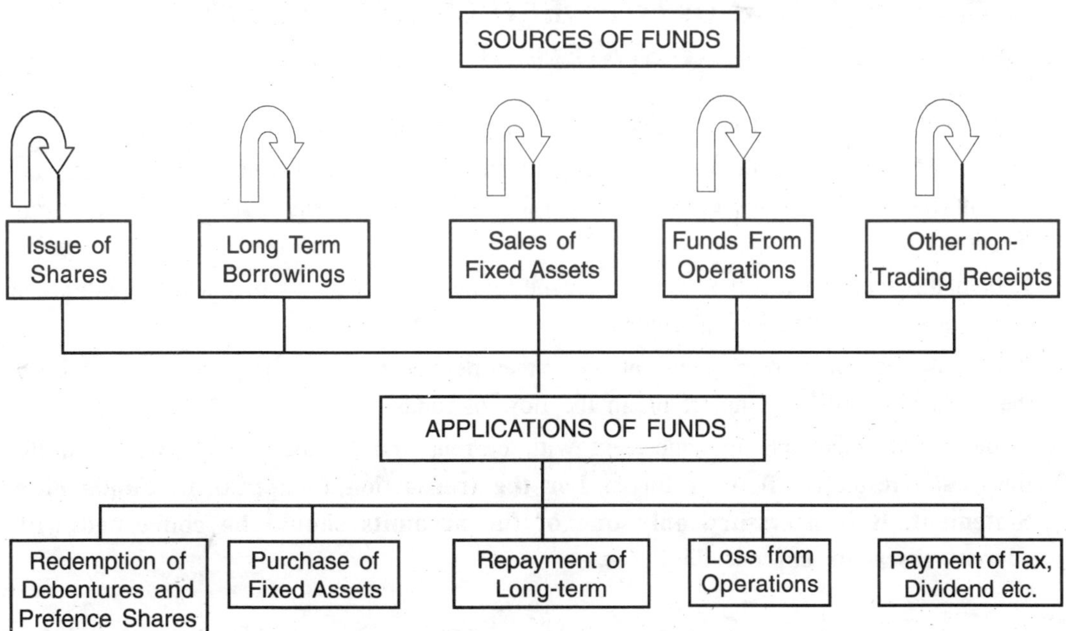

Sources and Applications of Funds

4.8 APPLICATION OR USES OF FUNDS

1. **Loss from Operations:** Result from trading operations may be a loss in a year. Such loss of funds in trading amounts to an application or outflow of funds. Working capital would be the first casualty when the firm sustains loss.
2. **Redemption of Preference Share Capital:** If preference shares are redeemed during a year, redemption decreases the funds and so it is an application. Where redemption happens at premium or discount, the net amount (including premium or after deducting discount) is the use. However, if preference shares are redeemed in exchange of some type of shares or debentures, it does not constitute as outflow of funds as no fund is involved in the transaction.
3. **Repayment of loans or redemption of debentures:** Similar to redemption of preference shares, repayment of loan and redemption of debentures are also uses.
4. **Purchase of Fixed or non-current Asset:** Purchase of fixed assets such as machinery or building results in application of funds. However, purchase of fixed assets in consideration of issue of shares, debentures or loans is not use as no funds are involved.
5. **Payment of Dividend and Tax:** Payment of dividend (including interim dividend) and tax are applications. The important point is their actual payment, and then only they become uses. Mere declaration of dividend and provision of tax are not uses.
6. **Any other non-trading payments:** Any other non-trading payments are also uses as they involve outgo of funds. Examples are loss of cash or theft in business.

4.9 PROCEDURE FOR KNOWING WHETHER A TRANSACTION FINDS A PLACE IN FUNDS FLOW STATEMENT

1. Make out the journal entry and find out the accounts involved.
2. Decide whether the accounts concerned are current (concerned with current assets and current liabilities) or non-current (concerned with non-current assets and non-current liabilities).
3. If both the accounts involved are current i.e. either current assets or current liabilities, it does not result in the flow of funds.
4. If both the accounts are non-current, i.e. either permanent assets or permanent liabilities, the transaction still does not result in the flow of funds.
5. If one of the accounts is concerned with current and the other is non-current, the transaction results in flow of funds. **For the transaction to appear in Funds Flow Statement, it is necessary only one of the accounts should be concerned with current assets or current liabilities.**

Examples:

	Transaction	Journal Entry	Category of Debit Account	Category of Credit Account	Result- Flow of Funds or not- Reason
1.	Cash collected from debtors	Cash A/c ...Dr To Sundry Debtors	Current	Current	NO Cash increases with similar decrease in debtors
2.	Goods purchased for cash or credit	Purchases ...Dr To Cash/CreditorsA/c	Current	Current	NO Working capital remains same
3.	Purchase of machinery in exchange of land	Machinery A/c ...Dr To Land A/c	Non -Current	Non -Current	NO Does not affect working capital
4.	Transfer to General Reserves	Profit & Loss A/c ...Dr To General Reserves	Non -Current	Non -Current	NO Does not affect working capital
5.	Issue of Debentures for cash	Cash A/c ... DR To Debentures	Current	Non -Current	YES Cash inflow increases working capital
6.	Redemption of Debentures	Debentures A/c...Dr To Cash	Non -Current	Current	YES Cash outflow decreases working capital
7.	Purchase of Trade Investment	Trade Investment A/c.. Dr To Cash	Non- Current	Current	YES Cash outflow decreases working capital
8.	Writing off fictitious assets, say goodwill	Profit and Loss Account...Dr. To Goodwill Account	Non -Current	Non -Current	NO Does not change working capital

Impact of Opening Stock/Closing Stock on Funds: Opening stock appears on the debit side of the Profit and Loss Account. Opening stock reduces profit so it is an application. Closing stock appears on the credit side of the profit and loss account and also appears on the assets side of the balance sheet. Profit is a source. Due to closing stock, profit increases. So, closing stock is a source. More so, working capital increases due to its inclusion in the current assets. This is also another argument why closing stock is a source.

4.10 PREPARATION OF FUNDS FLOW STATEMENT

To prepare Funds Flow Statement, first identify transactions relating to funds, as explained above. Two additional statements are required to be prepared. They are Statement of Changes in Working Capital and Statement of Funds from Operations. All the information may not be readily available, always. Hidden information has to be found out. The entire process of preparation of Funds Flow Statement can be summarised, as under:

(A) Statement of Changes in Working Capital
(B) Calculation of Funds from Operations
(C) Finding out hidden information, if required
(D) Preparation of Funds Flow Statement

(A) Statement of Changes in Working Capital

Working capital is the excess of current assets over current liabilities. Every current asset at the end of the year is to be compared with the amount at the beginning of the year to find out the increase or decrease of working capital. Increase or decrease of working capital is to be recorded in the relevant column. The same procedure is to be repeated in respect of all current liabilities.

All other information is not relevant for preparation of Statement of Changes in Working Capital.

Working capital = Current Assets – Current Liabilities

Increase in Current Asset	→	Increase in Working Capital
Decrease in Current Asset	→	Decrease in Working Capital
Increase in Current Liability	→	Decrease in Working Capital
Decrease in Current Liability	→	Increase in Working Capital

Effect on Working Capital

Illustration No.1

Prepare a Statement of Changes in Working Capital from the following Balance Sheets of THEER & Co, Bhopal.

	31st March, 2006	31st March, 2005
Assets		
Goodwill	20,000	15,000
Bank	70,000	60,000
Debtors	40,000	45,000
Bills Receivable	10,000	8,000
Closing Stock	20,000	22,000
Long-term Investments	5,000	3,000
Building	25,000	15,000
Preliminary Expenses	4,000	6,000
	1,94,000	**1,74,000**

Liabilities		
Trade Creditors	55,000	60,000
Bills Payable	30,000	25,000
Loans (Payable during 2007- Rs. 25,000)	40,000	———
Share Capital	50,000	80,000
Profit & Loss Account	19,000	9,000
	1,94,000	**1,74,000**

Solution:

Statement of Changes in Working Capital

Particulars	**2005**	**2006**	**Effect on Working Capital** **Increase Rs.**	**Decrease Rs.**
Current Assets:				
Bank	60,000	70,000	10,000	
Debtors	45,000	40,000		5,000
Bills Receivable	8,000	10,000	2,000	
Closing Stock	22,000	20,000		2,000
	1,35,000	**1,40,000**		
Current Liabilities:				
Trade Creditors	60,000	55,000	5,000	
Bills Payable	25,000	30,000		5,000
*Loans (Payable during 2007)	———	25,000	25,000	
	85,000	**1,10,000**		
Working Capital (CA-CL)Decrease in Working Capital	50,000 20,000	30,000 20,000		
	50,000	50,000	37,000	37,000

* **Note:** Out of the total Loan amount Rs. 40,000, only Rs.25,000 is repayable during the year 2007. Only Rs. 25,000 is current liability, as it becomes payable within one year and so working capital is affected to that extent only.

(B) Calculation of Funds from Operations

The net profit seen in the Profit and Loss Account need not necessarily be the funds from operations. Certain adjustments are to be made to get Funds from Operations. Follow the steps as under:

1. Take the net profit figure in Profit and Loss Account as the **BASE**.

2. **Depreciation:** Add back depreciation to the net profit, debited in the Profit and Loss Account, as it does not involve outflow of funds. Depreciation is an expense to be taken into account to arrive at accounting profit, but this has no relevance for calculation of funds from operations.
3. **Intangible Assets written off:** Add back expenses like preliminary expenses, discount on issue of shares and debentures, goodwill written off. These are intangible assets written off to arrive at profit but does not involve outflow of funds.
4. **Incomes not related to Operations or Business:** These are the incomes that are not related to operations but considered in Profit and Loss Account to arrive at net profit. These incomes – profit on sale of assets, income from investments and rent from buildings, not connected to business – are to be deducted from net profits.
5. **Non-operating Expenses:** Similarly, non-operating expenses like loss on sale of assets, loss on theft debited to Profit and Loss Account are to be added back to net profit to arrive at Funds from Operations.

The intention of the exercise is to find out funds from operations. Instead of net profit, net loss may appear in Profit and Loss Account. Simply, follow a reverse procedure to arrive at funds from operations in case of loss shown in Profit and Loss Account.

Income Statement or Profit and Loss Account is not given: If Income Statement or Profit and Loss Account is not given, information on net profit or loss may be, indirectly, given. Increase in General Reserve and Profit and Loss Account, balances appearing between opening and closing balance sheets, has to be taken as net profit i. e. increase in retained earnings. Suitable adjustments are to be made for the dividend paid and issue of bonus shares, capitalising profits. Funds from operations can be calculated by preparing Profit and Loss Adjustment Account.

Funds Flow Statement can be prepared in two types:

1. Report Form
2. T Form or Account Form or Self-Balancing Type.

Illustration No. 2

From the following information extracted from the Balance Sheets of Theer & Tarkh Ltd. Calculate Funds from Operations:

	As on 31 st March,2005 *(Rs.)*	**As on 31 st March,2006** *(Rs.)*
Share Capital	80,000	1,00,000
General Reserve	30,000	35,000
Profit and Loss Account	40,000	1,00,000
Depreciation Fund	15,000	18,000
Goodwill	15,000	10,000
Preliminary Expenses	3,000	2,000
Patents	10,000	8,000

Bonus shares have been issued for Rs.20,000 during 2005-06 capitalising profits from Profit and Loss Account. It is observed in the Profit and Loss Account that an income from sale of machinery Rs.6,000 has been received.

Solution:

	(Rs.)
Profit and Loss Account (as on 31st March, 2006)	1,00,000
+ Increase in share capital (Bonus issue)	
Transferring from Profit and Loss A/c	20,000
+ Transfer to General Reserve	5,000
+ Provision for Depreciation	3,000
+ Goodwill written off	5,000
+ Preliminary Expenses written off	1,000
+ Patents written off	2,000
- Income from sale of machinery	6,000
	1,30,000
- Balance in Profit and Loss Account (As on 31st March, 2005)	40,000
Funds from Operations	90,000

The funds from operations can be found out in an alternative way by preparing Profit and Loss Adjustment Account.

Adjusted Profit and Loss Account

Particulars	Amount (Rs.)	Particulars	Amount (Rs.)
To Transfer to Capital Account (Bonus issue)	20,000	By Balance b/d	40,000
To Transfer to General Reserve	5,000	By Income from sale of machinery	6,000
To Depreciation Fund (Provision for Depreciation)	3,000 5,000	By Funds from Operations	90,000
To Goodwill written off	1,000		
To Preliminary Expenses written off	2,000		
To Patents Written off	1,00,000		
To Balance c/d	1,36,000		1,36,000

(C) Finding out hidden information

While preparing the Funds Flow Statement, one has to analyse the Balance Sheets given. At the end of balance sheets, certain information may be given as notes that give clues for the hidden information. The hidden information may relate to provision and payment of tax, purchase/ sale of assets and issue/ redemption of shares and debentures.

1. **Provision for Taxation:** There are two ways of dealing with provision for Taxation.

   (i) As a current liability (ii) As an appropriation of profits

(i) **As a Current Liability:** Provision for tax may be treated as current liability as tax, generally, is an immediate obligation of the firm to pay to the Government. **It is preferable to treat 'Provision of tax' as current liability as such treatment is simple as nothing, further, is to be done. This approach is recommended for students if the problem does not stipulate any specific treatment.** When it is treated as current liability, provision for taxation will appear in the Schedule of Changes in Working Capital like other current liabilities. No further treatment is needed in respect of payment of tax and provision of tax made during the year. There is no need to prepare provision for taxation account. In this case, payment of tax shall not be shown as an application of funds. Provision for tax made during the year is not to be added back to the profits to arrive at funds from operations. The simple rule is to treat provision for tax as current liability and forget further treatment about this matter.

Illustration No.3

The opening balance in the Provision for Taxation Account as on 1st January 2005 was Rs. 40,000 and the closing balance as on 31st December 2005 was Rs. 50,000. The taxes paid during the year amounted to Rs. 35,000. Show the treatment of the item in the Funds Flow Statement:

(i) As Current Liability

(ii) As Appropriation of Profit

Solution:

(i) When provision for taxation is treated as Current liability

Provision for taxation is treated as current liability and is shown in the schedule of changes in working capital. No further effect on the Funds Flow Statement:

Schedule of Changes in Working Capital				
	1-1-2005 Rs.	31-12-2005 Rs.	Increase in Working Capital Rs.	Decrease in Working Capital Rs.
Current Liabilities				
Provision for Taxation	40,000	50,000		10,000

(ii) As Appropriation of Profit:

1. This item will not be shown in the Schedule of Changes in Working Capital.
2. Taxes paid during the year Rs. 35,000 is an Application of Funds and will appear on the application side of Funds Flow Statement.

Funds Flow Statement
for the year ended 31-12-2005

Sources	Rs.	Application	Rs.
		Payment of Tax	35,000

3. Provision for taxation made during the year Rs. 45,000 is calculated as below. This amount will be added back to net profit for finding Funds from Operations.

Calculation of Provision for Taxation made during the year

	Rs.
Opening balance of Provision for tax on 1-1-2005	40,000
Less : Tax paid during the year	35,000
	5,000
Closing balance of Provision on 31-12-2005	50,000
Provision made during the year	45,000

OR

Provision for Taxation A/c

			Rs.
To Cash (tax paid)	35,000	By Balance b/d	40,000
To Balance c/d	50,000	By Adjusted P/LA/c (Provision made-Balancing figure)	45,000
	85,000		85,000

Note: It is suggested to students to adopt 'Prepare Account' approach to find out the hidden information so that double entry concept can be applied, conveniently. More so, account preparation leaves no confusion about adding or subtracting the figures.

Proposed Dividend

Treatment of Proposed Dividend is similar to Provision for Taxation.

Proposed dividend can be treated as current liability or appropriation of profits.

(i) **As Current Liability:** Dividend recommended for payment by Board of Directors is, normally, approved for payment by Annual General Meeting. Till it is approved, it is appropriation of profits and after approval, it is an obligation on the part of company to make payment, so it is a current liability. **Students are advised to treat the amount of proposed dividend as current liability as the treatment is simple.** Show the amount as current liability in the Schedule of Changes in Working Capital. Information in respect of provision and its payment are to be ignored. Provision should not be added back to the net profits and payment should not be shown in application.

(ii) As non-current Liability: As proposed dividend is an appropriation of profit, it is not a current liability. Hence, the amount is not to be included in the Schedule of Changes in Working Capital. The appropriation of dividend, made during the year, is to be added back to net profits to calculate funds from operations. Actual dividend payment is to be shown as application in Funds Flow Statement.

Treatment of Proposed Dividend is similar to provision for Taxation

Interim Dividend: The expression 'Interim dividend' denotes dividend paid to shareholders of the company during the financial year, before the finalisation of accounts. This is the dividend paid or declared between two Annual General Meetings. Interim dividend should be added back to the figure of net profits (or debited to Profit and Loss Adjustment Account) to arrive at Funds from Operations. However, if the closing balance in the profit and loss account is given after payment of interim dividend, this adjustment is not required. To ascertain whether the closing balance in the Profit and Loss Account is after or before payment of interim dividend, it is desirable to prepare the Profit and Loss Account and incorporate the adjustments to find out the picture. Interim dividend is to be shown as an Application of funds.

Illustration No. 4

From the following Balance Sheets as on 31st March, 2005 and 31st March, 2006, prepare a Schedule of Changes in the Working Capital and Funds Flow Statement in T Form (Account Form or Self-Balancing Type) taking:

(i) the provision for tax and proposed dividend as current liabilities and

(ii) the provision for tax and proposed dividend as non-current liabilities.

Balance Sheet

Liabilities	31-12-2005 Rs.	31-12-2006 Rs.	Assets	31-12-2005 Rs.	31-12-2006 Rs.
Share Capital	1,00,000	1,50,000	Fixed Assets	1,00,000	1,55,000
Profit and Loss Account	4,000	6,000	Current Assets	13,000	14,500
Provision for tax	2,000	3,000			
Proposed Dividends	1,000	1,500			
Sundry Creditors	4,000	6,000			
Outstanding expenses	2,000	3,000			
	1,13,000	1,69,500		1,13,000	1,69,500

Additional information:

1. Tax paid during 2006 Rs.2,500
2. Dividends paid during 2006 Rs.1,000

Solution:

(i) When provision for tax and proposed dividends are taken as current liabilities.

Schedule of Changes in Working Capital

Particulars	31-12-2005	31-12-2006	Effect on Working capital Increase(+) Rs.	Decrease(-) Rs.
Current Assets	13,000	14,500	1,500	
Current Liabilities				
Sundry creditors	4,000	6,000		2,000
Outstanding expenses	2,000	3,000		1,000
Provision for tax	2,000	3,000		1,000
Proposed Dividends	1,000	1,500		500
Total Current Liabilities	9,000	13,500		
Net Working Capital (CA- CL)	4,000	1,000		
Decrease in Working Capital		3,000	3,000	
	4,000	4,000	4,500	4,500

Funds Flow Statement
for the year ended 31-12-2006

Sources	Rs.	Application	Rs.
Increase in share capital	50,000	Purchase of Fixed Assets	55,000
Funds from operations	2,000		
Decrease in Working Capital	3,000		
	55,000		55,000

(ii) When provision for tax and proposed dividends are taken as non-current liabilities:

Schedule of Changes in Working Capital

Particulars	Increase(+) Rs.	Decrease(-) Rs.
Sundry Creditors		2,000
Outstanding Expenses		1,000
Current Assets	1,500	
Decrease in Working Capital	1,500	
	3,000	3,000

Provision for Tax			
	Rs.		Rs.
To Cash (Tax Paid)	2,500	By Balance b/d	2,000
To Balance c/d	3,000	By P & L Adjustment A/c (Balancing figure)	3,500
	5,500		5,500

Profit and Loss Adjustment Account			
	Rs.		Rs.
To Provision for Tax	3,500	By Balance b/d	4,000
To Proposed Dividend	1,500	By Funds from Operations (Balancing figure)	7,000
To Balance b/d	6,000		
	11,000		11,000

Proposed Dividend Account			
	Rs.		Rs.
To Cash	1,000	By Balance b/d	1,000
To Balance c/d	1,500	By Profit and Loss Adjustment A/c	1,500
	2,500		2,500

Funds Flow Statement
for the year ended 31-12-2006

Sources	Rs.	**Application**	Rs.
Increase in share capital	50,000	Purchase of Fixed Assets	55,000
Funds from operations	7,000	Tax Paid	2,500
Decrease in Working Capital	1,500	Dividend Paid	1,000
	58,500		58,500

Illustration No. 5

The comparative Balance Sheets Kalyan & Kishore Ltd are indicated in a condensed form as under:

Liabilities	**31-3-06 Rs.**	**31-3-05 Rs.**	**Assets**	**31-3-06 Rs.**	**31-3-05 Rs.**
Share Capital	4,00000	3,60,000	Fixed Assets	5,20,000	4,80,000
General Reserve	60,000	1,10,000	Less: Depreciation	1,40,000	1,08,000

Profit & Loss Account	53,450	20,450		3,80,000	3,72,000
Sundry Creditors	1,75,350	1,83,650	Investments	50,000	1,00,000
Proposed Dividend	15,000	28,800	Debtors	1,67,800	1,18,300
Provision for Tax	32,000	—	Stock	90,500	55,600
			Bank Balance	47,500	49,800
			Preliminary Expenses	—	7,200
	7,35,800	7,02,900		7,35,800	7,02,900

Additional information:

1. The net profit for the year 2005-06 (after providing depreciation Rs. 40,000, writing off preliminary expenses of Rs. 7,200 and making provision for tax Rs.32,000) amounted to Rs.58,000.
2. The company sold during the year, an old machinery costing Rs. 9,000 for Rs. 3,000. The accumulated depreciation on the said machinery was Rs. 8,000.
3. A portion of company's investments became worthless and was written off to General Reserve during the year. The cost of such investment was Rs. 50,000.
4. During the year, the company paid an interim dividend of Rs. 10,000 and the directors have recommended final dividend of Rs. 15,000 for the current year.

Treat proposed dividend as non-current liability and prepare the Schedule of Change in Working Capital and the Funds Flow Statement.

Solution:

Schedule of Changes in Working Capital

Particulars	As on 31-3-2005	As on 31-3-2006	Increase in Working Capital	Decrease in Working Capital
Current Assets				
Debtors	1,18,300	1,67,800	49,500	
Stock	55,600	90,500	34,900	
Bank Balance	49,800	47,500		2,300
Total Current Assets	2,23,700	3,05,800		
Current Liabilities				
Creditors	1,83,650	1,75,350	8,300	
Total Current Liabilities	1,83,650	1,75,350		
Working Capital (CA-CL)	40,050	1,30,450		
Net Increase in Working Capital	90,400			90,400
	1,30,450	1,30,450	92,700	92,7000

Fixed Assets Account

To opening Balance b/d	4,80,000	By Sale of Old Machinery Account	9,000
To Cash- Purchase of Assets (Balancing figure)	49,000	By Closing Balance c/d	5,20,000
	5,29,000		5,29,000

Sale of Old Machinery Account

To Fixed Assets Account	9,000	By Cash (Sale Amount)	3,000
To Profit on sale of Machinery	2,000	By Depreciation Account	8,000
	11,000		11,000

Depreciation Account

To Old Machinery Account	8,000	By Opening Balance b/d	1,08,000
To Closing Balance c/d	1,40,000	By Depreciation for the year	40,000
	1,48,000		1,48,000

Profit and Loss Adjustment Account

To Proposed Dividend (2006)	15,000	By Opening Balance	20,450
To Interim Dividend paid	10,000	By Net Profit for the year	58,000
To Closing Balance	53,450		
	78,450		78,450

Funds from Operations

Net Profit for the year 1998	58,000	
Add:		
Depreciation	40,000	
Preliminary Expenses written off	7,200	
Provision for Tax	32,000	1,37,200
Less :		
Profit on Sale of Machinery		2,000
Funds from Operations		**1,35,200**

Sources & Application of Funds

Sources	Rs.	Application	Rs.
Sale of old Machinery	3,000	Purchase of Assets	49,000
Funds from Operations	1,35,200	Payment of Dividends:	
Issue of Share Capital	40,000	Interim Dividend	10,000
		Final Dividend	28,800
		Increase in Working Capital	90,400
	1,78,200		**1,78,200**

Note: 1. Profit and Loss Adjustment Account has been prepared to show that interim dividend and proposed dividend for the year 2006 have been appropriated.

2. The balance in the profit and loss account at the end of 2006 is after payment of interim dividend and provision for proposed dividend for the year 2006. To confirm that the closing balance in the Profit and Loss Account is after payment of interim dividend, Profit and Loss Adjustment Account is prepared and the adjustments have been incorporated. So, no adjustment is needed for them, except showing them in the application.

Illustration No. 6

The following information has been taken from the Balance Sheet of Tarkh & Company, Indore.

	31st March, 2005 Rs.	31st March, 2006 Rs.
Machinery	1,00,000	2,70,000
Accumulated Depreciation	45,000	60,000
Profit and Loss Account	15,000	40,000

The following additional information is also available:

(i) A machine costing Rs. 15,000 was purchased during the year by issue of equity shares.

(ii) On January 1st 2005, a machine costing Rs. 25,000 (with an accumulated depreciation of Rs. 10,000) was sold for Rs. 22,000.

Find out sources/application of funds.

Solution:

Machinery Account

	Rs.		Rs.
To Balance b/d	1,00,000	By Sale of machinery	25,000
To Share Capital	15,000	A/cBy balance c/d	2,70,000
To Cash- Purchase of machinery (Balancing figure)	1,80,000		
	2,95,000		2,95,000

Accumulated Depreciation A/c

	Rs.		Rs.
To Sale of Machinery A/c	10,000	By Balance b/d	45,000
		By Adjusted P/L A/c (Balancing figure)	25,000
To Balance c/d	60,000		
		70,000	70,000

Sale of Machinery Account			
To Machinery Account	25,000	By Depreciation	10,000
To Profit and Loss Adjustment Account	7,000	By Cash (sale of machinery)	22,000
	32,0000		32,0000

Adjusted Profit and Loss Account			
	Rs.		Rs.
To Accumulated Depreciation A/c	25,000	By Balance b/d	15,000
To Balance c/d	40,000	By Machinery A/c (Profit on sale)	7,000
		By Funds from Operations	43,000
	65,000		65,000

1. Purchase of Machinery for Rs.15,000 by issue of equity shares is neither a source nor an application of funds.
2. Sale of Machinery Rs. 22,000 is a source of funds.
3. Funds from Operations Rs. 43,000 are a source of Funds.
4. Purchase of machinery by cash Rs. 1,80,000 is an Application of funds.

Illustration No. 7

The following relevant information has been extracted from the following Balance Sheets:

	As on 31st December, 2005 Rs.	As on 31st December, 2006 Rs.
Equity Share Capital	6,00,000	10,00,000
Preference Share Capital	3,00,000	4,50,000

Additional Information:

1. Equity shares were issued during the year for purchase of Building for Rs.2,50,000.
2. 9% Preference Share Capital value Rs. 1,75,000 was redeemed during the year.

Prepare necessary accounts to find out Source/Application of Funds.

Solution

Equity Share Capital Account			
	Rs.		Rs.
To Balance c/d	10,00,000	By Balance b/d	6,00,000
		By Building A/c	2,50,000
		By Cash (Issue of shares-Balancing figure)	1,50,000
	10,00,000		10,00,000

9% Preference Share Capital Account

	Rs.		Rs.
To Cash (Redemption of shares)	1,75,000	By Balance b/d	3,00,000
To Balance c/d	4,50,000	By Cash (Issue of shares-Balancing figure)	3,25,000
	6,25,000		6,25,000

1. Issue of Equity Shares against purchase of Building Rs. 2,50,000 is neither a source nor application of funds. Issue of shares for Rs. 1,50,000 is a source.
2. Redemption of Preference Shares Rs. 1,75,000 is an application of funds.
3. Issue of Preference Shares Rs. 3,25,000 is a source of funds.

Issue of Shares other than cash: If shares are issued for cash, proceeds from issue of shares are a source. If shares are issued for acquiring non-current assets like fixed assets, the transaction is totally ignored, as the transaction does not appear anywhere, including in Sources and Application of Funds. However, the typical question comes when shares are issued for acquiring current assets as well as non-current assets, how the transaction is to be presented? Total value of the amount of shares issued is to be shown as a source. The current assets acquired increase working capital and the increased current assets are shown as application of funds. The non-current assets acquired too are to be shown as application.

The following problem explains the method of presentation.

Illustration No. 8

Prepare Statement Showing Changes in Working Capital and Source & Application of Funds from the following information:

	March, 2005 Rs.	March, Rs.
Creditors	1,40,000	1,30,000
Bills payable	40,000	30,000
Bank overdraft	50,000	—
Income Tax provision	75,000	65,000
Reserves	80,000	80,000
P & L Account	84,000	28,000
Share capital	5,00,000	6,00,000
	9,69,000	**9,33,000**
Cash in hand	50,000	70,000
Cash at bank	1,00,000	1,20,000
Debtors	1,65,000	1,00,000
Prepaid expenses	4,000	3,000
Stock	1,50,000	1,00,000
Fixed assets	5,00,000	4,80,000
Goodwill	—	60,000
	9,69,000	**9,33,000**

The following information was obtained:

(i) In 2006, a dividend of Rs. 84,000 was paid.

(ii) Assets of another firm were purchased at Rs. 1,00,000, payable in 10,000 shares of Rs. 10 each. The assets included stock Rs. 10,000; fixed assets Rs. 30,000; and goodwill Rs. 60,000.

(iii) Income tax paid in 2006 was Rs. 10,000.

(iv) Net profit in 2006 was Rs. 28,000.

Solution:

Schedule of Changes In Working Capital (Rs.)

	As on 31.3.05	As on 31.3.06	Increase in Working Capital	Decrease in Working Capital
Current Assets:				
Stock	1,50,000	1,00,000		50,000
Debtors	1,65,000	1,00,000		65,000
Cash in hand	50,000	70,000	20,000	
Cash at bank	1,00,000	1,20,000	20,000	
Prepaid expenses	4,000	3,000		1,000
	4,69,000	3,93,000		
Current Liabilities				
Creditors	1,40,000	1,30,000	10,000	
Bills payable	40,000	30,000	10,000	
Bills overdraft	50,000	—	50,000	
Income-tax provision	75,000	65,000	10,000	
	3,05,000	2,25,000		
Working capital	1,64,000	1,68,000		
Increase in working Capital	4,000			4,000
	1,68,000	1,68,000	1,20,000	1,20,000

Fixed Assets Account

To Opening Balance	5,00,000	By Depreciation (Balancing figure)	50,000
To Additions (Cash)	30,000	By Balance c/d	4,80,000
	5,30,000		5,30,000

Income Tax Provision Account

To cash	10,000	By Balance b/d	75,000
To Balance c/d	65,000		
	75,000		75,000

Funds from Operations	(Rs.)
Net Profits	28,000
Add : Depreciation	50,000
Funds from Operations	78,000

Statement of Sources and Application of Funds

Sources	Rs.	Application	Rs.
Funds from Operations	78,000	Increase in Fixed Assets	30,000
Issue of Shares	1,00,000*	Goodwill	60,000
Cash Dividends	84,000		
		Increase in working capital	4,000
	1,78,000		1,78,000

Note: Balance in Profit and Loss Account at the end of 31st March, 2005 is Rs. 84,000. The amount is totally paid as dividend, hence shown as Application. There is no balance left out for the previous year's profit. Net Profit for the year 2006 is Rs.28,000 , which is the balance in the Profit and Loss Account at the end of March, 2006.

*This represents the total value of shares acquired in consideration of stock Rs. 10,000 included the current assets shown in Schedule of Changes in Working Capital and non-current assets acquired shown as application.

Tip to Students: When shares are issued for acquiring current and non-current assets, the whole transaction has to be taken.

Treatment of Investments

Investments: Treatment of investments depends on the nature of investments purchased. i.e. current assets or fixed assets. They can be temporary investments or permanent investments.

Temporary Investments: When a firm has temporary excess funds, it is normal to purchase temporary investments. They are to be treated as current assets. They find a place in Schedule of Changes in Working Capital and they are to be treated like any other current assets. Just like any other current assets, they do not appear in Funds Flow Statement. **Dividend received on such investments is treated like business income.** Loss and profit on sale of such investments is like any other business loss/profit and is to be shown in Profit and Loss Account. If the amount is credited to Profit and Loss Account, it does not appear in Profit and Loss Adjustment account, again, as no adjustment is needed.

Long-term or non-current, Trade Investments: They are to be treated like fixed assets or non-current assets. As they are not current assets, they should not appear in the Schedule of Changes in Working Capital. If investments are purchased on the basis of 'cum-dividend', pre-acquisition dividend as and when received, subsequently, is to be credited to Trade Investment Account. The price of investments, paid, includes the amount of dividend, to be received later.

Here, dividend has been declared and the due date for receipt of dividend has not yet lapsed. Investments are to appear at cost. Investment Account has to be prepared to find out investments purchased or sold and profit/loss on sale/purchase of investment, if any.

Purchase of investment is to be treated as Application and sale as a source of funds. **Dividend received on these investments is not normal business income and is not to be credited to Profit and Loss Account.** This dividend amount is to be deduced from net profit to arrive at funds from operations. In case dividend is credited, the amount should be credited to Profit and Loss Adjustment Account to arrive at funds from operations.

The following problem explains the treatment of trade investments (fixed asset or non-current asset).

Illustration No.9:

From the following balance sheets of Beta Limited, make out

(i) Statement of changes in Working capital and

(ii) Funds Flow Statement:

Balance Sheets

Liabilities	2001 (Rs.)	2002 (Rs.)	Assets	2001 (Rs.)	2002 (Rs.)
Equity Share Capital	3,00,000	4,00,000	Goodwill	1,00,000	80,000
8% Redeemable Preference Share Capital	1,50,000	1,00,000	Land&Building	2,00,000	1,70,000
Capital Reserve	-	20,000	Plant	80,000	2,00,000
General Reserve	40,000	50,000	Investments	20,000	30,000
Profit & Loss Account	30,000	48,000	Sundry Debtors	1,40,000	1,70,000
Proposed Dividend	42,000	50,000	Stock	77,000	1,09,000
Sundry Creditors	25,000	47,000	Bills Receivable	20,000	30,000
Bills Payable	20,000	16,000	Cash in hand	15,000	10,000
Liabilities for Expenses	30,000	36,000	Cash at Bank	10,000	8,000
Provision for Taxation	40,000	50,000	Preliminary Expenses	15,000	10,000
	6,77,000	8,17,000		6,77,000	8,17,000

Notes:

1. A piece of land has been sold out in the year 2002 and profits on sales have been carried to capital Reserve.
2. A machine has been sold for Rs.10,000. The written down value of the machine was Rs.12,000. Depreciation of Rs.10,000 is charged on plant account in the year 2002.
3. The investments are trade investments. Rs. 3,000 by way of dividend is received including Rs.1,000 from pre-acquisition of profit, which had been credited to investments account.
4. An interim dividend of Rs.20,000 has been paid in the year 2002. **(M.B.A. –B.U., Bhopal 2003)**

Solution:

Statement of changes in Working capital

Particulars	2001	2002	Increase in Working Capital	Decrease in Working Capital
Current Assets				
Sundry Debtors	1,40,000	1,70,000	30,000	
Stock	77,000	1,09,000	32,000	
Bills Receivable	20,000	30,000	10,000	
Cash in hand	15,000	10,000		5,000
Cash at Bank	10,000	8,000		2,000
	2,62,000	3,27,000		
Current Liabilities				
Sundry Creditors	25,000	47,000		22,000
Bills Payable	20,000	16,000	4,000	
Liabilities for Expenses	30,000	36,000		6,000
Provision for Taxation	40,000	50,000		10,000
	1,15,000	1,49,000		
Working Capital	1,47,000	1,78,000	76,000	45,000
Increase in Working Capital	**31,000**			**31,000**
	1,78,000	1,78,000	76,000	76,000

Trade Investments Account

Funds from Operations	78,000	Increase in Fixed Assets	30,000
To Opening Balance b/d	20,000	By Dividend received, credited to this account	1,000
To Purchase of Investments	11,000	By Closing Balance c/d	30,000
	31,000		31,000

Plant Account

To Balance b/d	80,000	By Depreciation	10,000
		By Cash (Sale of machine)	10,000
To Machinery Purchased (Balancing)	1,42,000	By Loss on sale of Machine	2,000
		By Balance c/d	2,00,000
	2,22,000		2,22,000

Proposed Dividend Account

To Cash (Payment of dividend)	42,000	By Balance b/d	42,000
To Balance c/d	50,000	By Profit and Loss Account	50,000
	92,000		92,000

Adjusted Profit and Loss Account

	Rs.		Rs.
To General Reserve	10,000	By Balance	30,000
To Depreciation	10,000	By Dividend on Trade Investments	2,000
To Interim dividend	20,000	By Funds from Operations	1,33,000
To Loss on sale of machine	2,000		
To Preliminary expenses written off	5,000		
To Proposed Dividend Account	50,000		
To Goodwill Written off	20,000		
To Balance	48,000		
	1,65,000		1,65,000

Sources and Application of Funds

Sources	Rs.	Applications	Rs.
Sale of Land	50,000	Increase in Working Capital	31,000
Funds from Operations	1,33,000	Payment of Dividend	42,000
Sale of machine	10,000	Interim dividend paid	20,000
Dividend on Trade Investments	3,000	Redemption of 8% Redeemable Preference Shares	50,000
Issue of Equity Shares	1,00,000	Purchase of Machinery	1,42,000
		Purchase of Trade Investments	11,000
	2,96,000		2,96,000

Note:

1. Dividend received on Trade Investments is Rs.3,000. Out of Rs.3,000, only Rs.1,000 has been credited to Trade Investments Account. The balance amount Rs.2,000 has been credited to Profit and Loss Account. This is the interpretation of the problem. Many think Rs. 3,000 totally has been credited to Trade Investments Account. But, this is not so. Many a time, students' loose full marks, as answer would be different for incorrect interpretation.
2. The second part is reasoning for crediting part of dividend to Trade Investments Account. When trade investment is purchased on the basis of 'cum dividend', pre-acquisition dividend, subsequently received, is to be credited to Investment Account, as investment should appear at cost only.
3. Dividend received on investments (Fixed assets, non-current assets) is not operating income and so it is to be shown in Profit and Loss Adjustment account for calculating funds from operations. In other words, dividend is not part of normal business income.
4. Proposed Dividend has not been treated as current liability. It has been treated as appropriation of profit for better presentation. Interim dividend has been shown in application as the amount has been paid during the year. Another alternative way is to show Proposed dividend as current liability. In that event, both proposed and interim dividends are not to be shown as application.

Revaluation of Fixed Assets

Sometimes fixed assets are revalued and profit or loss on such revalued assets is transferred to Profit and Loss Account. Such change in the value of fixed assets is neither inflow nor outflow of funds.

At times, the profit on revaluation of the fixed asset may be credited to Capital Reserve Account. There is no inflow or outflow of funds as both the accounts are non-current. So, the transaction does not appear in Source and Application of Funds.

The following illustration explains the presentation.

Illustration No.10

In the following Balance Sheet, a part of machinery costing Rs.20,000 has been revalued at Rs.30,000 and transferred to Profit and Loss Account. Show the necessary accounts.

Liabilities	2005	2006	Assets	2005	2006
			Machinery	1,50,000	2,50,000

Solution:

Profit and Loss Adjustment Account

		By Machinery Account (Profit on Revaluation of Machinery)	10,000

Machinery Account

To Balance b/d	1,50,000		
To Profit and Loss Adjustment Account (Profit on Revaluation of Machinery)	10,000		
To cash- Purchase of machinery (Balancing figure)	90,000	By Balance c/d	2,50,000
	2,50,000		2,50,000

Funds Flow Statement

Sources		Applications	
		Purchase of Machinery	90,000

Redemption of Debentures by issue of Shares: If debentures are redeemed by cash, redemption of debentures is to be shown as application of funds. Instead of redeeming by cash, shares may be issued for redemption of debentures. As both the items are non-current, neither issue of shares nor redemption of debentures appears in Source and Application of Funds.

Illustration No.11

You are given the Balance Sheets of Sandhya & Co. as at the end of 2005 and 2006 as under:

Liabilities	2005 Rs.	2006 Rs.	Assets	2005 Rs.	2006 Rs.
Equity Share Capital	2,00,000	2,50,000	Building	2.,00,000	2,00,000
Share Premium	——	5,000	Plant at cost	1,04,000	1,00,000
General Reserve	50,000	60,000	Furniture at cost	7,000	9,000
Profit & Loss Account	10,000	17,000	Investments at cost	60,000	80,000
8% Debentures	70,000	50,000	Debtors	30,000	70,000
Provision for depreciation on plant	50,000	56,000	Stock	60,000	65,000
Provision for depreciation on furniture	5,000	6,000	Cash	30,000	45,000
Provision for taxation	20,000	30,000			
Sundry Creditors	86,000	95,000			
	4,91,000	5,69,000		4,91,000	5,69,000

Equity shares were issued, at par, for redemption of debentures. A dividend of 10% on share capital, at the end of the year, was paid.

A plant purchased for Rs. 4,000 (Depreciation Rs. 2,000) was sold for cash for Rs. 800 during the year. An item of furniture was purchased for Rs. 2,000. These were the only transactions concerning fixed assets during 2006.

Treat Provision for Tax as non-current liability.

Solution:

Schedule Of Changes In Working Capital

	2005	2006	Increase (+)	Decrease (-)
Current Assets :	Rs.	Rs.	Rs.	
Debtors	30,000	70,000	40,000	
Stock	60,000	65,000	5,000	
Cash	30,000	45,000	15,000	
	1,20,000	1,80,000		
Current Liabilities :				
Sundry Creditors	86,000	95,000		9,000
	86,000	95,000		
Working capital	34,000	85,000		
Increase in Working Capital	**51,000**			**51,000**
	85,000	85,000	60,000	60,000

Funds Flow Statement

Sources of Funds	Rs.	Applications of Funds	Rs.
Share Capital (including premium)	35,000	Purchase of Furniture	2,000
Sale of Plant	800	Dividend paid	25,000
Funds from Operations	82,200	Investments Purchased	20,000
		Tax paid	20,000
		Increase in Working Capital	51,000
	1,18,000		1,18,000

The increase in Working capital in Schedule of Changes in Working Capital is confirmed with the increase in working capital in Funds Flow Statement.

Note: Shares for Rs. 20,000 were issued at par for redemption of debentures and this transaction does not find a place in Funds Flow Statement and Schedule of Changes in Working Capita as both the items are non-current.

Working:

Adjusted Profit & Loss Account

	Rs.		Rs.
To Dividend paid	25,000	By Balance b/d	10,000
To Provision for taxation	30,000	By Funds from operations	
To Transfer to General Reserve	10,000	(Balancing figure)	82,200
To Plant (Depreciation)	8,000		
To Furniture (Depreciation)	1,000		
To Loss on Sale of Plant	1,200		
To Balance c/d	17,000		
	92,200		92,200

Plant Account

	Rs.		Rs.
To Balance b/d	Rs. 1,04,000	By Bank	800
		By P & L (loss on sale of plant)	1,200
		By Provision for Depreciation (on plant sold)	2,000
		By Balance c/d	1,00,000
	1,04,000		1,04,000

Furniture Account

	Rs.		Rs.
To Balance b/d	7,000	By Balance c/d	Rs. 9,000
To Cash (balancing figure)	2,000		
	9,000		9,000

Provision for Depreciation on Furniture			
To Balance b/d	Rs. 6,000	By Balance c/d	Rs. 5,000
		By P & L A/c (depreciation charged for the year – balancing figure)	1,000
			6,000

Provision for Depreciation on Plant			
To Plant Account (Depreciation on plant sold)	Rs. 2,000	By Balance c/d	Rs. 50,000
To Balance c/d	56,000	By P & L A/c (depreciation charged for the year – balancing figure)	8,000
	58,000		58,000

4.11 INCOME STATEMENT AND BALANCE SHEET FUNDS FLOW STATEMENTS

Funds flow statement is not a substitute of an income statement i.e. a profit and loss account and a balance sheet. Their purposes are different. Funds flow statement is not competitive but complementary to these financial statements.

Differences Between Funds Flow Statement and Income Statement

Base	Funds Flow Statement	Income Statement
1. Purpose	Shows the means the funds were obtained and ways these funds were used.	Find out profit or loss of the organisation.
2. Scope	Includes both capital and revenue items.	Only revenue items are considered.
3. Knowledge	Provides information on working capital and changes in financial position.	Depicts the items of expenses and income to arrive at profit or loss in business.
4. Format	No Prescribed format	Prescribed format exists for a limited company
5. Compulsory	A Voluntary statement in case of sole proprietor and partnership firms. In case of limited companies, now, it is mandatory.	Compulsory to prepare even in the case of proprietor and partnership firms for submission before tax authorities. Compulsory in case of limited companies under Companies Act.

6. Period	Prepared for short intervals.	Prepared yearly and sometimes half-yearly.
7. Preparation	Complementary to Income Statement. Income statement helps the preparation of Funds Flow Statement.	Income Statement is not prepared from Funds Flow Statement.

Differences Between Funds Flow Statement and Balance Sheet

Base	Funds Flow Statement	Balance Sheet
1. Nature	It is a statement of changes in financial position and hence is dynamic in nature.	It is a statement of financial position on a particular date and hence is static in nature.
2. Aim	Prepared to verify whether working capital is managed effectively or not.	To ascertain and verify the value of assets and liabilities on a particular date.
3. Publication	Not required to be published.	In the case of limited companies, Balance Sheet is published and required to be circulated among the shareholders.
4. Compulsory	A Voluntary statement in case of proprietorship and partnership firms. In case of limited companies, now, it is mandatory.	Compulsory in case of limited companies under Companies Act.
5. Period	Prepared occasionally.	Prepared at the end of the accounting period.
6. Preparation	Usually, Schedule of Changes in Working Capital is prepared before preparing Funds Flow Statement.	No Schedule of Changes in Working Capital is prepared. Rather Profit and Loss Account is prepared before the preparation of Balance Sheet

4.12 LIMITATIONS OF FUNDS FLOW STATEMENT

Funds Flow Statement is an important tool for analysis and serves several useful purposes. However, its limitations cannot be ignored and they are:

1. It is not an original statement. It is only a rearrangement of data taken from the financial statements (Profit and Loss Account and Balance Sheet).
2. It is based on the financial statements and so the limitations of financial statement are equally applicable to them.
3. It is essentially historic in nature and projected statement cannot be prepared with much accuracy.

4. Funds Flow Statement is not a substitute for basic financial statements like profit and loss account and balance sheet. At best, it can be a supplementary statement to explain the changes in working capital.

Despite the above limitations, Funds Flow Statement serves the basic purpose of explaining the causes for changes in the financial position of the firm between two periods.

Objective Questions

1. Explain the meaning, importance and objectives of Funds Flow Statement? **(4.1 to 4.4)**
2. Describe the significance of Funds Flow Statement to the different users? **(4.5)**
3. Describe the need and limitations of Funds Flow Statement? **(4.1 and 4.12)**
4. What are the different Sources and Applications in a Funds Flow Statement? **(4.6, 4.7 and 4.8)**
5. "Depreciation can be taken as a source of funds in a limited sense". Illustrate with a suitable example? **(4.7)**
6. "Depreciation is an indirect source of funds under certain circumstances – Explain? **(4.7)**
7. Explain briefly the procedure and steps to be followed for preparing Funds Flow Statement? **(4.9 and 4.10)**
8. Differentiate between :
   (a) Funds Flow Statement and Income Statement
   (b) Funds Flow Statement and Balance Sheet **(4.11)**

Check Your Understanding

(A). State whether the following statements are True or False

1. The term 'fund' in a fund flow statement refers to in working capital.
2. Loss on sale of machine should be added to net profit for calculating funds from operations.
3. Statement of change in financial position can be either funds flow statement or cash flow statement.
4. Income statements need not be prepared but funds flow statements are required to be compulsorily prepared.
5. Basic financial statements (Profit and Loss account and Balance sheet) fail to show the movement and causes of changes in assets and liabilities during the year.
6. Statement of change in financial position identifies changes in assets, liabilities and the shareholders' funds over a given period.
7. Funds flow statement points out the sources from which additional funds have been received during the year and the uses to which these funds have been applied.
8. In funds flow statement, if both the affected accounts relate to working capital only they appear.
9. As per existing legal requirement, in case of a limited company, it is not required to publish statement of changes in financial position along with other financial statements.
10. Flow of funds takes place from transactions, when one account is current and the other is non-current.
11. A company's funds flow statement shows diversion of working capital for purchase of fixed assets.

Answers

1.	True	2.	True	3.	True	4.	False	5.	True
6.	True	7.	True	8.	False	9.	False	10.	True.
11.	True								

(B). Pickup the correct answer:

1. Stock at the end results in the
   a. Application of fund.
   b. Source of funds.
   c. No flow of funds.
2. Sale of investments indicate
   a. Source of funds.
   b. Application of funds.
   c. None of the above.
3. Tax paid is
   a. Application of funds.
   b. Source of funds.
   c. No flow of funds.
4. Which of the following will result in flow of funds :
   a. Purchase of furniture on credit.
   b. Writing of goodwill.
   c. Depreciation of assets.
   d. Appreciation in Building.
5. Net profit earned plus non-working capital expenses is equal to
   a. Funds provided by operations.
   b. Use of funds.
   c. Sinking fund.
6. Depreciation is a source of funds
   a. Yes
   b. No
   c. Both Yes and NO
7. An increase in the share premium account is
   a. An application of funds.
   b. A source of funds.
   c. No flow of funds.
8. Increase in a fixed asset due to issue of shares is
   a. Source of funds.
   b. Use of funds
   c. None.

9. By preparing provision for taxation A/c, we can find out the missing figure of ...
   a. Taxes paid during the year.
   b. Taxes provided during the year.
   c. Either of a. & b. above.
   d. Neither of a. & b. above.
10. A company engaged in financial activities receives interest. Such interest is ...
   a. Operating income.
   b. Non-operating income.
   c. Loss from operation.
   d. Non-operational charge.
11. .... is not a current asset.
   a. Book debts.
   a. Short-term investment.
   b. Long-term investment.
   c. Book debts.
12. .... is not a current liability.
   a. Sundry Creditors.
   b. Bank overdraft.
   c. Outstanding expenses.
   d. Long-term loan
13. X Ltd has sales revenue of Rs.2,000. Depreciation for the period is Rs. 3000. Other operating expenses are Rs. 900. Net loss for the period is Rs.500.
   What is the amount of funds generated from operations during the period by X Ltd?
   a. 2,500
   b. 1,500
   c. 3,500
   d. 1,400

Answers

1. (b).	2. (a)	3. (a).	4. (a)	5. (a).
6. (c)	7. (b).	8. (c)	9. (c).	10. (a).
11. (c) .	12. (d).	13. (a)		

(C) Pick up the most appropriate answer:

1. If depreciation on furniture is in the additional information, it will be posted
   a. At the debit side of adjusted profit and loss A/c.
   b. At the credit side of plant A/c.
   c. Neither of a & b. above.
   d. At both a. & b. above
2. Current liabilities are equal to
   a. Working capital + Current assets.

b. Work-capital – Current assets.
c. Current assets – Working capital.
d. Current assets + Working capital.

3. Inflow of funds does not take place due to
   a. Funds from operation.
   b. Increase in capital.
   c. Increase in working capital.
   d. Sale of fixed assets.
4. Increase in working capital is
   a. Source of funds.
   b. Application of funds.
   c. Funds from operation.
   d. Loss from operation.
5. Vehicle sold for credit for a vehicle dealer results in...
   a. Increases working capital
   b. Decreases working capital
   c. Does not change working capital
6. Cash realisation from debtors increases working capital
   a. Yes
   b. No
   c. None of the above answers

Answers

1. (d) . 2. (c). 3. (c). 4. (b) 5. (c)
6. (c)

(D) Fill in blanks:

1. Any gain on sale of non-current assets should be ... from the net profit for determining funds from operations.
2. Difference between Current Assets and Current Liabilities is known as ...
3. Funds flow refers to changes in
4. Depreciation is sometimes treated as funds.
5. Goods purchased on credit in flow of funds.
6. Salary outstanding is of funds.
7. Vehicle sold on credit is of funds.
8. Furniture sold for cash funds flow.

Answers

1. Deducted. 2. Working Capital. 3. Working capital. 4. A source.
5. Does not result. 6. An application. 7. A source. 8. Increases

5

CASH FLOW STATEMENT

- *Importance of Cash*
- *Cash Flow Statement*
  - *Meaning*
  - *Need*
  - *Legal Requirement*
  - *AS - 3 (Revised)*
- *Objectives of Cash Flow Statement*
- *Classification of Cash Flows*
- *Steps involved in Preparing Cash Flow Statement*
- *Methods of Preparing Cash Flow Statements*
  - *Direct Method*
  - *Indirect Method*
- *Differences between Funds Flow Statement and Cash Flow Statement*
- *Limitations*
- *Statement of Changes in Financial Position (Total Resources Basis)*
- *Objective Questions*
- *Check Your Understanding*

5.1 IMPORTANCE OF CASH

Cash is one of the most significant and important current assets of an organisation. Cash is needed to make purchase of raw materials, payment of wages and meeting day-to-day expenses for every type of activity including entertainment expenditure. Development of business and faster growth are dependent on adequate and timely availability of cash. **In fact, what blood is to a human body, cash is similar to any business enterprise.** Firm may be profitable, yet may experience difficulty in arranging timely payments. It may not have adequate liquid resources to make payments for dividends and taxes in ready cash. It is due to poor management of cash. Though profits are earned, reason for insufficiency of cash could be of two types. Profits may not be realised in cash. Secondly, profits are diverted for purchase of fixed assets. The classical example is shelling cash for a premium car from profits, beyond means without planning, and searching cash for payment of daily wages. **Both adequacy and timely availability are essential for the success of any firm's activities.** Therefore, management of cash is of vital importance to any enterprise.

5.2 CASH FLOW STATEMENT

Meaning: Cash Flow Statement is a statement, which describes the inflows (sources) and outflows (uses) of cash and cash equivalents during a specified period. It is a summary of cashbook. **A Cash Flow Statement explains the causes of changes in cash position of a business enterprise between two dates of balance sheets.** Cash flow statement is a tool that is available to the management to assess, monitor and control the liquidity available in the enterprise. According to AS-3 (Revised), an enterprise should prepare and enclose the Cash flow statement for the same period for which the financial statements are prepared, in the prescribed format, by the listed companies.

The following terms, in the context of cash flow statement, are explained here:

Cash means physical cash on hand and demand deposits in bank. Balance in a current account in bank comes under the category of demand deposits as the amount can be withdrawn on demand, without any limit.

Cash equivalents are short term, highly liquid investments that can be converted into known amounts of cash within a reasonable period, without subjecting to any significant risk. **Short-term deposits in a bank, Government securities and treasury bills qualify the category of cash equivalents.** They are meant for meeting short-term obligations and not for long-term investment. They are to be converted into cash at short notice, without any significant risk at the time of conversion. Risk refers to financial risk, in particular, loss in value, at the time of conversion. So, equity shares of even reputed companies do not come into the cash category of cash equivalents though they are listed on stock exchange and are convertible into ready cash within a short period of three or four days. The reason for non-inclusion is there is no certainty about the amount of realisation as they are subject to fluctuations in price. Preference shares that are subject to redemption shortly in a very good company come into the category as the amount of realisation is predetermined and there is insignificant risk in respect of the failure of the company.

Cash flows are both inflows and outflows of cash and cash equivalents. Flow of cash is said to have taken place when a transaction makes change in cash and equivalents available before and after happening of the transaction. If cash and cash equivalents increase on account of transaction, it is called inflow of cash and if it causes decrease, it is said to be outflow of cash.

Conversion of cash into cash equivalents and vice versa does not constitute cash flows because they are not part of operating, financing and investing activities. Cash management includes the investment of cash into cash equivalents and vice versa.

Definition: A Cash Flow Statement may be defined as "**A financial statement that summarises the cash receipts and payments and net changes resulting from operating, financing and investing activities of an enterprise during a given period of time".**

5.3 NEED OF CASH FLOW STATEMENT

Basic financial statements i. e. Profit and Loss Account and Balance Sheet provide the essential basic information about the financial activities of the business. But, their utility is limited for analysis and planning purposes. To serve those needs, Funds Flow Statement is prepared to show the changes in assets and liabilities from one period of time to the end of another period. **The question arises when the Funds Flow Statement is prepared, what is the need to prepare Cash Flow Statement, separately?** Funds Flow Statement presents comprehensive picture of different components of working capital. However, working capital concept does not reveal the true picture of availability of cash. In the Funds Flow Statement, cash and inventories are treated alike. All the components of working capital are treated in the same manner as availability of fund, at the same time. However, this is not the correct picture as their time and quality of realisation, in respect of time, is different from the viewpoint of cash. Debtors take less time for converting into cash while inventories take more time for realisation. Similarly, inventories may consist of dead stock that has not been written off. Debtors may have bad debts that are not yet removed. But, Funds Flow Statement does not recognise this basic difference in their nature. An enterprise may have more slow paying debtors and non-moving stocks, with little cash or its equivalents. Due to comfortable working capital position, Funds Flow Statement does not throw the real picture about the inadequacy of cash. **Only when Cash Flow Statement is prepared, the real situation about the adequacy of funds, in the sense of cash, is known.** Firms prepare Cash Flow statements for short periods for proper cash planning.

Legal Requirement: To underline the importance of the funds flow statement; The Institute of Chartered Accountants of India had issued Accounting Standard-3 (AS-3) in 1981 that was made applicable to every listed company. However, the accounting standard provided more flexibility in implementation as the term "Funds" was meant for cash or cash equivalents or working capital. **In other words, companies had been given the option to prepare Funds Flow Statement or Cash Flow Statement along with the financial statement.** So, many firms had provided the Funds Flow Statement along with the financial statements based on working capital concept. This had served the useful purpose in understanding the changes in assets and liabilities between two different dates. However, this Accounting Standard had suffered the following **limitations**:

1. **Flexibility:** Many firms had prepared the statement on the basis of working capital, where as others prepared it on cash basis, due to flexibility of the Accounting Standard. **As inventories and prepaid expenses were treated similar to cash while preparing on working capital basis, firm's ability to pay short-term obligations, as and when they fall due, could not be assessed.**
2. **No Standard Format:** AS-3 did not provide the standard format. As such, firms had prepared different methods for preparing the Funds Flow Statement. **Lack of uniformity had made the comparison difficult.**
3. **Lack of Adequate Disclosure:** Even the firms that had prepared the Cash Flow Statement had provided the information merely in respect of inflows and outflows. They did not disclose information in respect of Operating, Financing and Investment activities, separately.

AS- 3 Revised: In view of the above limitations and recognising the importance of Cash Flow Statement, in 1995, Securities and Exchange Board of India (SEBI) had amended clause 32 of the Listing Agreement requiring every listed company to give along with the balance sheet and profit and loss account, a cash flow statement, in the prescribed format. The prescribed format requires the listed company to provide the information in respect of cash flows in respect of Operating, Financing and investing activities, separately. **AS-3 (Revised) issued in 1995 supersedes the requirement of AS-3, issued in 1981.**

Listed companies do not have the option of either preparing funds flow statement or cash flow statement, now. So, now, every listed company has to provide the cash flow statement along with the financial statements, in the prescribed format.

Applicability: AS-3 (Revised) applies to the following enterprises:

(i) If turnover of the enterprise exceeds more than Rs. 50 crores in a financial year, even though it is not a listed company.

(ii) Listed companies – shares of those companies listed on Stock Exchange.

Cash flow statement of listed companies should be presented only under the indirect method as prescribed in AS-3.

5.4 OBJECTIVES OF CASH FLOW STATEMENT

1. **Cash Management:** Cash flow statement is a tool for short-term financial planning. By preparing the statement, a firm can know how much cash can be generated by its operations and how much cash is needed. **It helps the firm to plan to arrange for excess cash requirements, in advance.**
2. **Cash Planning:** It helps in **planning repayment of loans, dividend policy, replacement of fixed assets and capital budgeting decisions.**

3. **Answers to Difficult Questions:** It explains the causes for financial difficulties. Even if the firm is profitable, firm experiences difficulty for cash. **The statement throws light on the intricate questions** like – What happened to the net profits. Where did the profits go? Why more dividends could not be paid, despite increase in profits?
4. **Discloses Reasons for success or failure:** It is an **important technique for evaluating success or failure of cash planning.** The actual cash flow is compared with the projected cash flow. If the results are not as per expectation, reasons can be analysed and corrective steps can be taken.

5.5 CLASSIFICATION OF CASH FLOWS

Cash flows as per Accounting Standard–3 are classified into three categories. They are:

1. **Cash Flows from Operating Activities:** Operating activities are the revenue producing activities of the enterprise and other activities that are not investing and financing activities. **Revenue producing activity is the key activity in the cash flows.** They generally result from the transactions and other events that determine the net profit or loss of the organisation.

For example, for a pickle industry, the main operation is to buy fruits like mangoes, lemon and apples, take out the pulp, mix the necessary ingredients and bottle them as different varieties of pickles with the help of human resources, plant and machinery etc. Therefore, the cash flows incidental to purchase of fruits and ingredients, payment of wages to labour and salaries, packing charges is operating outflows. Receipts from sale of pickles are to be regarded as operating cash inflows.

2. **Cash Flows from Investing Activities:** Investing activities are the acquisition of long-term assets and other investments that are not included in cash equivalent. In other words, long term assets such as plant and machinery, land and building etc that are held by the firm for long-term production, not meant for sale, fall in this category. Short-term securities, temporary excess funds, are cash equivalents and so are not to be included in this category. However, trade investments that are intended for long term are to be included in this category.

Separate disclosure is necessary to know the amount spent in acquiring the resources-long term assets such as plant and machinery and other fixed assets- intended to generate the future income and cash flows.

3. **Cash Flows from Financing Activities:** Financing activities are activities that result in changes in size and composition of owners' capital (including preference share capital in the case of company) and short-term and long-term debts of the firm.

Separate disclosure is important and necessary, as it is useful to predict the claims of the providers of funds as well as anticipated repayments on the future cash flows.

Inflows and outflows of these activities are:

Operating Activities

Cash Inflows

1. Cash received from Debtors.
2. Cash Sales.
3. Refund of Income Tax.

Cash Outflows

1. Cash Payments for Goods and Services.
2. Cash Payments to Employees for Wages & Others.
3. Cash Payments
4. Income Tax paid.
5. Other operating Expenses.

Investing Activities

Cash Inflows

1. Cash Sale of Plant, Equipments and other Long-term Assets.
2. Cash Sale of Investments in Shares, Debentures and other Securities.
3. Cash Collection of Loan from Borrowers.
4. Interest and Dividends received by Cash.

Cash Outflows

1. Cash Purchase of Plant, Equipment and other Long-term Assets.
2. Purchase of Shares, Debentures and Securities.
3. Loans given to other Firms.

Financing Activities

Cash Inflows

1. Cash Received from issue of Shares/Debentures.
2. Proceeds from Short-term and long-term Debts.

Cash Outflows

1. Payment of Cash Dividend.
2. Repayment of Loans.
3. Reacquiring Preference or Equity Shares.
4. Redemption of Debentures.
5. Interest Paid.
6. Dividends Paid.

Classification of Cash Inflows and Cash Outflows

5.6 PROCEDURE FOR PREPARING CASH FLOW STATEMENT

Cash Flow Statement is prepared from the following three sources:

1. **Balance Sheet at the opening and closing period:** If we are preparing cash flow statement for the financial year 2006, Balance Sheets for the years 2005 and 2006 are required. These balance sheets provide the information in respect of assets, liabilities and shareholders' funds.
2. **Profit and Loss Account of Current year:** We need Profit and Loss Account or Income Statement for the year 2006. This statement provides information in respect of operating, financing and investment activities. Interest/dividend paid come in financing activity. Interest/ Dividends received are instances of investing activity.
3. **Additional Information:** Both the above statements do not provide all the information required. Additional information such as purchase and sale of assets, payment of taxes, amount paid on redemption of debentures and funds raised in the form of shares including share premium etc are needed for preparing cash flow statement. This information may be hidden which is to be explored.

5.7 STEPS INVOLVED IN PREPARING CASH FLOW STATEMENT

The following steps are involved in its preparation:

Step 1: Calculate the increase or decrease in cash and cash equivalents by making a comparison of the opening and closing balance sheets.

Step 2: Calculate the net cash flow from operating activities by analysing the Profit and Loss Account, Balance Sheet and other additional information. For this purpose, they are two methods – Direct and Indirect Method. They are explained, subsequently.

Step 3: Calculate the net cash flow from investing activities.

Step 4: Calculate the net cash flow from financing activities.

Step 5: Prepare a formal cash flow statement indicating the cash flows from operating, investing and financing activities.

Step 6: Make an aggregate of net cash flows from three activities and ensure that the total net cash flow is equal to the net increase or decrease in cash and cash equivalents, as calculated in Step 1.

Step 7: Report the non-cash transactions that did not involve cash and cash equivalents in a separate schedule to the cash flow statement. Examples are redemption of debentures in exchange of issue of shares and purchase of machinery against issue of share capital etc.

5.8 CALCULATION OF CASH FLOWS FROM OPERATING ACTIVITIES

Cash flows generated from operating activities is an important indicator about the operating capability of the enterprise to pay dividends, repay loans and make new investments without recourse to external sources of financing.

This determines whether the firm can continue in the long run or not.

Separate non-operation items: The net effect of various transactions in a business is reflected in the form of net profit or net loss, shown in the Profit and Loss Account. A firm may be in net profit, even though the results from operations may be negative, due to non-operational gains. Similarly, firm may be in net loss even though the firm has made operational profits due to non-operational losses. To know whether the firm is operationally profitable or not, it is necessary to separate the non-operational expenses and income.

Replace Accrual System with Cash System: Net profit is not, normally, equal to net flow (difference of inflow and outflow). It is so because certain non-cash and non-operating items are charged to profit and loss account. While preparing profit and loss account, accrual system of accounting is followed as per the Generally Accepted Accounting Principles (GAAP). Whether the sales are realised or not (credit sales), they are accounted for.

All revenues are taken into account if they relate to the period whether they are actually received or not. Similarly, all expenses are charged to the profit and loss account if they relate to the period whether they are actually paid or not. Basic principle of accrual is followed both for expenses and revenues.

To calculate net flow from operating activities, it is necessary to replace revenues and expenses with actual receipts and payments in cash.

Effect of Opening and Closing Stocks

The amount of opening stock is charged to Profit and Loss Account. It thus reduces net profit without reducing cash from operations. Similarly, closing stock increases the net profit without increasing cash from operations. When net profit is taken as the base to arrive at cash from operations, they require adjustments.

The following illustration explains the concept more clearly.

Illustration No. 1

	Rs.
Opening stock	10,000
Purchases	25,000
Sales	30,000
Closing stock	15,000
Expenses (paid in cash)	3,000

Compute the net profit and cash from operations.

Solution:

The amount of net profit can be computed as follows:

Profit and Loss Account (in Rupees)			
Opening stock	10,000	Sales	30,000
Purchases	25,000	Closing Stock	15,000
Expenses	3,000		
Net Profit	7,000		
	45,000		45,000

The net profit for the year is Rs. 7,000. The cash from operations is computed as follows:

	Net profit for the year	7,000
Add	Opening stock	10,000
		17,000
Less	Closing stock	15,000
	Cash from operations	2,000

Alternatively, cash from operations can be calculated as under:

	Net Profit	7,000
Less	Outflow of cash on account of increase in stock	-5,000
	Cash from operations	2,000

5.9 METHODS OF PREPARING CASH FLOW STATEMENTS

There are two methods of preparing cash flow statement:

1. Traditional Method
2. Preparing under AS-3.

1. **Traditional Method:** The traditional method does not have any standard format. There is no classification of inflow and outflow under operation, investment and finance activities, separately.
2. **Preparing under AS-3: The basic difference from traditional method is presentation of cash flow statement.** They are two methods of reporting cash flows from operating activities: the Direct Method and Indirect method.

(A) Direct Method

Cash flows from operations include cash receipts from sale of goods and services, cash payments to suppliers of goods and services, other cash payments and receipts. Total cash receipts and payments are to be calculated. Only cash receipts and cash payments (known as cash flows) from operating activities are considered. Examples are:

(i) Cash receipts from the sale of goods and rendering of services;

(ii) Cash receipts from royalties, fees, commission and other revenue;

(iii) Cash payments to suppliers of goods and services;

(iv) Cash receipts and payments relating to insurance, taxes, claims, annuities and other benefits.

Under the direct method, actual receipt and payment in cash only are important.

Adjustments for depreciation, amortisation of preliminary expenses and intangible assets like goodwill, discount on issue of shares and debentures are not required. Similarly, profit or loss on sale of assets is not required because operating cash receipts and payments are directly reported in the cash flow statement.

(B) Indirect Method

Under the indirect method, net profit is taken as base and is adjusted instead of individual items appearing in the Profit and Loss Account to arrive at cash from operations.

Net profit or loss is adjusted for the following:

1. Non cash items such as depreciation, writing off goodwill and preliminary expenses etc.;
2. Changes during the period in inventories, operating receivables and payable and
3. All other items which affect cash included in financing and investing activities such as loss/gain on sale of fixed assets and loss/gain on sale of investments etc.

It is reminded, again, cash flow statement of listed companies should be presented only under the indirect method as prescribed in AS-3.

Traditional Method: There is no standard format for showing the method of calculation of cash from operations (Traditional Method).

Calculation of Cash from Operations (Traditional Method)		
	Rs.	Rs.
Net Profit for the year	–	
Add: Non-cash Expenses:		
Depreciation		
Goodwill written off	–	

	Loss on Sale of fixed assets	–	
	Discount on shares / Debentures	–	
	Provision for taxation etc.	–	
Less:	Non – Cash Incomes		
	Profit on sale of Fixed Assets	–	
			(–)
	Net profit after adjustment of Non – Cash items		–
*	Changes in inventories, operating receivables and payables		
Add:	Decrease in Current Assets	–	
	Increase in Current Liability	–	
Less:	Increase in Current Assets	–	
	Decrease in Current Liabilities	–	–
	Cash from Operations		–

* Calculation of changes in inventories, operating receivables and payables:

For example, decrease in debtors (current asset) indicates that cash has been collected without affecting net profits in any manner, hence added.

Increase in Creditors (current liability) occurs when credit purchases are made but not paid. This has reduced net profits and so added to arrive at cash flows.

Increase in Debtors (current assets) occurs when credit sales are made, but not realised. This has already increased profits. So, deduced to arrive at cash flows.

Decrease in creditors (current liability) occurs when cash is paid, without any effect on net profits. So, deducted to arrive at cash flows.

Note: Students have to think what impact the transaction has created on net profits to decide –add or deduct - to arrive at cash flows.

5.10 CALCULATION OF CASH FLOWS FROM OPERATING ACTIVITIES

1. **Calculation of Cash collected from Customers (Sales made):** Sales figure in Profit and Loss Account /Income Statement includes cash sales and credit sales. We are to collect total cash collected from customers. This figure can be arrived by adjusting credit sales with the opening and closing balance of Debtors and Bills Receivable as follows:

Calculation of Cash Collected from Customers	
Debtors and Bills Receivable at the Beginning of year	Xxx
Add: Credit Sales	Xxx
Less: Debtors and Bills Receivable at the end of year	Xxx
Cash Collected from total credit sales	Xxx

2. **Cash Paid for Purchase of Inventory:** The figure in the Profit and Loss Account/ Income Statement shows the total purchases. Total purchases include both cash and credit purchases. The credit purchases are to be adjusted with the opening and closing balance of creditors and Bills Payable to arrive at the cash paid for purchase of inventory.

Calculation of Cash Paid to Creditors	
Creditors and Bills Payable at the Beginning of year	Xxx
Add: Credit Purchases	Xxx
Less: Creditors and Bills Payable at the end of year	Xxx
Cash paid to total credit purchases	Xxx

3. **Cash Payments for Expenses:** Expenses in the Profit and Loss Account are charged on the accrual basis. There are outstanding expenses or prepaid expenses. They are to be adjusted to arrive on cash basis.

Cash Paid for Expenses-Adjustment of Prepaid Expenses	
Expenses appearing in Profit and Loss Account	Xxx
Add: Prepaid Expenses in Closing Balance Sheet	Xxx
Less: Prepaid Expenses in Opening Balance Sheet	Xxx
Cash paid for Expenses	Xxx
Cash Paid for Expenses-Adjustment of Outstanding Expenses	
Expenses appearing in Profit and Loss Account	Xxx
Add: Outstanding Expenses in Opening Balance Sheet	Xxx
Less: Outstanding Expenses in Closing Balance Sheet	Xxx
Cash paid for Expenses	Xxx

Let us explain with the following two examples:

(A) Salary expense in Profit and Loss Account is Rs.30,000. Salary outstanding at the beginning of the year is Rs.5,000 and salary outstanding at the close of the year is Rs. 3,000.

Here, cash paid for salary = Salary – Outstanding salary at the end + Outstanding salary at the beginning.

$$= 30{,}000 - 3{,}000 + 5{,}000$$
$$= 32{,}000$$

(B) Insurance premium appearing in Profit and Loss Account is 10,000. Premium Prepaid at the beginning of the year is Rs. 2,000 and premium prepaid at the end of the year is Rs. 1,500.

Here, cash paid for salary = Insurance premium – Prepaid premium at the beginning + Premium paid at the end.

$$= 10{,}000 - 2{,}000 + 1{,}500$$

$$= 9{,}500$$

After arriving at the answer, students are advised to check the correctness calculating in a reverse manner i.e. from cash to profit figure appearing in the Profit and Loss Account.

4. **Non-Cash items:** Certain non-cash expenses like depreciation, goodwill and preliminary expenses written off appear in the Profit and Loss Account. They are charged to arrive at true profits though there is no outgo of cash. So, these items are to be added.

The following illustration explains the Traditional Method of calculating cash from operations:

Illustration No.2:

Following information is available from the books of Suresh Ltd. for the year end 31-12-2005 and 31-12-2006.

	31-12-2005	31-12-2006
Profit made during the year	-	2,50,000
Income received in advance	500	400
Prepaid expenses	1,600	2,000
Debtors	80,000	20,000
Bills receivable	25,000	40,000
Creditors	45,000	65,000
Bills payable	13,000	5,000
Outstanding expenses	2,500	3,000
Accrued income	1,500	1,800

Calculate cash flow from operations for the year ending 31-12-2006.

Solution:

Calculation of cash from operations for the year ending 31-12-2006

		31-12-2006
Profit made during the year		2,50,000
Add:		
Decrease in Debtors	60,000	
Increase in creditors	20,000	
Increase in outstanding expenses	500	+80,500
	3,30,500	
Less:		
Decrease in income received in advance	100	
Increase in prepaid expenses	400	
Increase in bills receivable	15,000	
Decrease in bills payable	8,000	
Increase in accrued income	300	-23,800
Cash from Operations		2,06,700

5.11 DIFFERENCES BETWEEN FUNDS FLOW STATEMENT AND CASH FLOW STATEMENT

The term 'funds' has a variety of meanings. In a narrow sense, it means cash. When Statement of Changes in Financial Position is prepared on cash basis, it is called Cash Flow Statement. When Statement of Changes in Financial Position is prepared on working capital basis, it is called Funds Flow Statement. Both the statements are similar in several respects, yet there are some differences between the Funds Flow Statement and Cash Flow Statement. The differences are as under:

Base of Difference	Funds Flow Statement	Cash Flow statement
1. Meaning	It is a statement of changes in the financial position of business due to inflow and outflow of **funds**.	It is a statement of changes in the financial position of business due to inflow and outflow of **cash.**
2. Basis of Concept	It is based on the wider concept of funds i.e. working capital	It is based on the narrower concept of funds i.e. cash.
3. Basis of accounting	It is based on accrual system of accounting.	It is based on cash system of accounting
4. Concerned with	A funds flow statement is concerned with changes in working capital position between two balance sheet dates.	A cash flow statement is concerned with changes in cash position between two balance sheet dates.
5. Schedule of	Schedule of Changes in Working Capital is prepared to show the changes in working capital.	No such statement is prepared.

6. Purpose of Preparation Changes in Working Capital	This statement reveals sources and Uses of funds. The difference between sources and uses indicate the increase or decrease in working capital.	All inflows and outflows are classified in terms of operating, investing and financing activities. The net difference represents the net increase or decrease of in cash and cash equivalents.
7. Usefulness	It is useful for long-term planning and financing.	It is more useful for short-term analysis and cash planning of the business.

5.12 LIMITATIONS

Despite a number of uses, cash flow statement suffers from the following limitations:

1. **Ignores Basic Principles of Accounting:** Cash Flow Statement is prepared on the basis of cash accounting. It ignores the basic accounting concept of accrual basis.
2. **Not suitable for Judging Profitability:** Cash Flow Statement is prepared ignoring non-cash charges, while preparing cash flow from operations. So, this statement is not suitable for judging profitability of a firm.
3. **Statement does not reflect real liquid position:** The cash balance reflected in the cash flow statement may not represent the real liquid position. Purchases and payments can be postponed to present a better liquid position.
4. **Cannot be equated with Income Statement:** Cash flow statement cannot be equated with Income Statement. An income-statement takes into account cash as well as non-cash items and, therefore, net cash flow does not necessarily mean net income of the business.

In spite of these limitations, cash flow statement has its own role to play. It is a useful tool for financial analysis. It is a useful supplementary instrument. It discloses the volume of cash flows in different segments of the business. It helps the management in knowing the amount of capital tied up in each segment of the business. It serves as a barometer in measuring the profitability and financial position of the business.

Illustration No. 3

From the Balance Sheet of Dimpy Ltd. as at 31-3-2005 and 31-3-2006,

prepare Cash Flow Statement:

	31-3-2005	312-3-2006
Liabilities	Rs.	Rs.
Equity share capital	4,00,000	4,50,000
Share premium	—	30,000
General reserve	45,000	65,000
Profit and Loss	30,000	80,800
7% Debentures	—	70,000

Contd...

Sundry Creditors	85,000	90,700
Provision for Taxation	22,500	40,500
Proposed dividend	30,000	35,000
	6,12,500	8,62,000
Assets		
Land and Building	3,30,000	4,90,000
Plant and Machinery	85,400	1,40,000
Furniture	5,500	6,500
Stock	82,400	95,700
Sundry Debtors	75,000	85,500
Bank balance	34,200	44,300
	6,12,500	8,62,000

Additional information

Details of Depreciation written off on the following assets during the year are as under:

	(Rs.)
Land and Building	60,000
Plant and machinery	50,000
Furniture	1,200

Solution:

Calculation of operating profit, before working capital changes (Funds from operations) (Rs.)

Profit and Loss Account (31-3-2006)		80,800	
Add: Depreciation - Land and Building	60,000		
Depreciation- Plant and Machinery	50,000		
Depreciation – Furniture	1,200		
General Reserve	20,000		
Taxation Provision	40,500		
Proposed dividend	35,000	+2,06,700	
		2,87,500	
Less: Profit and Loss Account (31-3-2005)		-30,000	
Operating profit, before working capital changes (Funds from operations)			2,57,500

Land and Building A/c

To Balance b/d	3,30,000	By Depreciation	60,000
To Bank (Balancing figure)	2,20,000	By Balance c/d	4,90,000
	5,50,000		5,50,000

Plant and Machinery A/c

To Balance b/d	85,400	By Depreciation	50,000
To Bank (Balancing figure)	1,04,600	By Balance c/d	1,40,000
	1,90,000		1,90,000

Furniture A/c

To Balance b/d	5,500	By Depreciation	1,200
To Bank (Balancing figure)	2,200	By Balance c/d	6,500
	7,7,00		7,700

Provision for Taxation A/c

To Bank	22,500	By Balance b/d	22,500
To Balance c/d	40,500	By Profit & Loss A/c	40,500
	63,000		63,000

Proposed Dividend A/c

To Bank	30,000	By Balance b/d	30,000
To Balance c/ d	35,000	By Profit & Loss A/c	35,000
	65,000		65,000

Calculation of Cash from Operations

		(Rs.)
Operating profit, before working capital changes		2,57,500
Add : Increase in current liabilities		5,700
Sundry creditors (Rs. 90,700 - Rs. 85,000)		
		2,63,200
Less : Increase in Current Assets		
Stock (Rs. 95,700 - Rs. 82,400)	13,300	
Sundry Debtors (Rs. 85,500 - Rs. 75,000)	10,500	23,800
Cash inflow from operations		2,39,400

Cash flow statement for the year ended 31st March, 2006

		(Rs.)
Opening Bank balance		34,200
Add : Cash flow from Operations	2,39,400	
Issue of equity shares	50,000	
Share premium	30,000	
Issue of 7% Debentures	70,000	
		3,89,400
		4,23,600

Contd...

Less :		
Additions to land and buildings	2,20,000	
Additions to plant and machinery	1,04,600	
Additions to furniture	2,200	
Payment of dividend	30,000	
Payment of tax	22,500	3,79,300
Closing Bank Balance		44,300

Note: Operating profit, before working capital changes and Funds from operations are one and the same. They are different terms. Different authors use different terms. They mean the same.

PROFORMA OF CASH FLOW STATEMENT AS PER AS–3 DIRECT METHOD

Particulars	*Rs.*	*Rs.*
Cash Flows from Operating Activities		
Cash Receipts from Customers	–	
Cash Payment to Suppliers	(–)	
Cash paid to Employees as Salaries and Wages	(–)	
Other Operating Expenses	(–)	
Cash generated from Operations	–	
Income Tax Paid	(–)	
	–	
Income Tax Refund	–	
Cash Flow before Extra-ordinary Items	–	
Cash Flow from Extra-ordinary Items	–	
e.g. Proceeds from Earthquake Disaster Settlement	–	
Net Cash Flow from / used in Operating Activities		–
Cash Flows from Investing Activities		
Proceeds from Sales of Fixed Assets	–	
Cash Payment for Purchases of Fixed Assets	(–)	
Interest Received	–	
Dividend Received	–	
Net Cash Flows from / used in Investing Activities		–
Cash Flows from Financing Activities		
Proceeds from Issue of Shares	–	
Proceeds from Issue of Debentures	–	
Proceeds from Long-term Borrowings	–	
Redemption of Shares	(–)	
Redemption of Debentures	(–)	
Repayment of long-term borrowings	(–)	
Interest paid	(–)	
Net Cash flows from / used in Financing Activities		–
Net increase / decrease in cash and cash equivalents		–

Cash and Cash equivalent at the beginning of the period		–
Cash and Cash equivalents at the end of the period		–

INDIRECT METHOD

Particulars	*Rs.*	*Rs.*
Cash Flows from Operating Activities		
Balance of P & L A/c as per closing Balance Sheet	–	
Less: Balance of P & L A/c as per opening Balance Sheet	–	
or		
Increase in the balance of P & L A/c	–	
or		
Net Profit as per P & L A/c after appropriations	–	
Add: Appropriations during the year		
Transfer to General Reserve	–	
Transfer to Debenture Redemption Fund	–	
Transfer to Dividend Equalisation Fund	–	
Proposed Dividend	–	
Net Profit for the year		
Add: Non-Operating Expenses	–	
Interim – Dividend paid	–	
Loss by Fire –		
Interest paid –		
	–	
Less: Non-Operating Incomes	–	
Interest Received (–)		
Dividends Received	(–)	
Operating Net Profit	–	
Add: Non-cash Expenses		
Depreciation –		
Loss on Sales of Fixed Assets	–	
Loss on Revaluation of Fixed Assets	–	
Loss on Redemption of Shares	–	
Loss on Redemption of Debentures	–	
Goodwill written off	–	
Preliminary Expenses written off	–	
Discount on Shares written off	–	
Discount on debentures written off	–	
Provision for Taxation	–	
Less: Non-Cash Incomes		
Profit on Sale of Fixed Assets	(–)	
Profit on Revaluation of Fixed Assets	(–)	
Profit on Redemption of Debentures	(–)	
Profit on Redemption of Shares	(–)	
Operating Profit before Working Capital Changes	–	
Add: Decrease in Current Assets	–	
Less: Increase in Current Assets	(–)	

Add: Increase in Current Liabilities	–	
Less: Decrease in Current Liabilities	(–)	
Cash generated from Operations	–	
Less: Income Tax paid	(–)	
Add: Income Tax Refund	–	
Net cash from Operating Activities after Income Tax but before Extra-ordinary Items		
Add: Cash Inflows from Extra-ordinary Items	–	
Less: Cash Outflows from Extra-ordinary Items	–	
Net cash flows from / used in operating activities		–
Cash Flows from Investing Activities		
Proceeds from Sale of Fixed Assets	–	
Cash Payment for Purchases of Fixed Assets	(–)	
Interest Received –		
Dividend Received –		
Net Cash Flows from / used in Investing Activities		–
Cash Flows from Financing Activities		
Proceeds from Issue of Shares	–	
Proceeds from Issue of Debentures	–	
Proceeds from Long-term Borrowings	–	
Redemption of Shares	(–)	
Redemption of Debentures	(–)	
Repayment of long-term borrowings	(–)	
Interest paid	(–)	
Dividend paid	(–)	
Net Cash flows from / used in Financing Activities		–
Net increase / decrease in cash and cash equivalents		–
Cash and Cash equivalent at the beginning of the period		–
Cash and Cash equivalents at the end of the period		–

Illustration No.4

You are required to prepare cash flow statement from Balance Sheets of THEER & TARKH Company on 31.12.04 and 31.12.05 in the Traditional method and AS-3.

Balance Sheets

Liabilities	31.12.2004 Rs.	31.12.2005 Rs.	Assets	31.12.2004 Rs.	31.12.2005 Rs.
Equity Share Capital	1,25,000	1,53,000	Cash	10,000	7,000
	——	25,000			
Creditors	40,000	44,000	Debtors	30,000	75,000
Mrs. A's Loan	25,000	—	Stock	35,000	25,000
Loan from Bank	40,000	50,000	Machinery	80,000	55,000
			Land	40,000	50,000
			Building	35,000	60,000
	2,30,000	2,72,000		2,30,000	2,72,000

During the year a machine costing Rs. 10,000, accumulated depreciation Rs. 3,000, was sold for Rs. 5,000. The provision for depreciation against machinery as on 31.12.2004 was Rs. 25,000 and on 31.12.2005 Rs. 40,000. Net profit for the year 2005 amounted to Rs. 45,000. Building has been revalued and credited to capital reserve account.

Solution:

Cash flow statement
(Traditional Method)

Cash Balance as on 31.12.2004		Rs. 10,000
Add: Sources:		
Cash from Operations	Rs. 34,000	
Loan from Bank	10,000	+ 49,000
Sale of Machinery	5,000	
Less: Applications:		
Purchase of Land	10,000	
Mrs. A's Loan repayment	25,000	
Drawings 17,000	-52,000	
Cash Balance as on December 31, 2005		7,000

Working Notes:

Cash from operations

Profit made during the year		Rs. 45,000
Add: Depreciation on Machinery	18,000	
Loss on Sale of Machinery	2,000	
Decrease in Stock	10,000	
Increase in Creditors	4,000	34,000
	79,000	
Less: Increase in Debtors		45,000
Cash from Operations		34,000

Capital account

To cash-Drawings (Balancing figure)	Rs. 17,000	By Balance b/d	Rs. 1,25,000
To Balance c/d	1,53,000	By Profit	45,000
	1,70,000		1,70,000

Machinery account (at cost)

To Balance b/d	Rs. 1,05,000	By Bank	Rs. 5,000
		By Loss on Sale of Machinery	2,000
		By Provision for Depreciation	3,000
		By Balance c / d	95,000
	1,05,000		1,05,000

Provision for depreciation Account			
To Machinery A/c	Rs. 3,000	By Balance b/d	Rs. 25,000
To Balance c/d	40,000	By P & L A/c (Depreciation charged – Balancing figure)	18,000
	43,000		43,000

Note: Revaluation of Building is a non-cash item and so does not appear in cash flow statement.

Cash flow statement
(AS–3 (Revised) Method)

		Rs.	
I.	**Cash flows from operating activities**		
	Net profit made during the year	45,000	
	Adjustments for depreciation	18,000	
	Loss on sale of machinery	2,000	
	Operating profit before working capital changes	65,000	
	Decrease in stock	10,000	
	Increase in creditors	4,000	
	Increase in Debtors	(45,000)	
	Net Cash flows from operating activities		34,000
II.	**Cash flows from investing activities**		
	Sale of machinery	5,000	
	Purchase of land	(10,000)	
	Net Cash flow from investing activities		(5,000)
III	**Cash flows from financing activities**		
	Loan from bank	10,000	
	Ms. A' s loan repayment	(25,000)	
	Drawings	(17,000)	
	Net Cash flow from financing activities		(32,000)
	Net increase (decrease) in cash and cash equivalent		(3,000)
	Cash and cash equivalents at the beginning of the period		10,000
	Cash and cash equivalents at the end of the period		7,000

Illustration No.5

Following are the summarized balance sheets of Cherry and Dimpy Ltd as on 31st March 2005 and 2006, you are required to make the Statement of cash flow under the Traditional Method and AS-3 (Revised Method).

Liabilities	2005	2006
Share capital	2,00,000	2,50,000
General Reserve	50,000	60,000
Profit and Loss A/c	30,500	30,600
Bank Loan (Long Term)	70,000	—
Sundry Creditors	1,50,000	1,35,200
Provision for taxation	30,000	35,000
	5,30,500	5,10,800

Assets	2005	2006
Machinery	1,50,000	1,69,000
Land and Building	2,41,800	2,28,200
Goodwill	———	5,000
Stock	74,000	20,000
Debtors	64,200	80,000
Bank	———	8,000
Cash	500	600
	5,30,500	5,10,800

Additional Information

During the year ended 31st March, 2006.

(i) Dividend of Rs. 23,000 was paid.

(ii) Assets of another company were purchased for a consideration of Rs.50,000 payable in shares for purchase of the assets- stock : Rs. 20,000; Machinery Rs. 25,000.

(iii) Machinery was further purchased for Rs. 8,000.

(iv) Depreciation written off on machinery Rs. 12,000; Land & Buildings Rs. 13,600.

(v) Income tax provided during the year Rs. 33,000.

(vi) Loss on sale of machinery Rs. 200 was written off to General reserve.

Solution:

Machinery A/c

To Balance b/d	1,50,000	By General Reserve (Loss on sale of Machine)	200
To Share Capital a/c (Purchase by issue of shares)	25,000	By Depreciation	12,000
To Cash (Purchase of machinery)	8,000	By Cash (Sale of machine) Balancing figure	1,800
		By Balance c/d	1,69,000
	1,83,000		1,83,000

Provision for Taxation A/c

To Bank (Tax paid)	28,000	By Balance b/d	30,000
To Balance c/d	35,000	By Profit & Loss a/c(Tax provision)	33,000
	63,000		63,000

General Reserve Account

To Machinery account (Loss on sale)	200	By Balance b/d	50,000
To Balance c/d	60,000	By Profit and Loss Adjustment A/c	10,200
	60,200		60,200

Profit and Loss Adjustment Account			
To General Reserve A/c	10,200	By opening Balance b/d	30,500
To Provision for taxation	33,000	By funds from operations (Balancing figure)	91,900
To Machinery -Depreciation	12,000		
To Land and Buildings -Depreciation	13,600		
To Dividend paid	23,000		
To closing balance c/d	30,600		
	1,22,400		1,22,400

Decrease in Stock		
Opening Stock		74,000
Closing Stock	20,000	
Less Stock acquired* in acquisition	20,000	Nil
Decrease in Stock – Increase in cash		74,000

Cash Flow Statement for the year ending 31st March, 2006 (Traditional Method)		
Opening Cash & Bank Balance		
Sources:		
Funds from Operations	91,900	
Add: Sale of Machinery	1,800	
Decrease in stock	74,000	
Uses:		+ 1,67,700
Increase in Debtors	15,800	
Less: Purchase of Machinery	8,000	
Tax Paid	28,000	
Dividends paid	23,000	
Decrease in creditors	14,800	
Repayment of Bank Loan	70,000	-1,59,600
Closing Cash & Bank Balance		8,600

Note: Acquisition of business –stock and machinery- in exchange of share is a non-cash transaction.

Cash Flow Statement AS-3 (Revised Method)		
Cash Flows from operating activities		
Net profit made during the year (100+10,200+23,000+33,000)	66,300	
Adjustment for depreciation on Land and Building	13,600	

Contd...

Adjustment for depreciation on Machinery Operating profit before working capital changes	12,000	91,900
Decrease in stock	74,000	
Increase in Debtors	(15,800)	
Decrease in creditors	(14,800)	
Income Tax Paid	(28,000)	
1. Net cash Flows from operating activities		1,07,300
Cash flows from investing activities		
Sale of Machinery	1,800	
Purchase of Machinery	(8,000)	
2. Cash from investing activities		(6,200)
Cash Flows from financing activities		
Repayment of Bank Loan	(70,000)	
Dividend paid	(23000)	
3. Cash Flows from Financing Activities		(93,000)
Net increase in cash and cash equivalents		8,100
Cash and cash equivalents at the beginning of the period		500
Cash and cash equivalents at the end of the period		8,600

5.13 STATEMENT OF CHANGES IN FINANCIAL POSITION (TOTAL RESOURCES BASIS)

Here, the term "Funds" refer to all financial resources. The resources may be in any form- material, machinery, money and others- used in the business. The term 'funds' is used in the comprehensive way. This is a statement summarising the effect of changes in cash along with other significant investment and financing activities, which do not involve cash.

Preparation: Preparation of this statement is similar to the preparation of cash flow statement. In cash flow statement, transactions like conversion of debentures into shares and issuance of bonus shares do not get reflected as they do not affect cash. In this statement, these types of transactions are shown under the head '**Financial Resources not affecting cash** ' both under sources and uses in this **statement, additionally**. This is the only difference. This provides the comprehensive picture of total resources. There is no fixed standard format for presentation.

An illustration explains the concept better.

Illustration No.6

From the following comparative Balance Sheets of Kishore & Co. Ltd., prepare the Cash Flow Statement on Total Financial Resources basis.

Comparative Balance Sheets for the year ended 31st March, 2005 and 2006	2005	(Rs.) 2006
Current Assets		
Bank	65,000	1,65,000
Debtors	45,000	70,000
Inventory	90,000	62,000
Total current assets	2,00,000	2,97,000
Fixed Assets		
Goodwill	—	50,000
Land & Building	2,00,000	2,50,000
Equipment	2,50,000	2,95,000
Less: Accumulated Depreciation	(80,000)	(95,000)
Total net fixed assets	3,70,000	5,00,000
Total Assets	**5,70,000**	**7,97,000**
Current Liabilities		
Creditors	15,000	2,000
Salaries payable	22,000	60,000
Provision for tax	60,000	5,000
Provision for dividend	25,000	10,000
Total Current Liabilities	1,22,000	77,000
Long-term Liabilities		
Long-term loan	18,000	84,000
Debentures	1,30,000	1,06,000
Total long-term liabilities	1,48,000	1,90,000
Total Liabilities	2,70,000	2,67,000
Shareholders' Equity		
Equity share capital	2,35,000	3,75,000
Share premium	25,000	65,000
Reserves and surplus	40,000	90,000
Net Worth	3,00,000	5,30,000
Total Funds	**5,70,000**	**7,97,000**

The additional information is given below:

1. Debentures of Rs.24,000 were converted to share capital at par.
2. During the year equipment costing Rs. 40,000 (accumulated depreciation Rs.12,000) was sold for Rs. 32,000.
3. The company acquired another company for Rs.1,00,000 for which equity shares were issued. Assets acquired were Goodwill Rs.50,000 and Building Rs.50,000.

4. The company declared a cash dividend of Rs.25,000.
5. The company issued additional shares, par value Rs.100 per share, at a premium during the year.
6. Bonus shares were also issued at par for Rs.10,000.
7. Payment of tax Rs. 60,000 was made and a new provision for Rs.5,000 has been created.

Solution:

Cash from operations		**(Rs.)**
Net Profit during the year		70,000
Add: Depreciation	27,000	
Decrease in stock	28,000	
Increase in salaries Payable	38,000	
Provision for tax made	5,000	+98,000
Less: Profit on sale of Equipment	4,000	
Decrease in creditors	13,000	
Increase in debtors	25,000	-42,000
Cash from operations		1,26,000

Reserves and Surplus Account

To Provision for dividend	10,000	By Balance b/d	40,000
To Share capital (Bonus shares issue)	10,000	By Profit and Loss Account (Profit made during the year – Balancing figure)	70,000
To Balance c/d	90,000		
	1,10,000		1,10,000

Accumulated Depreciation Account

To Sale of asset (Depreciation on the asset sold)	12,000	By Balance b/d	80,000
To Balance c/d	95,000	By Profit and Loss Account (depreciation provided)	27,000
	1,07,000		1,07,000

Equipment Account

To Balance b/d	2,50,000	By sale of asset	40,000
To cash (purchase of new equipment - Balancing figure)	85,000	By Balance c/d	2,95,000
	3,35,000		3,35,000

Equity Share Capital Account

		By Balance b/d	2,35,000
		By Reserves and Surplus Account (issue of bonus shares)	10,000
		By Acquisition of company	1,00,000
		By Cash (Balancing figure)	6,000
		By Debentures Account (Conversion of debentures into shares)	24,000
To Balance c/d	3,75,000		
	3,75,000		3,75,000

Cash Flow Statement

Sources:		
Cash from operations	1,26,000	
Cash from issue of shares	6,000	
Cash from issue of shares at a premium	40,000	
Sale of equipment	32,000	
Receipt of long-term loan	66,000	
Financial resources not affecting cash		
Issue of Bonus shares from Reserves and Surplus	10,000	
Issuance of equity shares for purchase of Goodwill and Equipment	1,00,000	
Issuance of equity shares for conversion of Debentures	24,000	
Financial Resources Provided		**4,04,000**
Uses:		
Purchase of Equipment	85,000	
Payment of tax	60,000	
Payment of dividend	25,000	
Financial resources not affecting cash –Uses		
Purchase of Goodwill	50,000	
Purchase of Equipment	50,000	
Issue of Bonus shares from Reserves and Surplus	10,000	
Payment of Debentures through issuance of equity shares	24,000	
Financial Resources Applied		**3,04,000**
Increase in Bank Balance		1,00,000

Objective Questions

1. What is a Cash Flow Statement? Explain the meaning, need and its objectives? **(5.2,5.3 and 5.4)**
2. Describe the classification of cash flows from Operating, Investing and Financing Activities in a Cash Flow Statement? **(5.2 and 5.5)**

3. Explain the Procedure of preparing Cash Flow Statement and method of calculating fund from operating activities? **(5.6, 5.7, 5.8 and 5.10)**
4. Describe different methods of preparing Cash Flow Statement? **(5.9)**
5. Differentiate between Funds Flow Statement and Cash Flow Statement? **(5.11)**
6. What is a Cash Flow Statement and describe the different steps involved in preparing Cash Flow Statement? **(5.2 and 5.7)**
8. Describe Limitations of Cash Flow Statement? **(5.12)**

Check Your Understanding

State whether the following statements are true or false:

1. Every listed company has an option to prepare and enclose the cash flow statement or funds flow statement along with the financial statements.
2. Cash flow statement describes the inflows and outflows of cash.
3. Cash equivalents are short term, highly liquid investments that are readily convertible into cash.
4. As per AS-3 (Revised), cash flows resulting from the sale of fixed assets are classified as cash flows from investing activities.
5. Cash flow statement reveals the effects of transactions involving movement of cash.
6. Cash Flow Statement is a summary of cashbook.
7. Increase in provision for doubtful debts should be added back to net profit in order to find out cash from operations.
8. Funds Flow Statement and Cash Flow Statement are one and the same.
9. A "Cash Flow Statement" can very well be equated with an "Income Statement".
10. Cash flow statement is based upon accrual basis of accounting.
11. The term "Funds" means "Current Assets" in case of a cash flow analysis.
12. Cash flow statement is a substitute of a Cash Account.

Answers

1. False	2. True	3. True	4. True.	5. True
6. True	7. True	8. False	9. False	10. False
11. False	12. False			

Choose the correct answer:

1. In the context of Cash Flow Statement, the term "Fund" refers to
   (A) Working capital
   (B) Cash and cash equivalents
   (C) Total Resources

(D) None

2. Cash from operations is equal to:
   (A) Net profit plus increase in outstanding expenses;
   (B) Net profit plus increase in debtors;
   (C) Net profit plus increase in stock.
3. In the context of Cash Flow Statement, the term 'cash' is equivalent to
   (A) Physical cash on hand
   (B) Physical cash on hand and demand deposits in a Bank
   (C) Physical cash on hand and all types of deposits in a Bank

Answers

1. (B) 2. (A) 3. (B)

State the effect of each of the following transactions considered, individually, on funds (cash concept):

(a) Purchase of Furniture for cash.
(b) Purchase of Plant and Machinery against a long-term loan payable.
(c) Bonus shares issued, capitalising profits.

Answer

When fund denotes 'Cash', item (a) will result in decrease of cash while items (b) and (c) will have no effect on cash.

Fill in the Blanks:

1. Cash payments to suppliers for goods and services are classified as cash flows from .... activities.
2. Income from long-term investments is cash flow from .... activities.
3. Decrease in Debtors is ... of cash.
4. Net cash flow is the difference of... and...

Answers

1. Operating 2. Investing 3. Inflow 4. Inflow, Outflow

6

COST–VOLUME PROFIT ANALYSIS

6.1 INTRODUCTION

A firm's performance is measured by the profit it makes. Profits of a firm depend upon a large number of factors. But, the most important factors are costs of manufacture, volume of sales and selling price of the products. **The analytical technique employed to study the inter-relationship of cost, volume and price and its impact on the behaviour of profit is known as 'Cost-Volume Profit Analysis'.** In the short-run, profit planning can be made with the use of CVP analysis. It helps the management to achieve an ideal combination of costs and volume. This becomes possible with the understanding of the implications of variable cost, fixed costs and volume. CVP analysis helps the management in deciding the quantum of sales required to be made to avoid losses as well as reaching a particular level of sales to achieve the targeted amount of profit.

6.2 CVP ANALYSIS

Utility of CVP Analysis: CVP analysis studies the relationship of cost-volume-profit at different levels of output. This analysis is an important tool for profit planning. The three factors of CVP analysis–costs, volume and profit are interconnected and dependent on one another. For example, profits depend upon the selling price. Selling price largely depends upon cost of production. Cost of production, in turn, depends upon volume of production. It is only the variable costs that vary directly with production, whereas fixed costs remain constant regardless of the volume of production, in the short-run.

In some quarters, there is an opinion that business firms rarely operate at their break-even points. Therefore, the break-even analysis is of very limited use to the management. This is incorrect. Reason is many people consider CVP analysis and Break-even point are one and the same. It is not so. The scope of CVP analysis is quite wide while BEP is only a part of CVP analysis. Break-even analysis provides answer how much sales are to be made to avoid losses. CVP analysis provides not only this answer as BEP is a part of it, but provides answers in many areas to the management. Understanding CVP relationship is important in financial decision making to a dynamic management. It provides right answers to the following questions such as:

- How much sales are required to avoid losses?
- What level of sales is required to achieve a targeted amount of profit?
- What will be the effect of change in prices, costs and volume on profits?
- What will be the effect of change in sales mix on profits?
- What will be the new break-even point if there is change in prices, costs, volume or sales mix?
- Should we buy or manufacture some products or components?
- What will be the impact of plant expansion on the relationship of cost-volume-profit?
- Which product or product mix is most profitable and which one is least profitable?
- Should the sale of a product or operation of a plant be discontinued?
- Is it desirable to shut down the plant, temporarily?

These are some of the intricate questions for which management can find answers with the help of CVP analysis. All the above aspects have immense influence on the profitability of the firm. CVP analysis is concerned with entire profit planning, as management's main thrust is to build a good level of profit, at all times. This analysis provides the necessary insight to the management to take suitable decisions for necessary and timely action. It is of great use for profit planning, cost control and decision-making.

6.3 BEHAVIOUR OF FIXED AND VARIABLE COSTS

Fixed Costs: When a cost does not change with increase in volume, it is called Fixed Cost Fixed costs are constant. Fixed costs do not change irrespective of the level of production. Examples are rent, insurance, depreciation and repairs. The total fixed cost is one and the same whether one unit is produced or one hundred units are produced till the production does not exceed the capacity of machine. However, the unit fixed cost decreases as the volume of production increases. In the pictorial presentation of behaviour of fixed costs, unit fixed cost curve descends while total fixed cost is constant at all levels of production. In other words, unit cost decreases as and when volume increases. But, there is no change in fixed costs at different volume levels.

The graphical presentation of total fixed cost and unit fixed costs show as under:

Behaviour of Fixed Costs

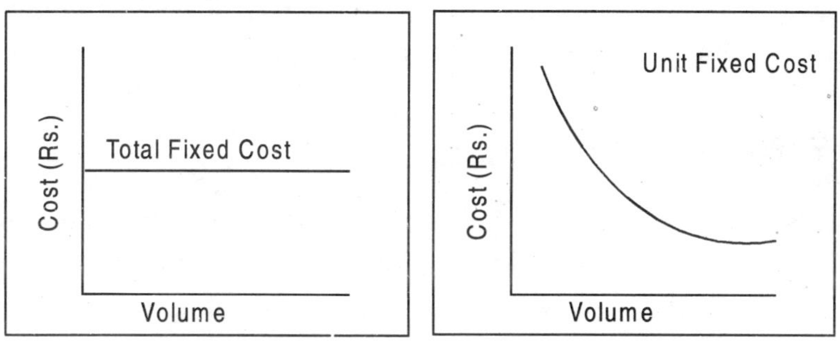

Total Fixed Cost **Unit Fixed Cost**

Variable costs: When a cost changes in proportion to the change in volume, it is called Variable Cost. The typical example is raw materials. If production increases, total cost of raw materials increases in the same proportion of level of production. If production is suspended or closed, cost of raw materials becomes zero. **Mathematically, a linear relationship exists between a variable cost and volume.** If volume increases or decreases by 20%, in the same proportion, the cost of production varies. So, unit cost is constant and total cost changes, proportionately, to volume.

The graphical presentation of total variable cost and unit variable cost shows:

Behaviour of Variable Costs

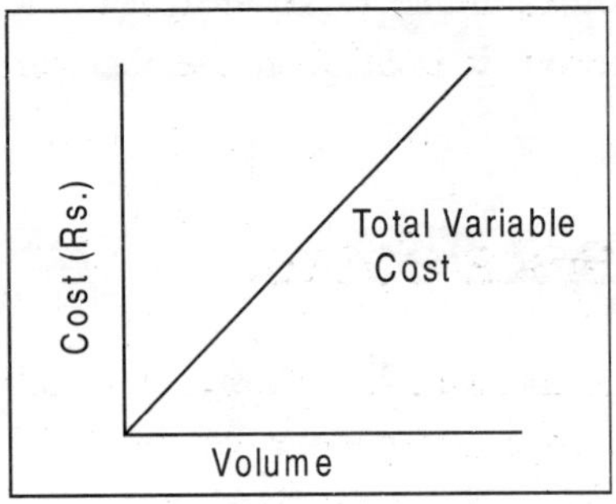

Total Variable Cost

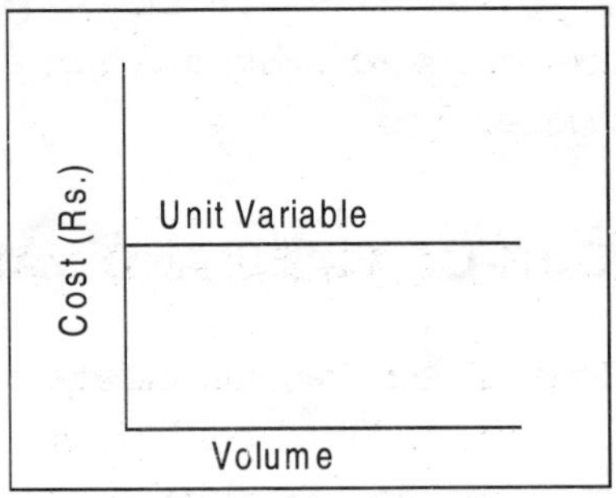

Unit Variable Cost

In CVP analysis, the presumption is fixed cost and variable cost can be separated.

6.4 CVP ANALYSIS AND BREAK-EVEN ANALYSIS

Many think break-even analysis and CVP analysis are one and the same. It is not so. **The Break-even analysis is the most widely known form of CVP analysis.** For this reason, both the terms are used interchangeably by many.

The purpose of CVP analysis is to examine the effect of change in costs, volume and price on profits. This is a comprehensive study. Break-even analysis is a part of CVP analysis.

6.5 BREAK-EVEN ANALYSIS

Break-even analysis establishes the relationship between revenues and costs with respect to volume. It indicates the level of sales at which total costs are equal to total revenues.

Breakeven analysis is a specific way of presenting information to management in a precise manner. Many a time, CVP analysis is popularly designated as break-even analysis. But, there is a narrow difference between the two. CVP analysis is concerned with the entire profit planning while the break-even analysis is one of the techniques used in that process.

Break-even point: Break-even point is the point at which the firm makes no profit or loss. At the break-even point, the firm is in the stage of equilibrium. The equilibrium point is commonly known as break-even point. **Break even point is the point where the revenue is just equal to total costs.** It is the point where the firm makes neither profit nor loss. This is a zero position. After this level, if the firm makes production and sells above the variable cost, it earns profit. If the sales fall below this level, firm sustains loss. There are two approaches to calculate the break-even point. They are:

(A) Break-even Formula Approach and

(B) Break-even Chart or Graphic Method break-even Analysis

(A) Break-even Formulae Approach: The break-even point can be calculated in terms of units, in terms of money value of sales volume or as a percentage of estimated capacity.

6.5.1 Contribution

When the selling price per unit is more than its variable cost, the excess is called contribution. Total contribution is calculated by multiplying the unit contribution with the number of units sold. Total contribution is the excess amount after covering total fixed costs that is incurred by the firm. After covering fixed costs, the amount left in the firm is gross margin. So, contribution covers total fixed costs and profit. If the contribution does not cover fixed costs, the difference is loss, sustained by the firm. Every firm looks to achieve break-even point, at the earliest. After the break-even level, whatever is sold that can leave in the form of contribution to the firm is a welcome decision. While making production and sales decisions, the firm chooses that product that gives the highest contribution. Contribution is vital in profit planning decision-making. Firm is always concerned to choose that product where it can sell and achieve the highest amount of contribution. Contribution is important to the finance manager and, equally, to marketing manager to show impressive performance of the firm, in terms of profitability.

The formulae for their calculation are

Contribution per unit = Selling price per unit – Variable cost per unit

Contribution per unit x Number of units sold = Total Contribution

Total Contribution = Total fixed costs + Profit

Profit = Total contribution – Total fixed costs

Loss = Total fixed costs – Total contribution

BEP in terms of Units: The break-even point, in terms of units, can be computed by dividing fixed costs by contribution per unit. The formula for break-even point (BEP), in terms of units, is as followss:

$$\textbf{BEP(units)} = \frac{\textbf{Total fixed cost}}{\textbf{Selling price per unit – Variable cost per unit}}$$

or

$$\textbf{BEP(units)} = \frac{\textbf{Total fixed cost}}{\textbf{Contribution per unit}}$$

The above formula is useful to find out break-even point in terms of number of units of sales.

From the above formula, it is evident that the selling price per unit should be higher than the variable cost per unit to have positive break-even point. Suppose, if the variable cost is higher than the selling price, a negative sales volume can be calculated, mathematically, to arrive at break-even point, but is of no help in the real life situation. In case, a firm has no fixed costs, what is the break-even point to that firm? Even if the firm does not produce anything, it does not incur any loss. So, no production level is the first break-even point. This is the safest situation for the firm. At each level, total contribution is equal to profit. So, every sales level will be the break-even point to that firm, if there are no fixed costs to the firm.

Illustration No.1

A firm produces a single product and its selling price is Rs.40. Its variable cost per unit is Rs. 32. Its fixed costs are Rs.2,40,000. What is its break-even point?

Solution:

Selling price per unit = Rs. 40

Variable cost per unit = Rs. 32

Contribution per unit = 8

$$\text{BEP (units)} = \frac{\text{Fixed costs}}{\text{Contribution per unit}} = \frac{2,40,000}{8}$$

= 30,000 units

Proof:

Total Sales	30,000 × 40	= 12,00,000
Total Variable cost	30,000 × 32	= 9,60,000
Contribution	30,000 × 8	= 2,40,000
Fixed costs		2,40,000
Profit		0

BEP in terms of Rupees: The break-even point can be calculated with the following formula:

BEP (in rupees) = BEP (in terms of units) × Selling price per unit

or

$$\textbf{BEP (in rupees)} = \frac{\textbf{Total fixed cost}}{\textbf{1 – (Variable cost per unit/Selling price per unit)}}$$

When we apply the same formula to the illustration No. 1, we can find out the BEP in terms of rupees:

$$\textbf{BEP (in rupees)} = \frac{\textbf{Total fixed cost}}{\textbf{1 – (Variable cost per unit/Selling price per unit)}}$$

$$\text{BEP (in rupees)} = \frac{2,40,000}{1\text{-}(32/40)}$$

$$= \frac{2,40,000}{8/40}$$

= 2,40,000 × 40/8 = 12,00,000

Note to Students: There are various formulae to calculate the same result. It is advisable to remember simple formulae. To facilitate students, required formulae to remember are put in bold.

6.5.2 PV Ratio or Contribution Ratio

PV Ratio is important for studying the profitability of operations of a business. This ratio establishes the relationship between contribution and sales value. PV ratio is useful to calculate the BEP, in terms of rupees. **The term P represents Profit that is equivalent to contribution when calculating BEP, in terms of rupees. The term V refers to Volume of sales.**

$$\textbf{Contribution ratio} = \frac{\textbf{Contribution per Unit}}{\textbf{Selling Price per Unit}}$$

or

PV Ratio

Alternatively,

$$\textbf{PV Ratio} = \frac{\textbf{Change in profit or Contribution}}{\textbf{Change in sales}} \times 100$$

PV Ratio can be used to calculate BEP and ascertain required sales to achieve a desired level of profit.

$$\text{BEP (in terms of Rupees)} = \frac{\textbf{Fixed cost}}{\textbf{PV Ratio}}$$

$$\text{To achieve target sales for a desired profit} = \frac{\textbf{Fixed cost + Desired Profit}}{\textbf{PV Ratio}}$$

Importance of PV Ratio: Management is interested to know which product is more profitable. Organization wants to reward the department, which is working efficiently and pull up the one, that is not working to the level expected. Higher the PV Ratio, more will be the profit. Thus, aim of management is at increasing the PV Ratio, identifying where the action is needed.

PV Ratio indicates availability of margin on sales made. So, firm that enjoys higher PV Ratio stands to gain, when demand for the product is growing.

Change in PV Ratio: If selling price is reduced, P/V Ratio gets reduced. In consequence, Break-even point becomes higher and margin of safety becomes lower. So, the effect of a price reduction is always to reduce P/V Ratio that raises break-even point and shortens margin of safety.

The above concept is explained, with a simple example.

Milk man teaches break—even point: Let us take the example of a milkman. He purchases milk packets @ Rs. 6 per packet and sells at Rs. 10. He distributes milk packets, hiring a motorcycle and the fixed hire charge is Rs. 100 per day. So, contribution per packet is Rs. 4. At this stage, his PV Ratio is 40% (contribution 4% selling price 10). If he sells 25 packets, he become break-even. If he sells 60 packets, his margin of safety is 35 packets (Actual sales 60—sales at break-even point 25)

Suppose, he reduces the selling price to Rs. 8 per packet and continues to sell 60 packets, as earlier. Now, his PV Ratio is 25% (Contribution 2/ selling price 8), As fixed cost is Rs. 100 and contribution is Rs. 2, break-even point is 50 packets. However, as he continues to sell 60 packets his margin of safety is reduced to 10 packets (Actual sales 60 — sales at new break-even point 50).

Now, the margin of safety is reduced to 10 packets, which was at 35 packets, earlier.

This explains reduction of selling price results in the following:

(i) Reduction of PV Ratio (40% reduced to 25%)

(ii) Break—even point is increased (in place of 25 packets, 50 packets are needed) and

(iii) Margin of safety reduced (earlier 35 packets reduced to 10 packets)

This situation is explained through pictorial presentation.

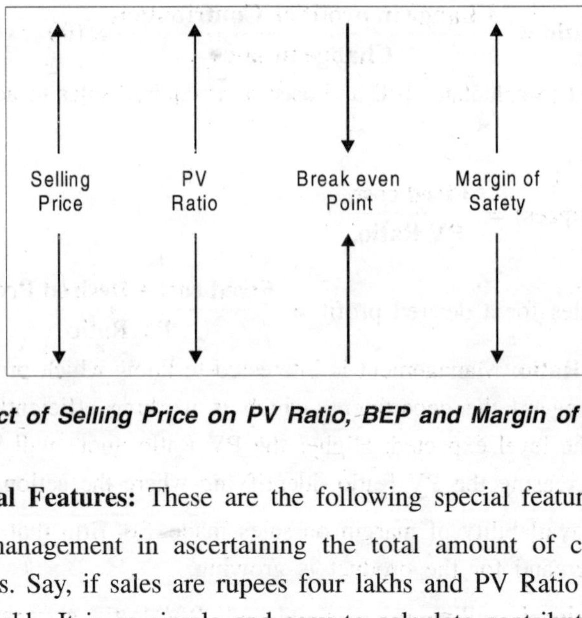

Impact of Selling Price on PV Ratio, BEP and Margin of Safety

Utility and special Features: These are the following special features.

1. It helps the management in ascertaining the total amount of contribution for a given volume of sales. Say, if sales are rupees four lakhs and PV Ratio is 25%, its contribution is rupees one lakh. It is so simple and easy to calculate contribution.
2. When the firm is engaged in producing more than one product, by calculating this ratio for each product, it can concentrate to produce that product which has higher PV Ratio as it gives more profitability. Leaving products that have less PV Ratio, the firm concentrates on those products having higher PV Ratio to boost profitability.

3. Management can increase this ratio by increasing selling price or reducing variable cost of the products.
4. PV Ratio remains constant so long as the selling price and variable cost per unit remain constant or fluctuate in the same proportion.
5. This remains unaffected by any change in the level of activity. In other words, it remains the same whether the sales are 1,000 units or 2,000 units.
6. This ratio also remains unaffected with any change in fixed cost, as they are not considered. It means even if the fixed cost increases or decreases PV ratio remains the same as fixed costs are not taken into account while calculating.
7. The above formula is of immense use to calculate break-even point when the firm is engaged in multiple products. A Multi-product firm experiences difficulty to calculate break-even point in terms of any common unit. Such firms can calculate break-even point, at the time of budgeting and actual sales, in terms of total rupee sales only.

BEP in terms of Capacity: Many firms compute the break-even point in terms of estimated sales or capacity of the manufacturing unit. Dividing the break-even sales with estimated sales or full capacity sales could do this. If break-even sales are, say, rupees ten lakhs and the estimated sales are rupees forty lakhs, the break-even point is 25%.

$$\textbf{BEP (\% of capacity)} = \frac{\textbf{Sales at break-even point}}{\textbf{Estimated sales}}$$

Alternatively, if the total contribution at the estimated sales or full capacity is known, it can be calculated directly.

$$\textbf{BEP (\% of capacity)} = \frac{\textbf{Total fixed cost}}{\textbf{Total contribution at the estimated sales}}$$

Impact of Break-even point: When two firms working with the same amount of sales and equal unit variable cost, with difference in fixed costs, which firm can withstand better? A firm enjoying lower break-even point is always at an advantage as its fixed costs get recovered early and can withstand better compared to a firm with higher break-even point.

BEP to achieve a desired amount of profit: The above formula requires a small change. In the numerator, the desired amount of profit is to be added. The formula is

$$\textbf{BEP (to achieve required amount of profit)} = \frac{\textbf{Total fixed cost + Desired profit}}{\textbf{PV Ratio}}$$

Illustration No. 2:

Calculate the sales required to earn a profit of Rs. 6,00,000 following from the following data:

Fixed Expenses = 1,20,000

Variable cost per unit:

Direct Material	=	Rs. 4
Direct Labour	=	Rs. 2
Direct Overheads	=	50% of Direct Labour
Selling price per unit	=	Rs. 14

Solution:

Selling price per unit		14
Less: Direct Material	4	
Direct Labour	2	
Direct Overheads	1	
	—	7
Contribution per unit		7

$$\text{PV Ratio} = \frac{\text{Contribution}}{\text{Sales}} \times 100$$

$$= \frac{7}{14} \times 100$$

$$= 50\%$$

Sales required to earn a profit of Rs. 6,00,000

$$= \frac{\text{Fixed Expenses + Desired Profit}}{\text{P/V Ratio}}$$

$$= \frac{1,20,000 + 6,00,000}{0.5}$$

$$= 14,40,000$$

Required sales are Rs. 14,40,000 to make a profit of Rs.6,00,000

(B) Break-even Chart or Graphic Method of Break-even analysis

The break-even point can be presented graphically. The pictorial presentation gives a better view of the relationship of cost, volume and profit. Graphical presentation gives immediate and clear understanding of the picture. This type of presentation always impresses the management as it gives instantaneous understanding of the situation.

The graphical chart of break-even analysis looks like this:

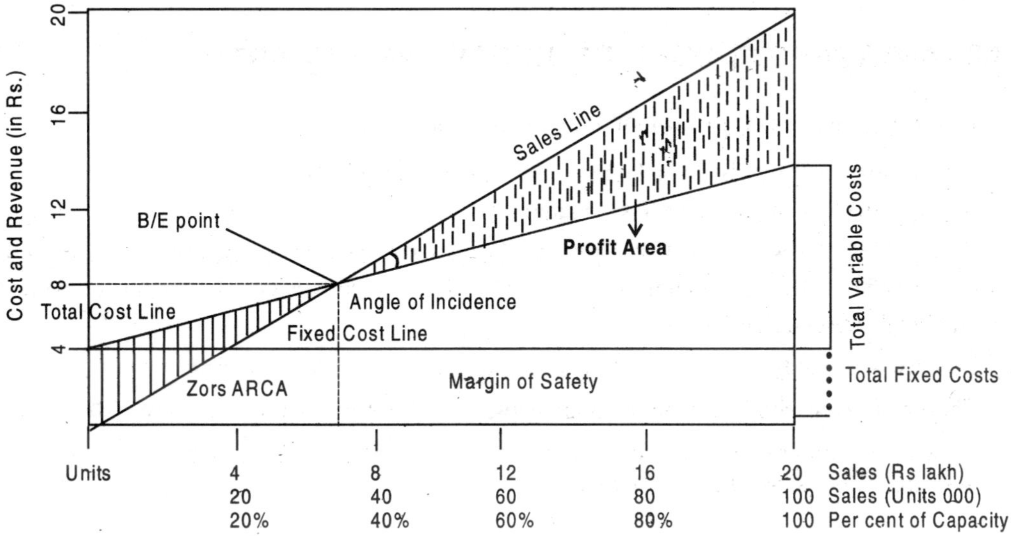

Break-even Chart

Following are the steps involved in preparing break-even chart:

1. Sales volume is plotted on the horizontal line i.e. X axis. Sales volume may be expressed in terms of units, rupees or as a percentage of capacity.
2. Vertical line i.e. Y axis is used to represent revenue, fixed costs and variable costs.
3. Both horizontal and vertical lines are spaced equally with the same distances.
4. The fixed cost line can be drawn parallel to the horizontal line.
5. A parallel line should be drawn to the vertical line.
6. Total sales line and Total cost line are drawn by plotting on the right hand vertical line.
7. As the vertical and horizontal lines are spaced equally, Total sales line and Total cost line intersect forming an angle of 45 degrees.

6.5.3 Angle of Incidence

The break-even point is indicated where the Total cost line and Total sales line intersect each other. The angle that is formed with their intersection is called 'Angle of incidence'. **Larger the angle of incidence, lower is the break-even point and vice versa.** A lower break-even point is an indication that the firm can withstand even if the sales fall. Firm does not go into loss immediately and remains, at least, with a small amount of profit.

Area of Contribution: Profit area is shown on the right side when total sales line is in excess of the total cost line while loss area is shown when the total cost line is above the total sales line. The variable cost is represented by the gap between the total cost line and fixed cost line.

6.6. ADVANTAGES OR USES OF BREAK-EVEN CHART

Following are the advantages or uses of break-even chart:

1. It is simple to form. Even a layman can understand, clearly.
2. It helps the management to take managerial decisions because the effects of changes in fixed cost and variable cost at various levels of output can be depicted, in a meaningful manner. The effect of changes in selling price on profits can be better explained by graphical presentation.
3. It is used to study the comparative profitability of various products.
4. The break-even chart is a better managerial tool for forecasting, planning and control.
5. Besides determining the break-even point, profit at various levels of output can be determined with the help of break-even charts.

6.7 ASSUMPTIONS OF BREAK-EVEN ANALYSIS

The break-even analysis is based on the following assumptions:

1. **Costs segregation:** It is based on the assumption that all costs can be segregated into fixed costs and variable costs.
2. **Constant Selling Price:** The selling price remains constant. That is, it does not change with volume or other factors.
3. **Constant Fixed costs:** Fixed costs are constant at all levels of activity. They do not change with change in sales.
4. **Constant Variable costs:** Variable cost per unit is constant. So, variable costs fluctuate, directly, in proportion to changes in volume of output. In other words, they change in direct proportion to sales volume.
5. **Synchronised production and sales:** It is assumed production and sales are synchronised. That is, inventories remain the same in the opening stock and closing stock.
6. **Constant sales mix:** Only one product is manufactured. Otherwise, sales mix of products sold does not change.
7. **No Change in operating efficiency:** There is no change in operating efficiency.
8. **No other factors:** The volume of output or production is the only factor that influences the cost. No other factors have any influence on break-even analysis.

6.8 LIMITATIONS OF BREAK-EVEN ANALYSIS AND BREAK-EVEN CHARTS

Despite many advantages, break-even analysis and charts suffer from the following limitations:

1. **Number of Assumptions:** Break-even analysis is based on several assumptions and they may not hold well under all circumstances. Fixed costs are presumed to be constant, irrespective of the level of output. It does not happen. When the production increases above the installed capacity, fixed costs change as new plant and machinery has to be installed for increased production. Variable costs do not vary in direct proportion to the change in volume of output due to the laws of diminishing and increasing returns. Selling price that is supposed to be constant, changes due to increased competition.
2. **Application in Short run:** Break-even analysis is a short run analysis. In long run, the cost analysis may not hold good as the assumptions may vary and situation may be totally different.
3. **Applicable in Single Product line:** This analysis is applicable for a single product only. If break-even point for each product is to be calculated, fixed costs have to be allocated to different products, which is a practical problem in the real life. Otherwise, BEP for the overall firm only is possible to calculate.
4. **No Remedial Action:** It does not suggest any remedy or action to the management for solving the problem.
5. **Other Factors ignored:** Other important factors such as amount of investment, problems of marketing and policies of Government influence the problem. Break-even analysis does not consider them. This analysis focuses only on cost-profit relationship.
6. **Limited information:** Break-even charts provide limited information. If we want to study the effects of changes in fixed costs, variable costs and selling prices on profitability, a number of charts have to be drawn. It becomes rather more complicated and difficult to understand.
7. **Static View:** More often, a break-even chart presents a static view of the problem under consideration.

Despite the limitations, it has great application for the basic problem of understanding the inter relationship of cost, volume and price on profits.

6.9 MARGIN OF SAFETY

The excess of actual or budgeted sales over the Break-even sales are called 'Margin of safety'. It is the difference between actual sales minus break-even sales.

Margin of safety = Estimated sales n Sales at Break-even point

It represents the amount of safety to the firm. If the firm makes break-even at 40% of its capacity, its margin of safety is 60%. Suppose, if the firm is able to break-even at a sale level of rupees ten lakhs and its actual sales are rupees forty lakhs, its margin of safety is rupees thirty lakhs. It means if the sales fall by rupees thirty lakhs, still, the firm does not incur loss. Higher the margin of safety, it is better for the firm. When two firms are compared, the firm having higher margin of safety can withstand any adverse conditions, such as fall in demand for the product or even recession.

Margin of safety ratio can be calculated as under:

$$\textbf{Margin of safety ratio} = \frac{\textbf{Actual sales – Break-even sales}}{\textbf{Actual sales}} \times 100$$

As margin of safety is the volume of sales beyond the break-even sales point, all the sales above the break-even point give some profit, which can be calculated as:

Profit = Margin of safety X P/V Ratio

OR

$$\textbf{Margin of safety} = \frac{\textbf{Profit}}{\textbf{p/V Ratio}}$$

The size of margin of safety is an important indicator of the strength of business. If the margin of safety is large, the firm can withstand fall of sales and can continue to be in some profit. If the margin of safety is thin, decline of sales would seriously affect the profit of business and may run into losses.

Steps to improve Margin of Safety: The margin of safety can be improved by taking the following steps:

1. Increasing the level of production and sales
2. Increasing the selling price
3. Reducing fixed costs
4. Reducing the variable cost
5. Substituting profitable products with the unprofitable products
6. Changing the business mix to improve contribution and dropping unprofitable products

6.10 CASH BREAK-EVEN POINT

Many a time, it is difficult for the industrial units to become break-even in the initial years. From that environment, the concept of cash-break even point has emerged. **The Cash break-even point may be defined as that point of sales volume where revenues are equal to cash costs.** Depreciation is, generally, a fixed cost. However, when plant and machinery is used for additional shifts, the additional depreciation is a variable cost. Reason for treating the additional depreciation as variable cost is the firm can avoid additional shift, at any time, and in such circumstances this cost would not be incurred. To calculate the cash-break even point, depreciation element (Additional depreciation component) is to be excluded from the fixed cost as well as variable cost. Similarly, deferred expenses are to be excluded from the fixed cost.

Thus, cash-break even point may be calculated as below:

$$\text{Cash break-even Point (in terms of units)} = \frac{\text{Cash Fixed Cost}}{\text{Cash Contribution per unit}}$$

Illustration No. 3

From the following information, calculate cash-break point.

Selling price per unit	60
Variable cost per unit	40
Additional Depreciation included in variable cost per unit	5
Fixed cost	1,50,000
Depreciation included in Fixed cost	25,000

Solution:

Cash fixed cost = 1,50,000-25,000

= 1,25,000

Cash Contribution per unit = 60- (40-5) = 25

$$\text{Cash break-even Point (in terms of units)} = \frac{\text{Cash Fixed Cost}}{\text{Cash Contribution per unit}}$$

$$= \frac{1{,}25{,}000}{25}$$

= 5,000 units

Cash break-even point (in sales value) = 5,000 × 60 = Rs. 3,00,000

6.11 MULTI-PRODUCT BREAK-EVEN POINT (COMPOSITE BREAK-EVEN POINT)

If a firm produces more than one product, it is known as Multi-product firm. As the firm is producing various products, the relative proportion of sales of different products is called the sales mix or product mix. In the case of a Multi-product firm, contribution of each product can be calculated by deducting variable cost from the individual revenue of the product. If contribution of all the products is aggregated, firm's total contribution can be arrived at. **The firm's overall break-even point can be calculated by dividing the total contribution by the total sales volume of the firm.**

$$\text{Composite Break-even point (in Rs.)} = \frac{\text{Total Fixed Cost}}{\text{Composite P/V Ratio}}$$

$$\text{Composite PV Ratio} = \frac{\text{Total Contribution}}{\text{Total Sales}} \times 100$$

P/V ratio of each product can be calculated without distributing the fixed costs of the firm over the different products. So, it is not, really, important to calculate the cost-volume-profit interrelations to allocate fixed costs to individual product lines. Even without allocating of fixed costs, individual product contribution can be calculated to decide priority amongst different products to take advantage of the available production capacity and maximise profits of the firm.

Illustration No. 4

The following data of Kish & Co. for the period ending 31st March, 2006 is as under:

	Product A	Product B	Product C
Sales	10,00,000	4,00,000	6,00,000
Variable Costs	6,00,000	2,80,000	4,00,000

Total Fixed costs are Rs. 2,00,000. You are required to calculate contribution of each product, firm's composite break-even point, profit and PV Ratio.

Solution:

	Product A	Product B	Product C	Total
Sales Mix	50%	20%	30%	100%
Sales Revenue	10,00,000	4,00,000	6,00,000	20,00,000
Variable Cost	6,00,000	2,80,000	4,00,000	12,80,000
Contribution	4,00,000	1,20,000	2,00,000	7,20,000
Fixed Cost				2,00,000
Net Profit				5,20,000
P/V Ratio	40%	30%	33.33%	36%
BEP for the firm (Rs.)				$\frac{\text{Total Fixed cost}}{\text{PV Ratio}}$
				$\frac{2,00,000}{0.36}$
				= 5,55,556

The firm's PV Ratio is 36%. i.e. $\frac{7,20,000}{20,00,000}$

This is the weighted average of the PV ratios for the individual products i.e. (40% × 50%) + (20% × 30%) + (30% × 33.33%)

Illustration No. 5

You are required to calculate the break-even point from the following information:

Selling price per unit	Rs. 20
Variable cost per unit	Rs. 04
Fixed costs for the year	Rs. 80,000
Estimated sales for the period	Rs. 2,00,000

The number of units involved coincides with the expected volume of output.

Calculate the margin of safety and advice its impact if there is a fall demand in business.

(B. U, Bhopal , MBA-2002)

Solution:

Selling price per unit	Rs. 20
Variable cost per unit	Rs. 04
Contribution per unit	Rs. 16

$$\text{Break-even point} = \frac{\text{Fixed costs}}{\text{Contribution}}$$

$$= \frac{80,000}{16} = 5,000 \text{ units}$$

Estimated sales for the period = Rs. 2,00,000

Selling price per unit = Rs. 20

$$\text{So, number of units expected to be sold} = \frac{\text{Estimated sales for the period}}{\text{Selling price per unit}}$$

$$= \frac{2,00,000}{20} = 10,000 \text{ units}$$

Expected sales = 10,000 units

Sales at Break-even point = 5,000 units

Margin of Safety (In terms of Units) = Expected sales – Sales at Break even point

= 10,000 – 5,000 = 5,000 units

Margin of Safety (In terms of Rupees) = Sales at BEP (in units) × Selling price per unit

= 5,000 × 20 = Rs. 1,00,000

$$\text{Margin of Safety (in terms of capacity)} = \frac{\text{Sales at break-even point}}{\text{Estimated sales}}$$

$$= \frac{5,000}{10,000}$$

= 50% capacity

Break-even point is 50% of the expected sales, in terms of number of Units (sales).

So, margin of safety is 50%. A high margin of safety indicates the soundness of business. Even if there is some fall in sales, still, the firm can withstand the loss. If the sales of the firm decline by Rs. 1,00,000, still the firm would not suffer any loss.

Illustration No. 6

The sales and profits of a company during two periods were as follows:

Period	Sales	Profit
I	1,00,000	10,000
II	1,50,000	20,000

(i) Find out the P/V ratio.

(ii) What amount of sales will generate a profit of Rs. 40,000?

(iii) What will be the profit if the sales are Rs. 1,20,000?

(B.U. Bhopal – MBA, 2003)

Solution:

(i) P/V Ratio $= \frac{\text{Change in profit}}{\text{Change in sales}} \times 100$

$= \frac{10,000}{50,000} \times 100$

$= 20\%$

(ii) Calculation of sales to generate a profit of Rs. 40,000:

P/V Ratio $= \frac{\text{Contribution}}{\text{Sales}}$

Contribution = Fixed Cost + Profits

P/V Ratio $= \frac{\text{Fixed Cost + Profit}}{\text{Sales}}$

Problem states sales of Rs. 1,00,000 gives a profit of Rs. 10,000

So, $20\% = \frac{\text{Fixed Cost + 10,000}}{1,00,000}$

$\frac{20}{100} = \frac{\text{Fixed Cost + 10,000}}{1,00,000}$

$(0.2) \times 1,00,000$ = Fixed cost + 10,000

Fixed cost = 20,000 –10,000

$$= 10{,}000$$

$$\text{Desired sales} = \frac{\text{Fixed Cost + Desired Profit}}{\text{P/V}}$$

$$= \frac{10{,}000 + 40{,}000}{\text{P/V Ratio}}$$

$$= \frac{50{,}000}{0.2}$$

$$= 2{,}50{,}000$$

So, Sales of Rs. 2,50,000 are needed to earn a profit of Rs. 40,000

(iii) Calculation of profit if sales are Rs. 1,20,000

$$\text{P/V Ratio} = \frac{\text{Fixed cost + Profit}}{\text{Sales}}$$

$$0.2 = \frac{10{,}000 + \text{Profit}}{1{,}20{,}000}$$

$$(0.2) \times 1{,}20{,}000 = 10{,}000 + \text{Profit}$$

$$\text{Profit} = 24{,}000 - 10{,}000$$

$$= 14{,}000$$

If sales are Rs. 1,20,000 profits would be Rs. 14,000

Illustration No. 7

Two firms, X Ltd. and Y Ltd sell identical products in the same market. Their budgeted profit and loss accounts for the year ending on 30th June 19XI are as follows:

	X Ltd		Y Ltd	
		Rs.		Rs.
Sales		4,00,000		4,00,000
Less: Variable cost	3,20,000		2,80,000	
Fixed cost	40,000	3,60,000	80,000	3,60,000
Net Profit		40,000		40,000

You are required to:

(a) Calculate the break-even point for each firm and

(b) State what shall be the likely effect on the profits of the firms in conditions of

(i) increasing demand for the products

(ii) falling demand for the products.

(c) Calculate the sales volume at which each business will earn Rs. 50,000 profit;

(B.U. Bhopal MBA- 2000)

Solution:

(a)

		X Ltd	Y Ltd
Sales		4,00,000	4,00,000
Less: Variable cost		3,20,000	2,80,000
Contribution		80,000	1,20,000
Fixed cost		40,000	80,000
PV Ratio	$\frac{\text{Contribution}}{\text{Sales}}\times 100$	$\frac{80,000}{4,00,000}\times 100$ = 20%	$\frac{1,20,000}{4,00,000}\times 100$ = 30%
Break-even point	$\frac{\text{Fixed cost}}{\text{PV Ratio}}$	$\frac{40,000}{20\%}$ = 2,00,000	$\frac{80,000}{30\%}$ = 2,66,667

(b)

(i) Effect on the profits of the firms in conditions of increasing demand for the products:

PV Ratio of X Ltd is 20% while it is 30% in case of Y Ltd. In case of high demand, Y Ltd will be in a position to earn higher profit because PV ratio is higher. PV Ratio indicates availability of margin on sales made. So, firm that enjoys higher PV Ratio stands to gain, when demand for the product is growing.

(ii) Effect on the profits of the firms in conditions of falling demand for the products:

Break-even point of X Ltd is 2,00,000 while it is 2,66,667 in case of Y Ltd.

Firm that has a low break even point would be in a position to withstand even if there is a fall in sales. So, X Ltd would have more profits, compared to Y Ltd, if there is a corresponding fall in sales to both the firms.

(c) Sales volume at which each business will earn Rs. 50,000 profit;

Sales required to earn a profit of Rs. 50,000

$$= \frac{\text{Fixed Expenses + Desired Profit}}{\text{P/V Ratio}}$$

$$\text{X Ltd} = \frac{40{,}000 + 50{,}000}{20\%}$$

$$= 4{,}50{,}000$$

$$\text{Y Ltd} = \frac{80{,}000 + 50{,}000}{30\%}$$

$$= 4{,}33{,}333$$

Objective Questions

1. What do you understand by the term cost-volume-profit relationship? Why is this relationship important in financial decision making? **(B.U, Bhopal, MBA- 2003) (6.1 and 6.2)**
2. What is CVP analysis? Explain its utility to management in decision making process? **(6.1 and 6.2)**
3. 'Profit volume analysis' is a technique of analysing the relationship of cost and profit at various levels of volume? Explain how such analysis helps the management in decision making? (6.1 and **6.2)**
4. Discuss the behaviour of fixed and variable costs in relation to volume? **(6.3)**
5. 'Break-even point is the point at which total cost and revenue are just equal' – Discuss? **(6.5 and 6.6)**
6. What is meant by contribution? How it is calculated? Discuss its role in the profit-decision making? **(6.5.2)**
7. "The break-even analysis is a useful device of profit planning." Do you agree? Discuss? **(B.U., Bhopal, MBA - 2000) (6. 5and 6.6)**
8. What is Break-even point? How would you compute it? **(6.5)**
9. "Business firms rarely operate at their break-even points. Therefore, the break-even analysis is of very limited use to the management." Is it correct? Discuss? **(6.1, 6.2 and 6.5)**
10. Discuss PV Ratio and its features to assist management in break-even analysis and achieving the desired level of profit? **(6.5.2)**
11. Would it be really important for the cost-volume-profit interrelations to allocate fixed costs to individual product lines? Defend your answer? **(B.U, Bhopal –2005) (6.2 and 6.11)**
12. Discuss the assumptions and limitations of break-even analysis? **(6.5, 6.7 and 6.8)**
13. Write short notes on:
    (A) Margin of safety **(6.9)**
    (B) Angle of Incidence **(6.5.3)**
    (C) Cash break-even point **(6.10)**
    (D) Multi product break-even point **(6.11)**

Check your understanding

Please state whether the following statements are True or False

1. CVP analysis helps the firm in understanding the impact of change in cost, volume and price on the behaviour of profit.
2. Break-even analysis is fundamentally a static analysis.
3. With the help of CVP analysis, it is possible to decide which product is most profitable and least profitable.
4. Mathematically, a linear relationship does not exist between a variable cost and volume of production.
5. Contribution is also known as Gross Margin.
6. At break even point, contribution covers total fixed costs and leaves a little towards profit.
7. It is not possible to calculate break-even analysis of the firm if the firm is engaged in producing and selling multiple products.
8. In break-even analysis, fixed costs and variable costs do not behave in the same manner.
9. In break-even analysis, unit variable cost decreases as and when the volume of production increases.
10. A large margin of safety indicates that the business is sound and even if there is some fall in sales, there will be profit.
11. Angle of incidence is the angle between the sales line and the total cost line formed at the break-even point.
12. Margin of safety = $\frac{\text{Fixed expenses}}{\text{P/V Ratio}}$
13. PV Ratio can be used to calculate BEP and ascertain required sales to achieve a desired level of profit.

Answers

1. True.	2. False.	3. True.	4. False	5. True
6. False	7. False	8. True	9. False	10. True
11. True	12. False	13. True		

(B) Pick up the right answer:

1. In the graphical presentation of break-even analysis, larger the angle of incidence ..... is the break-even point.
   (A) Lower
   (B) Higher
   (C) Similar
2. Angle of incidence is formed in break-even analysis when the intersection occurs between:
   (A) Fixed cost line and Sales line
   (B) Total cost line and Sales line
   (C) Fixed cost line and Total cost line

3. If Margin of safety is ….., the firm cannot withstand, if there is a large fall in sales.
   (A) Low
   (B) High
   (C) Does not exist
4. Margin of safety and break-even point are inter-connected
   (A) Yes
   (B) No
   (C) No relation exists
5. Contribution would occur early to a firm if fixed costs are ….
   (A) High
   (B) Low
   (C) Not relevant
6. P/V Ratio can be improved by reducing fixed costs.
   (A) True
   (B) False
   (C) No change

Answers

1. (A) 2. (B) 3. (A) 4. (A) 5. (B)
6. (B)

7

LEVERAGES

7.1 INTRODUCTION

It is the duty of finance manager in every firm to estimate the requirement of funds and procure them, at economic cost. There are various alternative sources to raise the funds. Sources are many and so costs are also different. In respect of some funds, firm has to pay fixed cost like interest on debentures while the return to shareholders varies, if the same amount is raised in the form of share capital. The finance manager has to determine the best mix of such funds or decide about the capital structure of the concern. The structure, finally, chosen influences the risk and return to the firm. **Leverage analysis is the technique used by the business firms to quantify the risk-return relationship of different alternative capital structures.**

7.2 MEANING OF LEVERAGE

The dictionary meaning of the term 'Leverage' refers to "an increased means for accomplishing some purpose." For example, leverage helps us in lifting heavy objects, which may not otherwise be possible. With a small amount of force in a particular direction, a heavy stone can be moved in a different direction, which is not possible if the same force is applied, directly. What we have done is application of leverage for moving the big stone. The concept of leverage is valid in business too. Simply, the term 'Leverage' means 'To improve or enhance'.

In general terms, leverage may be defined as relative change in profits **due to a change in sales.** A high degree of leverage implies that a large change in profits occurs for a relatively small change in sales.

In the area of finance, the term 'leverage' has a special meaning. **The term leverage is used to describe the firm's ability to use fixed cost assets or funds to magnify the returns to owners i.e. equity shareholders.**

Definition: James Horne has defined leverage as "the employment of an asset or funds for which the firm pays a fixed cost or fixed return".

Concept of Leverage: The term leverage, in general, refers to the relationship between two interrelated variables. In financial matters, one financial variable influences another variable. Those financial variables may be cost, sales revenue, earnings before interest and Tax (EBIT), output, earnings per share etc. In the leverage analysis, the emphasis is on the measurement of the relationship of the two variables, rather than on measuring the variables.

$$\textbf{Leverage :} \frac{\textbf{\% Change in dependent variable}}{\textbf{\% Change in independent variable}}$$

For example, a firm has increased sales promotion expenses from

Rs. 2,000 to Rs. @ 2,500 i.e. an increase of 25%. This has resulted in increase of sales from Rs. 40,000 to Rs. 60,000 i.c. an increase of 50%. The leverage between the promotional expenses and sales can be defined as:

$$\textbf{Leverage} = \frac{\textbf{\% Change in sales (dependant variable)}}{\textbf{\% Change in sales promotion expenses (independent variable)}}$$

$$= \frac{0.50}{0.25} = 2$$

This means that % increase in sales is 2 times that of increase in sales promotion expenses. If one hundred rupees sales promotion expenses were incurred, sales would increase by rupees two hundred.

7.3 TYPES OF LEVERAGES

Leverage is of there types:

(i) Operating Leverage,

(ii) Financial Leverage and

(iii) Combined Leverage

7.4 OPERATING LEVERAGE

Operating Leverage refers to the use of fixed costs in the operation of a firm. Due to the presence of fixed costs, (rent, salaries, insurance etc) operating Leverage results. Fixed costs do not change with sales. On account of fixed costs, the operating profit changes, disproportionately, with sales. In other words, increase or decrease in operating profit does not occur, proportionately, with sales.

A firm is said to have higher degree of operating leverage if it employs a higher proposition of fixed costs and smaller proportion of variable costs in the cost structure. On the other hand, a firm will have a low operating leverage when it employs a greater proportion of variable costs and a lesser proportion of fixed costs. Thus, **the degree of operating leverage depends upon the proportion of fixed element in the cost structure.**

Factors that Influence Operating Leverage: Operating leverage is a function of three factors in any firm:

1. The amount of fixed costs.
2. The contribution Margin.
3. The volume of Sales.

There will be no operating leverage, if there are no fixed costs. A firm will not have operating leverage if the ratio of fixed costs to total costs is nil. To such a firm, a given percentage of increase in sales produces the same percentage of operating profits i.e. EBIT.

Degree of Operating leverage: The degree of operating leverage may be defined as the percentage change in operating profit, resulting from a percentage of change in sales. It is calculated at a particular level of sales. It can be presented as a formula, as under:

$$\textbf{Degree of operating leverage} = \frac{\textbf{Contribution}}{\textbf{EBIT}}$$

Contribution = Sales – Variable Cost

EBIT = Contribution – Fixed Cost.

Alternative formula is

$$\textbf{Degree of operating leverage} = \frac{\%\ \text{Change in EBIT}}{\%\ \text{Change in Sales}} = \frac{\Delta\ \text{EBIT}/\text{EBIT}}{\Delta\ \text{Sales}/\text{Sales}}$$

Where, Δ (called delta) is change.

Here, operating profit and EBIT mean the same, in the as sank of other won-operating income.

Utility: The operating leverage indicates the impact of change in sales on operating income. Suppose, operating leverage is 2, it indicates if sales increases by 100%, operating income would increase by 200%.

Favourable & Unfavourable Leverage: Operating leverage may be favourable or unfavourable.

In case, contribution exceeds the fixed costs, there is favourable operating leverage. In the reverse situation, when fixed cost exceeds contribution, the operating leverage is termed as unfavourable leverage.

High Degree Operating Leverage: If a firm has a high degree of operating leverage, the percentage of change in operating income will be more than the percentage of change in sales. In other words, a small percentage of increase in sales results in a higher percentage of increase in operating income. As operating income (EBIT) is affected, increase or decrease also results in net income. Similarly, when the sales of a firm fall, a smaller percentage of fall in sales results in a larger percentage of fall in operating income.

A high operating leverage factor indicates the presence of automated production processes as heavy amounts are, normally, involved in fixed assets.

Operating Leverage is a Double Edged Sword: Operating profit of a highly leveraged firm would increase at a faster rate for any given increase in sales. However, if sales fall, the firm with a higher operating leverage would suffer more loss than the firm with no or low operating leverage. This is a very risky situation. **Operating leverage is a double-edged sword.**

Typical Examples: A retail firm and an airline are typical examples of low and high operating leverage. Proportion of fixed costs in the total cost structure is low in a retail firm, as the amount of investment is more on inventory, with a small investment in furniture and other fixed assets to support the business. So, to a retail firm, a small increase in sales does not produce a bigger increase in operating profit, due to low proportion of fixed cost in the total cost structure. To an airline, amount of fixed costs in the total cost structure is very high. Firm with high degree of operating leverage is more vulnerable to change in sales. So, profit is highly sensitive to the increase in revenue and passengers carried in an airline. Percentage of increase in revenue to an airline firm produces a higher percentage of operating profit. This is the reason why unsold tickets are sold at a cheap rate when the flight is about to depart to increase the operating profit. A retail firm and an airline are typical examples of low and high operating leverage, respectively.

Impact of Market Conditions on Operating Leverage

Times of Rising Prices or Inflation: During the time of inflation, sales of all firms rise. When sales are rising, the firms with high degree of operating leverage benefit more, in terms of increased profit. The percentage of increase in operating profit would be more than the percentage of increase in sales. Similarly, when sales are falling during depression or declining prices, firm with high operating leverage loses more. Indeed, during the later times, high operating leverage becomes a nuisance.

Firms having low operating leverage neither make money during inflation nor lose in the times of depression due to their special feature of low operating leverage.

Normal Conditions: When market conditions are normal, firm that has high degree of operating leverage would benefit more, if sales increase. Presumed, operating leverage is 3. For every 100% increase in sales, operating profit increase by 300%. Of course, if sales dip, its operating profit would dip by similar percentage too. However, as market conditions are normal, stable growth in sales can only be expected, normally. Firm that has high degree of operating leverage can gain advantage. **So, it is desirable for the firm to have high degree of operating leverage under normal market conditions.**

Impact of Technology: Whenever a company has to face the choice of technology, the company that opts capital-intensive technology incurs high fixed costs and low variable costs. On the other hand, low automated technology firms and production processes may involve less fixed costs and high variable costs. So, capital-intensive firms have higher operating leverage and so are more vulnerable. Low automated firms have lower operating leverage and are not so vulnerable.

Option of Higher Operating Leverage or Higher Operating Profit: If choice is to be made between higher operating leverage and higher operating profit, it is better to choose for a firm to have higher operating profit rather than having higher operating leverage. Reason is firm having higher operating leverage is vulnerable, in case sales fall due to high fixed costs. That firm suffers more loss, in case of decline in sales.

Significance of Operating Leverage: Operating leverage tells the impact of sales on income. Depending on the operating leverage, a given percentage of increase in sales results in a higher percentage of increase in operating income and net profit. Equally, a decline in sales may wipe out the operating profit or turn into loss, even.

If the fixed costs were higher, the operating leverage as well as operating risk of the firm would be higher. So, the break-even point of firm would also be high with low margin of safety.

The point is when the operating leverage can be said to be high. It is only a comparison of the firm with the industry to the category it belongs to.

7.5 FINANCIAL LEVERAGE

A firm would raise funds at the initial set up and subsequent expansion or diversification plans. Funds may be raised through two sources, in the form of owners' equity and external equity.

Owner's equity is share capital and reserves. External equity could be long term loans and debentures. Various means used to raise funds represent the capital structure of the firm.

Financing is a crucial matter in every business and, as a general rule, there should be a proper mix of debt and equity capital. **The use of long term** interest / fixed dividend bearing securities such as debt and preference share capital along with equity share capital is called financial leverage.

The process of magnifying equity shareholder's earnings through the use of low cost debt is known as 'Trading Equity'.

Purpose of Financial Leverage: The financial leverage is employed by a company to earn more on the fixed charges' funds than their costs. The surplus increases the return on total equity. An example clears the picture better. For example, if a company borrows Rs.100 at 10% per annum and earns 15% return (that is, Rs.15 per annum), after paying interest 10%, the balance 5% (Rs.5 per annum) belongs to the equity shareholders. In case, firm is able to earn only 8% per annum, the deficit 2% reduces the earnings of the shareholders. Thus, financial leverage provides the potentials of increasing the shareholders' earnings as well as creating risks to them. It is a double-edged sword.

So, both Operating Leverage and Financial Leverage are double-edged swords.

Measures of Financial Leverage: Debt ratio, Debt-equity ratio and interest coverage ratio are the measures of financial leverage, which have been discussed in detail in the Ratio Analysis, already. In the capital structure of the company, if the use of fixed interest/ dividend bearing securities is greater than the equity share capital of the company, the leverage is said to be larger. In a reverse case, the leverage is said to be smaller.

Degree of Financial leverage: The degree of financial leverage is defined as:

$$\textbf{Degree of Financial leverage} = \frac{\textbf{EBIT}}{\textbf{Profit before Tax}}$$

$$\textbf{Alternative formula is} = \frac{\textbf{\% Change in EPS}}{\textbf{\% Change in EBIT}}$$

Computation of profit before tax when share capital consists of Preference share capital: When share capital consists of preference shares, amount of preference dividend has to be grossed up (as per the tax rate applicable to the company) and deducted from EBIT to arrive profit before tax, **from the viewpoint of equity shareholders.** Reason is preference dividend is paid from profits, after payment of taxes. If tax rate is 30% and Rs.10 lakhs are 7% Preference share capital, preference dividend is Rs.70,000, available only after payment of tax. As we are to calculate profit before tax for the formula, this amount requires adjustment. So, if 70% (profit after tax) is Rs. 70,000 then 100% (profit before tax) would be Rs. one lakh. So, Rupees one lakh is to be deducted from operating profit (EBIT).

Income Tax Shield: Financial leverage is caused due to the use of fixed interest charge funds. Interest charges are also tax deductible. This income tax shield increases the earnings of the shareholders.

Utility: Financial leverage helps considerably the finance manager in designing the capital structure of the firm. **Financial leverage shows the impact of operating income on taxable income, in the same direction.** Assumed, the financial leverage is 2. It indicates if operating income increases by 100%, taxable profits increases by 200%.

Relationship between Financial Leverage and Financial Risk: For a given degree of variability of EBIT, the variability of EPS (and ROE) increases with more financial leverage. The variability of EPS by the financial leverage is called financial risk. The financial risk of two firms differs when the assets are financed, differently. Financial risk arises when the assets are financed by debt. A totally equity financed firm does not have financial risk. Financial risk is avoidable if the firm decides to finance the assets, totally, with equity.

7.6 MIX OF OPERATING LEVERAGE AND FINANCIAL LEVERAGE

Both operating leverage and financial leverage are quantitative tools to measure the return to the owners. The right combination is a great challenge to the management. A proper combination of both operating leverage and financial leverage is, indeed, a blessing for the firm's growth while an improper combination is a curse.

Now, the question is what is the right mix? There is no right mix; it all depends on the risk-bearing capacity and approach of the firm. A high operating leverage indicates presence of high fixed costs due to investment of heavy amount in fixed assets. A high financial leverage is an indication that it's financing is, largely, by debt capital. The fixed costs towards using the assets and fixed interest charges bring a greater business and financial risk to the firm. A firm with fluctuating earnings cannot afford to take such risk. So, a firm must make all possible efforts to combine the operating and financial leverage to suit its risk-bearing capacity.

A firm with high operating leverage should not have a high financial leverage. **The ideal situation is to have a low operating leverage and high financial leverage, provided the firm has enough profitable opportunities.** If the firm opts to have low operating leverage and low financial leverage, it shows the cautious policy of the management and, of course, the firm may be losing certain profitable business opportunities in this process.

Finally, the mix of financial and operative leverage shows the aggressive, cautious or prudent policy of the management.

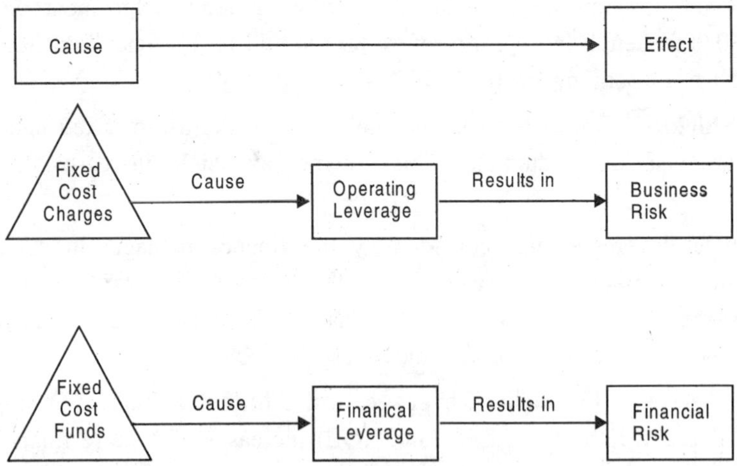

Operating Leverage and Financial Leverage —Cause and Effect

7.7 TRADING ON EQUITY

The aim of the finance manager is to increase the revenue available to the equity shareholders. A finance manager has to perform 'Financing Function' as well as 'Investment Function'. Funds are needed for the investment of projects. The required funds can be raised by way of equity alone or through the combination of debt and equity. The mix adopted for debt and equity in the capital structure of the organisation is significant. The process of magnifying the shareholder's earnings through the process of debt is called **'Trading on Equity', otherwise also known as Financial Leverage or Financial Gearing.** The objective is to give a high rate of return to the equity shareholders, above the general rate of earning on capital employed, in the company to compensate them for the risk they bear. **The term 'Trading on equity' is used for the financial leverage only when the financial leverage is favourable.** In other words, the quotient (financial leverage) should be more than one. Financial leverage could be positive as well as negative. But, Trading on equity is always positive.

Financial leverage shows the impact on EPS. Trading on equity shows the Impact on ROE.

Impact of Financial Leverage on Shareholders' Return: Interest is a fixed commitment, which must be paid irrespective of revenue earnings. The preference share capital also bears a fixed rate of dividend. However, the dividend to preference shareholders is paid only when there is a surplus in earnings. If the earnings of debt were more than cost, the leverage would be positive or favourable. If the revenue earned by the fixed cost funds is more than their cost (interest and / or preference dividend), the residual would be available to the equity shareholders. As the surplus earnings belong to the equity shareholders, earnings per share (EPS) increase and also return on equity (ROE) also increases. On the contrary, if the cost of debt is more than the earnings of debt, leverage would be negative or unfavourable. Then, earnings of equity shareholders get reduced and, in turn, return on equity and earnings per share also go down.

So, so long as return on investment (ROI) is greater than the cost of debt, the financial leverage is favourable. Otherwise, it gives a negative impact.

A simple example would explain the concept, clearer. A firm is raising funds by way of debentures at 8% per annum to employ them for earning. Its return on the project is 12% per annum. The firm pays the debenture holders only 8%, as committed, and leaves the balance 4% to equity shareholders. Additionally, the firm enjoys tax advantage on the interest paid. In case, the firm's earning, subsequently, is reduced to 6% per annum, still the firm has to pay 6% committed interest to the debenture holders and the loss of 2% has to be suffered by the equity holders. This borrowing is resorted to maximise the earning of the equity holders. The additional gain is for the risk taken by the equity share holders to pay the committed interest to the debentures holders, irrespective of the return to them.

Impact of financial leverage: Favourable and unfavourable impact to equity shareholders can be presented in the following way.

ROI > Cost of Debt	↑	**ROE & EPS**
ROI < Cost of Debt	↓	**ROE & EPS**

Double-edged weapon: So long as the return on investment is greater than cost of debt, return on equity goes up. Return on equity goes down when the return on investment falls lower than the cost of debt.

The use of the term 'Trading on Equity' is derived from the fact that it is the owner's equity that is used as a basis to raise debt. That is, equity is traded upon. The supplier of debt has limited participation (fixed interest) in the company's profits and, therefore, he will insist upon on protection in earnings and safety, which is provided by ownership equity.

The finance manager has to bear in mind both return and risk, while finalising the mix for raising funds. When the economic conditions are good and EBIT is increasing, EPS would grow faster with the increased debt in the capital structure. However, when economic conditions turn unfavourable and EBIT starts falling, the pace of EPS fall would be greater than the falling rate of EBIT. **Financial Leverage is a double-edged sword.** The finance manager has to remember its double-edged impact and design the capital structure, suitably.

Effect of Leverage

Favourable	**ROI > i**
Unfavourable	**ROI < i**
Neutral	**ROI = I**

Where 'i'= interest or cost of debt

Example to illustrate Financial Leverage is a double-edged sword:

	Company X	Company Z
Equity share capital of Rs. 10 each	20,00,000	8,00,000
10% Debentures	2,00,000	14,00,000
Total Capital Employed	22,00,000	22,00,000
Earning before interest and taxes (EBIT)-**40%** on Capital employed **(ROI)**	8,80,000	8,80,000
Less: Interest on Debentures	20,000	1,40,000
Profit before Tax (PBT)	8,60,000	7,40,000
Less: Tax @ 30%	2,58,000	2,22,000
Profit after Tax (PAT)	6,02,000	5,18,000
Earning available to Equity Shareholders	6,02,000	5,18,000
Number of Equity Shares	2,00,000	80,000
Earning per share (EPS)	3.01	6.5
Return on equity (ROE)	30.1%	65%

Both the companies X and Z have same amount of investment i.e. 22,00,000 and their return on investment is the same 40%. $\left(\frac{8,80,000}{22,00,000}\times 100\right)$

The interesting point is their EPS are totally different. In fact, EPS of company Z is more than double as compared to company A. What is the real reason? The difference in EPS is due to their diverse capital structure i.e. difference in financing the total capital employed.

Company Z has relied more on the fixed return source of funds. Z Company is earning 40% on total funds but paying only 10% interest. The difference between the return and cost and benefit of tax on interest (Tax shield) has increased the earnings of the shareholders.

Let us see what would happen to EPS if EBIT **increases** by similar 50% to both the companies.

	Company X	Company Z
Equity share capital of Rs. 10 each	20,00,000	8,00,000
10% Debentures	2,00,000	14,00,000
Total Capital Employed	22,00,000	22,00,000
Earning before interest and taxes (EBIT)-**60%** on Capital employed **(ROI)**	13,20,000	13,20,000
Less: Interest on Debentures	20,000	1,40,000
Profit before Tax (PBT)	13,00,000	11,80,000
Less: Tax @ 30%	3,90,000	3,54,000
Profit after Tax (PAT)	9,10,000	8,26,000
Earning available to Equity Shareholders	9,10,000	8,26,000
Number of Equity Shares	2,00,000	80,000
Return on equity	45.5%	103.3%
Earning per share (EPS)	4.55	10.33
Increase of EPS	51.16%	58.92%

Let us see what would happen to EPS if EBIT **decreases** by similar 50% to both the companies.

	Company X	Company Z
Equity share capital of Rs. 10 each	20,00,000	8,00,000
10% Debentures	2,00,000	14,00,000
Total Capital Employed	22,00,000	22,00,000
Earning before interest and taxes (EBIT)-**20%** on Capital employed **(ROI)**	4,40,000	4,40,000
Less: Interest on Debentures	20,000	1,40,000
Profit before Tax (PBT)	4,20,000	3,00,000
Less: Tax @ 30%	1,26,000	90,000
Profit after Tax (PAT)	2,94,000	2,10,000
Earning available to Equity Shareholders	2,94,000	2,10,000
Number of Equity Shares	2,00,000	80,000
Return on equity	15%	26%
Earning per share (EPS)	1.5	2.6
Decrease of EPS	50.16%	60%

$$\textbf{Degree of Financial Leverage} = \frac{\textbf{EBIT}}{\textbf{Profit before Tax}}$$

$$X = \frac{8,80,000}{8,60,000}, \quad Z = \frac{8,80,000}{7,40,000}$$

Degree of Financial Leverage

$$X = 1.02 \qquad Z = 1.19$$

Financial Leverage of Z Company is higher than X Company. So, when there is an increase of 50% in EBIT, EPS of Z Company has increased by 58.92% while X Company has increased on a lower side by 51.16%. However, when the fall of EBIT has been by 50%, again, EPS of Z Company has fallen by 60% while fall of X Company has been 50.16% only. Due to higher financial leverage, the percentage of increase as well as fall of EPS in Z Company is higher than X Company. This proves the financial leverage is a double-edged sword.

7.8 SIGNIFICANCE OF FINANCIAL LEVERAGE

Financial leverage is employed to plan the ratio between debt and equity so that earnings per share are magnified. The significance of financial leverage is as under:

1. **Planning of Capital Structure:** Financial leverage helps in planning the capital structure. The capital structure is concerned with the raising of long term funds, both from shareholders and long – term creditors. The structure has the implication of cost and risk that are to be borne in mind, while finalising the capital structure.
2. **Profit Planning:** The earning per share is affected by the degree of financial leverage. If the profitability of the concern is increasing, the fixed costs will help in increasing the availability of profits for equity shareholders. When profits decline and do not cover the interest on debt, the sufferers will be equity shareholders. Therefore, financial leverage is important for profit planning.

7.9 LIMITATIONS OF FINANCIAL LEVERAGE/TRADING ON EQUITY

These are the following limitations of financial leverage / trading on equity:

1. **Double-edged weapon:** Trading on equity is a double-edged weapon. It can be successfully used to increase the earning per share, as long as the return on the investment is higher than the cost of fixed-charge funds. If the cost of debt is more than the return on the investment, then it will work adversely and hence cannot be employed.
2. **Beneficial only to companies having stable earnings:** Trading on equity is beneficial only to companies having stable earnings. This is so because interest on debentures, a recurring expenditure, has to be paid, irrespective of the profits. If the company does not have profits in the lean years, it cannot pay. So, unless the company is assured of stable profits, it should not borrow and resort to financial leverage to take advantage.
3. **Moredebt Increases risk and rate of interest:** Every rupee of extra debt increases the burden of interest and along with it risks too. After a certain stage, it becomes difficult for the company to borrow without paying higher interest rate and offering additional securities. Payment of higher interest rate reduces profitability and makes the financial leverage not workable.
4. **Restrictions and covenants from financial institutions:** To prevent excessive borrowing and contain the risk, financial institutions stipulate conditions while sanctioning loans. This makes the ceiling for borrowing, even if the company wants to borrow and funds are available, without higher interest rate.

7.10 RELATIONSHIP BETWEEN OPERATING LEVERAGE AND FINANCIAL LEVERAGE

Operating Leverage and Financial Leverage are interrelated. The formulae for Operating Leverage and Financial Leverage are as under:

$$\text{Degree of operating leverage} = \frac{\%\text{Change in EBIT}}{\%\text{ Change in Sales}}$$

$$\text{Degree of Financial leverage} = \frac{\%\text{ Change in EPS}}{\%\text{ Change in EBIT}}$$

EBIT is dependent on sales. In turn, EPS is dependent on EBIT. **An ideal combination in a firm is to have low operating leverage and high financial leverage, provided opportunities are available to utilise borrowed funds, profitably.** Lower operating leverage indicates low fixed costs and in consequence break-even point would be low and margin of safety would be high. High financial leverage gives the benefit of a higher percentage of EPS for a given change in EBIT.

7.11 DISTINCTION BETWEEN OPERATING LEVERAGE AND FINANCIAL LEVERAGE

Operating leverage is concerned with the change of operating income with change in sales while financial leverage is concerned with change in earning per share with the change in operating income. High degree of operating leverage indicates large business risk and high degree of financial leverage shows large financial risk. High operating leverage with high financial leverage constitutes a very large risky situation.

The ideal situation is to have a high financial leverage and low operating leverage, provided profitable opportunities exist. The basic objective of both the leverages is to improve the profitability of the firm and earning per share. Both are to remain within the limits, comparable to the industry.

7.12 COMBINED LEVERAGE (COMPOSITE LEVERAGE)

Both financial and operating leverages magnify the earnings of the equity shareholders. **Operating leverage affects the income, which is the result of production and sales. On the other hand financial average is the result of financing decisions.** The high financial leverage may be offset by the low operating leverage or vice versa. The combined leverage focuses the attention on the entire income of the concern.

Computation:

Combined Leverage = Operating leverage × financial leverage.

$$= \frac{\text{Contribution}}{\text{EBIT}} \times \frac{\text{EBIT}}{\text{Profit before tax}}$$

$$= \frac{\textbf{Contribution}}{\textbf{Profit before tax}}$$

Alternatively

$$\frac{\%\ \text{Change in EBIT}}{\%\ \text{Change in Sales}} \times \frac{\%\ \text{change in EPS}}{\%\ \text{change in EBIT}}$$

$$= \frac{\%\ \textbf{Change in EPS}}{\%\ \textbf{Change in sales}}$$

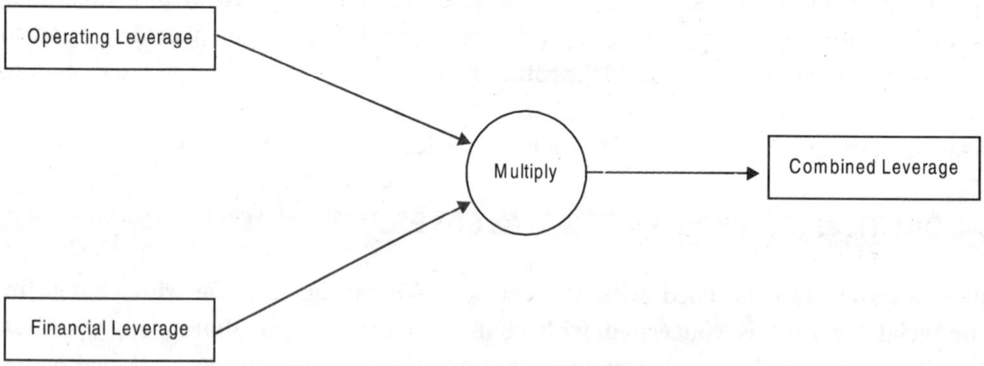

Formation of Combined Leverage

Illustration No. 1

Calculate the Degree of operating leverage, financial leverage and the degree of combined leverage for the following firms and interpret the results:

	P	*Q*	*R*
Output (Units)	3,00,000	75,000	5,00,000
Fixed Costs (Rs.)	3,50,000	7,00,000	75,000
Unit Variable Cost (Rs.)	1.0	7.50	0.10
Interest Expenses	25,000	40,000	Nil
Unit Selling Price	3.0	25.00	0.50

(B. U. MBA- 2004)

Solution:

	P	*Q*	*R*
Unit selling price	3.00	25.00	0.50
Unit Variable cost	1.00	7.50	0.10
Number of units	3,00,000	75,000	5,00,000
Total sales	9,00,000	18,75,000	2,50,000

Contd...

Total Variable cost	3,00,000	5,62,500	50,000
Total Contribution	6,00,000	13,12,500	2,00,000
Fixed cost	3,50,000	7,00,000	75,000
EBIT	2,50,000	6,12,500	1,25,000
Interest	25,000	40,000	Nil
Profit before tax	2,25,000	5,72,500	1,25,000
Operating Leverage $= \frac{\text{Contribution}}{\text{EBIT}}$	$\frac{6,00,000}{2,50,000} = 2.4$	$\frac{13,12,500}{6,12,500} = 1.07$	$\frac{2,00,000}{1,25,000} = 1.00$
Financial Leverage = $\frac{\text{EBIT}}{\text{Profit before tax}}$	$\frac{2,50,000}{2,25,000} = 1.11$	$\frac{6,12,500}{5,72,500} = 1.07$	$\frac{1,25,000}{1,25,000} = 1.00$
Combined Leverage = Operating Leverage × Financial Leverage	2.4 × 1.11 = 2.6	2.14 × 1.07 = 2.29	1.6 × 1.0 = 1.6

Interpretation: Operating Leverage, Financial Leverage and Combined Leverage are the highest for firm P amongst all the firms. This indicates P is exposed to the highest business risk as well as financial risk. The management of P is highly aggressive. A high operating leverage and financial leverage is a very risk situation to the firm.

If the firm's sales increase by 100%, the EPS increases by 267%. Equally, if sales fall by 100%, EPS also falls similarly.

R is exposed to the lowest risk of the above categories. This position indicates that the management of R is cautious.

Illustration No. 2

Consider the following data of ABC Company

	Rs.
Selling price per unit	60/-
Variable cost per unit	40/-
Fixed Cost	3,00,000
Interest burden	1,00,000
Tax Rate	50%
Preference Dividend	50,000

Calculate the 3 leverages if the number of units sold are 1,00,000.

Solution:

Contribution per unit = 60-40 =20

Total contribution = 20 × 1,00,000

= 20,00,000

EBIT = Contribution – Fixed Cost

= 20,00,000 – 3,00,000 : 17,00,000

$$\text{Operating Leverage} = \frac{\text{Contribution}}{\text{EBIT}}$$

$$\text{Operating leverage} = \frac{20,00,000}{17,00,000}$$

= 1.18

$$\text{Financial Leverage} = \frac{\text{EBIT}}{\text{Profit before tax}}$$

EBIT = 17,00,000

Interest = –1,00,000

16,00,000

*Less Preference

Dividend = 1,00,000

Profit before tax = 15,00,000

$$\text{Financial Leverage} = \frac{17,00,000}{15,00,000} = 1.13$$

Combined leverage = Operating leverage × Financial leverage

= 1.18 × 1.13 = 1.33

Or = Contribution / PBT

$$= \frac{20,00,000}{15,00,000} = 1.33$$

* Preference dividend is Rs. 50,000. Tax rate is 50%. We are to calculate 'profit before tax' **from the viewpoint of equity shareholders** for the formula of financial leverage. **Preference dividend is paid from the profits available, after payment of tax.** For the formula, we are to calculate corresponding amount of preference dividend, before tax. For the pre tax amount of Rs. 100, post tax amount is only Rs. 70. So before tax amount for dividend of Rs. 50,000 is Rs. 1,00,000 (grossed up).

Illustration No: 3

The following information has been given in respect of a company:

	Particulars	Rs.
1.	Equity share capital (divided into shares of Rs. 10 each)	10,00,000
2.	Debentures (14%)	30,00,000
3.	Selling price per unit	50
4.	Variable cost per unit	30
5.	Fixed costs	12,00,000

The company is producing, at present, 1,00,000 units. Now, the management of the company plans to increase output by 25%. The tax rate for the company is 40%.

On the basis of the above information, you are required to make out the following calculations for the existing as well as the planned level of output.

(A) Operating Leverage

(B) Financial Leverage

(C) Earnings per share

Analyse and interpret the results.

(B.U.-MBA, 2003)

Solution:

	Present Production	Planned Production
Production (in units)	1,00,000	1,25,000
Total Sales Realisation	50,00,000	62,50,000
Total Variable cost	30,00,000	37,50,000
Contribution	20,00,000	25,00,000
Fixed cost	12,00,000	12,00,000
EBIT	8,00,000	13,00,000
Interest	4,20,000	4,20,000
Profit before tax	3,80,000	8,80,000
Tax @ 40%	1,52,000	3,52,000
Profit after tax	2,28,000	5,28,000
Operating Leverage = $\frac{\text{Contribution}}{\text{EBIT}}$	$\frac{20,00,000}{8,00,000} = 2.5$	$\frac{25,00,000}{13,00,000} = 1.92$

Contd...

Financial Leverage = $\frac{\text{EBIT}}{\text{Profit before tax}}$	$\frac{8,00,000}{3,80,000} = 2.11$	$\frac{13,00,000}{8,80,000} = 1.48$
Earning per share = $\frac{\text{Profit after tax}}{\text{Number of equity shares}}$	$\frac{2,28,000}{1,00,000} = 2.28$	$\frac{5,28,000}{1,00,000} = 5.28$

Analysis and Interpretation: The Company has increased the production and sales by 25%. The operating leverage is 2.5. In other words, if sales increases by 100%, operating profit would increase by 250%. So, EBIT has increased by 62.5% (25% X 2.5). This has happened, as fixed costs have not increased.

However, EPS has increased from 2.28 to 5.28 ie. an increase of 131.57% $\left\{\frac{(5.28 - 2.28)}{2.28} \times 100\right\}$.

This is the combined effect of operating leverage and financial leverage.

Illustration No. 4

Consider the following data of XYZ Ltd.

	Rs.
Selling Price Per Unit	60
Variables Cost Per Unit	40
Fixed Cost	3,00,000
Interest Burden	1,00,000
Tax Rate	50%
Preference Dividend	50,000

Calculate the three types of Leverages, if the number of units sold is 10,000.

Solution:

	Rs.
Sales (10,000 x Rs. 60 per unit)	6,00,000
Less: Variable Cost (10,000 x 40)	4,00,000
Contribution	2,00,000
Less: Fixed Cost	3,00,000
EBIT	–1,00,000
Less: Interest	–1,00,000
EBT	–2,00,000

$$\text{Operating Leverage} = \frac{\text{Contribution}}{\text{EBIT}} = \frac{2,00,000}{-1,00,000}$$

$$= -2$$

$$\text{Financial Leverage} = \frac{\text{EBIT}}{\text{EBT}} = \frac{-1,00,000}{-2,00,000} = 0.50$$

$$\text{Combined Leverage} = \text{Financial Leverage} \times \text{Operating Leverage}$$

$$= 0.5 \times -2 = -1$$

Note: EBIT (operating profit) is negative. So, tax liability does not arise. In the absence of profits, preference dividend is not considered.

Illustration No. 5

The capital employed in a business has been financed as below:

	(Rs.)
Equity Share Capital	6,00,000
7% Preference Share Capital	4,00,000
6% Debentures	8,00,000
Reserves and Surplus	2,00,000
Total	20,00,000

The company earns a profit of Rs.4,00,000 before interest and tax.

Test for 'Trading on Equity' and explain the principles of 'Trading on Equity' by above illustration. Assume tax 30%.

(B.U.- MBA-2003)

Solution:

$$\text{Capital Gearing Ratio} = \frac{\text{Funds bearing fixed interest/dividend}}{\text{Funds not bearing fixed interest/dividend}}$$

(Equity share capital + Reserves and surplus)

$$= \frac{12,00,000}{8,00,000}$$

$$= 1.5$$

As the capital-gearing ratio is more than one, the capital structure is "high geared". There should be "Trading on equity". This can be verified as follows:

Profit as given	=	4,00,000
Less 6% Interest on Debentures	=	– 48,000
		3,52,000
Less Tax (30%)	=	1,05,600
		2,46,400
Less Preference Dividend	=	28,000
Profit available to equity shareholders	=	2,18,400

$$\text{Rate of Return on Equity Shareholders' funds} = \frac{\text{Profit available to equity shareholders}}{\text{Shareholders' funds}}$$

$$= \frac{2,18,400}{8,00,000}$$

$$= 27.3\%$$

$$\text{* Return on Investment} = \frac{\text{Profit after tax but before interest}}{\text{Capital employed}}$$

$$= \frac{2,46,400 + 48,000}{20,00,000}$$

$$= \frac{2,94,400}{20,00,000}$$

$$= 14.72\ \%$$

The Return on investment is 14.72 % while the return on equity is 27.3 %. This is due to the fixed cost of interest /dividend-bearing securities, which is lower than the return on investment. **Thus, there is trading on equity.**

It is to be noted that the **profits available to equity shareholders of a company, having a high gearing ratio, will be subject to wider fluctuations as compared to a company, which has a low capital-gearing ratio.** This is because after making payment of interest and dividend to the fixed income bearing securities, the total balance belongs to the equity shareholders, which would be distributed among the equity shareholders.

Note: * For calculating return on investment, normally, EBIT is taken. Then, the operating profit is before tax. Company is concerned with tax management too as tax involves outgo of funds, in a way, inevitable expenditure for making act profits. Finally, profits after tax, only belongs to equity shareholders. So, profits, after tax are considered, in the numerator as they only would be available to equity shareholders. As capital employed includes debt, profit before interest is considered so that numerator and denominator are uniform. Otherwise, there would be imbalance.

2.

In case, tax rate is not given in the problem, tax rate is to be assumed to explain the benefit of tax on interest, as interest is tax deductible.

Illustration No. 6

In the case of Illustration No. 5, calculate ROE and EPS if there is an increase and decrease of earning by 50% and draw the relationship between financial leverage and ROE and EPS.

Comments:

Trading on equity shows the impact on return on equity. As the firm is having financial leverage of 1.28, at the existing earning level, its Return on equity is 27.3 while it is paying only 6% and 7% to debenture holders and Preference shareholders respectively. The equity shareholders are benefited with the financial leverage. When the financial leverage is beneficial, it is called 'trading on equity'. Financial leverage is 1.28. Due to this Financial Leverage, ROE has increased from 27.3% to 44.8%. However, when there is a fall of 50% in earnings, ROE has fallen from 27.3% to 9.8%.

Financial leverage is a double-edged sword. In other words, when EBIT increases, ROE and EPS increase by a higher percentage. Similarly, when EBIT falls, ROE and EPS fall by a greater percentage than EPS.

When EBIT has gone up by 50%, both ROE and EPS have increased by 64%. Similarly, when the EBIT has fallen by 50%, both ROE and EPS have decreased by 64%.

Financial leverage shows the impact on EPS. Trading on equity shows the impact on ROE.

* Preference dividend is Rs. 28,000. Assumed tax rate is 30%. We are to calculate profit, before tax for the formula. The above preference dividend amount is after tax. We are to calculate corresponding amount, before tax. For Rs. 100, post tax amount is Rs. 70 so before tax amount for Rs. 28,000 is Rs. 40,000 (grossed up).

Illustration No. 7

A Ltd. Company has equity share capital of Rs. 5,00,000 divided into shares of Rs. 100 each. It wishes to raise further Rs. 3,00,000 for expansion cum modernisation plans. The company plans the following financing schemes.

(a) All equity stock.

(b) Rs. One lakh in equity shares and Rs. Two lakh in 10% debentures.

(c) All debt at 10% p.a.

(d) Rs. One lakh in equity shares and Rs. Two lakhs preference capital, with the rate of dividend at 8%.

The company's existing earnings before interest and tax (EBIT) are Rs. 1,50,000. The corporate rate of tax is 50%.

You are required to determine the earning per share (EPS) in each plan and comment on the implications of financial leverage.

If the concern suffers a loss of Rs. 70,000, discuss the impact of leverage under all the four plans.

Solution:

	Plan IRs.	Plan IIRs.	Plan IIIRs.	Plan IVRs.
Earnings before interest and tax	1,50,000	1,50,000	1,50,000	1,50,000
Less: Interest	——	20,000	30,000	——
	1,50,000	1,30,000	1,20,000	1,50,000
Less: Tax @ 50%	75,000	65,000	60,000	75,000
Earnings after tax	75,000	65,000	60,000	75,000
Less: Preference dividend @ 8%	— —	— —	——	16,000
Earnings available for equity stockholders	75,000	65,000	60,000	59,000
No. of equity shares	8,000	6,000	5,000	6,000
Earnings per share	Rs. 9.375	Rs. 10.83	Rs. 12	Rs. 9.83

Comments

In the four plans of fresh financing, Plan III is the most leveraged of all. In this case, additional financing is done by raising loans @ 10% interest. Plan II has fresh capital stock of Rs. One lakh while Rs. Two lakhs are raised from loans. Plan IV does not have fresh loans but preference capital has been raised for Rs. Two lakhs.

The earnings per share is highest in Plan III i.e. Rs. 12. This plan depends upon fixed cost funds and thus has benefited the equity shareholders by increasing their share in profits. Plan II is next best scheme where EPS is Rs. 10.83. In this case too Rs. 2 lakhs are raised through fixed cost funds. Even in Plan IV, where preference capital of Rs. 2 lakhs is issued, it is better than Plan I where equity shares of Rs. 3 lakh is raised.

Illustration No. 6 (Solution):

Rs.

	Existing capital structure	*Changed capital structure (50% increase in operating profits)*	*Changed capital structure II (50% decrease in operating profits)*
Equity Share Capital	6,00,000	6,00,000	6,00,000
7% Preference Share Capital	4,00,000	4,00,000	4,00,000
6% Debentures	8,00,000	8,00,000	8,00,000
Reserves and Surplus	2,00,000	2,00,000	2,00,000
Total Capital Employed	20,00,000	20,00,000	20,00,000
EBIT	4,00,000	6,00,000	2,00,000
Less: Interest	48,000	48,000	48,000
Profit before tax	3,52,000	5,52,000	1,52,000
Tax @ 30%	1,05,600	1,65,600	45,600
Profits after Tax	2,46,400	3,86,400	1,06,400
Less: Dividend to Preference shares	28,000	28,000	28,000
Profits after tax, available to equity shareholders	2,18,400	3,58,400	78,400
No. equity shares (assumed face value Rs.10)	60,000	60,000	60,000
Earnings per share PATNo. of equity shares	3.64	5.97	1.31
Profit before tax	3,52,000	5,52,000	1,52,000
Less: Preference Dividend (grossed up) *	-40,000	-40,000	-40,000
Earning before tax	3,12,000	5,12,000	1,12,000
Financial Leverage = $\frac{\text{EBITE}}{\text{Earning before tax}}$	$\frac{4,00,0003,}{12,000} = 1.28$	$\frac{6,00,000}{5,12,000} = 1.17$	$\frac{6,00,000}{5,12,000} = 1.79$
Return on equity = $\frac{\text{Profit after tax available to equity shareholders'}}{\text{Equity shareholders' funds}}$	$\frac{2,18,400}{8,00,000} = 27.3\ \%$	$\frac{3,58,400}{8,00,000} = 44.8\ \%$	$\frac{78,400}{8,00,000} = 9.8\ \%$

The analysis of this information shows that financial leverage has helped in improving earnings per share for equity shareholders. It helps to conclude that higher the ratio of debt to equity, the greater the return for equity stockholders.

Impact of Leverage on loss of Rs.70,000:

	Plan I Rs.	Plan II Rs.	Plan III Rs.	Plan IV Rs.
Loss before interest and tax	– 70,000	– 70,000	– 70,000	– 70,000
Add: interest	—	20,000	30,000	—
Loss: after interest	– 70,000	– 90,000	– 1,00,000	– 70,000
No. of Equity shares	8,000	6,000	5,000	6,000
Loss per share	Rs. 8.75	Rs. 15	Rs. 20	Rs. 11.67

Comments

The loss per share is highest in Plan III because it has the higher debt-equity ratio while it is the lowest in Plan I because all additional funds are raised through equity capital. The leverage with plan III will have an adverse impact on earnings, if the firm suffers losses because fixed cost securities are the highest that will magnify the losses.

Conclusion:

The plan that has the highest financial leverage would be the most advantageous so long as operating profits are increasing. However, if the firm starts incurring losses, that plan will magnify the losses per share.

Objective Questions

1. What do you understand by the term 'Leverage'? Define operating leverage. Explain its significance and impact on profits? **(7.1,7.2 and 7.4)**
2. What is Operating Leverage? Would you like to have higher operating leverage or higher operating profit, if you have to choose only one of those? Why? **(7.4)**
3. Would you prefer high degree of operating leverage or low degree of operating leverage under normal market conditions? Why? **(7.4)**
4. A retail firm and an airline are typical examples of low and high operating leverage, respectively. - Discuss? **(7.4)**
5. Explain the concept of 'Financial Leverage'. Show the impact of financial leverage on the earnings per share? **(7.5)**
6. In what manner is financial leverage related to operating leverage? Discuss with an example? **(B.U.- MBA 2003) (7.10 and 7.11)**
7. Compare the nature of financial leverage with operating leverage? **(7.10 and 7.11)**

8. 'Financial Leverage is a double-edged sword'- Explain and illustrate with a suitable example, taking hypothetical data? **(7.7)**
9. Leverages are double-edged weapons and should be used with care. Explain this statement and show practical uses of operating leverage and financial leverage? **(7.4 and 7.7)**
10. Write short notes on:

(A) Combined Leverage ***(7.12)***

(B) Significance and limitations of Financial Leverage ***(7.8 and 7.9)***

Check your understanding

(A) State whether the following statements are True or False

1. In financial management, the term 'leverage' is used to describe the firm's ability to use fixed cost assets or funds to magnify the return to its owners.
2. The use of debt funds in a profit making and tax paying business does not improve the return to equity shareholders.
3. A firm's use of fixed-charge securities like debentures and preference shares in its plan of financing the assets is called Financial Leverage.
4. Financial leverage occurs when a firm borrows funds.
5. A high operating leverage factor indicates the presence of automated production processes.
6. If a firm's fixed costs were higher; the operating leverage as well as operating risk of the firm would be higher.
7. A totally equity financed firm also has financial risk.
8. The earning per share is affected by the degree of financial leverage.
9. The ideal situation is to have a low operating leverage and high financial leverage, provided the firm has enough profitable opportunities.
10. If Company A has an operating leverage of '3' and company B has operating leverage of '4'; company B has less amount of business risk.
11. A high break-even point would indicate a high operating leverage.
12. Higher degree of operating leverage indicates larger business risk and higher degree of financial leverage shows larger financial risk.
13. Financial leverage shows the impact on EPS while trading on equity shows the impact on ROE.

Answers

1. True.	2. False	3. True	4. True	5. True
6. True	7. False	8. True	9. True	10. False
11. True	12. True	13. True		

(B) Fill in the blanks:

i. Trading on Equity is also known as ...., when it is positive.

ii. Firms that have a high ratio of fixed costs to variable costs are said to operate with a high degree of........

iii. A firm will have favourable leverage if its .... are more than the debt cost.

iv. A management would be considered too cautious if both operating leverage and financial leverage are kept ....

v. Operating Leverage x Financial Leverage = ...

vi. The shareholders of a company, which has a high financial leverage, stand to gain when the company's return on investment (ROI) is .... as compared to ...... of debt.

vii. Financial leverage indicates disproportionate change in taxable income as a result of change in ....

Answers:

i. Financial leverage	ii. Operating leverage	iii. Earnings	iv. Low
v. Combined leverage	vi. Higher, cost	vii. Operating income	

(C) Pick up the right answer

1. If a profit making and tax paying firm borrows at a rate of interest lower than the return on capital employed, the return on equity will be ... than / to return on capital employed.
   (i) equal
   (ii) more
   (iii) lower
2. Financial leverage always improves the total return on capital employed.
   (i) Yes
   (ii) No certainty
   (iii) No
3. Other things being constant, if firm A has more operating leverage than firm B, then a given percentage of declines in sales will cause a larger percentage of declines for firm A than for firm B in
   (i) EBIT
   (ii) Net Income
   (iii) Both EBIT and net income
   (iv) Neither EBIT nor net income
4. Other things being constant, if Firm A has more financial leverage than Firm B, then a given percentage of increase in operating income causes a large percentage of increase of.... for Firm A, compared to Firm B.
   (i) EBIT

(ii) Net income
(iii) Neither (i) nor (ii)
(iv) Both (i) and (ii)
(v) EPS

5. Financial leverage is different from operating leverage in that the former is concerned with
(i) capital structure
(ii) uncertainty of markets
(iii) inefficient finance manager
(iv) None of those

6. In general, financial leverage is more favourable, whenever the return on the asset exceeds
(i) total cost of capital
(ii) cost of debt
(iii) cost of equity share capital
(iv) net return after taxes

7. Highly leveraged companies are most likely to be found in industries where sales are
(i) increasing around a trend line
(ii) relatively stable
(iii) relatively unstable
(iv) expected to decline
(v) relatively uncertain with increasing margin

8. The term trading on equity is generally used for .... financial leverage.
(i) unfavourable
(ii) favourable
(iii) indifferent

9. The variability of. ...caused by the financial leverage is called financial risk.
(i) contribution
(ii) EPS
(iii) EBIT

10. Operating leverage affects earnings ...interest and tax while financial leverage affects earnings ... interest and tax.
(i) before, after
(ii) after, before
(iii) before, before
(iv) after, after

11. Highly automated firms contains high
    (i) Financial leverage
    (ii) Operating leverage
    (iii) Combined leverage

Answers

1. (ii)	2. (ii)	3. (iii)	4. (v)	5. (i)
6. (ii)	7. (ii)	8. (ii)	9. (ii)	10. (i)
11 (ii)				

8

TIME VALUE OF MONEY

8.1 CONCEPT OF TIME VALUE OF MONEY

The concept 'Time Value of Money' is based on the fact that the money has a time value i.e. a rupee today is much more valuable than a rupee that is received tomorrow. Even a child prefers today's enjoyment in preference for tomorrow's fulfilment.

8.2 MONEY HAS TIME VALUE

These are the following reasons that money has a time value.

1. **Uncertainty and Risk:** Future is always uncertain and risky. Outflows are in our control as payments to others are to be made by us. There is no certainty for future cash inflows. Inflows are dependent on others' convenience. People prefer to receive, immediately, than waiting for the uncertain tomorrow.
2. **Present needs are more important:** Individuals generally prefer current consumption. Even a child wants an ice cream today rather than tomorrow.
3. **Opportunity to invest:** An individual or firm can invest money for returns. An investor can profitably employ a rupee received today to give him a higher value to be received tomorrow or after a certain period.
4. **More Purchasing Power in Inflationary Economy:** In an inflationary economy, today's rupee has more purchasing power to buy, rather than the same amount of money can buy at a later date.

From the above, it is evident that money received, today, is more valuable than the money that may be received tomorrow. One can spend today, invest the amount for a return or can buy more goods, if the economy is passing through the period of inflation. Often, individuals or firms encounter difficulty in comparing inflows and outflows as they occur at different periods of time. **The logical solution is to recognise the principle of time value of money and make appropriate adjustments for time.** Otherwise, faulty financial decisions are likely to occur. Time value of money is of vital importance to reach a proper financial decision.

The following examples clarify the concept more clearly.

Example 1: A loan of Rs. 5,000 is given carrying an interest rate of 10% per annum. At the end of one year, the individual receives back Rs. 5,500. So, Rs. 5,000 at the beginning of the year is equivalent to Rs.5,500 received at the end of the year.

Example 2: A project needs an initial investment of Rs. 1,00,000. The return is spread over a period of eight years, with a return of Rs. 15,000 to be received annually. The question is whether the project is to be accepted or rejected. The outflow is at the 'Zero year', initially. The inflows are at different future periods. The firm has to ascertain the current value of the future annual returns or inflows, at the desired rate of interest or return. If the discounted value of the future inflows exceeds the initial investment or at least equals the initial investment, then only the project is accepted or otherwise rejected.

Example 3: A firm has an option to receive two types of returns for the initial investment of Rs. 20 lakhs. The first option is to receive annual return of Rs. 5 lakhs for a period of seven years, commencing from the end of the first year. The second one is to receive a return of Rs. 10 lakhs for five years, commencing from the end of the third year of investment. The firm can make the correct choice only when the present value of the inflows of both options is calculated.

8.2.1 Time Preference Rate and Required Rate of Return

The time preference for money is generally expressed by an interest rate: This rate will be positive, even in the absence of risk. Unless inducement is offered, no one would like to part present preference for future receipt. When an individual is offered a choice to receive Rs.100 today or Rs.110 at the end of one year, what is offered extra is compensation for parting with money for time. Here, this rate of return 10% is for time, not for risk. The individual is indifferent between the receipt of Rs. 100 today and Rs. 110 at the end of one year because he considers these two amounts equivalent in value.

Risk Factor: But, there is risk too when money is parted with as there is uncertainty of time of receipt or even for actual return of money. So, one expects compensation for the risk taken. **Higher the risk, the return expected is higher.** So, required rate of return has to compensate for time as well as risk too. It can be expressed

Required Rate of Return = Risk free Rate + Risk premium

The risk-free rate compensates for time while risk premium compensates for risk: The required rate of return may also be called opportunity cost of capital of comparable risk. In other words, risk premium increases when the risk is great. This is the reason why higher interest is charged when money is lent to a film producer as production of a movie is highly risky and return of money also depends on the success or failure of the picture too. The purpose for which money is utilised also influences the interest rate. This is the reason why speculative business has to pay higher interest in comparison to a stable business.

Time Preference rate is based on no risk, compensation for time only: The classical example is bank deposit, where there is no risk for return of money. Required rate of return involves compensation for time as well as risk. Example is money lent to a third party, where compensation is required for time as well as risk assumed.

8.3 IMPORTANCE OF TIME VALUE OF MONEY IN FINANCIAL MANAGEMENT

The objective of financial management is wealth maximisation rather than the profit maximisation as the later ignores the principle of 'Time value of money'. All financial decisions recognise the importance of this concept 'Time value of money'. When assets are purchased, funds outgo occurs, immediately, while returns in the form of 'inflow' occur in future period. Similarly, when funds are borrowed, 'inflow' is immediate while 'outflow' by repayment happens later. If these inflows and outflows are just identical, no financial decision take place as no one likes to part current sacrifice for future uncertain receipt. It is necessary that there should be some compensation for present sacrifice. When assets are purchased, the inflow has to be more than the outflow. In the same way, outflow has to be more than the inflow, if funds are to be raised. How the inflow and outflow can be matched? The logical answer is to make necessary adjustment for the flows that happen in the future date to compare them with the current flows so that financial decisions do not go wrong. This is recognition of time value of money, which is the basis for financial decisions. In this process, the owner's equity is maximised when the net present worth is created from such financial decisions.

Time Value of Money or Time Preference for Money means the same. This is one of the central ideas of finance for decision-making.

8.4 TECHNIQUES OF TIME VALUE OF MONEY

There are two techniques for adjusting time value of money. They are:

(A) Compounding Technique

(B) Discounted or Present Value of Technique

8.5 COMPOUNDING TECHNIQUE

Every one wants to have money, immediately, rather than at a later date. However, he may like to wait if he is duly compensated for the waiting time. If an individual is offered Rs. 100 immediately or Rs. 110 after one year, he may opt the later choice provided his preference is for an interest rate of 10%. In other words, to him the later preference is more attractive or Rs. 100 today and Rs.110 at the end of one year are at least the same. It means one has to receive, in future, more for a rupee than received today.

In case of this concept, the interest earned on the initial principal becomes a part of principal, at the end of the compounding period. For example, if Rs.100 is invested for a period of two years at an interest rate of 10% per annum, at the end of first year, the return is Rs.10. This interest Rs.10 becomes part of the principal amount at the beginning of the next year and interest is calculated on Rs. 110. Along with interest Rs.11 (10 % interest on Rs.110), the total amount at the end of the second year becomes Rs.121. This is the yearly compounding of interest. This compounding procedure continues for an indefinite period.

The general equation used to calculate the compounded value at the end of 'n' years is as under:

$$A = P(1+i)^n$$

Where A = Amount at the end of period 'n'

P = Principal at the beginning of the period

i = Interest rate

n = Number of years

Computation of this formula is cumbersome, manually, if the number of years is very large. The other alternative is to use compound value tables. These tables are available for a wide range of combinations of 'i' and 'n'.

Note: Many textbooks work out the problems, simply, with annuity tables. Annuity tables are not given to students, in the question paper. Life is not so simple for students in examinations. To assist the students in the right way for examination, problems are worked as if help of annuity tables are not available.

8.5.1 Multiple Compounding Periods

Interest may be compounded monthly, quarterly and half yearly. The above formula used for annual compounding requires suitable adjustment. If compounding is quarterly, annual interest rate is to be divided by 4 and number of years is to be multiplied by 4. Similarly, if monthly compounding is to be made, annual interest rate is to be divided by 12 and number of years is to be multiplied with 12.

The formula to calculate the compounded value is:

$$A = P(1 + i/m)^{m \times n}$$

Where m = number of times for which compounding is to be done.

With annuity table, compound value can be calculated even if the compounding is on half yearly, quarterly or monthly interest basis. If 12% interest per annum for 5 years on quarterly basis is to be calculated, then annuity table – 3% interest (dividing 12% by four) and for 20 years period (multiplying 5 by four) – provides the compounding interest on quarterly basis. Similar procedure can be adopted for half yearly and monthly interest.

The term Compounded value is also referred as terminal value i.e. value at the end of the period.

Illustration No. 1

Calculate the compound value when Rs.10,000 is invested for 3 years and interest 10% per annum is compounded on quarterly basis.

Solution:

The formula to calculate the compounded value is:

$$A = P(1+ i/m)^{m \times n}$$

$$A = 10{,}000(1+ 0.10/4)^{3 \times 4}$$

$$= 10{,}000(1 + 0.025)^{12}$$

$$= \text{Rs. } 13,\ 448.89$$

8.6 ANNUITY

The term 'Annuity' means a fixed amount, either receipt or payment, at regular intervals for a specified period. Annuity is an equal instalment, evenly spread over a specified period. The relevant point is annuity could be a payment or receipt. Importance is series of equal cash flows occurring over equally spaced periods, in time. The classical example for annuity is the instalment amount in a recurring deposit with a bank. Here, the instalment is fixed and the same amount is paid over a period, at regular intervals. Other examples are equated monthly instalments when a housing loan is taken. Insurance premium paid on the insurance policy, be it monthly, half-yearly or yearly, is also an annuity. Even if the house is taken for rent for a period of one year, even the fixed rent paid per month is also an annuity. **If the instalment differs from month to month or period to period, this is not called annuity.**

8.6.1 Compound Value of Annuity

The value of annuity at the end of the specified period is called compound value of annuity. So, compound value of annuity includes the total instalments paid and interest accrued on the instalments. Interest compounding may be annual, half-yearly or monthly, depending on the terms of the contract agreed.

Formula for Compound value of Annuity is as below:

$$F_n = A\left[\frac{(1+i)^n - 1}{i}\right]$$

Where F_n = Future value of Annuity
A = Annuity
i = Interest Rate

Illustration No. 2

Mr. X deposits Rs. 1,000 at the end of every year for 4 years and the deposit earns a compound interest of 10% per annum. Calculate the amount at the end of 4th year?

Solution:

$$F_n = A\left(\frac{(1+i)^n - 1}{i}\right)$$

Where F_n = Future value of Annuity
A = Annuity
i = Interest Rate

Value at the end of four years

$$= 1{,}000\left(\frac{1+.10^4 - 1}{.10}\right)$$

$$= 1{,}000\left(\frac{0.4641}{.10}\right)$$

$$= 1000 \times 4.641 = 4{,}641$$

8.7 SINKING FUND

The purpose of sinking fund is to create a fund when a big liability is to be repaid at the end of a known period like redemption of debentures that entails a huge cash outflow to the firm. The purpose can be even replacement of a fixed asset at the end of its useful or economic life. Here, when the events are likely to happen is known in the beginning. So, the firm plans and earmarks a fixed amount, every year, so that there would be no difficulty to meet the event. Normally, the annual payment is invested, outside the business, in certain safe investments, where the return is fixed like a bank deposit or Government securities that mature with interest at the end of the period.

The formula for sinking fund is reciprocal of the compound value annuity. The formula is as under:

$$A = FV\left[\frac{1}{(1+i)^n - 1}\right]$$

Where A = Annuity

FV = Future Value

Illustration No. 3

A Company has issued debentures of Rs. 50 lakh to be repaid after 7 years. How much should the company invest in a sinking fund, earning 12 percent in order to repay Debentures?

Solution:

Sinking fund: $FV \left(\frac{i}{(1+i)^n - 1}\right)$

$$50,00,0000 \left(\frac{0.12}{(1+.12)^7 - 1}\right)$$

$$50,00,000 \left(\frac{0.12}{2.210 - 1}\right)$$

$$50,00,000 \times \frac{0.12}{1.210} = \text{Rs. } 4,95,867.77$$

Illustration No. 4

Your father has promised to give you Rs. 1,00,000 in cash on your 25th birthday. Today is your 16th birthday. He wants to know the following things:

(a) If he decides to make annual payments into a fund after one year, how much cash will each have to be if the fund pays 8 percent?

(b) If he decides to invest a lump sum in the account after one year and let it compound annually, how much will be the lump sum?

(c) If in (a) the payments are made in the beginning of the year, how much will be value of annuity?

Solution:

(a) Sinking fund concept is to be applied to know the annual payment

Sinking fund: $FV \left(\dfrac{i}{(1+i)^n - 1} \right)$

A : Annuity

FV : Full Value – Rs. 1,00,000

i : Interest Rate – 8%

n : Number of years – 9 Years.

$$A : 1{,}00{,}0000 \left(\frac{0.08}{(1+0.08)^9 - 1} \right)$$

$$: 1{,}00{,}000 \times \frac{0.08}{1.999 - 1}$$

$$: 1{,}00{,}000 \times \frac{0.08}{0.999} = \text{Rs. } 8.008$$

Father has to contribute Rs. 8.008 every year, commencing from his 17th birthday. He has to contribute for 9 birthdays as 16th birthdays are already over.

(b) Compound Value of A lump sum : $P\ (1 + I)^n$

Where P = Principal at the beginning of the period

$$1{,}00{,}000 : P\ (1 + 0.08)^8$$

$$: P \times 1.8509$$

$$P : \frac{1{,}00{,}000}{1.8509} : \text{Rs. } 54.027/-$$

Father would be investing Rs. 54,027 at the end of 17th birthday, so that the amount would earn interest for a period of 8 years.

(c) As payments are made at the beginning of each year, first annuity would be paid at the end of 16th birthday and so there would be 10 annuities.

$$A \;:\; FV\left(\frac{i}{(1+i)^n - 1}\right)$$

$$:\; 1,00,0000\left(\frac{0.08}{(1+0.08)\ 10-1}\right)$$

$$:\; 1,00,000 \times \left(\frac{0.08}{2.1589-1}\right)$$

$$:\; 1,00,000 \times \frac{0.08}{1.1589} = \text{Rs. } 6.903/-$$

Father has to contribute Rs. 6.903 at the beginning of each year, commencing from 16th birthday.

8.8 COMPOUND VALUE OF AN ANNUITY DUE

The concepts of compound value and present value of annuity are based on the assumption that series of payments are made **at the end of the year.** A series of fixed payments starting **at the beginning of the year** for a specified number of years is called **Annuity Due**. When a fridge is purchased, first instalment is to be paid, immediately, and subsequent instalments in the beginning of each period. Its calculation is as under:

$$F_n = A\left(\frac{(1+i)^n - 1}{i}\right) \times (1+i)$$

Where F_n = Future value of Annuity

A = Annuity

Illustration No. 5

Mr. Rao deposits Rs. 5,000 at the beginning of each year for 5 years in a bank and the deposit earns a compound interest 8% per annum. Calculate the amount at the end of the five-year period?

Solution:

Formula for calculating the annuity due is as under:

$$\mathbf{F_n = A\left(\frac{(1+i)^n - 1}{i}\right) \times (1+i)}$$

Where $\mathbf{F_n}$ = Future value of Annuity

$$A = \text{Annuity}$$

$$= 5000 \left(\frac{(1+.08)^5 - 1}{.08} \right) \times (1 + .08)$$

$$= 5000 \times \frac{0.4693}{.08} \times 1.08$$

$$= 5000 \times 6.44 \times 1.08 = \text{Rs. } 31{,}678$$

8.9 DIFFERENCE BETWEEN ANNUITY AND ANNUITY DUE

When the cash flow or instalment occurs at the end of each period, it is called regular annuity or deferred annuity. When the cash flow or instalment occurs at the beginning of each period, it is called Annuity Due.

A depositor has deposited equal instalment of Rs. 1,000 every year for a period of five years, carrying an interest rate of 10% per annum. For calculating the compounding value of annuity, annuity table gives compound value of annuity of one rupee for 10% for five years –6.105 – that is to be multiplied with the constant amount Rs. 10,000 to arrive at the compound value of annuity.

8.10 DOUBLING PERIOD

We want to calculate the period that is needed to double the amount once the interest rate is given. This is called Rule of 72.

$$\text{Doubling period} = \frac{72}{\text{Rate of Interest}}$$

Illustration No. 6

If you deposit an amount of Rs.5,000 at 8 per cent rate of interest, in how many years will this amount double? Work out the problem by using Rule of 72.

Solution:

For calculating the double period, the formula is

$$\textbf{Doubling period} = \frac{\textbf{72}}{\textbf{Rate of Interest}}$$

$$= \frac{72}{8}$$

$$= 9 \text{ years}$$

8.11 EFFECTIVE RATE OF INTEREST IN CASE OF MULTI-PERIOD COMPOUNDING

Effective interest rate brings all the different bases of compounding such as yearly, half-yearly, quarterly and monthly on a single platform for comparison to select the beneficial base. **Now, the question is which works out highest interest amount? When interest is compounded on half-yearly basis, interest amount works out more than the interest calculated on yearly basis. Quarterly compounding works out more than half-yearly basis. Monthly compounding works out more than even quarterly compounding. So,** if compounding is more frequent, then the amount of interest per year works out more. **Now, we want to equate them for comparison. Suppose, an option is given as follows:**

Basis of Compounding	Interest Rate
Yearly	10
Half-yearly	9.5
Quarterly	9
Monthly	8.5

Now, the question is which basis of compounding is to be accepted to get highest interest rate. The answer is to calculate 'Effective Interest Rate'. Effective interest rate brings all the different bases of compounding on a single platform for comparison to choose.

Effective rate of interest (EIR) can be calculated in case of Multi-period compounding, using the following formula:

	EIR	=	[1 + i/m]m – 1
Where	EIR	=	Effective Rate of Interest
	i	=	Nominal interest rate (Yearly interest rate)
	m	=	Frequency of compounding per year

Take yearly interest rate (nominal interest rate) as the base and find out the comparable rate of interest for half-year, quarterly and monthly basis and select that is attractive.

Illustration No. 7

(i) A Company offers 12% rate of interest on deposits. What is the effective rate of interest if the compounding is done on

(A) Half-yearly

(B) Quarterly

(C) Monthly

(ii) As an alternative, the following rates of interest are offered for choice. Which basis gives the highest rate of interest that is to be accepted?

Basis of Compounding	Interest Rate
Yearly	12
Half-yearly	11.75
Quarterly	11.50
Monthly	11.25

Solution:

(i) The formula for calculation of effective interest is as below:

$$EIR = (1+i/m)^m - 1$$

Where EIR = Effective Rate of Interest

i = Nominal interest rate (Yearly interest rate)

m = Frequency of compounding per year

(A) When the compounding is done on half-yearly basis:

$$= [1 + .12/2]^2 - 1$$

$$= 1.1236 - 1 = 12.36\ \%$$

(B) When the compounding is done on quarterly basis:

$$= [1 + .12/4]^4 - 1$$

$$= 0.1255 = 12.55\%$$

(C) When the compounding is done on monthly basis:

$$= [1 + .12/12]^{12} - 1$$

$$= 0.1268 = 12.68\%$$

Basis of Compounding	Interest Rate	Effective Interest Rate
Yearly	12	12 %
Half-yearly	12	12.36 %
Quarterly	12	12.55%
Monthly	12	12.68%

(ii) When the compounding is done on half-yearly basis:

$$= [1 + .1175/2]^2 - 1$$

$$= 0.1209 = 12.09\ \%$$

When the compounding is done on quarterly basis:

$$= [1 + .1150/4]^4 - 1$$

$$= 0.1200 = 12.00\ \%$$

When the compounding is done on monthly basis:

$$= [1 + .1125/12]^{12} - 1$$

$$= 0.1184 = 11.84\ \%$$

Basis of Compounding	Interest Rate Offered	Effective Interest works out to
Yearly	12	12%
Half-yearly	11.75	12.09 %
Quarterly	11.50	12.00 %
Monthly	11.25	11.84 %

Out of all, interest rate of 11.75% on half-yearly compounding works out to be the highest effective interest rate i. e. 12.09%. So, this option is to be accepted.

8.12 PRESENT VALUE OF A PERPETUITY OR INFINITE LIFE ANNUITY

Annuity is a receipt or payment for a specific period while Perpetuity is for an indefinite period. Perpetuity is an infinite life annuity. Both are different concepts. Pension to a freedom fighter is perpetuity. In other words, the payment is made to him so long as the freedom fighter is alive. The formula for calculating the present value of an infinite life annuity is by simply dividing the regular receipt by interest rate.

$$V_o = \frac{R}{i}$$

Where
Vo = Present value of Perpetuity
R = Regular receipt
i = interest rate

Illustration No. 8

Calculate the present value of Rs. 2,000 received in perpetuity for an infinite period taking the discount rate of 10%.

Solution:

$$V_o = \frac{R}{i}$$

Where R = Regular receipt

i = interest rate

$$= \frac{2000}{10} = 20{,}000$$

8.13 DISCOUNTING OR PRESENT VALUE TECHNIQUE

Present value is the exact opposite of compound or future value. In case of compounding, we calculate the value of money at the end of the period, while in case of present value concept, we estimate the present worth of a future payment / instalment. Future value shows the amount receivable of present money on a future date. Principal amount always appreciates with interest. So, the future value is always higher than the present money. In case of present value, we calculate the value of future money receivable as on date, so it would be always lower than the future amount.

The present value approach is based on the concept that money has opportunity cost for money lying idle.

The formula for calculating discounting value is

$$V_o = \frac{V_n}{(1+i)^n}$$

Where V_o = Present Value

V_n = Future Value at the end of 'n' period

Illustration No. 9

X has an option to receive the value today for a debenture, face value Rs. 1,000 carrying interest rate of 10% per annum. The debenture falls due for payment after three years. Calculate the present value today?

Solution:

The formula for calculating discounting value is

$$V_o = \frac{V_n}{(1+i)^n}$$

Where V_o = Present Value

V_n = Future Value at the end of 'n' period

$$\text{Present value} = \frac{1,000}{(1+0.10)^3}$$

$$= \frac{1000}{1.331}$$

$$= \text{Rs. } 751.31$$

8.14 SERIES OF CASH FLOWS

There are two types of calculating series of cash flows. They are:

(A) Present value of Series of Cash Flows

(B) Future value of Series of Cash Flows

8.15 PRESENT VALUE OF SERIES OF CASH FLOWS

In a business situation, investment is made today and returns are spread over a future period. One would like to know whether the investment is desirable or not. Cash flows may be uniform or changing at periodical intervals. In other words, the following formula is useful to calculate the present value of annuity where the cash flow is constant or cash flows vary from period to period. For this, series of future cash flows are to be adjusted for the present value.

The present value of series of cash flows can be calculated by the following formula.

$$PV = \frac{A_1}{(1+i)} + \frac{A_2}{(1+i)^2} + \frac{A_3}{(1+i)^3} \frac{A_n}{(1+i)^n} = \frac{A_t}{(1+i)^t}$$

Where PV = Sum of individual present values of cash flows

A_1, A_2, A_3 = Cash flows after period 1,2,3 etc

i = Discount rate

t = time period

Illustration No. 10

Annuity received is Rs. 500 per annum. Calculate the present value for the annuity received for four years, if the discounting factor is 10%.

Solution:

$$PV = \frac{A_1}{(1+i)} + \frac{A_2}{(1+i)^2} + \frac{A_3}{(1+i)^3} \cdots\cdots \frac{A_n}{(1+i)^n}$$

Where PV = Sum of individual present values of cash flows

A_1, A_2, A_3 = Cash flows after period 1,2,3 etc

i = Discount rate

t = time period

$$PV = \frac{500}{(1+.10)} + \frac{500}{(1+.10)^2} + \frac{500}{(1+.10)^3} + \frac{500}{(1+.10)^4}$$

$$= 454.54 + 413.22 + 375.66 + 341.51$$

$$= \text{Rs.}1{,}584.93$$

Illustration No. 11

For the following future cash flows, calculate the present value assuming the time value of money is 10%. Decide its acceptance.

Year (Rs)	Cash flows (Rs.)
1	1,000
2	2,000
3	3,000
4	4,000

Solution:

We are to calculate the present value for the future cash flows.

Formula for calculating the present value of future cash flows:

$$PV = \frac{A_1}{(1+i)} + \frac{A_2}{(1+i)^2} + \frac{A_3}{(1+i)^3} \cdots\cdots \frac{A_n}{(1+i)^n}$$

Where PV = Sum of individual present values of cash flows

A_1, A_2, A_3 = Cash flows after period 1,2,3 etc

i = Discount rate

t = time period

$$Pv = \frac{1{,}000}{(1+.10)} + \frac{2{,}000}{(1+.10)^2} + \frac{3{,}000}{(1+.10)^3} + \frac{4{,}000}{(1+.10)^4}$$

$$= 909.09 + 1{,}652.89 + 2{,}253.94 + 2{,}732.05$$

$$= \text{Rs. } 7{,}547.97$$

Conclusion: The present value of future cash flows is Rs. 7,547.97. In case, 10% return is acceptable, it is desirable to accept the present value of future cash flows.

8.16 FUTURE VALUE OF SERIES OF CASH FLOWS

Earlier, we have considered the future value of a single payment made at the time zero. At times, different cash flows may occur at different periods of time. We may like to know the future value of series of payments made, at the end of the period.

Formula for future value at the end is

$$V_n = R_1 \,[(I+ i)^{n-1} + R_2(1+i)^{n-2} + R_3(1+i)^{n-3} + \ldots\ldots(R_{n-1})\,(1+i) + R_n]$$

Where V_n = Future value at the end of period 'n'

R_1 = Payment after period 1
R_2 = Payment after period 2
R_3 = Payment after period 3
R_n = Payment after period 'n'
i = interest rate

Illustration No. 12

Calculate the future value at the end of five years of the following series of payments at 10% interest rate:

At the end of Year (Rs.)	Cash Flow (Rs.)
1	1,000
2	2,000
3	3,000
4	2,000
5	1,500

Solution:

$V_n = R_1 [(I+ i)^{n-1} + R_2(1+i)^{n-2} + R_3(1+i)^{n-3} + ...(R_{n-1}) (1+i) + R_n]$

Where

V_n = Future value at the end of period 'n'
R_1 = Payment after period 1
R_2 = Payment after period 2
R_3 = Payment after period 3
R_n = Payment after period 'n'
i = interest rate

$= 1000(1 +.10)^4 + 2000(1+.10)^3 + 3000(1+.10)^2 + 2000(1+.10) + 1500$

$= 1464 + 2662 + 3630 + 2200 + 1500$ = Rs.11,456

Objective Questions

1. "A rational human being has a time preference for money." What are the reasons for such preference and illustrate with suitable examples? (7.1 and 7.2)
2. 'Generally individuals show a time preference for money.' Give reasons for such a preference and explain the relation between time preference rate and required rate of return? (7.1,7.2 and 7.2.1)
3. "The financial manager should take into consideration the time value of money in order to take correct financial decisions." Elucidate and explain importance in financial management? (7.1,7.2 and 7.3)

4. Define-
   - (a) Compound sum of annuity (7.6.1)
   - (b) Required Rate of Return (7.2.1)
5. Write short notes on:
   - (A) Annuity (7.6)
   - (B) Effective Interest Rate (7.11)
   - (C) Present and future Value of cash flows (7.15 and 7.16)
   - (D) Multiple compounding periods (7.5.1)
   - (E) Sinking Fund (7.7)

Check Your Understanding

(A) State whether the following statements are True or False

1. Value of money received today is more than the value of the same amount of money received tomorrow.
2. Discounting technique is also known as compounding technique.
3. An annuity is a series of receipts or payments of unequal amounts.
4. There are no differences between simple interest and compound interest value of money.
5. Time value of money and time preference for money conveys the same meaning.
6. Cash flows of different years in absolute terms are comparable.
7. The term 'annuity' does not necessarily apply to equal annual cash flows; it can even apply to monthly or quarterly cash flows occurring at equal intervals.
8. If cash flows occur at the end of the each period, the annuity is called regular annuity or deferred annuity.
9. Annuity and perpetuity are different concepts.
10. Even if the instalment differs from month to month or period to period, this is called annuity.
11. Effective interest rate brings all the different bases of compounding such as yearly, half-yearly, quarterly and monthly on a single platform for comparison to select the beneficial base.
12. Rule of 72 is useful to calculate period required for doubling principal amount, in the absence of interest rate.

Answers

1. True	2. False	3. False	4. False	5. True
6. False	7. True	8. True	9. False	10. False
11. True	12. False			

(B) Select the most appropriate one

1. Formula for sinking fund is

   (A) same as compounding annuity formula

(B) reciprocal of compounding annuity

(C) reverse of effective interest rate formula

2. Discounting technique is

(A) slightly different from compounding technique

(B) exactly opposite to compounding technique

(C) same as compounding technique

3. Formula for Compound value of a sum is

(A) $P(1+i)^n$

(B) $P(1-i)^n$

(C) $C(1+i)^n$

Where

P = Principal

i = interest rate

n = number of years

A = amount at the end of 'n' number of years

4. Effective Interest Rate means

(A) simple interest rate

(B) compound interest rate

(C) a single common interest rate for comparison between half-yearly, quarterly and monthly interest rates.

5. Cash flows of two years in absolute terms are

(A) comparable

(B) different

(C) same

6. When interest is compounded on half-yearly basis, interest amount works out .... than the interest calculated on yearly basis.

(A) less

(B) more

(C) same

7. The worth of money in hand today is ... than money receivable in future.

(A) same

(B) more

(C) less

Answers

1. (B) 2. (B) 3. (A) 4. (C) 5. (B)
6. (B) 7. (B)

9

INVESTMENT AND CAPITAL STRUCTURE DECISIONS

9.1 INTRODUCTION

Funds are needed to all business enterprises for investment, at every stage, from formation to expansion. Funds can be raised by two types, first through the ownership securities i.e. equity shares and preference shares and secondly through borrowing securities i.e. debentures and / or bonds. While raising funds, two factors are important, one is quantum and the other is mix. Investment is concerned with quantum; estimation of funds for current as well as future needs to run the business smoothly, without stress and strain. More importantly, every firm has to maintain a proper mix of both these types of securities in a manner that both their cost and risk are minimum. The mix of different securities is portrayed by the firm's capital structure. Capital structure deals with the composition of funds. Composition of funds is important to increase profitability, while minimising risk of the firm.

9.2 CAPITALISATION, CAPITAL STRUCTURE AND FINANCIAL STRUCTURE

Capitalisation refers to the total amount of securities issued by a company. The different securities are equity share capital, preference share capital and debentures.

Capitalisation refers to the total amount of long term-funds raised by the company. In other words, it refers to the par value of stocks and bonds, outstanding on a specific date.

Capital structure refers to the proportionate amount that makes up capitalisation. In other words, capital structure refers to the break up of the securities raised by the company.

Financial structure refers to the way the firm's assets are financed. In other words, it includes both long-term as well as short-term sources of funds. Thus, capital structure is only a part of financial structure.

Example: For example, the funds raised by a company are:

(Rs. in lakhs)

Nature of Funds	Amount	Break-up
Equity shares	4	50%
Preference Shares	2	25%
Debentures	2	25%
Capitalisation	**8**	**100%**
Reserves	1	
Short-term borrowing from bank	1	
Total	**10**	

Capitalisation: Rs.8 lakhs. This is the total long-term fund raised.

Capital Structure: Proportionate amount of capitalisation (50% equity shares, 25% preference shares and 25% debentures).

Some authors include retained earnings and reserves too for the purpose of capital structure.

Financial Structure: Rs.10 lakhs. This represents all the financial resources, short-term as well as long-term.

9.3 FORMS OR PATTERN OF CAPITAL STRUCTURE

The capital structure of a company may take any one of the following forms:

(A) Equity Share Capital

(B) Equity and Preference Share Capital

(C) Equity Share Capital and Debentures

(D) Equity Share Capital, Preference Share Capital and Debentures

9.4 IMPORTANCE OF CAPITAL STRUCTURE

The term 'Capital structure' refers to the mix of different sources of long-term funds such as equity share capital, preference share capital and long-term debt like long-term loans, debentures etc. The choice of an appropriate capital structure depends upon a number of factors such as nature of business, regularity of earnings the business can maintain, conditions of market and, finally, attitude of investors at the time of fund raising etc.

Borrowing is Cheap compared to Equity: Amongst the different determinants in designing the capital structure, the most important factor is 'mix of debt and equity' in the capital structure. Rising of funds through debt is cheaper compared to equity. This is because interest on debt is an admissible expenditure. In other words, it is allowed as an expense while computing profits for tax. Payment of Dividend is only an appropriation of profit. Dividend paid on equity is not allowed for income tax. In simple language, interest is an expense while dividend is not from the viewpoint of tax.

Let us explain through an example. Suppose a company is in the tax bracket of 50% and pays an interest of 12% on its debentures. As it is expenditure under income tax, the effective cost comes to only 6%. If funds were raised through equity, the cost would have been 12% as dividend is not an expense.

Role of Debt in Capital Structure: There is a basic difference between debt and equity. Debt is a liability. Interest on debt is a fixed commitment. Interest has to be paid, irrespective of the profits of the company. While equity is shareholders' funds on which dividend has to be paid only if there are profits, after payment of interest. So, there is no commitment for payment of dividend to equity shareholders.

Above all, debt is also risky too, beyond a certain point. If the proportion of debt in the capital structure increases, risk of the firm increases that may lead to the insolvency of the company, in adverse times.

Importance of Mix: The mix in capital structure has great implications. It is true that the mix of capital structure does not influence the total earnings of the firm but, definitely, mix has a great impact on the individual earnings of equity shareholders. Let us see how the mix works.

Suppose, a firm has an equity share capital of Rs. 1 lakh consisting of shares of Rs.10 each. When it is earning Rs.20,000, its return is 20% (ignoring tax). Now, the company plans to go for expansion involving Rs. 1 lakh. It has two options for raising funds through equity or debentures. It has decided to raise the funds by issue of

8% debentures as that option is profitable. As the available funds have gone up by 100%, earnings are also presumed to increase in a similar manner and so profits are, now, Rs. 2 lakhs. Company pays interest on debentures Rs.8,000 and balance

Rs. 12,000 goes to equity shareholders making the aggregate earnings available to equity shareholders Rs. 32,000. So, now their return is 32% against earlier 20% (ignoring tax). The return to equity shareholder's has increased by 60%, without any additional stake, due to use of debt.

Double-edged sword: What is the reason for increase in return? It is simple. The cost of debt is lower than the return on investment. In consequence, the earnings of the equity shareholders are magnified. This is called **'Trading on Equity' or 'Financial Leverage' or 'Financial Gearing'.** This concept has been explained already, in detail, in the Chapter No. 7- Leverages (Para No.7.7). Financial Leverage also behaves in an adverse manner, negative way, too. If the return on investment falls below the cost of debt, then the earnings of equity shareholders decreases compared to its earlier earnings. This situation may happen in recession or falling prices. That's why financial gearing is called Double-edged sword.

Approach to establish an Appropriate Capital Structure:

As and when firm is raising funds for expansion, it has to choose the mode of financing out of the different options available. The options - routes of financing - are equity, preference share capital, debt or a combination of the three, in different proportions. How to select the mode of financing , the route more rewarding to the firm?

EBIT - EPS Approach is the method followed by the firms to the firms to find the answer to the above question. This approach established the impact of different methods of financing on equity shareholder's value, reflected in the revised EPS, under the different method of financing. When EPS is at its maximum, that route of financing is to be accepted. When EPS is at peak, the value of the share would be at its highest level. The value of the firm is reflected in the value of the equity share price. So, firm has to accept that capital structure, when the revised EPS is at its maximum. When ROI is greater than the fixed charge funds, be it debt or preference share capital, ROE increases and in consequence EPS increases. Firm has to make up its mind; looking to the increased risk it may be exposed to once the route is accepted.

The following illustration explains the concept of EBIT-EPS Approach.

Illustration No. 1

A firm has an all-equity capital structure consisting of 1,00,000 equity shares of Rs.10 per share. The firm wants to raise Rs. 2,50,000 to finance its investments and is considering three alternative methods of financing:

(i) to issue 25,000 equity share at Rs. 10 each,

(ii) to borrow Rs. 2,50,000 at 8 per cent rate of interest,

(iii) to issue 2,500 Preference shares of Rs. 100 each, at 8% rate of dividend.

(a) If the firm's earnings before interest and tax after additional investment are

Rs. 3,12,500 and the tax rate is 50 per cent, which choice is to be made? Comment on the outcome of choice.

(b) Explain the effect on EPS, if EBIT decreases to Rs. 75,000.

(c) Draw conclusion in respect of relationship between EBIT and EPS.

Solution:

(a)

Eps Under Different Forms of Financing

	Equity Financing Rs.	Debt Financing Rs.	Preference Financing Rs.
EBIT	3,12,500	3,12,500	3,12,500
Less : Interest	0	20,000	0
PBT	3,12,500	2,92,500	3,12,500
Less : Taxes 50%	1,56,250	1,46,250	1,56,250
PAT	1,56,250	1,46,250	1,56,250
Less : Preference dividend	0	0	20,000
Earning available to equity shareholders	1,56,250	1,46,250	1,36,250
Equity shares outstanding	1,25,000	1,00,000	1,00,000
EPS	1.25	1.46	1.36

The firm is able to maximize the earnings per share, when it uses debt financing. Though the rate of preference dividend is equal to the rate of interest, both at 8%, EPS is high in case of debt financing the reason is interest charges are tax deductible, while preference dividends are not. This is an interesting point in mix of financing. **Change of form of financing has increased EPS.**

Higher is the ratio of debt to equity, the greater would be the return to the equity shareholders.

(b)

Eps Under Different Forms Of Financing - (Reduced Ebit)

	Equity Financing Rs.	Debt Financing Rs.	Preference Finance Rs.
EBIT	75,000	75,000	75,000
Less : Interest	0	20,000	0
PBT	75,000	55,000	75,000
Less : Taxes @ 50%	37,500	27,500	37,500
PAT	37,500	27,500	37,500
Less : Preference dividend	0	0	20,000
Earning available to equity shareholders	37,500	27,500	17,500
Equity shares outstanding	1,25,000	1,00,000	1,00,000
EPS 0.30	0.27	0.17	

With the use of debt financing, EPS has been the highest with 1.46 when EBIT has been at a high level of Rs. 3,12,5000. When EBIT has fallen to Rs. 75,000, EPS with debt financing has fallen to 0.27. EPS under debt financing has not fallen below preference share financing as interest paid is eligible for tax benefit, while dividend on preference shares is not eligible for tax benefit.

(c) **Relationship between EBIT and EPS:** With increasing levels of EBIT, EPS will increase at a faster rate with a high degree of leverage. However, if a company is not able to earn a rate of return on its assets higher than the interest rate (or the preference dividend rate), debt (or preference financing) will have an adverse impact on EPS. EPS decreases, drastically, in such an event. Use of Fixed charge funds such as debentures or preference share capital acts as a double-edged sword. So, these funds have to be selected, carefully, for the expansion of projects.

Conclusion: It can be concluded that if the level of EBIT is greater and its probability in the downward fluctuation is lower, it is more beneficial to employ debt in the capital structure.

9.5 CAPITAL GEARING

The term 'Capital gearing' is used to describe the relationship between equity share capital including reserves and surpluses to preference share capital and other fixed charge bearing securities. Preference share capital and Debentures / long-term loans are called fixed charge bearing securities.

Capital gearing ratio analyses the capital structure of the company. This is the ratio between fixed charge bearing securities and equity capital (equity shares plus reserves). Dividend on equity share capital is dependent on the profits of the company and so changes from year to year, while interest and dividend are fixed on debentures and preference shares, respectively.

Capital gearing ratio is calculated as under

$$\frac{\text{Preference share capital + Debentures + Long-term debts bearing fixed interest}}{\text{Equity share capital + Reserves and Surplus}}$$

If preference share capital and other fixed interest bearing loans exceed equity share capital and free reserves, the company is said to be highly geared. In case, the capital gearing is more than one, the firm is to be said to be highly geared. On the other hand, if preference share capital and other fixed interest bearing loans are less than the equity share capital and free reserves, the company is said to be low geared. In the low-geared firms, capital gearing is less than one. In case, both are equal, the firm is said to be even-geared.

Significance of Capital Gearing: Capital gearing is of immense importance to the company. As the fixed charge bearing securities carry a fixed amount of commitment in the form of interest and dividend, the balance amount of profits belong to the equity shareholders. In case of low-geared firms, the amount of interest and dividend would be low as the aggregate amount of preference share capital and debentures is low, compared to equity share capital. So, the amount of divisible profits would be high to equity shareholders. Whereas in case of high-geared firms, the amount of interest and dividend would be high as the proportion of debentures and preference share capital exceeds equity share capital. So, the amount of profit available to equity shareholders would be low. Proper gearing of the firm is important for the smooth running of an enterprise.

Comparison of Capital Gearing with Automobile: The capital gearing in the financial structure of a business is rightly compared with the gears of an automobile. To start the vehicle, we start with a low gear i.e. first gear and when the vehicle picks up the speed, we move into the higher gear i.e. second gear. Finally, when we want to pick up the real speed, we move the vehicle into the next higher gear i.e. third gear. Similar is the functioning of capital gearing in a business enterprise. Company is commenced, initially, with total equity share capital. After a couple of years, debt is introduced in the form of debt or issue of preference share capital. When the company totally stabilises and picks up momentum, a higher mix of fixed charge bearing funds, in the form of preference share capital and debt, is used to avail the advantage of financial leverage and magnify the earnings of equity shareholders. Capital gearing is important not only to equity shareholders but also creditors, debenture holders and financial institutions that have lent money to the firm.

9.5.1 Capital gearing and Trade Cycles

Company can use the technique of capital gearing, successfully, during the different conditions of inflation and deflation. Depending on the period, company has to change the technique either high gear or low gear, from time to time.

(A) **During inflation or Boom Period:** During boom, companies enjoy high profits. So, the interest on debt and rate of dividend on preference shares is always lower than the return on investment. To take advantage of the situation, firms borrow more and they adopt the policy of high gear. In consequence, the earning per equity share increases. **It is desirable that companies should adopt the policy of high gear during inflation or boom periods to magnify the earning per equity share.**

(B) **During deflation or depression Period:** Profits dip during the periods of depression. Companies experience difficulty to pay the fixed interest on debt or dividend on preference shares. So, a cautious approach is desirable to be adopted during that period. It is prudent for companies to raise equity funds as there is no commitment to pay fixed rate of dividend. During the periods of deflation, companies have to adopt the policy of low gear.

Illustration No. 2

Calculate the capital-gearing ratio from the following information. Comment on the ratio if the firm is passing through the period of inflation and planning expansion.

	(Rs.)
Equity share capital	7,00,000
7% Preference share capital	2,00,000
11% Debentures	4,00,000
Long-term Loan from MPSFC (term lending institution)	3,00,000
Reserves and Surplus	4,00,000
Current Liabilities	10,00,000

Solution:

Capital gearing ratio is

$$\frac{\text{Preference share capital + Debentures + Long-term debts bearing fixed interest}}{\text{Equity share capital + Reserves and Surplus}}$$

$$= \frac{2,00,000 + 4,00,000 + 3,00,000}{7,00,000 + 4,00,000}$$

$$= 0.82$$

Capital gearing is 0.82. As the capital gearing is less than one, the firm is low geared. During the inflation period, profits of the firm remain high and so does not experience difficulty to meet the fixed interest/dividend obligations. Firm can use more debt to improve the earning per equity share. In case, the firm is planning expansion, more debt is to be used in capital structure to improve the return on investment.

Objective Questions

1. Define the capital structure? Distinguish between Capitalisation, Capital Structure and Financial Structure? **(9.1and 9.2)**
2. Detail the different forms of capital structure and explain their importance? Illustrate the role of debt in capital structure as a means to increase the return on equity and magnify the earnings of equity shareholders, with suitable examples? **(9.3 and 9.4)**
3. Discuss the concept of capital gearing and explain its significance? What type of technique has to be adopted by prudent companies during various phases of trade cycle? **(9.5 and 9.5.1)**

Check Your Understanding

(A) State whether the following statements are True or False

1. Capital structure refers to the mix of different sources of long-term funds such as equity share capital, preference share capital and long term debt like long-term loans, debentures etc.
2. The terms 'Capitalisation' and 'Capital structure' are one and the same.
3. The term 'Capital gearing' is used to describe the relationship between equity share capital including reserves and surpluses to preference share capital and other fixed charge bearing securities.
4. In case of low- geared firms, the aggregate amount of preference share capital and debentures is more than equity share capital and free reserves.
5. Capital gearing affects only shareholders and does not affect the creditors, debenture holders and financial institutions that have lent funds to the concern.
6. It is prudent for companies to have low gear during the period of inflation and high gear during depression.
7. Capital structure is not a part of financial structure.

Answers

1. True 2. False 3. True 4. False 5. False.
6. False 7. False

(B) Pick up the right one:

1. Capital gearing refers to the relationship between equity capital and _____.
   (A) Preference share capital
   (B) Reserves and Surplus
   (C) Fixed charge bearing securities
2. It is better for a company to remain in …….. gear during the period of depression.
   (A) Low gear
   (B) High gear
   (C) Neutral gear
3. Capital structure deals with the …….. of long-term funds.
   (A) mix
   (B) quantum
   (C) quantum and composition
4. Capitalisation refers to the total amount of …….. raised by the company.
   (A) long term-funds
   (B) short-term funds
   (C) short-term and long term-funds

Answers

1. (C) 2. (A) 3. (A) 4. (A)

10

INSTRUMENTS OF LONG-TERM FINANCE

10.1 INTRODUCTION

Finance is said to be the life-blood of any enterprise. Without finance, no enterprise can accomplish its objectives. Capital required for any business enterprise can be classified under two main categories. They are

(A) Fixed Capital and

(B) Working Capital

Here, in this chapter, we deal with fixed capital. Fixed capital is provided by long-term securities. The two long-term securities available to a company are shares and debentures. Shares include Equity shares and Preference shares. Equity shares provide ownership status to investors. Debentures are a form of loan capital. Those who provide funds through debentures are only lenders. Long-term finance is also provided by term lending institutions too in the form of term loans. Different means of long-term finance enjoy merits and demerits, differently. What are those merits and demerits and why both types of securities are needed? Let us discuss.

10.2 KINDS OF OWNERSHIP SECURITIES

The Companies Act, 1956 permit issue of two types of shares. They are Equity shares and Preference shares. What is the need for a company to issue two types of shares? All investors are not alike. Some investors prefer higher returns, even uncertain, and, in tun, are prepared to take risk. Another category of investors wishes to have regular returns, though it may be low. Company may need to issue two types of shares to tap the required funds for the firm. Only one type may not serve all the requirements of the firm, adequately, and different types serve the individual wishes, suitably.

10.3 EQUITY SHARES

Equity shares are, earlier, known as ordinary shares or common shares. Equity shareholders are the real owners of the company as they have the voting rights and enjoy decision- making authority on important matters, related to the company. The shareholders' return is in the form of dividend, which is dependent on the profits of the company and capital gain / loss, at the time of their sale. They enjoy higher returns if the company performs well and may not get any dividend, at all, if the company does not do well or when the Board of Directors do not recommend any dividend for payment. **Therefore, equity shares are known as 'variable income security'.** They are the last one to get repayment in the event of liquidation of the company.

10.4 FEATURES OR CHARACTERISTICS OF EQUITY SHARES

Equity shares enjoy a number of special characteristics, which distinguish it from other securities. They relate to their rights and claims, which are:

(A) Claim on Income: Equity shareholders enjoy their claim on the residual income of the company. Residual income is that part of income which is left in the business after meeting all the expenses, taxes and preference dividend, if any. This income may be split into two parts: dividend and retained earnings. If income is distributed to shareholders, it is called dividend. If the income is not distributed, it remains with the company in the form of retained profits. Additionally, the shareholders stand to benefit in the form of enhanced value, capital gain, when the shares are sold. So, residual income benefits the shareholders immediately, in the form of dividend, or later by way of capital gains. Dividend is not tax deductible to the company.

Distribution of dividend is the discretionary right or prerogative of the Board of Directors. Even if the profits are sufficient and, in fact, even the profits increase compared to the earlier year, still, the equity shareholders cannot, legally, compel the company to declare dividend. Thus, equity share is not an assured security from the investors' point of view as they are not sure of dividend. More so, capital gains / loss depend on the market value at the time of their sale. So, equity shares are risky security too.

Though equity shareholders cannot compel the company to increase the rate of dividend, they can reduce the dividend, recommended by Board of Directors, in the interests of the company.

(B) Claim on Assets: Equity shareholders have a residual claim on the ownership of company's assets. In the event of liquidation of a company, the claims of creditors are paid first, later to preference shareholders, if any, and balance goes to the equity shareholders. Company, normally, goes into liquidation when the going is not good and so the equity shareholders do not get back much of their investment. So, equity shares provide cushion to absorb losses, in the event of liquidation of the company.

(C) Right to Control or Voting Rights: Equity shareholders are the real owners of the company. They have a voting right in the working of the company. The Board of Directors, appointed by the equity shareholders in the Annual General Meeting, exercise real control over the company. So, equity shareholders exercise an indirect control over the company. But, such control is often weak due to their indifference in casting their voting rights.

(D) Pre-emptive Rights: As and when a public limited company wants to issue fresh equity shares, they are to be offered first to the existing shareholders. This is known as pre-emptive right. The purpose is to enable the shareholders to continue to have proportionate share of ownership. For example, if a shareholder has 5% ownership, he has to be offered 5% of the new shares to be issued. The shareholders' option to purchase a stated number of new shares at a specified price during a given period is called 'Rights'. Rights are valuable to the existing shareholders as the company issues shares, normally, at a price lower than the market rate. This right is made available to prevent the management to issue shares to persons of their choice. This right protects the shareholders from dilution of their financial interest as well as to retain their control. If the shareholder does not want to exercise their rights, they can sell them too for a price, as they are valuable.

(E) Limited Liability: Another distinct feature is liability of the equity shareholder is limited to the face value of the shares. In case, he has paid the full amount of the face value, he is not liable, further, even if the company goes into liquidation and its liabilities are more than its assets. In case of sole proprietorship or partnership firm, liability is unlimited. This limited liability feature attracts even otherwise unwilling investors to invest in a company. This enables the firm to raise the risky funds in the market by issue of equity shares.

10.4.1 Pros and Cons of Equity Financing

Equity capital is the most important form of long-term source of financing. Its merits and demerits are as under:

Merits

1. **No outflow of Cash:** It is a permanent source of capital. The company need not have any fear of redemption with the outflow of cash. These funds are available as long as the company does not go into liquidation.
2. **Borrowing Base:** What a company can borrow depends on its capital base. Lenders feel confident to lend looking to the capital base and they lend in proportion to the company's equity capital.
3. **No obligation to pay Dividend:** There is no fixed obligation to pay dividend. In case of financial difficulties, it can reduce or even skip payment of dividend.
4. **Real Owners and Gainers:** They are the real owners of the company as they have the voting right. In case of profits, they are the real gainers by way of increased dividend as well as appreciation of market price.

Demerits

1. **Cost:** Cost of equity shares is the highest to a company as dividend is not tax deductible. More so, floatation costs are also high compared to debt. Floatation costs are those costs incurred by the company incidental to the issue of shares.
2. **Trading on Equity:** Trading on equity is possible when debt is issued along with equity shares. So, trading on equity is not possible with issue of equity shares only. Trading on equity magnifies the earnings of equity shares.
3. **Risk:** From the view - point of investors, equity is more risky compared to debt as there is no certainty of return. So, investors want higher return to invest in shares. It is more difficult and costly for the company to raise funds through equity.
4. **Earnings Dilution:** If company raises funds through equity and its earnings do not increase in the proportion of the additional issue of shares, the earnings per share gets diluted.
5. **Ownership Dilution:** Pre-emptive right enables the existing shareholder to maintain the proportionate ownership. For maintaining, additional funds are needed. In case of financial difficulty to invest, the existing control is likely to be lost. This is the threat with a closely held company.

10.5 PREFERENCE SHARES

As the very name suggests, Preference shares have certain preferences, compared to equity shares. They enjoy preference in respect of payment of dividend. Whenever company has surplus profits, before payment of dividend to the equity shareholders, dividend is to be paid to preference shareholders. The second preference relates to repayment in the event of liquidation of the company. After paying outside creditors, preference share capital is returned before repaying to equity shareholders.

10.5.1 Features

Preference shares have several features. They are:

1. **Claims on Income and Assets: Preference share is a senior security compared to equity share.** It has a prior claim on the company's income and repayment. Dividend is to be paid on preference share before payment on equity shares. Similarly, payment of claim is to be made to them, in preference to equity shareholders.
2. **Fixed Dividend:** The dividend rate is fixed in the case of preference shares. The payment of dividend to preference shareholders is not a legal obligation on the part of the company, similar to equity shares. However, companies honour payment of dividend when they make adequate profits. Otherwise, company's image would be adversely affected. The important point is company cannot pay dividend to equity shareholders without paying dividend to preference shareholders.
3. **Cumulative Dividend:** Dividend is cumulative in case of cumulative preference shares. This is a protective right to the preference shareholders as the dividend in arrears is to be paid to them before declaring dividend to equity shareholders. Preference shareholders cannot force the company to pay dividend and non-payment does not result in liquidation of company. As they do not have the enforcing right to pay dividend, cumulative feature is valuable to them.
4. **Voting Rights:** Preference shareholders do not have any voting right in the management of the company. However, they have a right to vote in respect of those matters that affect them.
5. **Maturity:** Preference shares are not repaid similar to equity shares in the normal course. They are perpetual. Their money is returned in the event of liquidation after payment of debenture holders. However, in case of redeemable preference shares, the amount is returned— on the due date— as per the terms of issue.
6. **Hybrid form of security: Preference share capital is a hybrid form security, in the real sense, as it carries some of the features of equity share as well as debenture.** It is similar to equity share, as non-payment of dividend does not compel the company to go into liquidation. Payment of dividend is not obligatory. Dividend is not tax deductible.

Similar to debenture, preference share has a fixed rate of dividend just like a fixed rate of interest. They do not share in the residual profits of the company.

10.5.2 Advantages and Disadvantages of Preference Shares

Preference shares provide a number of advantages both to the company as well as its investors.

(A) Company's Point of view: The company has the following advantages by issuing preference shares:

1. **No Legal Obligation:** Preference dividend is payable if the company has distributable profits only. Hence, there is no legal obligation or committed financial burden to the company.
2. **Fixed Dividend:** The preference dividend is restricted to the stated amount. Preference shareholders do not participate in the surplus profits of the company.
3. **Long-term Capital:** There is no threat of cash outflow to the company as the capital is permanent. In case of redeemable preference shares only, they are to be redeemed out of the proceeds of fresh issue of shares or accumulated profits of the company.
4. **Trading on Equity:** Company can take advantage of trading on equity when the return on investment is higher than the dividend rate. Raising funds through this source magnifies the earning of the equity shares, paying a fixed rate of dividend to preference shareholders. This is a risk-free leverage advantage with preference share capital. Even default in payment of dividend does not force the company into insolvency.
5. **Enhances Creditworthiness:** As preference share capital is, generally, regarded as part of net worth, it enhances creditworthiness of the firm.
6. **No Dilution of Control:** Preference shares carry voting rights only if the matter, directly, affects their interests. Under normal circumstances, they do not enjoy voting rights and, so, there is no threat of dilution of control.
7. **No Assets are pledged:** No specific assets are pledged while issuing preference shares. So, company's mortgageable assets are not disturbed, in any manner.

(B) Investors' Point of view: Investors enjoy the following advantages:

1. **Fixed Rate of Dividend:** In case of cumulative preference shares, even if the company has made loss in one year, dividend for that year has to be paid from the subsequent year's profits. In the case of non-cumulative preference shares, this is not the case. Dividend need not be paid for the year of loss.
2. **Super Security over Equity Shares:** Preference shareholders enjoy preference for payment of dividend and return of funds, compared to equity shares. So, investors prefer to invest in preference shares.
3. **Voting Rights:** If dividend is in arrears, preference shareholders can exercise voting rights on all resolutions.

10.5.3 Disadvantages of Preference Shares

Inspite of many advantages, they suffer from the following shortcomings:

(A) Company's Point of view

1. **Costly Source:** Investors expect a higher return compared to rate of interest on debentures, as risk with preference share capital is greater. So, Preference share capital is dearer compared to debentures.
2. **Tax Disadvantage:** Dividend on preference shares is not tax deductible while interest payment on debentures or debt enjoys tax shield or advantage.
3. **Affects Creditworthiness:** There is no legal obligation to the company for payment of preference dividend. However, non-payment affects the creditworthiness of the company. If preference shares are cumulative, company has to pay the dividend to them before the dividend is paid to equity shares.

Preference Shareholders' Point of view

1. **At Management's Mercy:** As preference shareholders do not have any voting rights, normally, they remain at the mercy of management for dividend as well as redemption of share capital.
2. **Lower Return:** Compared to equity shares, the return is always lower.
3. **No Charge on Assets:** Assets are charged to Debentures. Such charge of assets is not available to the preference shares and so they rank after debentures, in case of liquidation of the company.

10.6 DEBENTURES

A Company may raise long-term finance by issuing debentures. A debenture is a long-term promissory note for raising loan capital. Those who invest in debentures are called debenture holders. **An alternative form of debenture is Bond, in India.** Public sector companies in India, mostly, issue bonds.

A debenture holder is a creditor of a company. Company pays them interest and principal as per the terms of debentures issued. The interest that is paid is a charge to the profit and loss account. Debentures are, normally, secured by a floating charge on the assets of the company.

10.6.1 Features of Debentures

Debenture or Bond is a creditorship security with a fixed rate of interest and fixed maturity period. **Its nature is of low risk capital**. The salient characteristics of debentures are as follows:

1. **Interest Rate:** The interest rate is fixed and does not change during the tenure of debenture, irrespective of the profit / loss of the company. Interest is calculated on the face value of the debenture. Interest is tax deductible to a company. However, interest is an income and taxable in the hands of the debenture holder.

2. **Maturity:** Debentures are issued for a specific period of time. Normally, they provide long-term finance. Debentures are, normally, issued for a period of 7 to 10 years. They are to be redeemed on the specific date.
3. **Claim on income:** Interest is to be paid to the debenture holder, irrespective of the earnings of the income. Company is under a legal obligation to pay interest. Default in payment of interest empowers the debenture holder to move a petition in a court of law for the winding up of the company.
4. **Claim on Assets:** In the event of liquidation, debenture holders are to be repaid first before repayment is made to preference and equity shareholders. Debentures may have a specific charge or floating charge on the assets of the company. In that event, they are secured creditors. The sale proceeds of the assets, pledged to them, go towards repayment of principal and interest to them. In case, the sale proceeds are inadequate, they stand as unsecured creditors for the balance amount. For the balance, they rank Paripasu along with unsecured creditors. Paripasu means stand on the same footing. It means for the balance, they rank, equally, along with unsecured creditors.
5. **Control:** As debenture holders are creditors of the company, they do not have any voting right and cannot participate in the management of the company. They enjoy only a prior claim in payment over shareholders.
6. **Call Feature:** Debentures may provide a call feature. **Call feature enables the company to redeem the debentures before the due date of redemption.** Company invokes the call feature when the interest rate payable on debenture is high and the current interest rate is low. To save costs, company redeems the debentures, before the due date. Normally, call price is higher than the issue price. As company is gaining, it does not mind to share some of its gain with the debenture holders.
7. **Indenture or Trust Deed:** Indenture or trust deed is a legal agreement between the company issuing debentures, on one hand, and the debenture trustees, on the other hand, who represent the debenture holders. The trust deed provides the specific terms in respect of the description of debentures, security available, rights of debenture holders, rights of the issuing company and responsibilities of the trustees. It is the responsibility of the trustees to protect the rights of the debenture holders by enforcing the responsibilities of the company that has issued debentures. Normally, a financial institution or insurance company is appointed as trustees.

10.6.2 Pros and Cons of Debentures

(A) Debentures have a number of advantages as long-term source of finance:

1. **Less costly:** It involves less cost to the company as investors are prepared to invest in debentures accepting a lower rate of return compared to equity. Reason is investors consider debentures relatively less risky investment. To the company, interest is tax deductible and so the effective cost to the company is lower.

2. **No Dilution:** Debenture holders do not enjoy any voting rights and so there is no threat of dilution of ownership or control.
3. **Fixed Payment of Interest:** Debenture holders are entitled to a fixed rate of interest, specified in the debenture. They cannot claim any share in the extra earnings of the company. So, cost to the company is fixed.
4. **Advantage during Inflation:** Real cost of interest declines during the periodof inflation.
5. **Trading on Equity:** When the return on investment is more than the cost of debt, it is beneficial to the company to issue debentures as it can trade on equity and magnify the earnings of the equity shareholders. So, it is advantageous for a company to mix debentures in its capital structure, while raising funds in the market.
6. **Flexibility:** Debentures provide flexibility in the capital structure as company can redeem debentures as and when it has surplus funds and desire to do so. Normally, companies reserve this right at the time of issue to take advantage of the falling interest rates in the market.
7. **Easy to raise funds:** Even in depression period, when the market sentiment is low, it is relatively easy for the company to raise funds, through debentures. Investors appreciate the advantage of certainty of income, with low risk during those periods.

(B) Limitations of Debentures: Despite the above advantages, debentures have limitations too. They are:

1. **Obligatory Payments:** Payment of interest is a legal obligation, even if the company is not in profits. Redemption of debentures has to be made on the due date. Default may force the company into liquidation.
2. **Financial Risk:** To a firm that has fluctuating sales and earnings, it increases the financial leverage and financial risk.
3. **Cash outflows:** Debentures are to redeemed at one time or other. As and when redeemed, cash outflow occurs. Even a sinking fund is created, annual cash outflow occurs.
4. **Restrictive Covenants:** They are the restrictive conditions contained in the debenture indenture. For example, a condition can be incorporated in the indenture that the total borrowing by a company cannot exceed a specified limit. So, the restrictive covenants limit the operating flexibility of the company, in future.
5. **Not possible to All Companies:** Companies that do not have stable earnings or who deal in products with elastic demand cannot issue debentures as the interest is a fixed commitment. Similarly, companies that cannot offer assets as security experience difficulty in raising funds through this source.
6. **Stamp Duty:** Stamp duty increases the cost of financing.

10.7 DIFFERENCES BETWEEN SHARES AND DEBENTURES

The differences between the two corporate securities are as under:

Nature of Difference	Shares	Debentures
1. Type of Capital	Part of owned capital	Part of loan capital
2. Type of Security	Ownership security	Creditorship security, also known as debt capital.
3. Return	Dividend depends on profits in respect of equity shares. Preference shares get the stated rate of dividend.	Interest is fixed. Depends on contractual terms.
4. Impact on Profit and Loss	Appropriation of Profit.	Fixed expense.Charge on Profit and Loss Account.
5. Voting Rights	Equity shares enjoy voting rights on all matters of the company. Preference shareholders enjoy voting rights on matters that affect their interests only.	No say in management.No Voting Rights.
6. Redemption	Equity shares are not redeemable during the life of the company.Redeemable Preference shares are redeemed at the end of the specified period.	Redeemed at the end of the specified period, stated in the indenture.
7. Priority of Repayment	At the time of liquidation, first outside liabilities are repaid. Then, Preference shares are returned. If balance is left, it goes to equity shares.	Enjoy priority in repayment, over share capital.

10.8 TERM LOANS

Companies can raise long-term finance through term loans in addition to share capital and debentures. They are obtained for financing large expansion, diversification or modernisation projects. Term loans are meant for meeting medium-term and long-term financial needs. **This method of financing is also called project financing.**

10.8.1 Features:

1. **Purpose:** The purpose is mostly to meet the capital expenditure.

2. **Documentation:** When shares and debentures are issued, company issues share certificates and debenture certificates, respectively, to the investors. In case of term loan, agreement is entered into between the company and the financial institution that specifies all conditions of sanction, security, interest as well as repayment etc.

3. **Maturity:** Medium-term loans are for periods ranging from one to five years and long-term loans are granted for periods beyond five years.

4. **Repayment Schedule:** Normally, loans are repaid through instalment system. Interest is charged on the outstanding balance. So, interest burden declines over the years. Company has to pay interest as well as instalment amount fixed in the agreement.

Term loan is granted is for capital expenditure so project may not generate revenues, immediately. Certain period is needed for completion of the project and start generating revenues. During this period, payment of interest as well as instalment amounts are suspended by the financial institution, which is known as moratorium period. This aspect is also specified in the agreement.

5. **Security:** Term loans are always secured. The assets purchased through the term loan constitute the security. This is called primary security. The company's current and future assets also, generally, secure term loans. This is called secondary security.

6. **Direct Negotiation:** A company negotiates term loan for project finance with the term lending institution, directly. Thus term loan is a Private placement. It saves the company underwriting commission and floatation costs. The advantage of term loan is ease of negotiation and low cost of raising funds.

7. **Restrictive Covenants:** In addition to security, the lender may like to protect its financial interests, further. This is done through restrictive covenants incorporated in the agreement, while sanctioning term loan. The restrictive covenants can be categorised as follows:

(A) **Asset-related covenants:** Lender may impose a condition on the borrower to maintain certain minimum current ratio. Additional charge on assets may be prohibited, without the approval of the lender.

(B) **Liability-related covenants:** The company may be restrained from further borrowings or not allowed to repay the existing loans, without its approval.

(C) **Cash flow related covenants:** Lenders may be restrained to declare dividend, beyond a specified percentage, or further capital expenditure is not to be incurred, without its consent.

(D) **Management related covenants:** Financial institution may stipulate a condition, at the time of sanction, to appoint its nominee director on the Board of Directors. Certain conditions may be incorporated in the agreement about the appointment of suitable personnel to manage the affairs of the company and their competence. The nominee director has to protect the interests of the lending institution, contributing to the company's policies and sound financial management.

Objective Questions

1. Describe the main types of securities, which are considered useful for meeting long-term financial requirements of industries? **(10.2,10.3,10.4, 10.5, 10.5.1, 10.6 and 10.6.1)**
2. What do you understand by long-term finance? Critically examine the importance of instruments of long-term finance? **(10.2,10.3,10.4, 10.5, 10.5.1, 10.6 and 10.6.1)**
3. Examine the usefulness of Debentures as an instrument of long-term finance? **(10.6 and 10.6.1)**
4. Why a preference share is called hybrid security? Explain the advantages and disadvantages of preference shares from the viewpoint of company and investors? **(10.5, 10.5.1, 10.5.2 and 10.5.3)**
5. What are term loans? What are their features? **(10.8 and 10.8.1)**
6. What are the features of equity shares and explain their pros and cons? **(10.3, 10.4 and 10.4.1)**
7. Bring out the differences between shares and debentures? **(10.7)**
8. Write short notes on
   (A) Restrictive covenants **(10.8 and 10.8.1 – Point No.7)**
   (B) Indenture **(10.6.1 –Point No.7)**
   (C) Pre-emptive rights **(10.4 – Point D)**

Check your Understanding

(A) State whether the following are True or False

1. If Company distributes income to shareholders, it is called dividend and if not distributed, it remains with the company in the form of retained profits.
2. A Company, normally, goes into liquidation when it's going is not good and equity shareholders get back their investment.
3. The Board of Directors, appointed by the equity shareholders in the Annual General Meeting, exercise control over the company.
4. Preference share is often considered to be a hybrid security.
5. Payment of dividend to preference shareholders is not a legal obligation on the part of the company, similar to an equity share.
6. Ownership securities are represented by debentures.
7. Equity shareholders have a residual claim on the assets and profits of the company.
8. Debenture or Bond is a creditorship security with a fixed rate of interest and fixed maturity period.
9. The company's current and future assets , generally, secure term loans, which is called primary security.
10. The effective cost of debentures is low as compared to shares.
11. Preference shares are entitled to fixed dividend irrespective of the level of earnings.
12. Company cannot declare dividend to equity shareholders without paying dividend to preference shareholders.

Answers

1.	True	2.	False	3.	True	4.	True	5.	True
6.	False	7.	True	8.	True	9.	False	10.	True
11.	True	12.	True						

(B) Pick up the right answer:

1. This security is known as variable income security.
   (A) Debentures
   (B) Preference shares
   (C) Equity shares
2. Real ownership of a company rests with
   (A) Board of Directors
   (B) Equity shareholders
   (C) Preference shareholders
3. Preference share is a .... security compared to equity share.
   (A) senior
   (B) junior
   (C) equal

Answers

1. (C) 2. (B) 3. (A)

11

COST OF DIFFERENT SOURCES OF RAISING CAPITAL

11.1 COST OF CAPITAL

Cost of capital is the minimum rate of return expected by investors, the suppliers of capital. In other words, it is a price for obtaining capital. It is a compensation for time and risk. Investors are of different categories – equity shareholders, preference shareholders and debenture holders. They provide different sources of finance. Their risks are different. Debentures are paid interest whether the firm makes profit or not. They get back their money, before payment is made to preference and equity shareholders. They get a fixed interest rate. However, the debenture holders are exposed to the risk of default in payment. Since cash flows of a company are uncertain, there is probability for default in payment of principal as well as interest. Still, their risk is the lowest amongst the different long-term sources of finance. Risk and return always go in hand in hand. If risk is greater, one expects higher return. Here, their risk is lowest. So, they can expect a lowest rate of return amongst the different securities of the company. In other words, cost to the company on the funds raised through debentures is the lowest. Preference shares carry fixed dividend but the dividend is subordinated to interest on debentures. Return of funds to them is also only after payment of debentures. Looking to the relatively higher risk, the expectations of preference shareholders are higher than debenture holders. So, their cost is more to the company, compared to debentures. Equity shareholders are the residual claimants in profits as well as return of money. Their risk is the greatest and so cost to the company is the highest amongst all sources of finance.

Importance: The concept of cost of capital is very important in the financial management. Decision to invest in a particular project depends on the cost of capital. **The minimum return expected from the project is its cost of capital.** The minimum return expected by the investors depends upon their risk perception as well as risk-return characteristics of the firm. It is a cut off rate. If the return is above or equal to the cut-off rate, then only investment is made. If the return is below the cut-off rate, no investment is made. To achieve the objective of wealth maximization, the return has to be more than cut off rate.

The cost of capital to a company is the minimum return expected by the different group of investors who invest their money in the form of shares, debentures or term loans. If the company does not earn this minimum return, the investors will be tempted to pull their funds out of the company. They withdraw their investment from that company and prefer to invest elsewhere. The company concerned would not able to retain the investment, let alone attract fresh investment, at the current market rate and in consequence, the market price of the share falls. At the reduced market price, the company may receive the investment. In fact, cost of capital is the minimum rate of return, which will maintain the market value of the shares at its present level.

Definition: According to Solomon Ezra, "Cost of capital is the minimum required rate of earnings or the cut-off rate of capital expenditure".

From the above definition, there are three basic aspects of the cost of capital:

1. **Cost of capital is not cost as such:** It is not cost to the firm. In fact, it is the minimum rate of return that a firm requires.
2. **Minimum Rate of Return:** The rate of return is that minimum, expected by the investors, which maintains the market value of the shares.
3. **Composition:** The return should contain three components:
   (A) Normal return at Zero Risk
   (B) Premium for Business Risk and
   (C) Premium for Financial Risk on account of pattern of capital structure

Symbolically, the cost of capital may be represented as:

K = Normal return at Zero Risk level
+
Premium for Business Risk
+
Premium for Financial Risk

Where K = Cost of Capital

11.2 SIGNIFICANCE OF COST OF CAPITAL

Cost of capital plays a crucial role in financial management in the following areas.

(A) **Capital Budgeting Decisions:** Cost of capital helps the management in taking decisions about the selection of capital expenditure projects. It is a cut-off or discount rate for evaluating desirability of investment projects. In capital budgeting, according to the present value method, project would be accepted only if the present value of the expected future returns is more than or equal to the initial capital or investment, otherwise the project may be rejected. The present value is calculated by discounting the future cash flows at cut-off rate, which is the cost of capital. The discount rate is the cost of capital or cut-off rate. Discount rate is also known as implicit cost, which equates the present value of cash inflows with the present value of cash outflows. So, cost of capital is taken as a decision criterion in capital budgeting matters. Hence, the cost of capital concept is highly useful in capital budgeting decisions.

(B) **Designing Debt Policy:** Financing the firm's assets is a crucial problem in every business. There should be a proper mix of debt and equity in financing the assets of the company. When the return on investment is greater than the cost of debt, earning on equity share is magnified. While designing the capital structure of the firm, the management has to keep in mind to maximize the value of the share in the stock exchange. This becomes possible when the cost of capital is at its minimum and value of the firm is at its maximum. So, measurement of cost of capital from various sources of finance is essential in designing and planning the capital structure.

(C) **Measurement of Financial Performance:** The actual profitability of project is compared to the overall cost of capital of funds used. If the actual profitability of the project is more than the projected and actual cost of capital, the performance of the management is said to be satisfactory. When two managers are to be compared, ranking becomes possible with this concept.

11.3 CONCEPT OF COST OF CAPITAL: OPPORTUNITY COST

Decision-making is a process of choosing alternatives. Consider an individual having two investment opportunities, investing in 8 percent 3-year postal certificates and another 3 - year fixed deposit in a nationalised bank that fetches an interest rate of 9 percent interest. Government assures payment in respect of both the securities. Looking to the higher interest rate, now, the choice is made to deposit in a bank. By investing in a bank, the individual has foregone the alternative opportunity of investing in postal deposit that gives him 8 percent interest. So, the individual has incurred an opportunity cost. In this case, the cost is 8% for the individual. **The opportunity cost is the rate of return foregone on the next best alternative investment opportunity of comparable risk.** Thus, the required rate of return on an investment project is an opportunity cost. In other words, the minimum return required to invest in a project is the return foregone on the next best alternative, called opportunity cost.

Opportunity cost of capital and cost of capital mean the same.

11.4 RISK-RETURN RELATIONSHIP OF VARIOUS SECURITIES

Investors have numerous investment opportunities. Their returns as well as risks are different. Risk and return always go hand in hand. Why return in Postal deposit is low compared to interest rate on a debenture? Postal deposit is a risk-free security while debenture is not. As risk is more with a debenture, return is also high compared to postal deposit. Return in an equity share is still high because the risk is all the higher than the postal deposit as well as debenture. It may be observed that the required return of any security is composed of two rates – a risk-free rate and risk premium. A risk free rate is compensation for time value and its risk-premium, at that point, will be zero. Bank deposits and Government securities are the examples of risk-free securities. Investors expect a higher return on risky securities. The higher the risk of a security, the higher is risk-premium, and therefore, a higher required rate of return.

The risk-return relationship for various securities is shown in the following figure:

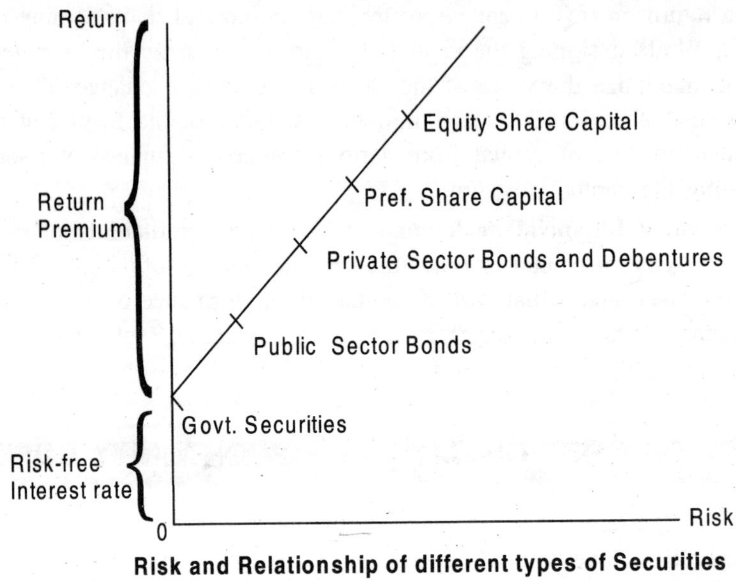

Risk and Relationship of different types of Securities

11.5 DETERMINING COST OF DEBENTURE

Debt includes all interest-bearing borrowings. Cost of debt to the company is the return (yield), which lenders expect from their investment. A Company can raise debt in various ways. It can borrow funds from financial institutions or public in the form of public deposits or debentures. A debenture is issued at par, discount or premium. The contractual rate of interest forms the basis for calculating the cost of any debt. **Contractual rate of interest on a debenture is called as coupon rate.** For example, if the interest rate of debentures is 12%, coupon rate is 12%. Though debenture is issued at discount or premium, interest is paid on the face value of the debentures.

So, for calculation of interest rate, face value of debenture is to be multiplied with interest rate or coupon rate.

Interest = Face value of the debenture × Interest rate

When the debenture is issued at par and to be redeemed at par, the cost of debt (before –tax), simply, is the contractual rate of interest. If the face value of a 10% debenture is Rs.100 and is issued at par and also to be redeemed at par, what is cost of debt (before-tax)? It is Rs.10.

In other words, when the debenture is issued at par and also to be redeemed at par, the cost of debt and interest rate mean the same. However, the cost of debt (before-tax) would be different if the debenture is issued/redeemed at discount and premium.

Interest tax shield: The interest paid on debt is tax deductible. In consequence, the actual cost of debt, interest amount less tax there on, would be lower. In other words, indirectly, Government is bearing a part of interest cost. As a result of the interest tax shield, the after-tax cost to the firm will be substantially lower than the investors' required rate of return. The before-tax cost of debt (k_d)should be adjusted for tax effect as follows:

$$\text{After-tax cost of debt} = k_d\,(I-T)$$

Where k_d = Before tax cost of debt

T = corporate tax rate

If interest rate is 15% on debenture and the tax rate is 35%, the after-tax cost of debenture would be

$$k_d\,(I\text{-}T) = 0.15(1-0.35) = 0.0975 \text{ or } 9.75\%$$

In other words, the actual cost of debt to the company is 9.75%, while the return to its investors is 15%. The difference between the two, in fact, is not borne by the company, but by the Government in the form of reduced tax.

It is to be noted that the tax benefit would be available if the firm is profitable and is paying taxes. A loss-making firm is not required to pay taxes. So, it would not gain any tax benefit associated with the payment of interest. So, cost of capital for a loss- making firm is its true cost of debt i.e. before tax-cost. In other words, effective cost of debt to a profit-making firm and loss-making firm is not the same.

For calculation of the average cost of capital, the after-tax cost of debt must be used, not the before cost-tax cost of debt.

11.6 DETERMINING COST OF PREFERENCE CAPITAL

Dividend paid on preference shares is not tax deductible so tax benefit is not available. Dividend payment is only an appropriation of profit, not a charge on Profit and Loss Account. More so, payment of preference dividend is discretionary on the part of the company. In other words, there is no legal obligation for payment of preference dividend. So, one may be tempted to think that preference capital does not have cost. It is not true. **The cost of preference capital is a function of the dividend expected by the investors.**

A company, with the intention not to pay dividend, never issues preference capital. Preference shareholders enjoy a prior claim on profits. So, only after payment of preference dividend, dividend to equity shareholders can be paid. More over, non-payment of dividend to preference shareholders, when profits are available, would adversely affect company's image. Preference shareholders would have voting rights, in the event of default of dividend payment. In case of default in payment of dividend, the market value of the equity shares would be affected. Though there is no legal obligation, company defaults in payment of dividend on preference capital only when it does not make profits. The default can also happen, if the cash position is tight.

Cost of Irredeemable Preference Share: The Irredeemable Preference Share is treated as perpetual security. The cost Irredeemable Preference Share is computed by the following equation:

$$**k_p = \frac{PDIV}{P_o}$$

Where

k_p = **Cost of Preference share**

PDIV = **Expected preference dividend**

P_o = **Price of preference share**

$$\text{*Cost of Capital of Preference share} = \frac{\text{Expected preference dividend}}{\text{Price of preference share}}$$

Note: For students, it is easy to remember the one star* type of definition at it gives meaning to remember rather than the two stars** definition as it contains a formula that is difficult to remember.

Illustration No. 1

A Company issues 12 percent irredeemable preference shares. The face value per share is Rs. 100. If the share is issued at a discount of Rs.5, what is the cost of preference share? What is the cost price, if the share is issued at a premium Rs.5?

Answer:

Issue price Rs. 95

$$k_p = \frac{PDIV}{P_o}$$

$$\frac{12}{95} = 0.126 = 12.63$$

Issue price Rs. 105

$$k_p = \frac{PDIV}{P_o}$$

$$= \frac{12}{105} = 0.114 = 11.42$$

11.7 DETERMINING COST OF EQUITY CAPITAL

The cost of equity is 'the minimum rate of return that a company must earn on equity financed portion of its investments in order to leave unchanged the market price of its stock'. The cost of equity capital is a function of the expected return by its investors. Payment of dividend on equity shares is not legally binding. It does not mean that equity share capital is a cost free capital.

The cost of equity can be calculated by the following methods:

(A) Dividend Yield Method:

According to this method, the cost of equity capital is calculated on the assumption the investors give prime importance to dividends and risk of the firm remains unchanged. This method does not consider the growth in dividends, in future, and does not consider the capital gains. This method is useful for the company that has stable dividend policy over a period of time.

$$K_E = \frac{\text{Dividend per share}}{\text{Market price per share}} \times 100$$

Where K_E = Cost of equity capital

Illustration No. 2

ABC Ltd. has disbursed dividend of Rs. 25 on each equity share of Rs. 10. The current market price of equity share is Rs. 60. Calculate the cost of equity as per dividend yield method.

Solution:

$$K_E = \frac{\text{Dividend per share}}{\text{Market price per share}} \times 100$$

$$\text{Cost of equity capital} = \frac{25}{60} \times 100 = 41.67\%$$

(B) Dividend Yield Plus Growth in Dividend Method:

When the company follows a constant dividend rate method and the dividend payout ratio is constant, this method is used to compute the cost of capital. In this method, an allowance for future growth in dividend is added to the current dividend yield. This method recognizes that the current market price of a share reflects expected future dividends.

The formula for calculation is

$$K_E = \frac{\text{Dividend}}{\text{Market price}} \times 100 + \text{Growth rate}$$

Illustration No. 3

XYZ LTD's shares are quoted in stock exchange trading at Rs. 120 each. Next year's dividend is expected to be Rs.30 per share and the subsequent dividends are expected to grow at an annual rate of 5% of the previous year's dividend. What is the cost of Equity shares?

Solution:

$$K_E = \frac{\text{Dividend}}{\text{Market price}} \times 100 + \text{Growth rate}$$

$$= \frac{\text{Rs. }30}{\text{Rs. }120} \times 100 + 5\% = 30\%$$

(C) Earning Yield Method:

This method is adopted when the following conditions are satisfied:

(i) When the earnings of the company are expected to remain constant, in future,

(ii) When all the expected profits would be distributed, without leaving any profits for retention i.e. pay-out ratio is 100% or retention ratio is Zero,

(iii) When the new equity capital is expected to earn the same current rate of earnings and

(iv) Market price is likely to be influenced only by the earnings per share and not by any other factors.

Formula for the calculation is

$$K_E = \frac{\text{EPS}}{\text{Market value per share}}$$

Illustration No. 4

Rani Ltd's shares are currently trading at a price of Rs.70 with outstanding shares of 5,00,000. Their expected profit after tax for the coming year is Rs. 84 lakhs. Calculate the cost of capital based on price/ earning method.

Solution:

$$K_E = \frac{\text{EPS}}{\text{Market value per share}}$$

$$\text{Earning per share} = \frac{84,00,000}{5,00,000} = 16.8$$

$$K_E = \frac{16.8}{70} \times 100 = 24\%$$

(D) Cost of Capital based on Net worth:

Based on the average net worth, the cost of capital is calculated. The following is the formula for calculation of capital based on net worth:

$$K_e = \frac{\text{Dividend}}{\text{Average net worth}} \times 100$$

Illustration No. 5

The Balance Sheet of Srinivas Ltd. as on 31-3-2006 is given below:

(Rs. lakhs)

Capital and Liabilities			Assets	
5,00,000 equity share of Rs. 10 each		50	Land	70
Share premium		10	Buildings	40
General Reserve as on 1-4-2005	20		Plant & Machinery	130
Added during the year	10	30	Current assets	60
P / L Appropriation A/c as on 1-4-2005	15			
Added during the year	5	20		
Term Loans		15		
Current liabilities and provisions		175		
		300		300

For the year 2005-06, the company has declared a dividend of 24% p.a. Calculate the cost of capital based on net worth of the company.

Solution:

$$\text{Dividend Paid} = \frac{50,00,000}{100} \times 24 = \text{Rs. } 12,00,000$$

Calculation of Net worth

Particulars	1.4.2005	31.3.2006
Equity Share capital	50	50
Share premium	10	10
General reserve	20	30
P & L appropriation A/c	15	20
Total	95	110

$$\text{Average Net worth} = \frac{95 + 110}{2}$$

$$= \text{Rs. } 1{,}02{,}50{,}000$$

$$\text{Cost of Capital} = \frac{\text{Dividend}}{\text{Average net worth}} \times 100$$

$$= \frac{12{,}00{,}000}{1{,}02{,}50{,}000} \times 100 = 11.7.\%$$

11.8 COST OF RETAINED EARNINGS

Retained earnings are that profit not distributed to the equity shareholders but retained in the business. Retained profits, normally, is a substantial amount used in the business. Does it have any cost? Yes, it has cost. Before, we explain this let us understand the meaning of implicit cost and explicit cost more.

Explicit cost: The explicit cost of capital of a particular source can be defined in terms of dividend or interest paid by the firm. There is an explicit flow of funds, in the form of return to its investors. If debt in the form of debenture is raised, interest is paid. Dividend, at a fixed rate, is paid on preference capital. There is some expected dividend on equity shares. These payments refer to explicit capital.

Implicit cost: Firm does not pay anything on retained profits. Then, where is the cost? If retained profits are distributed to the shareholders, shareholders could invest somewhere or other. If they invest elsewhere, they would get some return. By not distributing the profits and retaining in the business, the equity shareholders have foregone their expected return. So, the cost of retained earnings is the return foregone by the investors on the amount of profit not distributed to them and kept in the business. In other words, retained earnings have implicit cost.

The opportunity cost of the retained earnings is the rate of return on dividends foregone by the equity shareholders. In other words, retained earnings have implicit cost.

Objective Questions

1. What do you understand by cost of capital? Explain its significance? **(11.1 and 11.2)**
2. Explain Risk – Return relationship of various securities through pictorial presentation? **(11.4)**

3. How cost of debentures and preference capital is calculated?
   (11.5 and 11.6)
4. Explain the different methods of cost of equity capital?
   (11.7)
5. Write Short notes on:
   (A) Opportunity cost of capital
   (11.3)
   (B) Cost of retained earnings
   (11.8)

Check Your Understanding

State whether the following statements are True or False

1. Cost of capital is the minimum rate of return required by investors.
2. Cost of capital is taken as a decision criterion in capital budgeting decisions.
3. Cost of capital is equal to Normal return at any risk level.
4. According to the present value method in capital budgeting, project would be accepted only if the present value of the expected future returns is more than or equal to the initial cost of capital or investment, otherwise the project may be rejected.
5. Implicit cost is the discount rate, which equates the present value of cash inflows with the present value of cash outflows.
6. Risk and return do not go hand in hand.
7. Dividend on preference shares is a charge on Profit and loss account and so is tax deductible.
8. Contractual rate of interest on debenture is called as coupon rate.
9. When the debenture is issued at par and also to be redeemed at par, the cost of debt and interest rate are one and the same.
10. In case of default in payment of preference dividend, the market value of the equity shares would be affected.
11. Equity share capital is a cost free capital.
12. Cost of capital comprises both business and financial risks.

Answers

1. True	2. True	3. False	4. True	5. True
6. False	7. False	8. True	9. True	10. True
11. False	12. True			

12

WEIGHTED AVERAGE COST OF CAPITAL

- Specific cost of Capital
- Importance of Overall Cost of Capital
- Calculation of Overall Cost of Capital
- Capitalisation
    - Value of Capitalisation
- Objective Questions
- Check your Understanding

12.1 INTRODUCTION

Different sources of finance such as debentures, preference share capital, equity share capital and retained earnings have their individual cost of capital, dependent on the risk each carries.

12.2 SPECIFIC COST OF CAPITAL

The cost of each source of capital is known as specific cost of capital. Amongst the different sources, debt is cheap due to tax deductibility. Preference share capital is dearer compared to debt, as dividend is not admissible under the income tax. Amongst the different sources of capital, equity is the costliest as the risk is maximum with this source of capital.

12.3 IMPORTANCE OF OVERALL COST OF CAPITAL

What is the need of for calculating overall cost of capital when the specific cost of capital is known? Let us take an example to explain. A Company's internal rate of return (IRR) for project A is 10% and has an option to finance the project with debt whose cost is 8%. The company has accepted the project, as its IRR is more than the cost of debt. Later, in the same year, another project B has come up for its consideration, with the same level of risk, similar to project A. For funding the project, debt funds are not forthcoming. So, company has explored the option to choose financing through equity. Equity is available at 12%. Using the component cost of capital as the cut-off rate, the company has rejected the proposal to go ahead with project B, as the cost of equity is higher than the IRR of that project. Is it a right decision? The firm is associating the method of financing (equity) with the investment project (Project B). The firm is not appreciating the aspect that the various sources of capital are related to each other. No doubt, equity is always dearer compared to debt. However, with the increasing usage of debt, risk of the firm increases. The firm's decision to use the debt reduces the future capacity of the firm to use debt more and makes it more costly, compared to the earlier situation. Reason is it increases the risk of equity shareholders. Over a long run, every firm has to maintain a balance between debt and equity to have balanced or target capital structure. **It is, generally, agreed that the cost of capital should be used in the composite or overall sense.** This is known as weighted average cost of capital.

12.4 CALCULATION OF OVERALL COST OF CAPITAL

Once the specific cost of capital of each of the above long-term sources is ascertained, the next step is to calculate the overall cost of capital. The overall cost of capital may be defined as the rate of return that must be earned by the firm in order to satisfy the requirements of different investors. What is its importance? The overall cost of capital is of utmost importance. **The overall cost of capital is used as the discount rate or cut-off rate in evaluating the capital budgeting proposals.**

The overall cost of capital is the minimum return required on the assets of the firm. The formula for the calculation is as follows:

$$WACC = k_e * w1 + k_d * w2 + k_p * w3$$

Where WACC = Weighted average cost of capital

k_e = Cost of equity capital

k_d = After tax, cost of debt

k_p = Cost of Preference capital

w1 = Proportion of equity in capital structure

w2 = Proportion of debt in capital structure

w3 = Proportion of Preference capital in capital structure

For calculating the overall cost of capital, first the different long-term sources of finance are to be identified. Their relative proportion or weight, in the aggregate, is to be found out. Their individual weight is to be multiplied with the respective cost and the aggregate is the overall cost of capital. The aggregate cost is to be divided by the total amount of long-term sources of finance to arrive at weighted averege cost of capital.

Illustration No. 1

The following is the capital structure of XYZ ltd.

Source	Amount Rs.	Interest rate / Dividend
Equity share capital	25,000	11%
Preference share capital	20,000	10%
Retained earnings	10,000	8%
Debentures	20,000	10%

Tax rate is 50%. Calculate the overall cost of capital.

Solution:

$$WACC = k_e * w1 + k_d * w2 + k_p * w3$$

Where
- $WACC$ = Weighted average cost of capital
- k_e = Cost of equity capital
- k_d = After tax cost of debt
- k_p = Cost of Preference capital
- $w1$ = Proportion of equity in capital structure
- $w2$ = Proportion of debt in capital structure
- $w3$ = Proportion of Preference capital in capital structure

Source	Amount	Cost of capital	Amount X cost of capital
Equity share capital	25,000	0.11	2,750
Preference share capital	20,000	0.10	2,000
Retained earnings	10,000	0.08	800
Debentures	20,000	0.05*	1,000
Total	75,000		6,550

$$WACC = \frac{6,550}{75,000} \times 100 = 8.73\%$$

* Interest payable on debentures is 10%. However, tax-rate is 50%. So, the after-tax cost is 5%.

12.5 CAPITALISATION

Capital and capitalisation are two different terms. They convey different meanings. The term 'Capital' refers to the total investment of a company in money, tangible and intangible securities. The term 'Capitalisation' is used in the context of companies only, and not in relation to sole proprietorship and partnership concerns. **In common parlance, capitalisation refers to the par value of stocks and bonds outstanding.**

Value of capitalisation: According to Earnings theory of capitalisation, the capitalisation of a company depends upon its earnings and the expected fair rate of return on its capital invested. If a company is making net profit of

Rs. 5 lakhs and its fair rate of return is 10%, capitalisation of the company will be

$$5,00,000 \times \frac{100}{10} = \text{Rs. } 50,00,000$$

Illustration No. 2

A Company with net operating earnings of Rs. 3,00,000 is attempting to evaluate a number of possible capital structures, given below. Which of the capital structures will you recommend, and why?

Capital structure	Debt in capital structure (B) (Rs.)	Cost of debt (K_1) %	Cost of equity (K)%
1	3,00,000	10.0	12.0
2	4,00,000	10.0	12.5
3	5,00,000	11.0	13.5
4	6,00,000	12.0	15.0
5	7,00,000	14.0	18.0

Solution:

					(Rs.)
Particulars	Capital structure plans having debts of various amounts				
I	II	III	IV	V	
EBIT	3,00,000	3,00,000	3,00,000	3,00,000	3,00,000
Less interest (K_1 x B)	– 30,000	– 40,000	–,55,000	–72,000	– 98,000
Net income (NI) for equity share holders	2,70,000	2,60,000	2,45,000	2,28,000	2,02,000
K_e(equity capitalisation rate	0.12	0.125	0.135	0.150	0.180
S (market value of equity)	22,50,000	20,80,000	18,14,815	15,20,000	11,22,222
B (market value of debt)	3,00,000	4,00,000	5,00,000	6,00,000	7,00,000
Total market value (S + B) = V	25,50,000	24,80,000	23,14,815	21,20,000	18,22,222
Overall cost of Capital $(K_0) = \frac{(EBIT)}{V}$	V11.76%	12.10%	12.96%	14.15%	16.46%

Capital structure having debts of Rs. 3,00,000 (capital structure 1) is recommended, as the cost is the lowest.

Objective Questions

1. Explain the concept and method of calculating the weighted average cost of capital? **(12.1 to 12.4)**
2. Distinguish the difference between capital and capitalisation? **(12.5)**

Check your Understanding

1. The overall cost of capital may be defined as the rate of return that must be earned by the firm in order to satisfy the requirements of different investors.
2. For calculation of the average cost of capital, the before-tax cost of debt must be used.
3. The terms capital and capitalisation convey the same meaning.
4. It is, generally, agreed that the cost of capital should be used in the composite or overall sense, which is known as weighted average cost of capital.

Answers

1. True 2. False 3. False 4. True

13

OPTIMUM CAPITAL STRUCTURE

- *Introduction*
- *Concept and Significance of Optimum Capital Structure*
- *Optimal Capital Structure – Difficult Task*
- *Essential Features of an Appropriate Capital Structure*
- *Factors Determining Capital Structure*
- *Balanced Capital Structure*
- *Relevant Ratios for Analysing Capital Structure*
- *Objective Questions*
- *Check Your Understanding*

13.1 INTRODUCTION

Debt in capital structure is profitable. Reason is its tax deductibility. If debt is so profitable, why companies are not totally financed by debt? As debt is risky compared to other forms of financing such as preference and equity share capital, proportion of debt financing is contained. There are several considerations for limiting debt. What are those considerations that prevent to have major debt component in financing, even sacrificing higher profits? Why companies try to achieve optimum capital Structure? There is no mathematical formula to achieve optimal capital structure. Then, what issues govern to achieve the optimum capital structure? Let us discuss them.

13.2 CONCEPT AND SIGNIFICANCE OF OPTIMUM CAPITAL STRUCTURE

The optimum capital structure is obtained when the market value per share is maximum while the average cost of capital is minimum. The optimum capital structure may be defined as "that capital structure or combination of debt and equity that leads to the maximum value of firm". So, the optimum capital structure is that relationship of debt and equity, which maximises the value of the company's equity share in the stock exchange. Normally, every firm uses debt and equity in financing its assets. In case, company's borrowing helps the company in increasing its market value of share in the stock exchange, it can be said that the company is moving towards its optimum capital structure. However, if the use of borrowing results in the fall of market value of share in the stock exchange, it can be said that the company is moving away from its optimum capital structure.

So, the objective of the firm is to select that type of financing or debt-equity mix, which leads to maximise the value of equity share in the stock exchange.

CONSIDERATIONS

The following considerations should be kept in mind while achieving the goal of achieving optimum capital structure.

(A) **Borrow when cheap:** Company should borrow as long as its cost of debt is lower than the return on investment. **If the interest paid on debentures/long term loans or dividend payable on preference share capital is lower than the return on investment, it is preferable to borrow.** It will increase the market value of the share. So, every effort has to be made to take possible advantage of leverage.

(B) **Tax Advantage of Corporate Taxes:** Interest paid on borrowing is eligible for tax benefit. So, effective cost of debt goes down in comparison to other forms of financing. So, **tax advantage comes with borrowing.**

(C) **Avoid Perceived High Risk:** Beyond a point, increased debt financing is attached with undue risk. If the shareholders perceive excessive amount of debt in the capital structure, the price of the equity share may drop. **The finance manager should not, therefore, borrow whether risky or not if the investors perceive borrowing as an excessive risky proposition.** Investor's perception is likely to depress the market price of equity share of that company. So, firm should avoid undue financial risk, attached with borrowing.

(D) **Flexible structure:** The flexibility of capital structure refers to the ability of the firm to raise additional capital funds, whenever needed to finance viable and profitable investment opportunities. The capital structure should enable the firm to take advantage of the opportunities that may come up due to changing conditions. **Precisely, it means firm should have always untapped borrowing power.** It facilitates to take advantage of the favourable government policies or capital market. **If the capital market is conducive, the firm should raise additional funds through equity market rather than the issue of debt.**

Continuous Process: Achieving balanced or optimum capital structure, practically, is a difficult task. The Board of Directors or chief operating officer develops the capital structure, which is most advantageous to the company. As many factors affect the determination of the capital structure, the judgement of the person who is making the capital structure decision plays an important role. Two similar companies may have different capital structure, if the decision-makers differ in their judgement.

The capital structure decision is a continuous process and has to be taken, whenever firm needs additional finances.

13.3 OPTIMAL CAPITAL STRUCTURE –DIFFICULT TASK

There are two extremes in financing, one is 0% debt financing and the other is 99.99% debt financing, because 100% debt financing is not possible. Between these two extremes, particular debt-mix finance is to be decided. As already stated, there is no mathematical formula or method to determine the optimal capital mix. This is a formidable task. This is not possible to achieve overnight. At optimum capital structure, the value of equity share is at its maximum and average cost of capital is at its minimum. As long as the return on investment is more than the cost of debt, every rupee of borrowing brings in more profits. Then, why firms do not have more debt content in their capital structure? **The simple reason is debt brings risk. Once investors perceive the risk, they may retreat from the share market and in consequence, the share price may fall.** However, if they consider the risk is reasonable and would bring in more profits, instead of share price declining, it may as well increase on account of investors' speculation. Share market is highly complex, does not work on theories and capital markets are never perfect. The exact optimal capital structure may be impossible and, therefore, every effort is to be made to achieve the best approximation to the optimum capital structure. The capital structure so arrived may not be optimum but appropriate in those circumstances. Optimum capital structure is a hypothetical concept. So, some people prefer to use the term 'sound or appropriate capital structure' in place of optimum capital structure as the former appears to be more realistic. Let us see what optimal capital structure requires.

13.4 ESSENTIAL FEATURES OF AN APPROPRIATE CAPITAL STRUCTURE

A capital structure will be considered to be appropriate, if it possesses the following features:

(A) **Profitability:** The capital structure of a company should be the most profitable. **The most profitable capital structure is one, when the cost of financing is at its minimum and earning per share is at peak.**

(B) **Risk:** The use of excessive debt threatens the solvency of the firm. To the point debt does not add significant risk, the debt should be used. Beyond that level, debt should be avoided. So, the content of the debt should not, therefore, increase the financial and business risk, beyond the manageable limits. **While designing the capital structure, the finance manager has to design the capital structure in such a manner that the cost and risk are minimum.**

(C) **Flexibility:** The capital structure should be flexible. Flexibility means the capital structure should always have an untapped borrowing power, which can be used in conditions, which may arise due to favourable capital market, government policies etc. The structure should be such that it can be manoeuvred to meet the changing requirements and conditions. The company should not borrow to its maximum extent. Whenever, the firm finds profitable opportunities, it should be in a position to take advantage. **Borrowing scope should be left to avail profitable opportunities.**

(D) **Capacity:** The capital structure should be within the debt capacity of the company. The debt capacity depends on its ability to generate future cash flows. In other words, the **borrowing should be commensurate with the company's ability to generate future cash flows.** The firm should be in a position to meet its obligations in paying the loan and interest charges as and when they fall due.

(E) **Control: The firm should so devise its capital structure that it involves minimum risk of loss of control.** When additional funds are raised, the controlling interest of the existing owners gets diluted, automatically, unless they invest additional funds, suitably. Even the preference shareholders would get the voting right if the dividend is not paid for two consecutive years. In such an event, the composition of the board of directors may change that may result in reduced level of control. More so, the owners of closely held companies are, particularly, always concerned with the dilution of control.

Conflicting Approach: The above mentioned are the general principles of an appropriate capital structure. Some of the features are conflicting with each other. For example, rising funds through debt is cheap and so complies with the principle of profitability. However, debt is risky and so goes against the principles of conservatism and solvency.

Degree of Emphasis: Companies give different degrees of emphasis to these features. For example, a company may give more importance to control while another company is concerned with solvency. Further, relative importance of these requirements may change with shifting conditions.

Conflicting interests: The finance manger is responsible to design the appropriate capital structure, which is most advantageous to the interests of different groups that may be conflicting. Equity shareholders are the owners of the company. Therefore, their interest is primary and due consideration has to be given to them. However, there are other interested groups such as customers, employees, society and the government. So, due consideration is also required to be given to them.

Final Compromise: The prudent finance manager should try to have the best out of the circumstances within which the company is operating. **The fact remains that the finance manager has to make a satisfactory compromise to suit the management's desires and prevailing trends in the capital market when market is tapped for raising funds.**

13.5 FACTORS DETERMINING CAPITAL STRUCTURE

The factors that determine the capital structure are of different importance and not possible to rank. The influence of the individual factors depends on the preferences of the management and also change over a period of time. For example, a closely held company may give more importance to the question of control. As and when funds are needed, the finance manager has to study the pros and cons of the various sources of finance so as to select the right combination for raising funds.

The 'Essential features' detailed above also determine the structure. Following are the **additional factors**:

1. **Financial Leverage or Trading on Equity:** The use of long-term fixed interest bearing debt and preference share capital alongwith equity share capital is called financial leverage. **Financial Leverage is the most important factor that determines capital structure.** Financial leverage is used as long as the cost of debt is lower than the return on investment. The use of debt increases the return on equity and magnifies the earnings per share. However, leverage can operate adversely if the expected rate of earnings of the firm falls below the cost of debt. Interest on long-term debt is fixed with a commitment over a long period. In the light of inherent greater risk with financial leverage, caution is required in planning the capital structure.
2. **Stability of Sales and Growth:** If the sales of a firm were fairly stable, the earnings of the firm would reasonably be constant. **If there is no great risk for decline in earnings, firm can utilise the financial leverage to its optimum advantage.** When there is assured growth, firm can plan to utilise the borrowing for expansion, without much risk. In case of those firms, firm can plan to use more debt in its capital structure for increased earnings.
3. **Cost of Capital:** Every rupee invested in business has a cost. Cost of capital is the minimum return expected by its suppliers. There are different sources of finance. Amongst the different sources, long-term debt is the cheapest. The reasons for its cheapness are
   (*A*) Fixed interest rate,

   (*B*) Long-term debt is, normally, secured by those assets for which finance is sanctioned. Suppliers get **priority for repayment of principal and interest** on debt compared to Preference share capital and Equity Share Capital, so they would be willing to invest at a lower cost.

   (*C*) Admissibility of interest as an expense under income tax so it's effective cost becomes the lowest.

Preference share capital has a legal obligation for a fixed rate of dividend. The dividend paid to preference shareholders is not an admissible expense under the tax. So, cost of preference share capital is higher than the cost of debt. Equity share capital is costlier compared to preference share capital. The reason is equity share capital does not have any fixed obligation for payment of dividend. So, comparatively, equity share capital is dearer to preference share capital.

Preference share capital is cheaper to Equity share capital while long-term debt is still cheaper in terms of cost implication. While formulating capital structure, every effort has to be made to keep the over-all cost of capital lowest to boost up the earning per equity share.

4. **Cash Flow Ability to Service Debt:** This ability is measured through fixed charges coverage ratio. This is calculated by

$$\frac{\text{Earning before Interest and Tax}}{\text{Fixed Interest Charge}}$$

Comparison of the existing coverage ratio with the future ratio, after the anticipated borrowings, gives idea about the risk the firm would be exposed to. If the future cash flows grow in line with the increased amount of borrowing, the firm would able to service the debt, without difficulty. **In case, the interest coverage ratio falls, after borrowing, this would be an indicator that the changed capital structure would create problems to that firm.**

Cash flows are more important than absolute amount of profit. Firms with stable and growing cash flows can employ more debt in comparison to those firms with unstable and lesser ability firms.

5. **Nature and Size of Business: Nature and size of business also influence the capital structure.** A public utility concern, for example, electricity-generating unit requires more funds on account of heavy investment in fixed assets. These types of concerns enjoy regular and assured cash flows so they can afford more debt. Similarly, big firms can raise funds through debt as investors consider them less risky. Small firms, not well known in the market, experiences more difficulty to raise funds through debt and so have to rely considerably upon the owners' funds for financing.
6. **Legal Requirements:** The promoters of the company have to comply with legal requirements while deciding about the capital structure of the company. For example, banking companies are not allowed to issue any other type of securities other than equity share capital for raising funds. SEBI governs regulatory framework. Approval of SEBI is needed for capital issue, which is accorded only after the stipulated guidelines are complied with. Such approval is not necessary while raising a long-term loan from financial institution. So, **the finance manager has to take into account the legal and regulatory framework while designing the capital structure.**
7. **Capital Market Conditions and Market Sentiment:** Capital market conditions play an important role for raising funds in the market. Capital market conditions always do not remain the same. There are boom and depression periods. **The choice of the securities is influenced by market conditions.** During the period of depression, investors are cautious and do not intend to take risk. So, they prefer investment in debentures as they consider them less risky. In times of boom, market sentiment is always high and so preference is towards investment in equity shares as the market considers investment in shares would be more profitable with anticipated appreciation in market value, at a faster pace. So, depending upon the capital market conditions and sentiment, companies have to plan their capital structure for raising funds.
8. **Corporate Tax Rate: High corporate tax rate compels the companies to raise funds through debt as interest on debt is an admissible expenditure so taxable profits would be low.** In consequence, tax liability would be low. On the other hand, dividend on shares is not an admissible expenditure so companies give lower preference for raising funds through equity for tax planning.

13.6 BALANCED CAPITAL STRUCTURE

In the capital structure, debt is used to improve profitability. The advantage of debt is that it saves tax since interest is tax deductible. On the other hand, its disadvantage is it can cause financial distress if there is a major fall in earnings when debt component is heavy. What is a financial distress? Financial distress arises when the fixed obligations of the firm affect the firm's normal operations. For example, if a firm has to dispose off some of its fixed assets to meet its fixed financial obligations, the firm is said to be in distress. One extreme of financial distress is its liquidation when it is not able to meet its financial obligations. Therefore, a trade-off is necessary between tax advantage and cost / risk of financial distress.

Conclusion: The firm's debt capacity may be best defined not as the maximum amount which the lenders or debt investors are willing to lend or its legal capacity, but the amount of debt the firm should use.

So, every company aims at balanced capital structure to take maximum advantage within the manageable limits.

13.7 RELEVANT RATIOS FOR ANALYSING CAPITAL STRUCTURE

The following ratios are relevant for analysing capital structure.

Ratio name	Formula	Purpose
1. Debt Equity Ratio	Total Debt (Net Worth)	To measure the extent of debt in financing the business
2. Financial Leverage Ratio	EBIT (Profit before tax)	To find out the impact of operating income on shareholders' income
3. Capital Gearing Ratio	Preference share capital + Debentures + Long-term debts bearing fixed interest/Equity share capital + Reserves And Surplus	To ascertain the influence of fixed-charge bearing securities in the financing pattern of business
4. Fixed charges coverage Ratio	Earning before Depreciation, Interest and Tax/Fixed Interest Charged	A test for firm's debt servicing capacity

Objective Questions

1. Explain the concept and significance of optimum capital structure? What do you mean by flexibility of capital structure? **(13.2)**
2. 'Optimum capital structure is a hypothetical concept'. Explain your views on the above statement. **(13.2 and 13.3)**

3. What do you understand by a balanced capital structure? Why should a company aim at balanced capital structure? **(13.2, 13.3 and 13.6)**
4. Discuss the essential features of an appropriate capital structure? **(13.4)**
5. If debt is a cheaper source of finance, then why every firm is not a 99% debt firm? **(13.1 and 13.3)**
6. What ratios would you like to compute to analyse the capital structure? **(13.7)**

Check Your understanding

(A) State whether the following statements are True or False

1. Achieving an optimum capital structure, practically, is a difficult task
2. Preference share capital is cheaper to equity share capital, while long-term debt is still cheaper in terms of cost implication.
3. The board of directors or chief operating officer develops the capital structure, which is most advantageous to the company.
4. Equity share capital is described as fixed charge bearing securities.
5. Raising funds through debt is dearer compared to equity.
6. When additional funds are raised, the controlling interest of the existing owners gets diluted, automatically, unless they invest additional funds, suitably.

Answers

1. True 2. True 3. True 4. False 5. False
6. True

(B) Pick up the right answer

1. Fixed cost bearing securities should be mixed with equity when the rate of earnings is........ than the rate of interest of the company.
   (A) More
   (B) Less
   (C) Equal
2. The optimum capital structure is obtained when the market value per equity share is at ....
   (A) maximum
   (B) minimum
   (C) zero
3. If the use of borrowing results in the fall of market value of share in the stock exchange, it can be said that the company is ....from its optimum capital structure.
   (A) moving away
   (B) moving towards
   (C) moving towards or moving away

Answers

1. (A) 2 (A) 3 (A)

14

VALUATION AND RATES OF RETURN

14.1 INTRODUCTION

Assets are, broadly, divided into two categories. They are real assets and financial assets. For example, Physical assets like building and machinery are real assets. Securities like equity shares, preference shares and debentures are financial assets. The fundamental concepts of risk and return determine the value of real assets as well as financial assets.

14.2 CONCEPT OF VALUE

How bonds and shares are valued? Earnings per share (EPS) and Price-Earnings (P/E) ratios play a significant role in the valuation of financial securities. These have been discussed, already, in the ratio analysis. The concept 'value' has different meanings. They are:

Book Value: Book value is an accounting concept. Assets are recorded at historical cost in books of accounts. Depreciation is provided on fixed assets and the depreciated value (cost minus depreciation provided) is shown in the financial statements. Intangible assets (goodwill and preliminary expenses etc.) are amortised. Acquisition cost minus amortisation is shown as book value. The book value of debts is shown at the outstanding amount. The difference between the assets and liabilities is equal to net worth or shareholders' funds. To arrive at the book value per share, the net worth is to be divided by the number of equity shares outstanding. **Book value reflects the historical cost, not value.** Value is what an asset is worth as on date, in terms of potential benefits.

Replacement Value: Replacement value is the amount company has to spend to acquire the same asset in the existing condition. In times of inflation, replacement value is always higher than the book value of the asset that is already depreciated.

Liquidation Value: Liquidation value is the value one would get on the assets, after the termination of the business. As the business is closed, assets do not get much value. Intangible assets such as goodwill get nothing as the business is closed.

Going Concern Value: Going concern value is the amount that a company could realise if sold when the business is still on. In other words, it is an operating business. So, the value that can be realised is, normally, higher than the liquidation value. Even intangible assets command value, even though not shown in the financial statements, due to the prosperous condition of business.

Market Value: Market value of an asset or security is the price at which it is bought or sold in the market. Market value of a share is higher than the book value, if the business is profitable. A number of factors influence the market value of the share. What is important is the long-term trend of the share in the market. In other words, what the market considers more important is about the potentialities of the share, in future, rather than the condition of business today. In an ideal situation, when the capital market is efficient, the market price reflects the intrinsic value of a share.

14.3 FEATURES OF BOND/DEBENTURE

A bond or debenture is a long-term debt instrument. **Government or public sector companies, normally,** issue bonds. **Bonds are, generally, secured.** The private sector companies issue debentures. They may be secured or unsecured.

Features: The features of a bond or debenture are as under:

1. **Face Value:** Face value is called par value. A bond/debenture is issued at the face or par value, which is, normally, Rs. 100 or Rs.1,000. Interest is paid on the face value, whether debentures are issued at par, premium or discount.
2. **Interest Rate:** Interest rate is fixed and known to the investor. Interest is tax deductible to the firm that issues. Interest is paid quarterly, half-yearly, annually or at the time of

redemption. The interest rate is also called coupon rate. Interest rate is mentioned on the face of the certificate.

3. **Maturity:** A bond/debenture is issued for a specified period of time. It is repaid on maturity.
4. **Redemption Value:** The value, which a bond holder/debenture holder will get on maturity, is called redemption value. It can be redeemed at par or at premium or at discount.
5. **Market Value:** A bond/debenture may be traded in the stock exchange. It can be bought or sold at the market value. Market value may be different from par value or redemption value.
6. **Risk:** The risk in holding a government bond is lower than the risk associated with the debenture issued by a company. So, if both carry same rate of interest and other terms such as redemption period and value of security remain the same, debenture would be quoted in stock exchange at a lower price, compared to a bond of the same face value.

14.4 VALUATION OF SECURITIES

Present value concept helps the investor in decision making for buying or selling the securities. If the present value is more than the current market price, he chooses to buy. In case, the present value is less than the current market price, the investor can sell the securities to make a profit. The basis for this decision-making is the required rate of return that he wishes to have and the forecast about the behaviour of the future return. In case of debentures and preference shares, the return is fixed while the dividend in the case of equity shares is only a planned estimate on which the decision is taken.

14.5 CALCULATION OF PRESENT VALUE-BOND WITH A MATURITY PERIOD

A bond or debenture may be issued for a specified period. Till the date of maturity, the holder gets interest, periodically. At the end of the period, he gets the maturity value. Every investor wants to have certain rate of return. If the bond or debenture is quoted at a particular rate, the investor wants to know whether the bond or debenture is worth buying at that rate or not. In other words, he wants to buy if the value satisfies the required rate of return. The required rate of return may be defined as the minimum rate of return necessary to induce the investor to hold or buy the security. Present Value concept gives him the answer for taking the decision. By comparing the present value of the bond with the current market value, it can be determined whether the bond is overvalued or undervalued. Accordingly, investor can decide whether to buy or sell the security.

Formula for calculating present value of a debenture is

$$B_o = \frac{INT_1}{(1+k_d)} + \frac{INT_2}{(1+k_d)^2} + \ldots\ldots + \frac{INT_n + B_n}{(1+k_d)}$$

Where B_o = Present value of a bond/debenture

INT = Amount of interest

K_d = Required rate of return on bond (%)

B_n = Maturity value in period 'n'

n = number of years to maturity

The above formula works if return is paid on an annual basis. Return can be calculated on monthly, quarterly, half-yearly basis. In such a case, the formula requires a small change. To calculate return on quarterly basis,

K_d is to be divided by four and n is to be multiplied by four. Interest amount is to be divided by four to show quarterly interest in place of INT_1 and INT_2 etc. For half yearly basis, this exercise is to be done by two and for monthly return, it is to be done by twelve.

Illustration No. 1

An investor is considering to purchase a five year, Rs. 1,000 par value bond bearing a coupon rate of 7 per cent. The investor's required rate of return is 8 percent. The bond is quoted at Rs. 950. The bond will be redeemed at par value. Advise him for purchase?

Solution:

The bond gives him interest of Rs. 70 per annum for a period of 5 years.

$$\mathbf{B_o = \frac{INT_1}{(1+k_d)} + \frac{INT_2}{(1+k_d)^2} + \ldots\ldots + \frac{INT_n + B_n}{(1+k_d)}}$$

Where B_o = Present value of a bond/debenture

INT = Amount of interest

K_d = Required rate of return on bond (%)

B_n = Maturity value in period 'n'

n = number of years to maturity

$$= \frac{70}{(1+.08)} + \frac{70}{(1+.08)^2} + \frac{70}{1+.08)^3} + \frac{70}{1+.08)^4} + \frac{70}{1+.08)^5} + \frac{1000}{(1+.08)^5}$$

= 65 + 60 + 56 + 51 + 48 + 681 = 961

The bond is worth buying for Rs. 961, with the required return of 8% . It is available at Rs. 950. So, it is worth buying.

Perpetual Bonds

Bonds, which never mature are known as perpetual bonds. **Perpetual bonds are rarely found in practice. In respect of these bonds, interest is received, infinitely.**

Formula for calculation of present value is

$$B_o = \frac{\mathbf{INT}}{\mathbf{K_D}}$$

Where B_o = Present value of a bond/debenture

INT = Amount of interest

K_d = Required rate of return on bond (%)

Illustration No. 2

If a 7 % perpetual bond of Rs. 1,000 that gives interest monthly is quoted at Rs. 900 and your required rate of return is 8%. Is it worth buying?

Solution:

$$B_o = \frac{INT}{K_D}$$

Where B_o = Present value of a bond/debenture

INT = Amount of interest

K_d = Required rate of return on bond (%)

$$= \frac{70/12}{0.08/12} = \text{Rs. } 870.14$$

The bond is quoted at Rs 900. So, the bond is not worth buying.

14.6 PRESENT VALUE OF PREFERENCE SHARES

The holders of the preference shares get a fixed rate of dividend on a continuous basis. They enjoy preference over equity shareholders in respect of receipt of dividend. Preference shares may be issued with or without a maturity period. A company can issue convertible preference shares. After the stated period, they get converted into equity shares.

The formula for calculating the value of irredeemable preference share is

$$P_o = \frac{PDIV}{K_p}$$

Where P_o = Value of Preference share

PDIV = Preference dividend

K_p = Required Return on Preference share

Similar to bonds, it is relatively easy to estimate the cash outflows associated with irredeemable preference shares as dividend is constant. It may be observed the above formula is similar to the calculation of the value of the bond or debenture.

Illustration No. 3

A company has issued irredeemable preference shares with a face value of Rs.100, with a dividend rate of 9%. The value of the preference share is Rs.82? What is the yield on the preference share?

Solution:

$$P_o = \frac{PDIV}{K_p}$$

Where P_o = Value of Preference share

PDIV = Preference dividend

K_p = Required Return on Preference share

$$K_p = \frac{PDIV}{P_o}$$

$$= \frac{8}{82} = 0.11 \text{ or } 11\%$$

The yield on the preference share is 11%.

14.7 PRESENT VALUE OF EQUITY SHARE

Valuation of equity shares is relatively difficult. There are two types of difficulties. The rate of dividend on equity shares is not constant. More so, it is not known, in advance for calculating present value. Secondly, dividend is discretionary and not compulsory. In case of debentures and preference shares, the rate of interest and dividend is certain. It is, therefore, easy to forecast those cash flows. But, it is not the case with the equity shares. The earnings on equity shares are, generally, likely to grow. This feature of variable and uncertain dividend on equity shares makes the calculation of the value of equity share rather difficult.

Dividend Capitalisation Model

Dividend capitalisation model is a basic valuation model for equity shares valuation. The value of an equity share is a function of cash flows in the form of dividends expected by the investors and the risk associated with the cash inflows. So, the value of a share, today, is the present value of its future stream of dividends plus the present value of the expected price at the time of sale.

(A) **One-Period Valuation Model:** Suppose, an investor wants to hold the share for a period of one year. The value of the share for him will be the present value of the expected dividend at the end of one year plus the present value of the expected sale price at the end of one year.

The formula for calculation is

$$P_o = \frac{D_1}{1+k_e} + \frac{P_1}{1+k_e}$$

Where P_o = Current value of share

D_1 = Expected dividend at the end of first year

P_1 = Expected price at the end of first year

k_e = Required rate of return on equity

Illustration No. 4

Mr. Kalyan is planning to buy an equity share for holding it for a period of one year and then sell it. The expected dividend at the end of one year is

Rs. 8 and the expected sale proceeds at the end of one year are Rs. 300. Determine the value of the share to the investor, assuming the expected required return is 20%. If the current market price is Rs.225, is it worth buying?

Solution:

$$P_o = \frac{D_1}{1+k_e} + \frac{P_1}{1+k_e}$$

Where

P_o = Current value of share

D_1 = Expected dividend at the end of first year

P_1 = Expected price at the end of first year

k_e = Required rate of return on equity

$$= \frac{8}{(1.20)} + \frac{300}{1.20} + \frac{308}{(1.20)}$$

=Rs. 257

The present value of equity share is Rs. 257. It is available at Rs. 225. So, it is worth buying.

(B) Two-Period Valuation Model: Suppose, the investor wants to hold the share for two years, then the formula would be:

$$P_o = \frac{D_1}{(1+k_e)} + \frac{D_2}{(1+k_e)^2} + \frac{P_2}{(1+k_e)^2}$$

Where

P_o = Current value of share

D_1 = Expected dividend at the end of first year

D_2 = Dividend at the end of the second year

P_2 = Expected selling price at the end of second year

k_e = Required rate of return on equity

Illustration No. 5

Mr. Kishore is planning to buy an equity share and wants to hold it for two years and then sell it. The expected dividend at the end of first year is 8% and 9% at the end of second year. The expected selling price at the end of second year is Rs.900. Calculate the value of share today, taking the required rate of return as 18%. The share is, now, quoted at Rs.780. Advise about its buying?

Solution:

$$P_o = \frac{D_1}{(1+k_e)} + \frac{D_2}{(1+k_e)^2} + \frac{P_2}{(1+k_e)^2}$$

Where P_o = Current value of share

D_1 = Expected dividend at the end of first year

D_2 = Dividend at the end of the second year

P_2 = Expected selling price at the end of second year

k_e = Required rate of return on equity

$$= \frac{8}{(1.18)} + \frac{9}{(1.18)^2} \frac{900}{(1.18)^2}$$

$$= 7 + 6 + 646 = \text{Rs. } 659$$

For the required return, the share is worth buying for Rs. 659 and the current market rate is Rs. 780. So, it is not worth buying.

(C) **n-Period Valuation Model:** Similarly, if the share holder wants to retain for 'n' years, the formula for calculating present value of share is

$$P_o = \frac{D_1}{(1+k_e)} + \frac{D_2}{(1+k_e)} + \frac{D_n}{(1+k_e)^n} \ldots\ldots + \frac{P_n}{(1+k_e)^n}$$

Objective Questions

1. Explain the concept "Value' and its meaning? **(14. 1 and 14.2)**
2. Distinguish between bond and debenture and explain their features? **(14.3)**
3. **Explain the method of calculating present value of debentures, preference shares and equity shares that help in decision making for buying or selling? (14.4, 14.5 14.6 and 14.7)**

Check Your Understanding

State whether the following statements are True or False

1. Present Value concept helps the investor in taking a decision to buy or sell the securities, once the required rate of return is known.
2. Bonds, which mature at a specified period are known as perpetual bonds.
3. Present value concept compares the present value of the bond with the current market value to determine whether the bond is overvalued or undervalued for decision making.
4. The value of a share is the present value of its future stream of dividends and selling price.

5. Physical assets like building and machinery are financial assets.
6. The difference between the assets and liabilities is equal to net worth or shareholders' funds.
7. Replacement value is the amount company has to spend to acquire the same asset in the existing condition.
8. Liquidation value is the value one would get on the assets, when the business is in progress.
9. Market value of a share is lower than the book value, if the business is profitable.
10. When the capital market is efficient, the market price reflects the intrinsic value of a share.
11. Debentures are always secured.
12. Bonds/debentures can be redeemed at par, premium or discount.

Answers:

1. True	2. False	3. True	4. True	5. False
6. True	7. True	8. False	9. False	10. True
11. False	12. True			

15

BUDGETING AND BUDGETARY CONTROL

- *Meaning of Budget and Budgeting*
- *Meaning and Nature of Budgetary Control*
- *Objectives of Budgetary Control*
- *Requisites for Successful Budgetary Control System*
- *Essential Steps for Installation of Budgetary Control System*
- *Advantages of Budgetary Control*
- *Limitations of Budgetary Control*
- *Classification of Budgets*
  - *Classification on the basis of Time*
  - *Classification on the basis of Functions*
  - *Classification on the basis of Flexibility*
- *Differences between Fixed and Flexible Budget*
- *Zero Base Budgeting*
  - *Benefits of Zero Base Budgeting*
- *Objective Questions*
- *Check your understanding*

15.1 INTRODUCTION

Planning is a management function. In this competitive environment, the business enterprise becomes successful only with planing. Plans are framed to achieve better results. However, planning for the sake of it is of no use.

Plans should work to achieve the results planned. This is possible through co-ordination, as all the tasks cannot be performed, in isolation. Where more than one individual is involved; only co-ordination can bring the required results. For it, control is needed. **Management is termed efficient, if maximum results are achieved with minimum costs and efforts.** To achieve the anticipated targets, planning, co-ordination and control are the important main tasks of management, achieved through budgeting and budgetary control.

15.2 MEANING OF BUDGET AND BUDGETING

A budget is a monetary and/or quantitative expression of business plans and policies, prepared in advance, to be pursued in the future period of time. According to Certified Institute of Management Accountants, Budget is defined as **"A budget is a financial and/or quantitative statement prepared prior to a defined period of time, of the policy to be pursued during that period for the purpose of attaining the objective".** In brief, it is a systematic plan for utilisation of manpower and other resources. It acts as a barometer of a business as it measures the success from time to time, against the standard set for achievement.

Budgeting is a technique for formulating budgets.

Characteristics of a Budget: The main characteristics of a budget are:

(A) A comprehensive business plan showing what the enterprise wants to achieve

(B) Prepared in advance

(C) For a definite period of time

(D) Expressed in quantitative form, physical or monetary terms, or both

(E) For achieving a given objective

(F) A proper system of accounting is essential

(G) System of proper fixation of authority and responsibility has to be in place.

15.3 MEANING AND NATURE OF BUDGETARY CONTROL

Budgetary control is the process of determining various budgeted figures for the enterprise and then comparing the actual performance with the budgeted figures for calculating the variances, if any. In this process, first budgets are to be prepared. Second, actual results are to be recorded. Third, comparison is to be made between the actual with the planned action for calculating the variances. Once the discrepancies are known, remedial measures are to be taken, at proper time. Then only, planned results can be achieved. A budget is a means and budgetary control gives the end result.

Definition of Budgetary Control: The Chartered Institute of Management Accountants, London, defines the Budgetary Control as

"The establishment of budgets relating to the responsibilities of executives to the requirements of a policy, and the continuous comparison of the actual with the budgeted result, either to secure by individual action the objective of the policy or to provide a basis for its revision".

Thus, establishment of budgetary control involves the following:

1. Establishment of budgets.

2. Continuous comparison of actual with the budgets for achievement of targets and fixing the responsibility for failure to achieve the budget figures.
3. Revision of budgets in the light of changed circumstances.

The position of budgetary control can be likened or compared to the navigation of a ship, across the seas. The navigating officer works out the course ahead and records the happening of the position of the ship from hour to hour in a log-book. To navigate the ship across the seven seas, safely, the captain wants the navigating officer to check his ship's position, constantly, against the predetermined one. If the ship is off its course, the navigating officer must report, immediately, to the captain for prompt action to regain the course. Valuable lessons are learnt by the captain of the ship from a study of the factors that have caused misadventure in the past. Exactly, so it is with the industrial ship. **What the modern management requires for day to operating purposes is detailed forecasts and immediate reporting of variances, with explanations of the reasons for variations.** This facilitates the management to take the required corrective action by the persons who are made responsible, but contributed for the failure.

15.4 OBJECTIVES OF BUDGETARY CONTROL

The main objectives of budgetary control are as under:

1. To co-ordinate the activities of different departments.
2. To operate various cost centres and departments with efficiency and economy.
3. Fixation of responsibility of various individuals in the organisation.
4. To ensure a system for correction of deviations from established standards.
5. To centralise the control system and
6. To ensure planning for future by setting up various budgets.

15.5 REQUISITES FOR SUCCESSFUL BUDGETARY CONTROL SYSTEM

The following requisites are essential for effective budgetary control system.

1. **Determination of the Objectives:** There should be clear perspective of the objectives to be achieved through the budgetary control system. In most of the cases, the basic objective is to achieve desired/increased profits. To achieve, the following problems are to be sorted out:

   (A) Laying down the Plan for implementation to achieve the objectives,

   (B) Bringing **co-ordination** amongst the different departments and

   (C) Controlling each function so as to bring the best possible results.

   The steps needed to be followed to achieve the above are explained further here.

2. **Proper Delegation of Authority and Responsibility:** The first step is to have clear organisation chart explaining the authority and responsibility of each individual executive.

There should be no uncertainty regarding the point when the jurisdiction of one authority ends and that of another begins.

3. **Proper Communication System:** The flow of information should be quick so that the budgets are implemented. **Two way communications is important.** What is required to be achieved and how it is to be achieved should reach the lowest level. Similarly, upward communication in respect of implementation difficulties should reach the top level to sort out, without loss of time. The performance reports at the various levels help the management in monitoring and leading to the achievement of the budgeted goals.
4. **Participation of All Employees:** Budget preparation and control are done at the top level. However, involvement of all persons, including at the lower level, is necessary in framing the budget and its implementation for the success of budgetary control. In practice, budgets are executed at the lower level. With experience, they can offer practical suggestions that can lead to success. **The success depends more on the active participation of all employees of the organisation.**
5. **Flexibility:** Future is uncertain. Despite the best planning and foresight, still there may be occurrences that may require adjustments. Budgets should work in the changed circumstances. **Flexibility in budgets is required to make them work under changed circumstances.**
6. **Motivation:** Budgets are executed by human beings. **There should be incentive in achieving the required targets.** All persons should be motivated to improve their working to achieve the goals set in the budgets.

15.6 ESSENTIAL STEPS FOR INSTALLATION OF BUDGETARY CONTROL SYSTEM

In order to have effective budgetary control system, it is appropriate to take the following steps:

1. **Budget Manual:** This is a written document specifying the objectives and procedures of budgetary control. **It spells out the duties and responsibilities of executives.** The budget manual defines the sanctioning powers of the various authorities.
2. **Budget Centres:** A budget centre is that part of organisation for which the budget is prepared. **Budget centre can be a department, section of a department or any other part of department.** Budget centres are necessary for the purpose of ascertaining cost, performance and its control.
3. **Budget Committee:** In a large concern, all the functional heads are the members of the budget committee. They discuss their respective budgets and finalise the budget, after collective decisions. **The committee is responsible for its execution and achievement of the goals set.**
4. **Budget Officer:** The chief executive appoints some person as the budget officer. He is conversant with the functioning of the various departments. All budgets are presented to him who places before the budget committee, after making the necessary changes, for its approval. The actual performance of each department is communicated to the budget officer.

He determines the variances, analyses the reasons and reports to the top management to take the necessary steps to remove the deviations. **As the convenor of the budget committee, his function is co-ordination to ensure achievement of the budgeted targets.**

5. **Budget Period: A budget period is the length of the period for which budget is prepared.** Normally, budgets like purchases and sales budgets are prepared for one year. However, a capital expenditure budget is prepared for a longer period i. e. 3 to 5 years.
6. **Determination of Key Factor:** Budgets are prepared for all the functional areas such as production, sales, purchases, finance, human resources and research and development. These activities are inter-connected and inter-dependent and so the budgets are. For example, raw material supply may be limited. So, production and sales budgets are prepared based on the purchase budget. To some of the firms, finance may be a constraint. Then, all other budgets are prepared based on the availability of finance. **A factor, which influences all other budgets, is known as key factor or principal factor.** A better co-ordination brings better performance, even while facing constraints.

The influence of key factor may neither be permanent nor the same factor may be constant. Limited supply of raw materials may be the key factor till an alternative source of supply for that material is found. When the raw material supply problem is cleared, another factor may create the problem and assume the rde of key factor. After raw materials problem is eased, sales may become a problem and turn to be a key factor, due to change in trends. The management would be constantly endeavouring to remove the problems associated with key factor for better performance.

15.7 ADVANTAGES OF BUDGETARY CONTROL

Budgetary control acts as an important tool for the management to economise costs and maximise profits. The system helps the management to set the goals. The current performance is compared with the pre-planned performance to ascertain deviations so that corrective measures are taken, well at the right time. In this way, **budgetary control system acts as a friend, philosopher and guide to the management. The following are the advantages of budgetary control system.**

1. **Profit Maximisation:** The resources are put to best possible use, eliminating wastage. Proper control is exercised both on revenue and capital expenditure. To achieve this, proper planning and co-ordination of various functions is undertaken. So, the system helps in reducing losses and increasing profits.
2. **Co-ordination:** The budgets of various departments have a bearing with each other, as activities are inter-related. As the size of operations increases, co-ordination amongst the different departments for achieving a common goal assumes more importance. This is possible through budgetary control system.
3. **Communication:** A budget serves as a means of communicating information through out the organisation. A sales manager for a district knows what is expected of his performance. Similarly, production manager knows the amount of material, labour and other expenses

that can be incurred by him to achieve the goal set to him. So, every department knows the performance expectation and authority for achieving the same.

4. **Tool for Measuring Performance:** Budgetary control system provides a tool for measuring the performance of various departments. The performance of each department is reported to the top management.
5. **Economy:** Planning at each level brings efficiency and economy in the working of the business enterprise. Resources are put to optimum use to achieve economy. All this leads to elimination of wastage and achievement of overall efficiency.
6. **Determining Weaknesses:** Actual performance is compared with the planned performance, periodically, and deviations are found out. This shows the variances highlighting the weaknesses, where concentration for action is needed.
7. **Consciousness:** Budgets are prepared in advance. So, every employee knows what is expected of him and they are made aware of their responsibility. So, they do their job uninterrupted for achieving what is set to him to do.
8. **Timely Corrective Action:** The deviations will be reported to the attention of the top management as well as functional heads for suitable corrective action, in time. In the absence of budgetary control, deviations would be known, at the end of the period, and there is no time and opportunity for necessary corrective action.
9. **Motivation:** Success is measured by comparing the actual performance with the planned performance. Suitable recognition and reward system can be introduced to motivate the employees, at all levels, provided the budgets are prepared with adequate planning and foresight.
10. **Management by Exception:** The management is required to exercise action only when there are deviations. **So long as the plans are achieved, management need not be alerted.** This system enables the introduction of 'Management by Exception' for effective delegation and control.

15.8 LIMITATIONS OF BUDGETARY CONTROL

Budgetary control is a sound technique of control but is not a perfect tool. Despite many good points, it suffers from the following limitations:

1. **Uncertainty of Future:** The budgets are prepared for the future periods. So, budgets are prepared with certain assumptions. There is no certainty that all the assumptions prevail in future. With the change in assumptions, the situation in future changes. Due to this, the utility of budgetary control reduces.
2. **Problem of Co-ordination:** The success of budgetary control, largely, depends upon effective co-ordination. The performance of one department depends on the performance of the other department. To ensure necessary co-ordination, organisation appoints a budget officer. All organisations can not afford the additional expenditure involved with the appointment of a budget officer, separately. In case, budget officer is not appointed, lack of co-ordination results in poor performance.

3. **Not a Substitute for Management:** Budgetary control helps in decision-making, but is not a substitute for management. A budgetary programme can be successful, if there is proper administration and supervision.
4. **Discourages Efficiency:** Every person is given a target to achieve. So, every one is concerned only achieving the target of his own. This is the common tendency. Even capable and competent people too would concentrate just to achieve their individual targets. So, budgets may serve as managerial constraints, unless suitable award or incentive system is introduced. In the absence of award system to recognise efficiency and exceptional talents, budgets dampen the people with initiative and enthusiasm.
5. **Timely Revision Required:** Budgets are prepared on certain assumptions. When those conditions do not prevail, it becomes inevitable to revise the budget. Such frequent revision of budgets reduces the reliability and value. Revision of budgets involves additional expenditure too.
6. **Conflict among Different Departments:** For the success of budgetary control, co-ordination of the different departments is essential. Every department is concerned with the achievement of the individual department's goal, not concerned with the final goal of the enterprise. In this process, each department tries to secure maximum fund allocation and this creates conflict among the different departments.
7. **Depends upon Support of Top management:** The success of budgetary control depends upon the support of top management. If the top management is not enthusiastic for its success, the budgetary control will collapse. So, the whole-hearted interest of top management is highly essential for its implementation, in its true spirit, to make it workable and succeed.

15.9 CLASSIFICATION OF BUDGETS

Budgets can be classified on the basis of time, function and flexibility.

(A) **Classification on the basis of Time:** Budgets can be long-term and short-term. Long term budgets relate to a period ranging from 5 to 10 years. Only the top level knows these budgets and lower level would not be aware of. These budgets are prepared for certain areas of the enterprise such as capital expenditure and research and development. Short-term budgets are for one or two years. Generally, budgets are prepared to coincide with the financial year so that comparison of the actual performance with budgeted estimates would facilitate better interpretation and understanding.

(B) **Classification on the basis of Function:** Budgets are divided on the basis of different functions performed in the organisation. They are sales budget, production budget, purchase Budget, Direct Labour Budget, Overheads Budget, cash budget and, finally, master budget. **The master or final budget is a summary budget, which incorporates all functional budgets, in a summarised form.**

(C) **Classification on the basis of Flexibility:** There are two types of budgets on the basis of flexibility.

(i) **Fixed Budgets:** The budget is prepared on the basis of fixed level of activity. In other words, **a fixed budget remains unchanged irrespective of the change in volume or level of activity.** It is presumed that the forecast and the actual level of activity, both production and sales, would be one and the same. In other words, if the budget is prepared for a particular quantity of production and sales, at a particular cost, and selling price, the same should happen. Then only, this type of budgeting would be useful. Where static conditions occur, this is useful. In practical life, it does not happen on account of changes that cannot be anticipated or foreseen. It is not practically possible to anticipate the likely production and sales, accurately. Due to this limitation, fixed budgets are not followed, where the forecast can not be done, accurately, both for production and sales.

(ii) **Flexible Budgets:** Flexible budget is a good budgeting technique as well as tool of control. **Flexible budgets are prepared where the level of activity cannot be estimated with accuracy.** This type of budget is prepared for a range of production activity say 15,000 to 25,000 units. A flexible budget recognises the difference between fixed, semi-fixed and variable cost and is designed to change in relation to the change in level of activity.

The flexible budgets will be useful where the level of activity changes and cannot be estimated at the time of preparation of budget.

15.10 STEPS IN PREPARATION OF FLEXIBLE BUDGET:

1. Decide the range of activity (say 15,000 to 25,000 units) to which the budget is to be prepared.
2. Decide the behaviour of each element of cost, which are included in the budget, into fixed, semi-fixed and variable cost.
3. Select the activity levels (say 15,000, 18,000, 20,000, 22,000 and 25,000 units) in terms of production.
4. Prepare the budget for each level of activity by associating the corresponding cost with each level of activity.

15.11 DIFFERENCES BETWEEN FIXED AND FLEXIBLE BUDGET

Base of Difference	Fixed Budget	Flexible Budget
1. **Level of activity**	It is based on single level of activity.	It is based on more than one level of activity.
2. **Assumptions**	Assumes that conditions and level of activity remain constant.	Assumes that level of activity may change.
3. **Cost classification**	Costs are not classified according to their nature.	Costs are classified as per their nature i.e. fixed, semi-fixed and variable.

4. **Comparison**	If the level of activity changes, budget and actual cannot be compared.	If there is a change in the level of activity, budget can be recast to make it possible for comparison.
5. **Adjustment**	Fixed budget is not able to provide any automatic adjustment when the volume changes.	Flexible budget is automatically geared to changes in production activity.
6. **Utility**	A fixed budget has limited utility and it may give misleading results when level of activity changes.	Flexible budget provides wider acceptance to several organisations as it provides a reliable basis for changed level of activity.

Illustration No.1

Following are the budget estimates of a repairs and maintenance department, which are to be used to construct a flexible budget for the ensuing year:

(Rs.)

Details of cost	Planned at 6,000 direct hours	Planned at 9,000 direct hours
Employee salaries	28,000	28,000
Indirect repair material	42,000	63,000
Miscellaneous cost	16,000	20,500

(i) Prepare a flexible budget for the department up to activity level of 10,000 direct repair hours using increment of 1,000 hours.

(ii) What would be the budget allowance for 9,500 direct repair hours?

(B.U. MBA- 2002)

Solution:

(i)

Flexible Budget of Repairs and Maintenance Department

Details of Cost	Planned Activity (Direct Hours)					
	6,000 hours	**7,000 hours**	**8,000 hours**	**9,000 hours**	**9,500 hours**	**10,000 hours**
Fixed Cost Employee salaries	28,000	28,000	28,000	28,000	28,000	28,000
Variable Cost Indirect repair material (@ Rs.7 per hour)	42,000	49,000	56,000	63,000	66,500	70,000
Semi-fixed cost Miscellaneous cost	16,000	17,500	19,000	20,500	21,250	22,000
Total cost	86,000	94,500	1,03,000	1,11,500	1,15,750	1,20,000

(ii) At 9,500 hours, for the incremental increase of 500 hours, the cost increases by Rs.4,250 due to the following:

Variable cost	
Indirect repair material (@ Rs.7 per hour) = 500 × 7 =	3,500
Semi-fixed cost	
Miscellaneous cost (@ Rs. 1.50 per hour) = 500 × 1.50 =	750
–Variable cost component)	
Total incremental cost	4,250

15.12 PREPARATION OF CASH BUDGET

A cash budget is an estimate of cash receipts and disbursements during a future period. The anticipated cash receipts from various sources are taken into account. Similarly, the amount to be spent on various heads, both revenue and capital, are taken into cash budget. In short, it is a summary of cash intake and outlay.

Illustration No.2

Prepare a cash-budget of a company for April, May and June 2003 in a columnar form using the following information;

(Rs.)

Month, 03	Sales	Purchases	Wages	Expenses
January (Actual)	80,000	45,000	20,000	5,000
February (Actual)	80,000	40,000	18,000	6,000
March (Actual)	75,000	42,000	22,000	6,000
April (Budgeted)	90,000	50,000	24,000	7,000
May (Budgeted)	85,000	45,000	20,000	6,000
June (Budgeted)	80,000	35,000	18,000	5,000

You are further informed that:

(a) 10% of the purchases and 20% of the sales are for cash;

(b) The average collection period of the company ½ month and the credit purchases are paid off regularly after one month;

(c) Wages are paid half monthly, and the rent of Rs. 500 included in expenses is paid monthly;

(d) Cash and Bank Balance as on April, was Rs. 15,000 and the company wants to keep it at the end of every month approximately this figure, the excess cash being put in fixed deposits in the bank.

(B.U. MBA-2003)

Solution:

(Rs.)

Cash Budget
For the months from April to June, 2003

	April	May	June
Receipts:			
Opening balance of cash at bank	15,000	15,000	15,000
Cash Sales	18,000	17,000	16,000
Collections from debtors	66,000	70,000	66,000
Total receipts	**99,000**	**1,02,000**	**97,000**
Payments			
Cash purchases	5,000	4,500	3,500
Payments to credit purchases	37,800	45,000	40,500
Wages	23,000	22,000	19,000
Expenses	6,500	5,500	4,500
Rent	500	500	500
Total Payments	**72 ,800**	**77,500**	**68,000**
Cash Balance left	26, 200	24,500	29,000
Fixed Deposit placed	11,200	9,500	14,000
Closing cash balance	15,000	15,000	15,000

Calculation of cash sales and realisation of credit sales

Month	Total sales	Cash sales (20% of total sales)	Credit sales	Collections during month
March (Actual)	75,000	15,000	60,000	Current month 30,000 + previous month 32,000 =62,000
April (Budgeted)	90,000	18,000	72,000	Current month 36,000 + Previous month 30,000 = 66,000
May (Budgeted)	85,000	17,000	68,000	Current month 34,000 + Previous month 36,000 = 70,000
June (Budgeted)	80,000	16,000	64,000	Current month 32,000 + Previous month 34,000 = 66,000

Calculation of Payments for Purchases

Month	Total Purchases (10%)	Cash Purchases	Credit purchases	Payments for credit Purchases
March (Actual)	42,000	4,200	37,800	36,000
April (Budgeted)	50,000	5,000	45,000	37,800
May (Budgeted)	45,000	4,500	40,500	45,000
June (Budgeted)	35,000	3,500	31,500	40,500

Calculation for Payment of Wages				
	Total Wages current month's wages (50 %)	Payment for Previous	Payment for month's wages	Total Payment of wages
March (Actual)	22,000	11,000	9,000	20,000
April (Budgeted)	24,000	12,000	11,000	23,000
May (Budgeted)	20,000	10,000	12,000	22,000
June (Budgeted)	18,000	9,000	10,000	19,000

15.13 ZERO BASE BUDGETING

Meaning of Zero Base Budgeting: Zero base budgeting is the latest technique of budgeting. Initially, the former President of America, Jimmy Carter, has developed this technique when he was working as the Governor of Gorgia for controlling state expenditure.

The term 'Zero Base Budgeting' means starting from the scratch. In zero base budgeting, justification of expenditure is to be made for the past as well as new projects. In the traditional budgeting, the figures of the previous years are taken as base and additions are made for the current year. But, in zero base budgeting, even the running projects are to be justified for continuation. If the past projects were allowed to continue, without justification, the past inefficiencies would continue, automatically. So, the manager has to justify why he wants to spend. The manager has to justify the essentiality of the new projects for their starting and continuation of previous projects, every year. Equally, the concerned manager has to justify the amount of spending there on is reasonable.

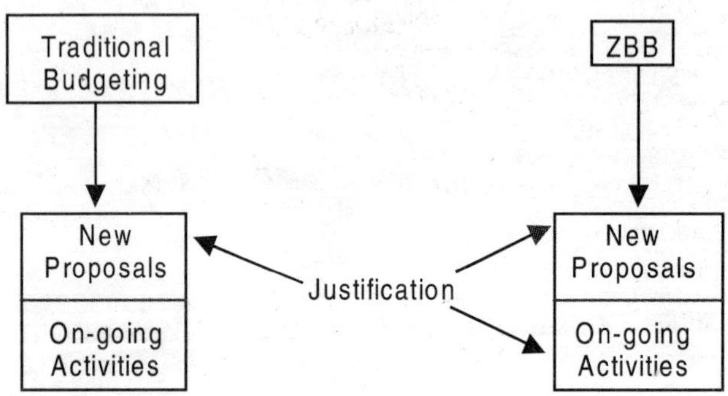

Zero-Base Budgetingh

15.14 DIFFERENCES BETWEEN TRADITIONAL BUDGETING AND ZERO BASE BUDGETING

The differences between the two are as under:

Traditional Budgeting Vs Zero base budgeting

		Traditional Budgeting	Zero Base Budgeting
1.	**Emphasis**	Lays emphasis on 'How much'	Lays emphasis on 'Why'
2.	**Focus**	Focus is on increase or decrease in expenditure.	Focus is on cost benefit analysis.
3.	**Communication**	Communication is usually vertical.	Communication is, usually, both vertical and horizontal.
4.	**Approach**	Past is taken for granted and never questioned for continuation.	Past is questioned and justification needed for continuation and fund allocation.

15.15 STEPS FOR PREPARATION OF ZERO BASE BUDGETING

The following steps are involved in Zero Base Budgeting:

(A) **Determining the Objectives:** Determination of the objectives is the first step. The objective can be cost reduction in staff overheads or dropping those projects that do not fit in the organisational objectives.

(B) **Extent of Coverage:** It relates to the decision whether Zero Base Budgeting is to be introduced in all areas or certain select areas on trail basis.

(C) **Developing Decision Units:** Decision can be a functional department, a programme, a product-line or sub-line. Each decision unit must be independent. Then only, they come under consideration. Cost benefit analysis is to be done to the decision units. Decision is to be taken whether the units are to be continued or dropped. If the cost benefit analysis is favourable, the decision unit can be implemented, otherwise can be dropped. If the decision unit is dropped, no further thinking is needed for those decisions.

(D) **Developing Decision Packages:** This is the most important step involved in the ZBB process. After decision for selection of the units, the concerned manager of the activity is given the freedom to come out with the alternatives to achieve. He summarises the plans and resources required to achieve.

(E) **Preparation of Budgets:** This is the last stage involved in ZBB process. Once the top management has ranked the various decision packages keeping in view of the cost benefit analysis and availability of funds, a cut-off point is established. All packages (programmes, products etc) which come with in the cut-off point are accepted and others rejected. The resources are then allocated to the different decision units and budgets relating to units are approved.

The above analysis shows that the Zero Base Budgeting is simply extension of the Cost Benefit Analysis method to the area of corporate budgeting.

15.16 BENEFITS OF ZERO BASE BUDGETING

ZBB is a revolutionary concept. The benefits are as under:

1. **Proper Allocation of Funds:** Priority in allocation of funds is made on cost-benefit analysis.
2. **Systematic Evaluation:** Every manger has to justify the demand for resources. So, it provides the organisation a systematic way to evaluate different programmes and operations undertaken.
3. **Links Budgets with Goals of Enterprise:** Those projects that do not fit in within the overall goals of the enterprise are not continued, even if they were commenced. Goal oriented approach of the enterprise would be developed.
4. **Improvement of Efficiency:** Only those activities and programmes that are essential only will be undertaken which improves the efficiency of the enterprise. Alternative courses of action will be studied and economies would be achieved, eliminating wastage.
5. **Optimum use of Resources:** As cost-benefit analysis is the guiding principle in fixing priorities, resources are used to the optimum advantage of the organisation.

15.17 LIMITATIONS OF ZERO BASE BUDGETING

Inspite of the many advantages, it suffers from the following limitations:

1. Computation of cost-benefit analysis is essential for ZBB. This is not possible in respect of non-financial matters.
2. The system of ZBB has no scope to adjust for changes and so flexible budgeting is not possible.
3. ZBB involves lot of time and cost of operating is also high.
4. Formulation of decision package is a difficult process and all the managers may not have the necessary expertise.
5. ZBB has no scope in flexible budgeting.

Objective Questions

1. What is Budget? Discuss, in brief, the objectives and advantages of budgetary control? **(15.1, 15.2, 15.3, 15.4 and 15.7)**
2. Discuss the essentials of a good budgetary control system. Explain briefly the steps in setting up of a budgetary control system so that its working efficiency is ensured? **(15.3, 15.5 and 15.6)**
3. Define 'Flexible Budget' and explain its importance as a budgeting technique and tool of control? Detail the steps for introducing flexible budget? **(15.9 and 15.10)**
4. Explain the classification of budgets? **(15.9)**
5. Detail the advantages and limitations of budgetary control? **(15.3, 15.7 and 15.8)**
6. What does zero-base budgeting mean? What are the different steps involved in it and how is it useful to the business? Explain its limitations? **(15.13 to 15.17)**
7. Write short notes on:
   (A) Budget and budgeting **(15.2)**
   (B) Differences between fixed and flexible budget **(15.11)**
   (C) Zero-Base Budgeting **(15.13 and 15.16)**

Check Your Understanding

(A) State whether the following Statements are True or False

1. A budget is a means and budgetary control is the end result.
2. To achieve the anticipated targets, planning, Co-ordination and control are the important main tasks of management, achieved through budgeting and budgetary control.
3. A key factor or principal factor does not influence the preparation of all other budgets.
4. Budgetary control does not facilitate introduction of 'Management by Exception'.
5. Generally, budgets are prepared to coincide with the financial year so that comparison of the actual performance with budgeted estimates would facilitate better interpretation and understanding.
6. A fixed budget is preferable to flexible budget.
7. A flexible budget recognises the difference between fixed, semi-fixed and variable cost and is designed to change in relation to the change in level of activity.
8. Cash budget is a summary of cash intake and outlay in respect of both revenue and capital items.
9. Zero base budgeting is the latest technique of budgeting.
10. Sales budget, normally, is the most important budget among all budgets.
11. The principal factor is the starting point for the preparation of various budgets.
12. A budget manual is the summary of all functional budgets.

Answers

1. True	2. True	3. False	4. False	5. True
6. False	7. True	8. True	9. True	10. True.
11. True	12. False			

(B) Choose the appropriate answer:

1. The basic difference between a fixed budget and flexible budget is that a fixed budget ....
   (A) is concerned with a single level of activity while flexible budget is prepared for different levels of activity.
   (B) is concerned with fixed costs while flexible budget is concerned with variable costs.
   (C) is fixed while flexible budget changes.
2. A flexible budget requires a careful study of
   (A) Fixed, semi-fixed and variable expenses
   (B) Past and current expenses
   (C) Overheads, selling and administrative expenses.
3. Sales budget is a ...
   (A) Expenditure budget
   (B) Functional budget
   (C) Master budget
4. The budget that is prepared first of all is ...
   (A) Master budget
   (B) Budget with key factor
   (C) Cash budget
5. Materials becomes key factor if
   (A) quota restrictions exist
   (B) insufficient advertisement prevails
   (C) there is low demand

Answers

1. (A)	2. (A)	3. (B)	4. (B)	5. (A)

16

METHODS OF CAPITAL BUDGETING

- *Introduction*
- *Definition and Meaning of Capital Budgeting*
- *Need and Importance of Capital Budgeting*
- *Types of Investment Decisions*
- *Investment Evaluation Criteria*
- *Capital Budgeting or Investment Techniques*
  - *Discounted techniques*
  - *Non-Discounted techniques*
- *Net Present Value Method*
- *Internal Rate of Return Method*
- *NPV versus IRR*
- *Pay Back Method*
- *Objective Questions*
- *Check Your Understanding*

16.1 INTRODUCTION

A capital expenditure may be defined as an expenditure, the benefit of which is spread over a period exceeding one year. The main feature of a capital expenditure is that the heavy expenditure is incurred at one period of time while the benefits of the expenditure are spread at different points of time, in future. **Capital expenditure involves exchange of current assets to acquisition of fixed assets.** Some of the examples of capital expenditure are

(A) Purchase or acquisition of permanent assets such as machinery, building, goodwill etc.

(B) Cost of improvement, addition, expansion or alteration in the fixed assets.

(C) Cost of replacement of fixed assets.

(D) Research and development expenditure.

Capital expenditure decisions are also called as long-term investment decisions.

16.2 DEFINITION AND MEANING OF CAPITAL BUDGETING

Definition: The investment decisions of a firm are generally known as capital budgeting or capital expenditure decisions. Capital budgeting is concerned with allocation of the firm's scarce financial resources in long-term projects, the benefits occur over a future period. **Capital budgeting may be defined as the firm's decision to invest current funds in long-term assets to get the benefits over the years.**

The characteristics of capital budgeting or long–term Investment decisions are:

(A) Exchange of current assets for future benefits.

(B) Investment of funds in non-flexible and long-term assets or activities.

(C) Huge Funds are involved.

(D) Future benefits or cash flows occur over a series of years.

(E) Decisions are irreversible.

(F) Significant impact on the profitability of the concern.

16.3 NEED AND IMPORTANCE OF CAPITAL BUDGETING

Investment decisions are of great importance to any concern. These decisions involve commitment of a large sum of money. They affect the profitability of the enterprise, greatly. These decisions are difficult to make.

The need, significance or importance of these decisions is due to the following reasons:

1. **Large Investments:** Funds are limited and opportunities are abundant. Capital expenditure decisions involve commitment of large sums of money. If funds are committed to one project, other projects are denied. So, a great deal of planning is necessary before the capital expenditure.
2. **Growth and Profitability:** The direction of growth is set by the capital expenditure. If the expenditure goes in the right direction, the organisation gets a boost in the profitability. If the decision is wrong, it is fatal for its growth or at times, even the profitable concern may suffer due to their heavy financial implications.
3. **Irreversible Nature:** Most investment decisions are irreversible. Once these assets are acquired, their disposal is difficult as there is no ready market and, often, results in heavy losses. Due to this long-term implication, decisions are taken after careful planning. More often, the decisions cannot be reversed, without substantial loss.
4. **Difficulties of Investment Decisions:** The impact of investment decision is not limited for one year. Its influence spreads over a series of years. Future is uncertain and so it is difficult to forecast its impact over the period of the life of the asset. It is difficult to estimate the future cash flows, accurately. Economic, political, social and technological forces cause the uncertainty of the cash flows.

5. **Risk:** Long-term commitment of funds changes the risk profile of the firm. Adoption of a profitable investment increases the earnings per share but causes a change in the earning pattern. As future is uncertain, there is no guarantee for the continuation of the same earnings, positively. Thus, investment decisions shape the basic character of the firm.

16.4 TYPES OF INVESTMENT DECISIONS

They are many ways to classify the investments. One way of classification is as follows:

1. **Expansion and Diversification: A company may add capacity to its existing capacity, which is known as expansion.** If the present capacity of an enterprise is 10, 000 mt of urea and it decides to manufacture another 5, 000 mt by adding a new plant, it is expansion. A firm engaged in soft drinks invests in a package manufacturing; it is diversification, as it has not engaged in packing activity, earlier.
2. **Replacement and Modernisation:** Replacement is needed when the life of the existing asset is over. Normally, replacement and modernisation go together as technology chages occur over a period. Benefit of technological advancement can be taken at the time of replacement. The main objective of modernisation and replacement is to improve operating efficiency and reduce costs. A cement manufacturing company may replace an existing semi-automatic with fully automatic machine. This reduces costs and increases profitability, while the revenue remains unchanged. However, substantial modernisation and replacement, with modern technological improvements, expands revenues as well as reduces costs.

Another classification may be as follows:

(A) **Mutually exclusive investments: Mutually exclusive investments serve the same purpose, but compete with each other.** The best example is when a stone crusher is planning to replace the existing manual operations either with semi-automatic machine or fully automatic machine. Both the machines are, simultaneously, not needed. One of the machines serves the purpose.

(B) **Independent Investments: Independent investments do not compete with each other and serve different purposes**. For example, a company may plan to purchase machinery for increasing production and vehicle for improved transportation and reduction of costs. Both these investments do not compete with each other. One purchase does not dispense another. Depending on the availability of funds and the profitability planned, the company can undertake both the investments.

(C) **Contingent Investments:** Contingent investments are dependent investments. **The choice of one investment necessitates undertaking one or more investments.** When a company plans to start a new factory in a remote and backward area, it may have to invest in houses and roads to attract the employee force to join and work. The total expenditure will be treated as one investment. Factory alone cannot be commenced without the required infrastructure and necessary support to the employees to live under suitable working conditions.

16.5 INVESTMENT EVALUATION CRITERIA

A finance manager is faced with several investment opportunities. There are several investment techniques. **The essential property of a sound investment evaluation criterion is that it should maximise the shareholders' wealth.** So, the finance manager should have clear understanding of the features of a sound investment evaluation criterion for proper selection.

Evaluation criteria for choice: The following are the sound characteristics or criteria for choice of an investment decision:

- All cash flows over the life of the project are to be considered.
- Criteria should be clear and objective to separate a good project from a bad one.
- Help in ranking the projects, according to their profitability.
- Should recognise the fact that bigger cash flows are preferable to smaller ones and the early cash flows are better than the later ones.
- Should help to choose among mutually exclusive projects that maximise the shareholders' wealth.
- Should be applicable to all conceivable projects for selection.

16.6 CAPITAL BUDGETING OR INVESTMENT TECHNIQUES

Capital Budgeting techniques are, broadly, divided into two categories. They are discounted and non-discounted techniques.

(A) Discounted techniques:

- Net Present Value (NPV)
- Internal Rate of Return (IRR)
- Profitability Index (PI)
- Discounted Payback Period

(B) Non-Discounted techniques:

- Payback Period (PB)
- Accounting Rate of Return (ARR)

16.7 NET PRESENT VALUE METHOD

The best method for evaluation of investment proposals is the net present value method or Discounted cash flow technique. The net Present Value technique explicitly recognises the time value of money. These techniques recognises the cash flows, arising at different time periods, differs in value and are comparable only when their present values are found out.

Steps for calculation of NPV:

1. Cash flows of different investment projects are to be forecasted, based on the realistic assumptions.
2. Choose the appropriate discount rate.
3. The appropriate discount rate is the firm's opportunity cost of capital. This is equal to the rate of return expected by the investors on investments of equivalent and comparable risk. Investors want compensation for time and risk, they assume. This is the meaning of 'Required Rate of Return'.
4. The cash flows are to be discounted, applying the discount rate, to arrive at the present value of the cash flows.
5. Net Present Value should be found out by subtracting the present value of cash outflows from the present value of the cash inflows.
6. Accept the Project if the NPV is positive. (i.e. NPV > 0)

Formula for calculation of NPV: The formula for calculating NPV is as under:

$$\textbf{Net Present Value} = \frac{C_1}{(1_0+k)} + \frac{C_2}{(1+k)^2} + \frac{C_n}{(1+k)^{\eta}} - C_0$$

$$= \sum_{t=1}^{n} \frac{C_t}{(1+k)^t} - C_0$$

Σ = Sigma (sum)

C_1 and C_2 = Net cash inflows in year 1 and $2..._n$

k = Appropriate discount rate (cost of capital)

tassumes values from 1 to η

C_0 = Initial cost of investment

In case, present value factors (PVF) are given, the cash flows of the different years are multiplied with the respective present value factors to arrive at the present values of the cash flows.

Importance of Net Present Value: NPV is the true measure of firm's profitability. When different independent projects compete, the projects can be ranked, in the order of net present value, for selection. The NPV method can also be used to select between mutually exclusive projects.

Acceptance Rule: A project may be accepted, if NPV is positive. The net present value would be positive if the project generates cash flows at a rate higher than the cost of capital. **Positive NPV increases the value of the firm's share price and contributes to the maximisation of the shareholders' wealth.** A zero NPV implies that the project generates enough cash flow at a rate, just equal to the opportunity cost of capital.

Thus, the NPV acceptance rules are:

- Accept if NPV > 0
- Reject if NPV < 0
- May Accept or Reject if NPV = 0

Advantages of NPV Method: The advantages of NPV method for evaluating investment proposals are as follows:

1. **Recognition of Time Value of Money:** NPV method recognises the time value of money. This is suitable for evaluation of investment proposals whether the cash flows, both inflows and outflows, are uniform or uneven.
2. **All cash flows considered:** It takes into account the cash flows arising during the total life of the projects and true measure of the profitability can be evaluated.
3. **Profitability Objective Achievement:** It takes into consideration the objective of maximum profitability.
4. **Value Additivity Principle:** It satisfies the value-additivity principle (i.e. NPV of two or more projects can be added).

Limitations of NPV:

1. In practice, it is difficult to obtain the estimates of cash flows, due to uncertainty of future.
2. It is difficult to measure precisely, the discount rate.
3. When alternative projects with unequal lives are evaluated, caution must be exercised.
4. Equally, caution is necessary when the firm has constraints of funds. Even if the alternative project's NPV were higher, the firm would not be in position to select due to higher commitment of funds of that project.
5. As compared to the easy traditional method of Payback period, this is difficult to calculate and understand.

Illustration No. 1

A machine purchased six years ago for Rs. 1,50,000 has been depreciated to a book value of Rs. 90,000. It originally had a projected life of 15 years and zero salvage value. A new machine will cost Rs. 4,30,000 and result in a reduced operating cost of Rs. 30,000 per year for the next nine years. The older machine could be sold for Rs. 50,000. The cost of capital is 10%. The new machine will be depreciated on a straight line over nine year's life with Rs. 25,000-salvage value. The company's tax rate is 55%.

Decide whether the old machine should be replaced?

(B.U. MBA- 2004)

Solution:

Incremental Net Investment or Net Initial outflow:

Cost of the Proposed Machine	=	4,30,000
– Current scrap value of existing machine	=	50,000
Incremental net investment		3,80,000
(Net outflow)		

Incremental annual cash inflows:

	Existing machine	Proposed machine
Depreciation of existing machine	10,000	45,000
$= \dfrac{\text{Dpreciated value}}{\text{Balance life of asset}}$		
$= \dfrac{90,000}{9}$		
Depreciation of new machine		
$= \dfrac{\text{Cost} - \text{salvage value}}{\text{life of asset}}$		
$= \dfrac{4,30,000 - 25,000}{9}$		
Reduction in operating cost		– 30,000
Eligible for tax benefit	10,000	15,000
Tax Benefit @ 55%	5,500	8,250
Net tax benefit 8,250 – 5500		2,750
Savings in annual operating cost		30,000
Increase in annual Inflow		32,750

NPV of the proposal (cost of capital 10%)

= Present value of inflows–Present value of outflow

$$\text{Net Present Value} = \frac{C_1}{(1+k)} + \frac{C_2}{(1+k)^2} + \ldots + \frac{C_n}{(1+k)^\eta} - C_0$$

C_1 and C_2 = Net cash inflows in year 1 and 2 $\ldots_n$

k = Appropriate discount rate (cost of capital)

C_0 = Initial cost of investement

$$= \frac{32,750}{(1.10)} + \frac{32,750}{(1.10)^3} + \frac{32,750}{(1.10)^4} + \frac{32,750}{(1.10)^5} + \frac{32,750}{(1.10)^6} + \frac{32,750}{(1.10)^7} + \frac{32,750}{(1.10)^8}$$

$$+ \frac{32,750}{(1.10)^9} - 3,80,000$$

= 29,773 + 27,066 + 24,606 + 22,369 + 20,335 + 18,487 + 16,806 + 15,278 + 13,889 – 3,80,000

= 1,88,607 – 3,80,000 = Rs. – 1,91,393

By replacing the existing machine with the new machine, there would be a loss of Rs. 1,91, 393 with a cost of capital @ 10%. So, it is not desirable to replace the machine.

Tutorial Note: In case, the problem gives PVAF value:

NPV = 32,750 X PVAF (present value of annuity factor of 10% for 9 years) –3,80,000

= 32,750 X 5.759 –3,80,000

= Rs. 1,88,607 –3,80,000

= Rs. –1,91, 393

16.8 INTERNAL RATE OF RETURN METHOD

The internal rate of return (IRR) method is another discounted cash flow technique which takes into account the magnitude and timing of cash flows. IRR is simple to understand, in case of one-period project. For example, a deposit of Rs. 1,000 in a bank would get Rs. 1,010 after one year, the rate of return is calculated as under:

$$\text{Rate of Return} = \frac{1{,}010 - 1{,}000}{1{,}000} = 0.10 = 10\%$$

Formula for rate of return on an investment is

$$\mathbf{r} = \frac{C_1 - C_0}{C_0}$$

Where r = Rate of return

C_1 = Single cash flow after one year

C_0 = Initial Investment

In the equation, the 'Rate of Return' can be defined as that rate which equates the investment outlay with the present value of inflow received at the end of one year. This also implies that the rate of return is the discount rate that makes NPV = 0.

In IRR technique, the future cash inflows are discounted in such a way that their total present value is just equal to the present value of the total cash outflows. The time schedule of occurrence of the future cash flows is known, but the discount rate is not known. The discount rate is ascertained by the trail and error method, where the present value of future inflows is equal to the present value of outflows, which is known as Internal Rate of Return. **In simple words, future inflows are discounted to become equal to the present value of the outflows and the discount rate is IRR.**

Formula for Calculation: The formula for calculation of IRR in case of series of cash flows is as under:

$$C_0 = \frac{C_1}{(1+\mathbf{r})} + \frac{C_2}{(1+\mathbf{r})^2} + \frac{C_3}{(1+\mathbf{r})^3} + \ldots + \frac{C_n}{(1+\mathbf{r})^n}$$

It may be noted that the IRR equation is the same as the one used for the NPV method. The difference is the required rate of return, k, is assumed to be known in NPV method while in the IRR method the value of 'r ' has to be determined at which the present value is zero.

Trail and Error Method: The value of 'r ' can be determined through trail and error method. If the calculated present value of the discounted inflows is higher than the present value of the outflows, a higher discount rate should be tried. In case, the present value of the discounted inflows is lower than the present value of the outflows, a lower discount rate is to be tried. This process has to be repeated till the net discounted value of inflows and outflows are equal to each other. Only through the process of trail and error method, the correct discount rate can be calculated.

Acceptance Rule: In order to take a decision about the acceptance or rejection of the project, the IRR is to be compared with the required rate of return (k), fixed by the management of each firm, which is also known as cut-off rate or hurdle rate. In case, IRR is greater than the cut-off rate, the project would be accepted. If IRR is lower than the cut-off rate, the project would be rejected. In case, IRR is equal to required rate of return, the project may be accepted or rejected, in other words, the firm is indifferent about its acceptance or rejection. **The virtue of the IRR rule is that it does not require the computation of the required rate of return.** Symbolically, it can be presented as under:

- Accept if IRR > k
- Reject if IRR < k
- May Accept or Reject, if IRR = k

Evaluation of IRR-Merits: Let us evaluate IRR against the principles of sound investment evaluation criteria. The merits of IRR can be summarised as under:

1. **Recognition of Time Value:** IRR method recognises the time value of money. All the cash flows happening, at the different periods of time, are adjusted to make them comparable.
2. **All cash flows:** All the cash flows occurring over the entire life of the project are considered for calculating rate of return.
3. **Shareholders' Wealth Maximisation:** It is consistent with the objective of shareholders' wealth maximisation.
4. **Proposal Selection:** It helps in selecting the proposals, which is expected to earn more than the required rate of return.
5. **More Practical:** Since IRR is expressed as a percentage, it is easy to compare IRR of different projects and make proper selection, in the order of ranking.
6. The IRR id based on the cash flows rather than the accounting profit. Hence, IRR is more justified.

Drawbacks of IRR: Though IRR has the qualities of sound investment evaluation criterion, still, this technique suffers the following disadvantages.

1. Its calculation is complicated, based on trail and error method.
2. It is based on the assumption future cash outflows are reinvested at a rate equal to the IRR. Practically, it is not essential that every firm would have reinvestment opportunities.

3. In evaluating mutually exclusive projects, the IRR rule may give misleading results in a number of situations.
4. IRR violates the value-additivity principle. It means IRR of two or more projects cannot be added, unlike NPV method.

16.9 NPV VERSUS IRR

The NPV and IRR are closely related investment criteria.

Superiority of IRR over NPV: In the following respects, IRR may be considered to be superior to NPV for the following reasons:

1. **Basis: IRR gives the percentage result, while NPV gives the result in absolute amount.**
2. **Required Rate of Return:** For calculating IRR, the required rate of return is not a pre-requisite while it is a must to NPV.

Superiority of NPV over IRR: NPV is superior to IRR for the following reasons:

1. NPV shows the expected increase in the wealth of the shareholders.
2. The NPV of different projects are additive while the IRRs can not be added.
3. NPV gives better ranking as compared to IRR.

Comparison between NPV and IRR: Both are modern techniques of capital budgeting and take the time value of money into account. Still, there are certain basic differences between them.

Basis	NPV	IRR
1. **Cash flows**	Cash flows are discounted at predetermined discount rate, based on cost of capital.	Cash flows are not discounted at predetermined rate and arrived at by trail and error method.
2. **Reinvestment**	Cash flows are presumed to be reinvested at the cut-off rate.	Cash flows are presumed to be reinvested at the internal rate of return.

Similarity between NPV and IRR: It must be remembered that both NPV and IRR methods show the same results in respect of independent investment proposals, which do not compete with one another.

Different Results: In case of mutually exclusive projects, both the projects compete with each other and acceptance of one project, automatically, excludes the acceptance of the other. Both may give contradictory results when evaluating mutually exclusive projects for the following reasons:

(A) Requirement of cash outlays for the projects may be different. One project may require more funds while the other may demand less.

(B) The projects have unequal lives.

(C) The projects have different patterns of cash flows.

16.10 PAY BACK METHOD

The Payback Method (PB) is one the most popular and widely recognised traditional methods of evaluating investment proposals. **Payback method is defined as the number of years required to recover the original cash outlay invested in a project.** If the project gives constant annual cash inflow, the payback period can be calculated by dividing cash outlay by the annual cash inflow.

Equal Cash inflows: The formula for calculation of payback period, when the cash inflows are constant is as follows:

$$\text{Payback Period} = \frac{\text{Initial Investment}}{\text{Annual cash inflow}}$$

Unequal Cash inflows: In the case of unequal Cash inflows, the payback period can be found out by adding up the cash inflows until the total is equal to the initial cash outlay.

So, payback method is useful when the cash flows are equal or unequal.

Acceptance Rule: On account of simplicity, many firms follow pay back method as an Accept or Reject criterion as well as a method for ranking projects. First, management sets the standard payback period. If the payback period calculated is below the standard payback period, the project is accepted. In case, the payback period is more than the standard period, the project is rejected. It is very simple to operate and decision-making. For example, if the standard payback period is 3 years, fixed by the management, and the payback period calculated is 2 years, the project is accepted. In case, the payback period is, say, 4 years, the project is rejected. So, simple the operation is. If there is more than one project for consideration, all the projects are ranked, according to the payback period. The project that has the shortest payback period is ranked first and the project that has the longest period is placed at the last, in the order of ranking. Thus, if a firm has to choose among the mutually exclusive projects, project with shorter payback period is selected.

Evaluation of Payback Method: If we analyse the payback method against the standard investment evaluation criterion, the positions is as follows:

Merits: It has the following advantages.

1. **Simple to Operate:** The most significant merit is it is simple to understand and easy to calculate. Its simplicity is considered as a virtue, which is evident from the popularity with business executives.
2. **Calculation costs Low:** Its calculation costs less while the other sophisticated techniques require lot of analyst's time and even use of computers.
3. **Risk of Obsolescence high:** This method is ideally suitable in those industries where the risk of obsolescence is high. There is no guarantee that the same technology would continue, in future. In such industries, projects that have shorter payback period only are to be financed.

Demerits: In spite of its simplicity, it suffers from the following limitations.

1. **All cash flows not considered:** Cash inflows through out the life of the projects are not considered, totally. It fails to take into account the cash inflows after the payback period.

In other words, if the standard payback period, say 5 years, the cash inflows after 5 years, even though available, are ignored. It is not an appropriate method for measuring the profitability of the project as it ignores the time value of money.

2. **Equal weightage to all cash flows:** It fails to consider the pattern of cash inflows i. e. magnitude and timing of the cash flows. It gives equal weights to all the cash inflows though they may happen at different periods of time.
3. **No rational in fixing standard Period:** The firm may experience administrative difficulty to fix the standard payback period, as there is no rational in fixing the period.
4. **Not consistent with Shareholders' Wealth Maximisation:** The payback period is not consistent with the maximisation of the shareholders' wealth.

Illustration No. 2

Delhi Machinery Manufacturing Company wants to replace the manual operations by new machine. There are two alternative models of X and Y for the new machine. Using payback period, suggest the most profitable investment. Ignore taxation:

(Rs.)

	Machine X	Machine Y
Original Investment	9,000	18,000
Estimated Life of the Machine (Years)	3	5
Estimated Savings in Scrap	500	800
Estimated Savings in Wages	6,000	8,000
Additional cost of Maintenance	800	1,000
Additional cost of Supervision	1,200	1,500

(B.U. MBA- 2004)

Solution:

	Machine X	Machine Y
Estimated Savings in Scrap and Wages	6,500	8,800
Less: Estimated additional costs on maintenance and supervision	2,000	2,500
Net savings	4,500	6,300
Depreciation (Cost/Life of asset)	3,000	3,600
Net gain	1,500	2,700
Add: Depreciation	3,000	3,600
Annual inflow	4,500	6,300
Payback period (years)	9,000	18,000
Initial Investment	4,5002	6,3002.86
Annual cash inflow	2	2.86

Conclusion: Under Payback method, machine that gives the earliest recovery of outlay is selected. The management has not fixed any standard period. Machine X has 2 years payback period while the payback period of Y is 2.86 years. So, machine X has to be selected, based on Payback Method.

Objective Questions

1. What is Capital Budgeting? Detail its significance for a firm? **(16.1 to 16.3)**
2. What do you mean by Capital Investment Decision? Write its importance? **(16.1 to 16.3)**
3. Detail the different classification of capital expenditure and their evaluation criteria for the choice? **(16.4 and 16.5)**
4. What is Net Present Value Method? Why it is regarded as best method for evaluation of investment proposals? **(16.7)**
5. "The virtue of the IRR rule is that it does not require the computation of the required rate of return." Comment? **(16.8)**
6. Write a note on different methods of Capital Budgeting? Choose any three methods and analyse their strength and weakness against the standard evaluation criteria? **(16.5 to 16.8)**
7. Compare Net Present Value and Internal Rate of Return? **(16.9)**
8. 'Pay Back method is a traditional capital budgeting technique and simple to calculate'. Why this method is not universally applicable in all capital budgeting decisions? **(16.10)**

Check Your Understanding

State whether the following Statements are True or False

1. Capital expenditure decisions are also called as long-term investment decisions.
2. Net Present Value of Inflows is arrived at by deducting outflow investment from of present values of cash inflows.
3. Capital rationing and capital budgeting mean the same thing.
4. Net present value method takes into account the earnings over the entire life of the project.
5. Mutually exclusive investments do not serve the same purpose.
6. Contingent investments are dependent investments and the choice of one investment necessitates undertaking one or more investments.
7. Positive NPV does not contribute to the maximisation of the shareholders' wealth.
8. NPV method is not suitable for evaluation of investment proposals when the cash flows, both inflows and outflows, are uneven.
9. The internal rate of return (IRR) method, another discounted cash flow technique, does not take into account the magnitude and timing of cash flows.
10. Both NPV and IRR methods show the same results in respect of independent investment proposals, which do not compete with one another.
11. In payback method, if a firm has to choose among the mutually exclusive projects, project with longer payback period is selected.
12. Capital Investment decisions are generally of irreversible nature.

Answers

1.	True	2.	True	3.	False	4.	True	5.	False
6.	True	7.	False	8.	False	9.	False	10.	True
11.	False	12.	True						

17

SHORT-TERM FINANCING AND INVESTMENTS

17.1 INTRODUCTION

Short-term finance means availability of funds for a period of one year or less than that period. The basic purpose of short-term financing is to meet the working capital requirements of the company.

Types of Short-term Financing

There are two main types of short-term financing: Trade credit and Bank borrowing.

17.2 TRADE CREDIT

Meaning: Trade credit refers to the credit received by a customer from the supplier of goods, in the normal course of business. When a retailer buys goods from a wholesaler, retailer is the customer to whom credit is extended by the wholesaler. In India, buying goods on credit is a normal feature. In India, this is a major source of short-term financing. In many areas of business, unless credit is extended business can not be made. Very few trades are lucky not to extend credit and make a good business. In that trade, there are no credit sales and all sales are made on cash basis.

In trade credit, payments are deferred. Small traders heavily depend on the trade credit as they still experience difficulty in securing borrowing from banks, though credit is made liberal by the banks. Small traders cannot raise the needed finance by other means.

Trade credit is mostly an informal arrangement and is granted on open account basis. Normal procedure is supplier sends the goods, with an agreed understanding, that the payment is to be made after a certain credit period. Buyer accepts the invoice and so, in effect, he acknowledges the debt. There is no other formal legal document. Once a link is established between the supplier and buyer and payment is regularly made as per the terms of the invoice, the wholesaler supplies the goods for an increased amount, as and when the business of the retailer increases. To a wholesaler, credit extended to the retailers appears as 'Sundry debtors' in its balance sheet. In the balance sheet of the buyer (retailer), the trade credit is shown in the form of sundry creditors. In U.S.A., trade creditors are called accounts payable.

Bills Payable: Bills payable may take the form of trade credit. When the supplier of the goods is less sure of receiving the payment on the due date, supplier draws the bill of exchange on the buyer and buyer accepts for payment on the due date. In other words, **trade credit is documented in the form of bills payable.** Bills payable take the place of sundry creditors in the accounts of the retailer. In the accounts of the wholesaler, bills receivable appears in the place of sundry debtors.

Supplier would be in a position to discount these bills with his banker and can raise the finance. Even when there is no doubt of creditworthiness of the buyer, seller may adopt the mode of payment through bill of exchange when he wants to have the option of raising finance through discounting the bills of exchange.

Credit Terms: Credit terms refer to those terms under which the supplier sells on credit to the buyer. There are two important terms and they are due date and cash discount. Due date is the date on which the buyer has to make the payment for the goods supplied. On the due date, supplier can expect the payment. Credit terms refer to the length of credit period and the date of commencement of credit. Cash discount is the incentive provided by the supplier to the buyer for early payment, before the due date. The typical way of expressing credit in an invoice is 2/15, net 30 days. This means 2% cash discount would be given, if the buyer makes the payment within 15 days from the date of invoice. If the buyer does not want to avail the cash discount, payment can be made at the end of 30 days from the date of invoice.

Benefits and costs of Trade credit: Trade credit is a spontaneous source of financing. As the volume of business grows, the amount of credit also, automatically, increases. Suppose, the buyer is in the habit of receiving credit for 30 days and his daily purchases are Rs.10,000 per day. If his business increases and makes purchases for Rs.15,000 per day, his trade credit has increased from Rs. 3,00,000 (30X 10,000) to Rs. 4,50,000 (30X 15,000). In an informal way, the buyer receives the extra credit as he makes the prompt payment at the end of 30 days.

Advantages: The major advantages of trade credit are as under:

1. **Easy Availability:** Unlike other sources of finance, trade credit is easier to obtain. **Trade credit is automatic and no negotiation is needed to obtain.** On this credit, many small firms survive. In many trades, it is an accepted way of conducting business. Even a new shop gets trade credit, after a couple of transactions. It is not possible to secure borrowing from the banks in the initial periods. Even for a new company, trade credit is easier to secure and is highly difficult to raise finance in the capital market.
2. **Flexibility: Flexibility is the unique feature of trade credit.** If business expands, more purchases are made and with higher purchases, more trade credit is received. In contrast, when the business declines, automatically, firm makes lower purchases and with it, lesser trade credit is received.
3. **Informality:** Trade credit is informal. **No legal documents are involved.** Generally, even a formal agreement is not entered into, while extending trade credit.

Cost of Trade Credit: Is trade credit a free source of finance? Many think, trade credit does not have any additional cost. It is wrong. Supplier of trade credit has to borrow more funds, paying interest, if trade credit is to be extended. This cost of credit is passed on by the supplier via increased price to the buyer. It is common knowledge cash purchase attracts a lower price, compared to purchase on credit.

17.3 ACCRUED EXPENSES AND DEFERRED INCOME

Accrued Expenses: Accrued expenses represent a liability for the services already received, yet to be paid. They permit payment after the services are received. The classical examples are salaries, rent and electricity where services are received first and payments are made at the end of the specified duration, normally, at the end of the month. In case of salaries and wages, employees render their services and so benefit of the services is received by the firm, immediately, while payments are made at the end of the month. So, even employees too provide a source of spontaneous short-term finance to the organisation they work! In case of corporate taxes, they are paid, quarterly, while the profits are made as and when sales are made. When payment is not made and accounts are to be finalised, provision for accrued expenses is made in accounts.

Accrued expenses represent spontaneous and interest-free source of financing. The longer the period of payment, higher the benefit firm derives. However, due to legal constraints and practical difficulties, firm cannot postpone their payment. Till their payment, firm enjoys the benefit as short-term financing.

Deferred Income: Deferred income represents funds received, in advance, for the services to be rendered, in future. The receipts improve liquidity of the firm. In turn key projects or where goods are to be made for a specific requirement, advance payments are insisted. This avoids the possibility for the cancellation of the sale, after the commencement of the execution of the order. Normally, clause remains in those contracts that the advance payment would be forfeited on cancellation of the contract. These advances are adjusted when the goods and services are supplied. Till the date of supply of services, the amount stands as liability.

17.4 BANK FINANCE FOR WORKING CAPITAL

Banks are the main institutions that provide working capital, which is a short-term source of financing. Bank credit is the most important source for working capital. There are various forms of bank finance for short-term requirements. They are discussed hereunder:

(A) Cash Credit

Cash credit is the common form of financing for meeting working capital requirements, with greatest flexibility, to the borrower in conducting the account. Bank considers the firm's sales and production plans to sanction a particular working capital limit, which is called sanctioned limit in cash credit account. In case of seasonal industries, bank sanctions peak credit limit to meet the working capital requirements during the season which is always higher in comparison to the limit sanctioned for non-peak period. So, bank sanctions separate limits for peak and non-peak periods as working capital requirement is maximum during peak season. These cash credit limits are against the security of current assets such as stocks and book-debts.

Margin: Bank does not finance 100% of current assets. Banks stipulate the required margin. The drawing power (amount that can be drawn) is calculated, after deducting the required margin from the value of stocks. Borrower has to submit the stock statement, monthly, as per the terms of sanction, declaring the physical stocks and value on the specified date. If the margin requirement is 30%, bank lends only up to 70% of the value of stocks. The amount so calculated is called drawing power and the borrower is allowed to draw to the extent of the drawing power. Based on the value of stocks, drawing power is fixed, not exceeding the sanctioned limit. Against the stocks of Rs.80,000, borrower can avail the drawing power of Rs. 56,000 (80,000 -30% of 80,000).

Additional temporary over drawings: Bank allows the borrower to draw, beyond the sanctioned limit, for temporary periods. This would be allowed, if stocks cover the borrowing, with the stipulated margin. An example would clarify the picture, better.

Sanctioned limit	1,00,000
Stocks	1,50,000
Margin	20%
Drawing power	1,20,000
Outstanding balance	90,000

In the above situation, borrower has approached the bank for temporary over drawings of Rs. 20,000. Normally, bank allows Rs. 10,000, up to the sanctioned limit only. As the stocks cover the additional drawings, with the required margin, bank can permit the over drawings for a temporary period, normally, not exceeding 30 days. Once the over drawings are allowed, the outstanding balance becomes Rs. 1,10,000 (90,000 + 20,000), which is in excess of sanctioned limit, but covered by the drawing power.

Ideal Form for Business: The greatest convenience of cash credit account is its flexibility. Borrower can deposit the sale proceeds, daily, to reduce the outstanding balance in the cash credit account and can draw as and when needed, to the maximum extent of drawing power or cash credit limit, which ever is lower. Interest is charged on the outstanding balance only. In other words, borrower is required to pay interest for the amount utilised only and not on the total sanctioned limit. In the loan account, this facility of withdrawing money, again, does not exist. Once deposited in the loan account, the amount is not available for withdrawal as the money is deemed towards the closure of the loan account. This feature in the cash credit account is the greatest convenience to the borrower. On account of this convenience, the actual rate of interest on the sanctioned limit would work out lower than the rate offered by the bank as no borrower requires money on a continuous basis. Moreover, there is no commitment charge for the limit not utilised. By virtue of margin, bank is secured even if the value of the stocks falls to the extent of the margin.

Period of sanction: Cash credit limits are, normally, sanctioned for one year. At the end of the year, the limits are reviewed. Technically, the advances are repayable on demand. However, bank recalls the advance only when the conduct of the account is not satisfactory.

Pledge/Hypothecation: Cash credit facility can be sanctioned either in the form of pledge or hypothecation of goods. In case of pledge, goods are kept in the godowns, under lock and key of the bank. So, the possession of goods and control thereon is not with the borrower. As and when payment is made, goods are released, even proportionately, to the customer. Normally, banks sanction this facility to new borrowers or when their credit worthiness is not fully known. However, Borrower does not enjoy total convenience with the pledge facility. In case of hypothecation, possession of goods is with the borrower and can deal with the goods in the manner he likes, even selling the goods, without the bank's prior approval. However, borrower is required to deposit sale proceeds of the goods into the cash credit–hypothecation account. So bank assumes more risk while sanctioning the hypothecation limit. So, hypothecation facility is extended to such borrowers whose creditworthiness is well known to the bank.

(B) Overdraft

Bank sanctions overdraft in the current account of the customer as and when cheques are received, in excess of the balance in the current account. This is a temporary arrangement. Banks also sanction regular overdraft limits, normally, against the security of fixed deposit receipts, shares, life insurance policy, postal certificates etc. Interest is charged on the amount utilised. Cheque facility is made available in the overdraft account. Cash credit is a normal feature in business and overdraft facility is, normally, availed by professionals for their working capital requirements.

(C) Purchase or Discounting of Bills

This category of finance is a self- liquidating character, with greater control for the bank to monitor the utilisation of the finances, sanctioned by the bank, for working capital requirements. Banks often experience difficulty to check and control diversion of funds i.e. utilisation for purposes other than the sanctioned. In that context, this form of finance is ideal as banks can control better in respect of utilisation as well as monitoring the end use of funds.

Banks sanction limit against the bills of exchange drawn by the suppliers on its customer. Supplier can avail the limit for the bills drawn on the buyers. If the bill of exchange is payable on demand, the bill is purchased by the bank. If the bill of exchange is drawn on acceptance basis, bank discounts the bill, after acceptance by the buyer of the goods. Buyer has to make the payment, only on the due date. In both the cases, working capital is provided by the bank by purchasing or discounting the bills, as the case may be. Banks credit the customer's account, after deducting their commission.

The greatest convenient feature of the advance is its self-liquidating character. Once, the buyer makes the payment, the advance sanctioned against the bill is recovered. The amount sanctioned for working capital is, normally, divided between the stocks and bills.

Banks can monitor the utilisation of the limit in this scheme, better as chances for abuse of the cash credit limit are more. Diversion of funds for other purposes is difficult in the bill scheme. To encourage bills as an instrument of working capital, Reserve Bank of India had introduced the new bill market scheme in 1970. However, the scheme has failed to work.

(D) Letter of Credit

The purpose of letter of credit is that the payment is assured to the supplier of goods or services by the bank. Here, responsibility for payment is assumed by the bank and so supplier is not concerned with the credit worthiness of the buyer. In case, payment is not made by the customer, bank makes payment to the party in whose favour the letter of credit is opened. So, bank assumes the risk. Simply, credit worthiness of the buyer is not relevant to the supplier, once letter of credit is opened. In other words, credit worthiness of the borrower is substituted by the creditworthiness of the bank.

Letter of credit is a non-fund based limit. It means there is no outgo of funds, when the letter of credit is opened by the bank in favour of the customer. Bank opens the letter of credit in favour of financially sound customers. While sanctioning letter of credit limit, banks, normally, insist on margin from the customers.

Additional Working Capital through Letter of Credit

Borrower may face a difficult situation, when its cash credit limit for working capital is exhausted and suppliers are unwilling to give further trade credit. This situation, occasionally, happens in practical life. Many a time, sanctioned letter of credit limit may remain unutilised. In such circumstances, borrower can utilise the letter of credit limit for working capital purposes by requesting bank to open letters of credit in favour of suppliers. Even an unwilling supplier would gladly accept to supply goods on credit, if letter of credit is opened in his favour. Supplier is confident with the letter of credit as there would be no default in payment by bank. So, buyer can negotiate with the supplier for the length of credit and open letter of credit on 'Documents against Acceptance' basis. Once bill of exchange is accepted, buyer can get possession of RR/LR, as the case may be. Taking delivery of goods, buyer can sell the goods and make payment on the due date of bill of exchange. This is an ingenious way of utilising a non-fund based limit for working capital purposes.

Margin-Earmarking from Cash Credit Account: Normally, banks insist on cash margin for opening letter of credit. This margin amount is kept in short term deposit and it attracts low interest rate while the funds, drawn from cash credit, bear a higher interest rate. Instead of cash margin, one can intelligently request the bank to earmark the margin amount from the cash credit limit. Bank reduces the cash credit drawing power to the extent of margin on letter of credit and allows only reduced drawing power for operations of the business. By this exercise, interest can be saved. This is one more way for the finance manager to boost up profitability.

The author, humbly, submits that he had successfully negotiated with the suppliers in working capital crunch situations to accept letter of credit with documents on acceptance basis and could overcome working capital constraints. To improve profitability, earmarking of cash credit limit towards margin was also accepted by the bank.

(E) Working Capital Loan: Working capital loan is, normally, sanctioned by banks for adhoc or temporary purposes of the customers, which are not foreseen by the borrower. This is an additional sanction, in excess of the cash credit limit sanctioned. Once repayment is made, the loan account would be closed. In other words, customer cannot utilise this mode of finance on a continuous basis, like cash credit account. Banks charge higher rate of interest for extending this type of facility, compared to the normal cash credit limit extended to the same borrower.

17.5 COMMERCIAL PAPER

Commercial paper is an unsecured instrument, issued in the form a promissory note. They are issued by the highly rated corporate firms to diversify their sources of short-term financing. Equally, they provide an outlet to invest the temporary excess funds by the individual, corporate sector and non-corporate sector in safe and liquid instruments to secure higher returns, compared to the interest rates offered by banks on short-term deposits. Even non residents and foreign institutional investors can invest in commercial paper. As the gamut of investors is more, commercial paper provides the real opportunity to raise finances from varied types of investors. Commercial paper is an ideal route to raise funds as well as investing excess short-term funds.

Recent Importance: With reduction in interest rates, the importance of commercial paper has diminished, of late. However, issue of commercial paper has, again, regained its erstwhile importance to raise finances, at a cheaper rate of interest, compared to the rates of interest offered by banking industry, due to increase in interest rates charged by the banking industry.

The Indian economy has started witnessing the unprecedented increasing trends on inflation, from the middle of the year 2006. In consequence, bank interest rates have been hardening, more significantly, from the year 2007. Increase in interest rates, offered by banks, is also in consequence of different stringent initiatives taken by RBI. The different measures are increase of credit reserve ratio and statutory liquidity ratio to contain or control the galloping inflation trends, prevailing more than 6%, during the year 2007. So, commercial paper has regained its importance to work as a potent weapon to raise short-term finances, by highly rated companies, to improve their bottom line. In other words, commercial paper has become attractive as an alternative way to finance short-term requirements, instead of borrowing from the banks.

Commercial paper is an important money market instrument for raising short-term finance, at a cheap interest rate. Reserve Bank of India stipulates conditions for issue of commercial paper, from time to time. Conditions, as amended up to 30th June, 2006 are as under:

(i) **Eligibility:** Companies, which have net worth not less than Rs.4 crores only, can issue commercial paper. They should be enjoying working capital limits. Their advance should have been categorised at 'Standard Asset' by the financing bank.

(ii) **Rating requirements: All eligible participants have to obtain the credit rating from CRISIL or CARE or any other recognised credit rating agency.** The minimum credit rating required for issue of commercial paper is P-2 of CRISIL or any other equivalent rating from other rating agencies.

(iii) **Minimum Investment and Denomination:** Amount that can be invested by a single investor cannot be less than Rs.5 lakhs (Face Value). Commercial paper can be issued in denomination of Rs. 5 lakhs or multiples there of.

(iv) Maximum Limit: Company can issue commercial paper up to a maximum of 100% of net owned funds, as per the latest audited balance sheet. This over-all limit covers issues of commercial paper, alongwith other instruments such as term money borrowings, term deposits, certificates of deposit and inter corporate deposits.

(v) Reduction of cash credit limit, no longer, now: Earlier, banks used to reduce the cash credit limit to the extent commercial paper is issued by the borrowing firm. This restriction is no longer, in force.

(vi) **Working Capital Limits:** Banks and financial institutions have the flexibility, now, to fix working capital limits, duly taking into account the resources pattern of companies' financing, including commercial paper.

(vii) **Period of Raising Subscription:** Commercial paper has to be raised within two weeks, from the date of opening the issue for subscription.

(viii) **Maturity:** Maturity runs between a minimum of 7 days and maximum of one year, from the date of issue.

(ix) **Credit Enhancement:** CP is a 'stand alone' product. However, banks have the flexibility to provide credit enhancement, by way of stand-by assistance, based on their commercial judgement.

In other words, in case of default in payment by the issuer, the responsibility would be cast on the bank that has provided credit enhancement. This credit enhancement provides the necessary cushion to the investor's confidence to invest. It may be made clear that the credit enhancement is not compulsory for the issue of commercial paper. The issuer, normally, seeks the credit enhancement, when the credit rating for the commercial paper is not adequate, though enough to issue commercial paper, to attract the investors' response, to raise finance at a cheaper rate of interest. This credit enhancement strengthens the rating of the commercial paper.

These conditions change from time to time and the conditions existing at the time of issue govern the commercial paper.

Cheaper interest rate is the attraction for issue of commercial paper. Investors would, generally, invest in commercial paper issued by sound and creditworthy companies. Commercial paper gives higher interest rate compared to interest rate offered by banks on short-term deposits.

17.6 PUBLIC DEPOSITS

Acceptance of deposits by the manufacturing companies and non-banking financial companies has been the unique feature of Indian Financial System. The restrictive credit policy of Government of India has not allowed the companies to enjoy liberal credit, without regulations. To fill the substantial credit gap existing in the market, the corporate sector has explored the avenue of attracting deposits from the public. When the corporate sector has offered higher interest rate than the interest rate prevailing in banks and post offices, the public has been tempted to invest their savings in corporate deposits. In fact, the public savings have found their way towards corporate deposits, in preference to the banking channels. Corporate sector too has found an easy way to get the money they wanted to have, without restrictions and regulations. Though they have been offering higher interest rate, still, the effective cost to the company has been lower than the total cost incidental on their borrowing from the banks. Even the public sector (government Companies) too has started accepting deposits.

Government Regulation: In that scenario, to regulate acceptance and protect the interests of depositors, Government of India has framed the Companies (Acceptance of Deposits) Rules, 1975 in exercise of the powers conferred under section of 58A of Companies Act. These rules relate to the maximum amount, company can accept in the form of deposits, interest rate and other features to protect the interests of depositors. The Company deposits are unsecured in their character and many investors have overlooked this important aspect while investing, attracted by the higher interest rate, alone. Several investors have burnt their fingers and lost their hard earned savings. Despite the rules for acceptance of deposits, still, many depositors are, yet, to receive their money back from non-banking finance companies as well as manufacturing companies, despite the maturity of deposits and expiry of several years thereafter.

Under the current provisions, interest on public deposits is not exempted from income-tax, in the hands of depositors.

17.7 SHORT-TERM INVESTMENTS

Cash is the most liquid asset held for business operations. Excess cash, amount in excess of the operating cash balance, is held for two reasons. When the business is seasonal, after the season, firm would have excess cash during non-peak season. Other reason is to hold cash for precautionary motive i.e. for meeting unforeseen contingencies and unpredictable financial needs. However efficient the finance manager may be, cash flows cannot be predicted with certainty. So, company would experience the need to park excess cash balance in short-term investments.

Need of short-term investments: Idle cash does not earn anything. The excess cash balance is to be, temporarily, invested in marketable securities, which can be considered as near moneys.

Features of Marketable Securities: Cash is parked in marketable securities for a temporary period. **The primary criterion in selection of marketable securities is quickest convertibility into cash.** If conversion into cash takes time, the very purpose of holding excess cash is defeated. Conversion should be immediate. While converting into cash, there should be no financial loss for the original investment. The investment should yield certain gain, which is only secondary. In choosing the investment opportunities, the firm is guided by the following principles.

Safety: It is the desire of every firm to make maximum gain while investing. But, risk and return always go hand in hand. This cardinal principle should not be forgotten. If the firm looks for return, risk would exist. The risk referred here is default risk. Risk may relate to principal or interest or both. **In choosing the investment opportunity, the default risk should be zero both in respect of principal and return that is assured at the time of investment.** So, the finance manger does not have the option other than choosing low-return investments. Low-risk securities always earn lower return. The finance manager should not be tempted to invest the excess balance in risky securities. Once this primary objective is forgotten, selection goes wrong.

Maturity: Maturity refers to the period when the principal amount is realised. Interest may be paid during the period of security or at maturity. The price of a long time security fluctuates more widely. Longer the maturity the price variation would be higher. So, **selection should be made for short-term securities to avoid fluctuations in price realisation.**

Liquidity and Marketability: Liquidity refers to the ability to convert into cash, immediately without any significant loss of value. Marketability refers to the convenience and speed of conversion into cash. So, securities should be selected that have a ready market so that they are realisable before maturity, if necessary.

Return or Yield: Other things equal, firm should go for those securities that give the highest return. However, this criterion should be the last in selection and return should not influence the selection, at any time. Restraint is necessary for the finance manager in selection process.

Avenues of Investment: The following are the different types of short-term investment opportunities available in India for investing surplus cash:

1. **Treasury Bills: Treasury bills are Government securities.** They are issued by Reserve Bank of India on behalf of the Central Government. There is no default risk with them as issue is made by Government. Normally, the treasury bills are issued at a discount and redeemed at the

face value. The difference is the return for investment in treasury bills. They are issued in the bearer form and purchaser's name does not appear on the bills. So, they are easily transferable. Secondary market exists for sale so they are highly liquid. However, return is very low due to safety and backing of the Government for repayment.

2. **Bank Deposits:** Excess cash balance can be placed with the banks in the form of deposits. The minimum period for short-term deposit is 14 days. As failure of banks does not exist, there is no risk, virtually, with the bank deposits. In case of need, they can be cancelled, before maturity, and funds are available, immediately. However, if the deposit does not run for a minimum period of 14 days, no interest would be paid on cancellation.

3. **Commercial Paper:** Commercial Papers are short-term and unsecured securities issued by highly creditworthy large companies. CPs are negotiable instruments that make them marketable securities. Detailed coverage has been made, already, above.

4. **Inter-corporate Deposits:** Inter-corporate lending/borrowing or deposits are a popular form of investment. Excess funds are placed with the sister/ associate companies or outside companies of high repute and creditworthiness. Risk default is very high, but returns are attractive.

As they are unsecured in nature, the credit worthiness of the borrower should be beyond question. Section of 370 of Companies Act has placed certain restrictions on inter-corporate deposits, which are to be complied with. The main provisions are as follows:

(A) A company cannot lend more than 10% of its net worth (aggregate of equity and free reserves) to a single company.

(B) The total lending of a company can not exceed 30% of its net worth, without passing a special resolution and obtaining the approval of the central government for such lending.

5. **Money Market Mutual Funds:** Money market instruments are forms of debt that mature in less than one year and are very liquid.

The fund so raised by the money market mutual funds would be invested in the money market instruments such as Call Money, Treasury bills, Re-discounted bills, GOI Securities, and Certificates of Deposits and Commercial Papers, with ratings of PI and above.

Money Market Mutual Funds like Unit Trust of India and private players like Kothari Pioneer invest the funds received in short-term marketable securities such as treasury bills, commercial and call money. Investors can withdraw the money at short-notice or over the counter and so highly liquid. They offer attractive yields. The key features are they are easy to trade, liquidated easily and no tax is deducted at source.

Check Your Understanding

State whether the following are true or false

1. Trade credit refers to the credit received by a customer from the supplier of goods in the normal course of business.

2. Trade credit is mostly an informal arrangement and is granted on open account.
3. Cash discount is offered as and when cash sale is made.
4. Trade credit is a spontaneous source of financing that is made available increasingly, with the expansion of business.
5. Trade credit does not involve any additional cost to the buyer, while it is an easy source of finance.
6. Accrued expenses are an asset.
7. Technically, cash credit advance is repayable on demand, but, bank does not recall the advance, if the conduct of the account is satisfactory.
8. Commercial paper is an important money market instrument for raising short-term finances at a cheap interest rate.
9. Commercial paper is unsecured in character.
10. Public deposits are secured.

Answers

1. True	2. True	3. False	4. True	5. False
6. False	7. True	8. True	9. True	10. False

Objective Questions

1. Detail the different sources of short-term finance and explain whether these forms of finance involve any additional cost to the buyer? **(17.1 to 17.6)**
2. **Explain the importance and advantages of trade credit as a source of working capital. Whether provision of this source involves any cost to the provider and who bears it, finally? (17.1 and 17.2)**
3. **Describe the different types of short-term finance provided by commercial banks for meeting working capital requirements? Is there a way to utilise non-fund based limit for working capital purposes? (17.4)**
4. **Enumerate the various facilities available for meeting working capital requirements, identify the ideal facility of borrowing for business and justify? (17.4)**
5. Explain the criteria that a firm should use in choosing short-term investments and detail the available avenues of investment? **(17. 7)**

18

MANAGEMENT OF WORKING CAPITAL

18.1 INTRODUCTION

Working capital may be regarded as the lifeblood of a business enterprise. It is, closely, related to the day-to-day operations of the business. Every business needs funds for two purposes. Long-term funds are required for creation of production facilities such as plant and machinery, land, building and furniture etc. Investment in these assets represents that part of firm's capital, which is permanently blocked on a permanent or fixed basis and is called fixed capital. The form of these assets does not change, in the normal course.

Funds are, also, needed for purchase of raw materials, payment of wages and other day-to-day expenses etc. These funds are known as working capital. Funds invested in these assets keep revolving, fast. These assets are converted into cash and, again, cash is converted into current assets. So, working capital is also called revolving or circulating capital. The assets change the form, on a continuous basis. In other words, **working capital refers to that part of the firm's capital, which is required for financing short-term or current assets such as cash, debtors, inventories and marketable securities etc.**

18.2 MEANING OF WORKING CAPITAL

The term 'working capital' refers to

(i) Those current assets, which are **convertible into cash, within a period of one accounting year** and

(ii) Those **funds needed for meeting day-to-day operations.**

18.3 CONCEPTS OF WORKING CAPITAL

There are two concepts of working capital–gross and net.

Gross working capital: Gross working capital refers to the firm's investment in total current assets of the enterprise. Current assets are those, which can be converted into cash, within an accounting year (or operating cycle). They include cash, debtors, bills receivable, stock and marketable securities etc. In a broader sense, working capital refers to gross working capital.

Net working capital: In the narrow sense, working capital refers to net working capital. **Net working capital is the difference between current assets and current liabilities.** Current liabilities are those claims of outsiders, which are expected to mature for payment, within an accounting year. They include creditors, bills payable, bank overdraft/cash credit account and outstanding expenses.

If the payment of current liabilities is delayed, the firm gets the availability of funds to that extent. So, a part of the funds required to maintain current assets is financed by the current liabilities. The firm is required to invest in the current assets, to that extent, not financed by the current liabilities.

If current assets are in excess of current liabilities, net working capital is positive. A negative working capital occurs when the current liabilities exceed current assets.

Treatment of Bank overdraft/cash credit account: Bank overdraft/cash credit account is treated as current liability as the sanction of bank is for one year. It is a different matter bank renews these facilities on a continuous basis, at the request of the borrower, on submission of the required data and particulars. Some authors treat bank overdraft/cash credit account as permanent borrowing, not as current liability, as the funds remain with the firm, on a continuous basis. As already discussed in ratio analysis, in detail, we consider bank overdraft/cash credit account, as current liability as the firm has to repay, at the end of one year, as the official written sanction of the bank is available for one year, only.

Gross and Net working capital not exclusive: The two concepts of gross and net working capital are not exclusive. It means both have equal significance or importance from the management's view point. The gross working capital concept is a financial or going concern concept while net working capital is an accounting concept of working capital. A finance manager must consider both the aspects, as they provide different interpretation.

Gross Working Capital Concept: Gross working capital requires consideration from two angles:

(A) How to optimise investment in current assets?

There are two danger points in respect of working capital, excessive or inadequate investment in current assets. Both are equally dangerous. **The basic objective of working capital management is to manage firm's current assets and current liabilities, in such a way, that working capital is maintained, at a satisfactory level.** Then, what is a satisfactory level? **The working capital should be neither more nor less, but just adequate.** Cash is tied in current assets and funds involve costs. If investment in current assets is excessive, profitability will be greatly affected. If investment in current assets is inadequate, firm experiences difficulty, in meeting the current obligations, as and when they fall due. Inadequate working capital threatens the solvency of the firm, due to inability to pay current obligations, in time. Both profitability and solvency are equally important. So, the management should be prompt to initiate the necessary action to keep working capital, adequate to the changing needs of business.

Moreover, different components of working capital are to be balanced. If inventory level is too high in the total current assets, due to slow moving stocks, it does not provide any cushion in the form of liquidity. Similar is the case with the high proportion of accounts receivable, which are difficult to recover. If cash and bank balances are more in total current assets, they are idle and do not contribute to profitability. So, **it is important to maintain proper level of current assets, in aggregate, as well as their individual proportion.**

(B) How should current assets be financed?

The second aspect is arranging funds for financing current assets. Working capital requirement is not static. The requirement keeps on changing. If business increases, more working capital is needed. If the business shrinks, idle funds arise. Thus, the finance manager should have adequate knowledge to tap the different sources of working capital funds, at short notice, as well as investment avenues, where idle funds may be, temporarily, invested.

Net Working Capital Concept: Current assets are financed by current liabilities, to a large extent. The balance amount of working capital, not financed by current assets, is financed from the long-term sources of the firm. Long-term sources are shareholders' funds and long-term borrowings. Net working capital, excess of current assets over current liabilities, measures the firm's liquidity. This also gives an idea about the buffer available to current liabilities. It indicates the margin of protection available to the short-term creditors. Net working capital gives more assurance to the creditors. So, **creditors look for higher net working capital for their safety and promptness in payments. In all, net working capital indicates the financial soundness of the firm.** So, to the finance manager, net working capital concept is also important to send signals of safety to creditors.

(C) Importance of Working Capital

Cash inflows and outflows are never synchronised. Cash inflows occur with the realisation of current assets, such as stock and debtors. Their realisations are highly unpredictable as the inflows depend on outsiders' actions. Outflows are related with the payments to creditors, bills payable and outstanding expenses. They are more predictable and controllable as they depend on the behavior of the firm. However efficient the finance manager may be, certainty of both cash inflows and outflows cannot be predicted, with total accuracy. To meet the gap between the cash inflows and outflows, working capital is needed. **The more these cash flows are predictable, lesser amount is needed for working capital.** If these cash flows are uncertain, higher amount of working capital is essential for the enterprise.

Working capital Level: It is a conventional rule to maintain level of current assets twice the level of current liabilities. In other words, **current ratio should be 2:1.** However, this is only a crude rule. It all depends on the quality of current assets. If the current assets are totally realisable and qualitative, even a lesser current ratio may be adequate and the firm may not experience any difficulty in meeting current obligations. If the current assets consists more slowly moving stocks and more time taking debtors, even a higher ratio may not put the firm at ease for making the payments, in time. **The mix of current assets is more important then its mere quantity.**

Working capital should be a judicious mix: Working capital should be a judicious mix of long-term and short-term funds for financing its current assets. The permanent component of current assets should be financed by long-term sources such as equity share capital, preference share capital, debentures, long-term loan and retained earnings. Each firm should decide the mix of short-term and long-term funds, depending on their availability and risk the firm is prepared to assume. There is no hard and fast rule for deciding the exact quantum of working capital as the requirements of business fluctuates. Similarly, there is no specific rule how the current assets are to be financed. But, one thing is clear, there should be proper judicious mix and whatever funds are raised, they should be put to productive use.

18.4 NEED FOR WORKING CAPITAL

Every enterprise is not fortunate enough to conduct its total business with cash sales. Credit sales are common in, almost, every form of business. To support credit sales, working capital is needed in the form of current assets. Working capital is required to carry on day-to-day business activities. While every firm requires working capital, its quantum differs from business to business, dependent on nature of activity the business is engaged in. A retail firm may require lower amount of working capital, while a wholesale firm needs more. Similarly, where the gestation period is long for production, the manufacturing firm requires more amount of working capital. It needs no further emphasis that the requirement of working capital is vital for every business, more so, when the objective of each firm is wealth maximization. The amount of working capital depends on the operating cycle, involved in conversion of sales into cash or the total period needed for bringing cash into cash again as cash is the starting for business while cash, again, is the end point of transaction.

18.5 OPERATING CYCLE

Operating cycle is the length period required to convert sales, after acquisition of the resources such as materials, power etc, into cash. The operating cycle of a manufacturing firm, typically, involves three phases:

- **Acquisition of Resources** such as raw material, labour, power and fuel etc.
- **Manufacture of the Product** which includes conversion of raw material into work-in-process into finished products.
- **Sale of the product** either for cash or credit sales. Credit sales result into debtors or accounts receivable.

The operating cycle can be presented in a pictorial form.

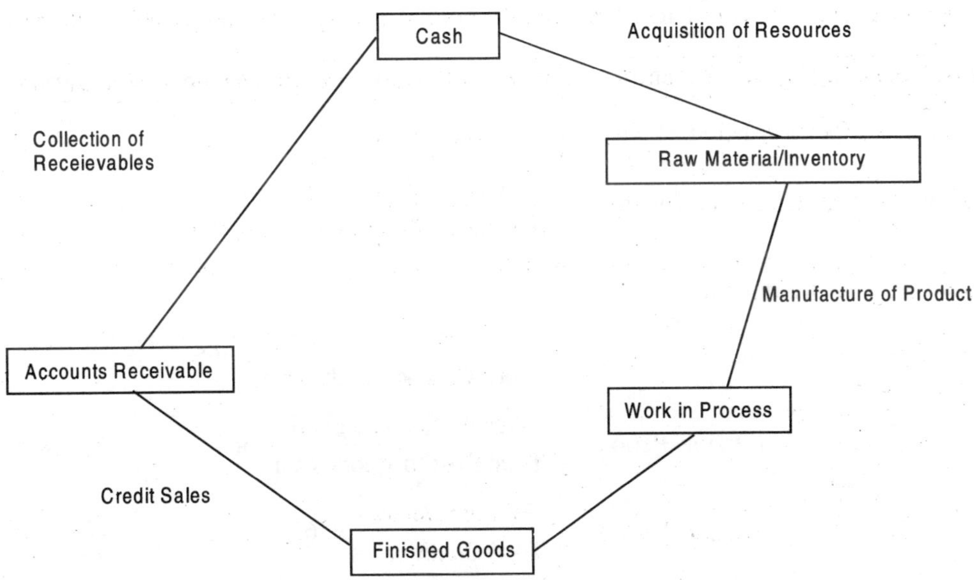

Operating Cycle

The length of the operating cycle is the sum of:

(i) **Inventory Conversion Period:** The inventory conversion period includes raw materials conversion period, work-in-process conversion period and finished goods conversion period. So, it is the total period required for converting raw materials into finished goods.

(ii) **Debtors Conversion Period:** It is the period required for collecting credit sales into cash.

The aggregate of Inventory conversion period and debtors' conversion period is known as gross Operating Cycle. Firms are able to purchase raw materials on credit and also postpone payments for services such as wages, rent etc. and the period is known as payables deferral period. The difference between gross operating cycle and payables deferral period is known as Net operating cycle.

When cash sales are involved, the length of the operating cycle is short as there is no debtors' conversion period.

Estimation of Working Capital with Operating Cycle: With operating cycle method, working capital can be calculated in the form of length of operating cycle i.e. number of days. As depreciation is a non-cash expense, depreciation is to be excluded from the expenses to compute cash operating cycle. Actual operating cycle would be compared with the anticipated operating cycle to evaluate the performance of working capital management. If net operating cycle increases, requirement of working capital would increase and vice versa.

The method of calculation of operating cycle is as under:

$$\boxed{\textbf{Net operting cycle : Gross operating cycle} - \textbf{Payables Deferral period}}$$

Inventory Conversion Period (ICP) is the sum of raw materials Conversion Period (RMCP), work-in-process Conversion Period (WIPCP) and Finished Goods Conversion Period (FGCP).

$$ICP = RMCP + WIPCP + FGCP$$

Net Operating Cycle is the difference between the gross operating cycle and payables deferral period.

$$\boxed{\textbf{Gross Operating Cycle} = \textbf{Inventory Conversion Period} + \textbf{Debtors's Conversion period}}$$

The formulae for calculation of the different components are:

$$\text{Raw Materials Conversion Period} = \frac{\text{Average Raw Materials held}}{\text{Total Raw Meterial consumption}}$$

Average is calculated by averaging the total of opening and closing balance of the raw materials stock, held by the firm.

$$\text{Work-in-progress Conversion Period} = \frac{\text{Average Work-in-progress}}{\text{Total Cost of Production}} \times 365$$

$$\text{Finished Goods Conversion Period} = \frac{\text{Average finished goods}}{\text{Total Cost of goods sold}} \times 365$$

$$\text{Debtors' Conversion Period} = \frac{\text{Average Debtors}}{\text{Total Credit Sales}} \times 365$$

$$\text{Payables Deferral Period} = \frac{\text{Average Creditors}}{\text{Total Credit Purchases}} \times 365$$

Illustration No.1

From the following information, extracted from the books of a manufacturing company of Kalyan & co, compute the operating cycle in terms of days and amount of working capital needed for the firm.

Period covered	365 days
Average period of credit allowed by suppliers	20 days
	(Rs. In '000)
Average Total of Debtors Outstanding	480
Raw Material Consumption	4,400
Total Production Cost	10,000
Total Cost of Sales	10,500
Sales for the year	16,000
Value of Average Stock maintained :	
Raw Material	320
Work-in-progress	350
Finished Goods	260

Solution:

Computation of Operating Cycle

(i) Raw materials held in stock:

$$= \frac{\text{Average stocks of raw materials held}}{\text{Total consumption}} \times 365$$

$$= \frac{320 \times 365}{4400} = 27 \text{ days}$$

Less : Average credit period granted by suppliers = $\frac{20 \text{ days}}{7 \text{ days}}$

(ii) Work-in-progress:

$$= \frac{\text{Average stocks of raw materials held}}{\text{Total consumption}} \times 365$$

$$= \frac{320 \times 365}{4400} = 27 \text{ days}$$

(iii) Finished Goods held in stock:

$$= \frac{\text{Agerage finished goods}}{\text{Total cost of sales}} \times 365$$

$$= \frac{360 \times 365}{10{,}500} = 27 \text{ days}$$

(iv) Credit period allowed to debtors:

$$= \frac{\text{Average debtors}}{\text{Total credit sales}} \times 365$$

$$= \frac{480 \times 365}{16{,}000} = \frac{11 \text{ days}}{40 \text{ days}}$$

Total operating cycle period: (i) + (ii) + (iii) + (iv) = 40 days

Number of Operating cycles in a year = 365/ 40 = 9

$$\text{Amount of Working Capital required} = \frac{\text{Total Cost of Sales}}{\text{Number of Operating Cycles in a year}}$$

= 10,500/9

= Rs. 1,167

Illustration No. 2

Dimpy Ltd. has obtained the following data concerning the average working capital cycle for other companies in the same industry:

Raw material stock turnover	20 Days
Credit received	- 40 Days
Work-in-progress turnover	15 Days
Finished goods stock turnover	40 Days
Debtors' collection period	60 Days
	95 Days

Using the following data, calculate the current working capital cycle for XYZ Ltd. and briefly comment on it.

(Rs. in '000)

Credit sales	5,000
Total cost of sales	4,000
Cost of Production	3,000
Purchases	3,500

Total raw materials consumed	600
Average raw material stock	80
Average work-in-progress	85
Average finished goods stock	180
Average creditors	700
Average debtors	350

Solution :

Operating cycle of Dimpy Ltd.

1. Raw material

$$= \frac{\text{Average stocks of Raw Material}}{\text{Total Raw Materials consumed}} \times 365$$

$$= \frac{80}{600} \times 365 = 49 \text{ Days}$$

2. Work-in-Progress

$$= \frac{\text{Average Work-in-progress}}{\text{Total Cost of Production}} \times 365$$

$$= \frac{85}{3{,}000} \times 365 = 10 \text{ Days}$$

3. Finished Goods

$$= \frac{\text{Agerage finished goods Stock}}{\text{Total Cost of sales}} \times 365$$

$$= \frac{350}{5{,}000} \times 365 = 16 \text{ Days}$$

4. Debtors

$$= \frac{\text{Average Creditors}}{\text{Credit Sales}} \times 365$$

$$= \frac{350}{5{,}000} \times 365 = 26 \text{ Days}$$

5. Gross operating cycle

$(1 + 2 + 3 + 4) = 101$ days

6. Creditors

$$= \frac{\text{Average Creditors}}{\text{Purchases}} \times 365$$

$$= \frac{700}{3,500} \times 365 = 73 \text{ Days}$$

Credit period granted by creditors = –73 days

7. Net operating (5-6) cycle =28 days

Comments: Dimpy Ltd's operating cycle is 28 days, which is below the industry average of 95 days. No doubt, a lower operating cycle involves a lower investment in net current assets. However, the following points deserve specific consideration about the individual elements of working capital. This is necessary to find out the business opportunities, the firm may be missing to improve the overall efficiency of the business:

(a) The stock holding of raw materials is 49 days, considerably higher than average of 20 days, for the industry. So there is a need to review stock control procedures.

(b) The period of credit availed from creditors is 73 days, against the average of 40 days. This indicates that Dimpy Ltd. is delaying the payment to creditors, beyond the normal credit period of the industry. This factor is an indication of inadequacy of working capital, for the abnormal delay. Although this is an additional source of finance, it may result in a higher cost of raw materials or loss of goodwill, among the suppliers. When supplies are aware of the abnormal delay in payment schedule, they may be charging a higher price to compensate the interest loss.

(c) The finished goods stock holding is 16 days, which is below the average of 40 days for the industry. This may be due to high demand for the firm's goods or efficient stock control. A low finished goods stock can, however, reduce sales since it can cause delivery delays. Another reason may be the firm may not be maintaining the total range of stocks and may be concentrating only on the fast moving goods. This may be a reason for missing the sales opportunities, otherwise available.

(d) Debts are collected more quickly than average. The firm is extending a credit period of 26 days only, against the average of 60 days. The company might have shortened the period of credit extended, deliberately, due to working capital inadequacy. May be, the firm could have employed good credit control procedures or offered heavy cash discounts for early payment.

Any abnormal feature requires detailed investigation. It is advisable to inquire the policy regarding the credit period allowed for the debtors. We have the information about the industry, alone, but not about the firm's policies, which is also vital for commenting about the efficiency of working capital management.

Conclusion: It shows the firm is grossly inadequate with the working capital, as finished goods holding are highly below the industry level. Another indicator is debtors' credit period, very low, compared to the credit, normally, extended by industry. If the firm makes necessary arrangements for improving the working capital, the firm is likely to improve sales and profitability, further.

18.6 CLASSIFICATION OF WORKING CAPITAL

Permanent and variable working capital

The working capital is classified in two ways:

(A) On the basis of Concept

(B) On the basis Time

On the basis of concept, working capital is classified as gross and net working capital, as discussed earlier.

On the basis of time, working capital is divided into two types:

(A) Permanent or fixed working capital

(B) Temporary or variable working capital

(A) **Permanent or fixed working capital:** Permanent or fixed working capital is that portion of working capital, which is necessarily required to carry on the business operations. This amount is permanent in the business, as fixed assets are. For example, a certain amount of inventory or receivables is permanent in the business, irrespective of the volume of sales. This level would remain constant during the peak as well as non-peak season. In other words, this level does not fluctuate, with the change in volume of business.

(B) **Fluctuating or Variable Working Capital:** The extra working capital needed to support the changing production and sales is called the fluctuating or variable working capital. The classical example is Divali period, when sales are normally high. To manufacture the increased inventory, more raw materials are needed and equally work-in-process would also be more, during the period of production. Once, the season is over, the increased inventory held for the season disappears. This picture appears in the seasonal business too. In seasonal industries, the inventory would be the highest during the peak season. During the sugar cane crushing season, the inventory level would be the highest when the season is in progress. Once season is over and inventory is sold, the working capital level would be the lowest.

Trends in Stable and Growing Firms: In case of stable firms, the permanent working capital is constant while the variable working capital increases and decreases, in other words fluctuates. This trend is seen in the following diagram.

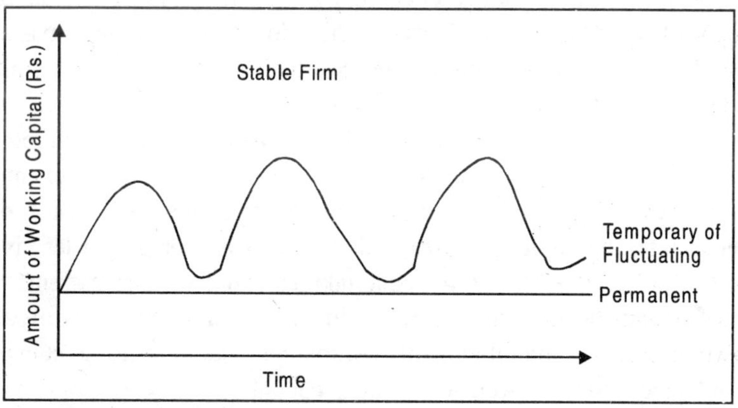

Stable Firm- Permanent and Temporary Working Capital

In progressive or growing firms, the permanent working capitals increases on a continuous basis to support the increasing trend of production and sales, unlike in stable firms. The temporary working capital increases or decreases, similar to stable firms. So, the requirements of working capital would continuously increase in the growing firm, as seen in the diagram.

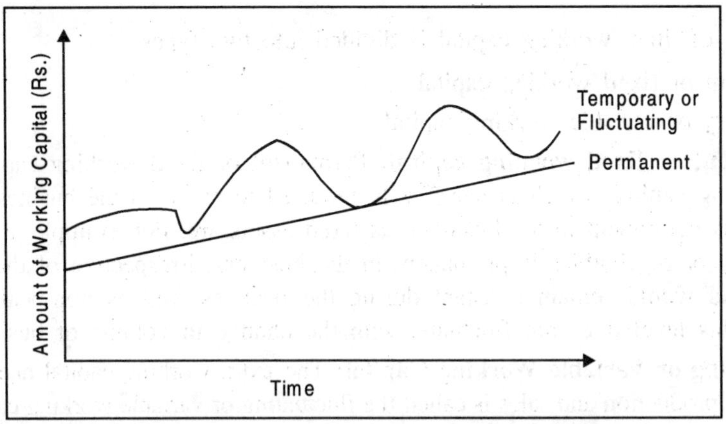

Growing Firm- Permanent and Temporary Working Capital

18.7 FACTORS OR DETERMINANTS OF WORKING CAPITAL

There are no set rules or formulae to determine the working capital requirements. The factors that influence the requirements vary from time to time. They cannot be ranked in the order of importance as the importance of each factor differs, over time. However, the following is the description of the factors, which, generally, influence the requirement of working capital.

1. **Nature or Character of Business: Working capital requirement, basically, depends on the nature of business.** Public utility undertakings like railways, Water supply and Electricity firms deal in supply of services, not products, so they do not require any investment in inventory and receivables as their sales are total cash sales. So, their working capital requirement is limited, while they abundantly invest in fixed assets. However, Trading and Financial Companies invest heavy amount in inventory and receivables so their working capital requirement is large. For example, a retail shop maintains heavy inventory to suit the varied tastes of clientele. For a housing construction firm, houses built for sale are the current assets as they are meant for sale, not to live in. So, investment in working capital (houses built for sale) is more, with less investment in fixed assets. So, it can be said that public utility undertakings stand on one extreme while trading and financial companies remain on the other extreme, in the requirement needs of working capital. In between these two extremes, manufacturing companies' stand with a substantial amount of investment, both in fixed assets as well as working capital.

2. **Size of Business/Scale of Operations:** The working capital requirements are largely determined by the size of the unit or scale of operations. **If the enterprise is big, the requirements are large and to a small firm, the requirements are low.** In some cases, even small units may

require more working capital due to inefficient utilisation of funds, high overhead charges and other economic disadvantages.

3. **Sales and Demand conditions:** The working capital needs of a firm are directly related to sales. The firm has to build the inventory, before the sales are expected. It is a normal feature to see heavy piles of stock before the festival season. During the festive season, demand is large and to meet the anticipated demand, firms plan building up stock, in advance. This type of demand is seasonal and during the seasonal period only, additional working is needed. Once the season is over, stocks disappear and the need for additional working capital also goes off. Similarly, during the slack season, the demand falls and inventory level goes down and, in consequence, requirement for working capital decreases. In case, the firm believes that the demand for the product has gone up, steadily, it has to invest in fixed assets to increase the production facilities. Then additional current assets are needed to match the increased volume of production and sales. So, the **firms need more working capital, when the sales are more and demand for the product is high.**

4. **Technology and Manufacturing Policy: In manufacturing business, the requirement of working capital is in direct proportion to the length of the manufacturing process.** If the manufacturing process is long, the requirement of working capital is more. For example, BHEl, which produces boilers, takes one to two years to manufacture each boiler, as the manufacture cycle is long. To reduce the requirement of working capital, industries engaged in tailor-made products insist on advance payment. They insist on advance as the products are specific and do not meet the general demand in the market. In contrast, requirement of working capital is low in firms, engaged in manufacturing chocolates, soaps and detergent powders, where the manufacturing cycle is short.

During the manufacturing process, raw materials and other supplies have to be carried in the form of work-in-process. The investment is substantial and cannot be avoided in these forms as the manufacturing process demands. So, it is prudent to choose the shortest manufacturing process, when there are alternative manufacturing processes to facilitate for lower working capital requirement. It is also necessary to ensure the manufacturing process is completed as per the schedule to avoid accumulation of larger work-in-process, due to delays.

Non-manufacturing and service industries do not have manufacturing cycle and so their working capital requirement is uniform, normally, through out the year, if they are not engaged in seasonal products.

5. **Credit Policy:** The credit policy influences the level of debtors. **Where a firm buys on cash and extends credit to its customers, the requirement of working capital would be substantial.**

In certain industries, credit is a must. They buy on credit and sell on credit. Their need for working capital would not be too high as they enjoy and extend credit. In certain industries, credit terms depend upon the norms of the industry, it belongs to. In textiles, wholesalers, normally, extend three months credit to the retail shops and so the individual firms cannot influence the credit policy. So, the requirement of working capital of any firm, normally, would be in line with the pattern of industry. Whatever be the policy, every firm has to ensure collections from debtors, in terms of the original credit period allowed, to contain the working capital requirements. Firms have to keep a close watch on the prompt collections to ensure the chance of bad debts to the absolute minimum level as bad debts erodes the profitability, severely.

6. **Availability of Credit:** When the firm is confident of raising additional finance from the banks, they manage with lower amount of working capital, in contrast to those firms not enjoying that type of facility or support. Similarly, firms enjoying liberal credit may not require much working capital. They can sell on cash, enjoying credit.

7. **Operating Efficiency:** Firms may not able to control the prices of raw materials and wages of labour, but are certainly capable of utilizing the resources, efficiently, without wastage of materials and idle labour. **Efficient firms can manage with lower working capital.**

8. **Seasonal Business:** In certain industries, the business is seasonal. The classical example is firecrackers. Even though firecrackers are used in marriages, now held through out the year, yet, the main demand for firecrackers is during Divali season. To meet the huge demand during that period, production in those industries is carried out through out the year. When there is no off take during the non-peak season, the inventories accumulate creating more need for working capital. The convenience is financial arrangements can be made, well in advance, for meeting seasonal requirements, as they are known from the beginning.

9. **Variable Production Competencies:** When the industry is able to develop alternative products, it can manufacture its main product during the period of increasing demand and other products during the non-peak season to use the production capacities, evenly. This enables the firms to have uniform working capital requirement, through out the year.

10. **Business Cycles:** Business cycles alternate to general expansion and contraction of business activity, generally. During periods of boom, sales increase and the situation demands higher working capital. In depression, there is an all round dullness or declining trend in every activity and there would be a great fall in sales, which reduces the working capital requirement.

11. **Price Level Changes:** When the prices of raw materials increase, same level of assets need increased investment in current assets. The increasing shifts in price level result in increased requirement of working capital, if the firm is not able to revise the selling prices, immediately. This situation creates difficulty to the finance manger as he has to arrange additional working capital, at short notice, which has not been foreseen. However, those firms do not get affected, if the firms are able to pass on the increased prices of raw materials and inputs to their buyers.

12. **Working Capital Cycle:** The working capital cycle commences with purchase of raw materials and ends with realisation of cash, in a manufacturing enterprise. The raw materials move into work-in-process and, finally, to finished products. Later sales are made and, often, they are on credit. The credit period depends on the industry norms as well as the policy of the firm. Once,

credit sales are realised, finally, the firm ends with cash, which has been the starting point in the working capital cycle. The speed with which the entire cycle is completed determines the working capital requirement. It is evident **longer the operating cycle, need for working capital is more.**

18.8 ESTIMATION OF WORKING CAPITAL REQUIREMENT

The most appropriate method for calculating working capital requirement is the concept of operating cycle. In operating cycle method, working capital requirement is expressed in terms of length of operating cycle, i.e. number of days. As already discussed, efficiency of working capital management is evaluated in terms of actual days, against the original operating cycle planned or anticipated.

Another popular method is the current assets holding period. The holding period method is based on the operating cycle concept, but expressed in terms of amount. This method is popular with the banks, as bank would like to know the working capital requirement, in terms of amount.

Illustration No. 3

A newly formed company has applied for a loan to a commercial bank for financing its working capital requirements. You are requested by the bank to prepare an estimate of the requirements of the working capital for the company. Add 10 per cent to your estimated figure to cover unforeseen contingencies. The information about the projected profit and loss account of this company is as under:

		(Rs.)
Sales		21,00,000
Cost of goods sold		15,30,000
Gross Profit		5,70,000
Administrative Expenses 1,40,000Selling Expenses	1,30,000	2,70,000
Profit before tax		3,00,000
Provision for tax		1,00,000
Profit after tax		2,00,000

Note: Cost of goods sold has been derived as follows:

	(Rs.)
Materials used	8,40,000
Wages and manufacturing expenses	6,25,000
Depreciation	2,35,000
	17,00,000
Less stock of finished goods (10 per cent not yet sold)	1,70,000
	15,30,000

The figures given above relate only to the goods that have been finished and not to work in progress; goods equal to 15 percent of the year's production (in terms of physical units) are in progress on an average, requiring full materials but only 40 per cent of other expenses. The company believes in keeping two months consumption of material in stock; Desired cash balance Rs. 40,000.

Average time lag in payment of all expenses is 1 month; suppliers of materials extend 1.5 months credit; sales are 20 per cent cash; rest are two months credit; 70 per cent of the income-tax has to be paid in advance, in quarterly installments.

You can make such other assumptions as you deem necessary for estimating working capital requirements.

(B.U. MBA- June, 2004)

Solution:

Estimate of Working Capital Requirement

	Rs.
Current Assets	
Cash	40,000
Inventories:	
Closing stock $*14{,}65{,}000 \times \frac{10}{100}$	1,46,500
Raw Materials $8{,}40{,}000 \times \frac{2}{12}$	1,40,000
Work-in-progress	
Raw Materials $8{,}40{,}000 \times \frac{15}{100} = 1{,}26{,}000$	1,63,500
Wages and other mfg. Exp = 37,500	
$6{,}25{,}000 \times \frac{15}{100} \times \frac{40}{100}$	
Debtors $15{,}30{,}000 \times \frac{80}{100} \times \frac{2}{12}$	2,04,000
Total Current Assets	**6,94,000**
Current Liabilities	
Sundry Creditors $8{,}40{,}000 \times \frac{1.5}{12}$	1,05,000
Outstanding Wages $6{,}25{,}000 \times \frac{1}{12}$	52,083
Outstanding Administrative & Selling Expenses	22,500
$2{,}70{,}000 \times \frac{1}{12}$	

Total Current Liabilities	1,79,583
Working capital (current assets- current liabilities)	5,14,417
Unforeseen contingencies 10%	51,414
Total estimated working capital needed	5,65,831

Assumptions:

1. * Depreciation is a non-cash expense, so not included in the valuation of closing stock. From the cost of production Rs. 17,00,000, depreciation Rs. 2,35,000 is deducted and the balance Rs. 14,65,000 is taken as the basis for valuation of closing stock.

2. Taxes are not included in the estimate of total working capital as tax has to be paid only after the sale is made. Banks do not finance for payment of taxes, as they are collected at the time of sale.

3. Debtors are calculated on the basis of cost of sales as profit is not financed by banks.

Illustration No. 4

The cost sheet of Kalyan & Kish Ltd provides the following data:

	Cost per unit
Raw material	Rs. 50
Direct labour	20
Overheads (including depreciation of Rs. 10)	40
Total cost	110
Profits	20
Selling price	130

Average raw materials, in stock is for one month. Average material in work-in-progress is for half month. Credit allowed by suppliers: one month; credit allowed to debtors: one month; Average time lag in payment of wages: 10 days; average time lag in payment of overhead is 30 days. 75% of the sales are on cash basis. Cash balance expected to be Rs. 1,00,000. Finished goods lie in the warehouse for one month.

You are required to prepare a statement of the working capital needed to finance a level of the activity of 54,000 units of output. Production is carried on evenly, throughout the year and wages and overheads accrue, similarly. State your assumptions, if any, clearly.

Solution:

As the annual level of activity is given at 54,000 units, it means that the monthly turnover would be 54,000/12 = 4,500 units. The working capital requirement for this level of turnover is as follows:

Estimation of Working Capital Requirement

		Amount (Rs.)	
I.	**Current Assets:**		
	Minimum Cash Balance Inventories:	1,00,000	
	Raw Materials (4,500 x Rs. 50)	2,25,000	
	* Work-in-progress		
	Materials (4,500 x Rs. Rs. 50)/2	1,12,500	
	Wages 50% of (4,500 x Rs. 20)/2	22,500	
	Overheads 50% of (4,500xRs.30)/2	33,750	
	Finished Goods (4,500xRs.100)	4,50,000	
	Debtors (4,500xRs.100) X 25%	1,12,500	
	Gross Working Capital	**10,56,250**	**10,56,250**
II.	**Current Liabilities:**		
	Creditors for Materials (4,500xRs.50)	2,25,000	
	Creditors for Wages (4,500xRs.20)/3	30,000	
	Creditors for Overhead (4,500xRs.30)	1,35,000	
	Total Current Liabilities	**3,90,000**	**3,90,000**
	Net Working Capital		**6,66,250**

Assumptions:

1. The Overheads of Rs. 40 per unit include a depreciation of Rs. 10 per unit, which is a non-cash item. This depreciation cost has been ignored for valuation of work-in-progress, finished goods and debtors. The overhead cost, therefore, has been taken only at Rs. 30 per unit.
2. * In the valuation of work-in-progress, the materials have been taken at full requirement for 15 days; but the wages and overheads have been taken only at 50% on the assumption that, on an average, all units' work-in-progress is 50% complete.
3. Since, the wages are paid with a time lag of 10 days, the working capital provided by wages has been taken by dividing the monthly wages by 3 (assuming a month to consist of 30 days.)

18.9 METHODS OF RAISING WORKING CAPITAL

Short-term funds are used to finance working capital. Two most significant sources of short-term sources of finance for working capital are: Trade credit and bank borrowings.

Trade credit refers to the credit granted by the suppliers in supplying goods, in the normal course of business. Accrued expenses and deferred income are the spontaneous sources of finance for meeting the working capital needs.

Next is, bank borrowing, which is the next important source of working capital finance. The different forms of bank finance are overdraft, cash credit, purchase or discounting of bills and Working capital loan etc. Banks, normally, sanction working capital facilities for a period of one year. Borrowers can request the bank for enhancement of the limits, on submission of the required data. Now, banks are flush with funds and they are also looking for good borrowers for better funds utilisation and improving their own profitability. Good borrowers do not experience any difficulty for increasing limits for their genuine business needs. Though initial sanction is given for one year, banks, often, renew the sanction of the limit, at the same level or increase the limit, depending on the past conduct of the account, business projected and assessment of their working capital needs. Letter of credit is another important source of indirect finance for meeting the working capital needs, in particular, to those firms engaged in import of goods. This area is covered, in detail, in the chapter on short-term sources of finance.

Another final and more important source of working capital is long-term funds. The long-term funds have to finance both the fixed assets as well the permanent component in the working capital. Long-term funds are equity share capital, preference share capital, reserves, debentures and long-term loans. There should be a judicial mix of funds both from short-term and long-term sources for meeting the working capital needs of the organisation.

Temporary Finance: Banks, normally, allow additional overdrawing in the cash credit account to meet the unforeseen requirements of the borrowers, provided drawing power is available in the cash credit account. Normally, they are allowed for a temporary period only and the borrowers are required to repay, at the earliest. Banks insist the additional overdrawing to be cleared off, before the last Friday of the concerned month.

Check Your Understanding

1. State whether the following Statements are True or False

1. The gross working capital concept is a financial or going concern concept while net working capital is an accounting concept.
2. Permanent working capital is that portion of a firm's current assets, which is financed by long- term funds.
3. To meet the gap between the cash inflows and outflows, working capital is needed.
4. The working capital should be neither more nor less, but just adequate.
5. With the change in price levels, firms require more working capital, even if they are able to pass on the increased prices of raw materials and inputs to their buyers.
6. The excess of current assets over the current liabilities can be expressed as gross working capital.
7. Every firm is interested in increasing the period of operating cycle.

8. Working capital is different from revolving or circulating capital.
9. Growing firms require more variable working capital on a continuous basis.
10. Permanent working capital is constant in a stable firm.
11. Net working capital refers to the capital invested in the total assets of a business.
12. Smaller the size of a business unit, higher will be the requirements of working capital.

Answers

1. True	2. True	3. True	4. True	5. False
6. False	7. False	8 False	9. False	10. True
11. False	12. False			

2. Detail brief reasons whether the following action would result in increase or decrease of total working capital requirements, presuming other factors being constant.

(A) Increase in the credit period allowed to customers from 15 days to 30 days.
(B) Realisation of book debts by cash.
(C) Acquisition of additional fixed assets to increase production facilities.
(D) Change in the method of packing the product, involving no additional costs, which improves the selling price.
(E) Credit sales.
(F) The decision to store, in a larger quantity, the new material, whose price is expected to go up in future.
(G) Change in the method of deprecation.
(H) Bills receivable are received in place of sundry debtors
(I) A decision to pay immediate cash to raw materials' suppliers for enjoying cash discounts.
(J) Receipt of sanction of cash credit limit communication from bank for working capital needs.
(K) Implementation of a scheme for reducing the production period.
(L) Strict recovery of debtors with close follow-up.
(M) A decision to increase the wages rates.

Answers

(A) Increase – since the sundry debtors will increase.
(B) No Change– one form of current asset is changed to another, increase of cash and decrease of debtors.
(C) Increase – since increased production requires increased investment in debtors, inventories and cash, etc.
(D) Increase – Improved sales result in higher profitability that increases the current assets.
(E) No change– Inventory goes down and debtors increase

(F) No change– inventory increases and on the other hand sundry creditors increase resulting in no change in working capital.

(G) No change– Neither the production time nor the inventory level is affected.

(H) No change– one form of current asset is changed to another.

(I) Increase- To avail cash discounts more cash is needed and so working capital has to increase from long-term sources.

(J) No change– No change in the status of current assets and current liabilities.

(K) Decrease– investment in inventories decreases.

(L) No change– debtors decrease and cash increases.

(M) Increase– Cost of inventories goes up and work-in-process would be more

Objective Questions

1. Explain the concept of working capital. Are gross and net concepts of working capital exclusive? Discuss? **(18.2 and 18.3)**
2. To a Finance Manager, both Gross Working Capital and Net Working Capital are equally important - Justify. **(18.2 and 18.3)**
3. What is the importance of working capital in a business? Whether the working capital should be met from long-term or short-term capital? **(18.3 and 8.3.1)**
4. Discuss the factors, which influence the need for working capital management for a manufacturing concern? **(18.7)**
5. What is the impact of 'excess' or 'paucity' of working capital on the operations and profitability of the undertaking? **(18.3)**
6. Discuss the importance of operating cycle for estimating working capital requirement? **(18.5)**
7. Write a note on the classification of working capital and its role in a stable and growing firm, with suitable pictorial presentation to explain the difference between the two categories? **(18.3 and 18.6)**
8. Explain the concept of 'Working Capital Flow'. Give examples of transactions that affect working capital, and that do not affect working capital? **(18.2, 18.3 and check your understanding question & answer no. 2)**
9. Suggest the methods you consider most suitable for raising the required amount of working capital in the short and long run? **(18.9)**

19

MANAGEMENT OF CASH RECEIVABLES

- *Introduction*
- *Importance of Receivables*
  - *Meaning*
  - *Characteristics*
- *Objectives of Receivables Management*
- *Dimensions of Receivables Management*
- *Credit policy*
  - *Credit Standards*
  - *Credit Terms*
  - *Collection Efforts*
- *Optimum Credit Policy*
- *Monitoring Receivables*
  - *Aging Schedule*
- *Review Questions*
- *Test your Analytical Skills*
- *Check Your Understanding*

19.1 INTRODUCTION

Accounts receivables or debtors are created, as and when goods are sold on credit. Debtors occupy a predominant place, next to inventories, in current assets. In India, debtors constitute about 30% in the current assets. When it is the practice of the industry, as a whole, to sell on credit, it is not possible for an individual firm to avoid credit sales.

19.2 IMPORTANCE OF RECEIVABLES

Meaning: Book debts arise with credit sales. It is not possible for the firms to make cash sales, totally. Credit sales have serious implications in the form of investment and risk. Investment, additionally, is necessary as funds are tied up in current assets. To contain the risk, at the acceptable level, managerial control is essential for efficient management of debtors.

Characteristics: Book debts have three peculiar characteristics. The first and most important feature is 'risk', they carry. If payment is not received, sale turns into a bad debt, eroding the profitability of the firm. In other words, profit made on other sales is at stake, till realisation of proceeds of sale. Second, the 'economic value' in the goods or services is transferred from the seller to the buyer, immediate to the sale. After sale, seller stands at the convenience of the buyer to receive payment. The third characteristic is its 'uncertainty' feature. The seller receives payment, at a later date. This future event of 'receiving the payment' is a contingent or uncertain event. Payment depends on the willingness and capacity of the buyer, on the due date. This picture cannot be foreseen, at the time of sale.

19.3 OBJECTIVES OF RECEIVABLES MANAGEMENT

The objectives of receivables management are to improve sales, eliminate bad debts, and reduce transaction costs incidental to maintenance of accounts and collection of sale proceeds and, finally, enhance profits of the firm. Credit sales help the organisation to make extra profit. It is a known fact, firms charge a higher price, when sold on credit, compared to normal price.

Book debts are used as a marketing tool for improvement of business. If the firm wants to expand business, it has to, necessarily, sell on credit. After a certain level, additional sales do not create additional production costs, due to the presence of fixed costs. So, the additional contribution, totally, goes towards profit, improving the profitability of the firm.

Optimum Level of Investment in Receivables: To support sales, it is necessary for the firm to make investment in receivables. Investment in receivables involves costs as funds are tied up in debtors. Further, there is also risk in respect of bad debts too. On the other hand, receivables bring returns. If so, till what level investment is to be made in receivables? **Investment in receivables is to be made till the incremental costs are less than the incremental return.** Thus, the objective of receivables management is to make a sound investment in debtors. In the words of Bolton , S.E., the objective of receivables management is "to promote sales and profit until that point is reached where the return on investment in further funding of receivables is not less than the cost of funds raised to finance that additional credit".

In simple words, **the objective of receivables management is to make a sound investment in debtors till such a point, where the cost of investment is less than the return on investment.** Risk perception of the firm also plays a key role in the decision making process of deciding the level of investment in receivables.

19.4 DIMENSIONS OF RECEIVABLES MANAGEMENT

Receivables Management involves consideration of the following two dimensions or facets:

(A) Credit Policy

(B) Monitoring Receivables

19.5 CREDIT POLICY

For efficient management of receivables, each firm has to design its own credit policy. Credit Policy involves decisions relating to

(a) Credit standards or selection of customers,

(b) Credit terms and

(c) Collection efforts

(a) Credit standards or Selection of Customers: Credit standards are the criteria followed for selection customers for extending credit. The volume of sales is influenced by the credit policy adopted by the firm. More sales can be created from more customers. But, before credit is extended, investigation about the creditworthiness of the potential customer has to be made to avoid bad debts and ensure repayment, in the agreed time schedule. This process involves costs. In consequence, there is increased clerical work to maintain more debtors' accounts in books of accounts and manage them. So, additional staff is needed to make collections from them, in time. Above all, book debts may turn into bad debts. All this involves additional costs. On the other hand, more sales also result in more profits. So, the firm has to strike a balance or bring a trade-off between incremental costs and incremental revenue that can be generated, with additional sales. The optimum sales would be that point, where both additional costs and additional revenue are equal.

Selection of the customers should neither be too liberal nor too stringent. More liberal sales may add more revenue, but they also involve additional costs in the form of transaction costs for verifying the creditworthiness, clerical costs involved with maintenance of accounts and, finally, bad debts. With a liberal credit policy, firm sells to those whose creditworthiness is not known. However, stringent policy also involves rejecting the customers who want to buy, but the firm is not willing to sell, as it is not sure of their creditworthiness. In other words, the firm sells only to selective customers with a stringent policy. Both the policies of extreme stringent and lenient policies have shortcomings of their own. So, in practice, firms follow credit policies ranging between stringent and lenient policies.

The finance manager should consider these three C' s to form a reasonable Judgment about the chances of default:

Character refers to customer's willingness to pay. Before sale is made, it is necessary for the seller to judge whether the customer would make efforts to honour the credit obligations, he makes.

Capacity fefers to the ability to pay. Ability is reflected in the financial position of the buyer. Financial position is found from ration anlysis.

Condition refers to the prevailing economic and other conditions which may affect the customer's ability to pay. Adverse economic conditions can affect the ability of the buyer to make payment, on the due date.

Conflict between Liquidity and Profitability: Both liquidity and profitability do not go together. Let us see the situation when the firm follows liberal credit policy. More credit sales require more working capital, as more funds would be tied up in receivables. So, when the a firm follows liberal credit policy, it experiences liquidity crunch. However, it would have higher profits. When the firm switches to follow stringent credit policy, it would discontinue sales to those customers who have been taking longer time for payments or their creditworthiness has become doubtful. Lesser sales ease the problem on liquidity front. As a result, firm would not have liquidity problems. However, less sales result in lesser profits and profitability problem commences. So, profitability and liquidity are the two conflicting issues.

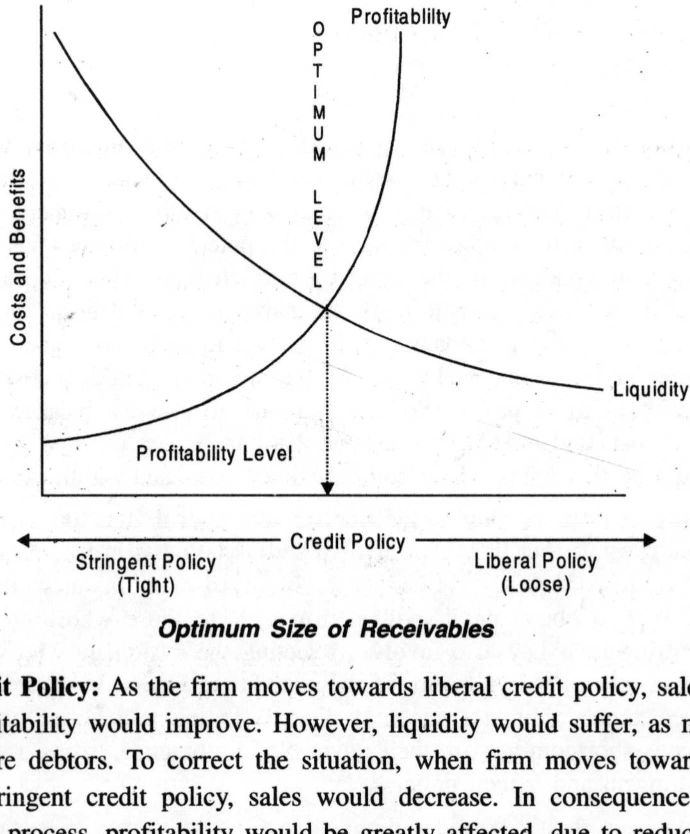

Optimum Size of Receivables

Optimum Credit Policy: As the firm moves towards liberal credit policy, sales would increase and, as a result profitability would improve. However, liquidity would suffer, as more funds would be tied up with more debtors. To correct the situation, when firm moves towards contraction of sales, adopting a stringent credit policy, sales would decrease. In consequence, liquidity would improve. But, in the process, profitability would be greatly affected, due to reduction of sales. So, **every firm has to strike a balance between liquidity and profitability and this level can be achieved when the incremental costs is equal to revenue.** That level would be the optimum size of receivables. So, optimum credit policy is the objective of management of receivables.

(b) Credit Terms: Credit terms refer to duration of credit and terms of payment extended to customers such as payment of interset, after due date of payment. Credit terms include

(i) Credit period and

(ii) Cash discount.

(i) **Credit Period:** Length of credit is influenced by the practice or custom prevalent in the industry. If a firm extends lower credit below the credit period allowed by the rest of the firms, its sales decline. So, by necessity, firms have to adopt similar practices followed by the industry. To attract new customers, some firms may give more credit than its competitors. It may extend more credit period, provided the existing customers agree to buy more quantity than their normal purchases. In other words, credit period is used as a marketing tool to improve the existing sales or arrest sales falling. But, more working capital is needed to extend more liberal period of credit. This also involves additional cost, as there is cost of capital for the funds. The finance manager has to allow the firm so long as the incremental revenue is more than the additional costs that may be incurred by the firm, by allowing liberal credit period, after analysing the risk implications. Though credit period is allowed, firms allow cash discount to those firms, who pay earlier than the stipulated period of credit.

(ii) **Cash Discount:** A cash discount is a reduction in payment, provided the payment is made, earlier, to the stipulated credit period allowed. So, the invoice should clearly state the rate of cash discount offered, period within which payment is to be made to avail the discount and if discount is not availed, the normal credit period available. If the invoice states '2/20, net 30' it means discount of 2% is available, provided the payment is made within 20 days from the date of invoice. Otherwise, payment has to be made within the normal period of credit allowed, i.e. 30 days. The discount is usually expressed as a percentage of sales.

(c) Collection efforts: Collection efforts influence the collection period. If customers take longer period, higher amount would be blocked in receivables. The lower the collection period, the lower the investment and vice versa. If collection efforts become slack, investment in receivables becomes more and becomes unprofitable for the firms. Slackness in collections is the main cause for creation of bad debts. Debtors turn often bad because there is no follow up with them for payment in the form of reminders, personal as well as in writing. Bad debts happen on account of default on the part of delinquent customers. In case, results do not materialize in recovery, timely legal action is essential before the debts become time barred. Fixation of credit period itself is not sufficient, its execution in terms of follow up and recovery are important.

19.6 MONITORING RECEIVABLES

To monitor receivables, calculation of average period and comparing the actual period of credit with the credit period allowed is the first step for the purpose of monitoring the receivables, in aggregate. The next step is preparation of aging schedule for identifying the group, where action is needed.

Average Collection Period: The average collection period is determined as follows:

$$\text{ACP} = \frac{\text{Debtors}}{\text{Credit Sales}} \times 365$$

This collection period is to be compared with the credit terms fixed. This shows the efficiency or otherwise of the collection department. For example, if the credit period allowed is 30 days and the average collection period shows 60 days, it shows the laxity of the collection department. The average collection period is based on the aggregate data and it suffers from the limitation of showing specific picture, where exact concentration or action is needed to tone up efficiency for improving the recoveries. This problem can be solved with the aging schedule.

Aging Schedule: Aging schedule breaks down the debtors to the length of the time for which they have been outstanding. This helps in identifying the slow-paying debtors' group. Now, the individual debtors have to be identified, who have exceeded the period of credit allowed. Concerted action has to be initiated in respect of those debtors. Legal action is the last step one has to resort, when all other follow up measures have failed.

The following illustration is explained for understanding the picture better.

So, credit policy plays a vital role in determining the efficiency of receivables management.

Illustration No. 1

Atul Ltd has Rs. 7,50,000 in receivables on 31-12-2004. The amount contains the selling amount of December Rs. 3,00,000; November

Rs. 2,25,000; October Rs. 1,50,000 and remaining prior to October 2004. If the term of credit offered by the company is 'Net 30 days', prepare an ageing schedule of receivables, keeping in view the credit period and comment on the collection efforts of the company.

Solution:

Outstanding Period (Months)	Outstanding amount of receivables (Rs.)	Percentage of Total Receivables
0-1	3,00,000	40 %
Above 1 –Below 2	2,25,000	30 %
Above 2 –Below 3	1,50,000	20 %
Above 3 Months	75,000	10 %
Total Debtors	7,50,000	100

Assessment of Collection efforts: The first category is 40%, which is within the normal period of credit granted by the firm. This category does not cause any anxiety as the outstanding is within the normal period of credit allowed.

The rest is 60%, which is overdue for payment. This is an abnormally high and anxiety causing.

This shows the collection department is inefficient and its follow up is not adequate. On account of the slow collections, firm must be experiencing liquidity problem. Delayed collections affect the profitability of the firm too as funds carry cost.

Immediate action is needed for the last category, which is above 3 months. In fact, examination of individual debtors' accounts, falling in this group, is immediately required. If necessary, legal action may be initiated in respect of chronic cases, before the cases are time barred by limitation.

Suggestion: It has to be examined whether the firm has made any assessment to introduce cash discounting inducement to accelerate the collections. The collection policy indicates the payment system as 30 days credit, showing it does not offer any inducement for earlier payments. (Period of limitation is three years from the date of sale. Unless suit is filed, against the debtor, in court of law, before the date of limitation, debt would be time barred. In other words, debt connot be recovered through legal means.) It is advisable to adopt discount system, after carefully examining the incremental costs as well as incremental revenue that may generate.

The risk the firm, already exposed too, has to be examined.

Review Questions

1. What is 'Receivables Management'? How is it useful to business operations? **(19.1 and 19.2)**
2. Explain the meaning and objectives of receivables management? **(19.2 and 19.3)**
3. What should be the considerations in formulating a credit policy? **(19.4 and 19.4.1 and 19.5)**
4. Explain the objective of credit policy? What is an optimum credit policy and show it with pictorial presentation? **(19.4 and 19.4.1)**
5. 'Liquidity and Profitability are conflicting with each other while following credit policy'. How a firm can bring trade-off between the two? **(19.4 and 19.4.1 -a)**
6. What are the different dimensions of 'Receivables Management'? **(19.4, 19.4.1 and 19.5)**

Test your Analytical Skills

Explain the impact of receivables, individually, and other incidental implications, in case of the following events, making the necessary valid assumptions:

(A) Boom

(B) Interest rate increases

(C) Production and selling costs increase due to inefficiency of the staff.

(D) Firm changes the credit terms from '3/10, net 30 to 4/10, net 30'

(E) Depression

Answers

(A) Receivables increase. During boom, sales increase. So, more funds would be tied up in receivables.

(B) Receivables increase. Increase in interest rate causes increase in cost of production, so firm increases the selling price to meet the increased cost of production to have the same profit margin. This is the likely situation, as the interest rate increase would affect the industry, totally. A higher selling price results in increased receivables. However, if the firm absorbs the increase in cost, from its profit margin, and decides not to pass on the burden to its customers, there would be no impact on receivables.

(C) No impact on receivables. The increase in cost of production and selling costs is confined to this firm, alone. The increase in costs is not applicable for all the firms, in the industry. If it increases the selling price to retain the profit margin, it is likely the firm's sales would reduce. So, firm does not take any action on the front of increasing the selling price.

(D) Decrease in receivables. Firm is offering a higher discount rate of 4% instead of the existing discount rate of 3%. So, more buyers would be tempted to avail the benefit of cash discount. So, realisations would be fast and investment in receivables goes down, improving the liquidity of the firm. So, receivables go down. There may be impact on profitability, due to higher discount rate unless the firm utilises the improved liquidity in a better manner.

(E) Decrease in receivables. During depression, there would be lesser sales and the market would be dull. Lesser sales reduce the investment in receivables.

Check your Understanding

State whether the following statements are True or False

1. There is no change in working capital to extend more liberal period of credit, than normally allowed.
2. The lower the collection period, the lower the investment and vice Versa.
3. Credit policy plays a vital role in determining the investment in receivables.
4. Bad debts happen on account of default on the part of delinquent customers.
5. It is desirable to follow stringent credit policy to avoid bad debts.
6. Aging schedule does not help in making assessment of the age of debtors' outstanding period.
7. Firm can extend the credit if the incremental revenue is higher than the incremental costs.
8. Credit standards indicate the selection criteria for the choice of customers to whom credit extension can be made.
9. The objectives of receivables management are to expand sales and to increase profit.
10. Both the policies of extreme stringent and lenient policies have shortcomings of their own.
11. The volume of sales is influenced by the credit policy adopted by the firm.
12. Firm sells only to selective customers when it follows a liberal credit policy.
13. Optimum credit policy is the objective of management of receivables.
14. Cash discount is usually expressed as a percentage of sales.
15. Slackness in collections is the not cause for creation of bad debts.

Answers

1. False	2. True	3. True	4. True	5. False
6. False	7. True	8. True	9. True	10. True
11. True	12. False	13. True	14. True	15. False

20

INVENTORY MANGEMENT

20.1 INTRODUCTION

Inventories constitute a major component in current assets. It constitutes around 60% in the public limited companies, in India. For the smooth running, every enterprise needs inventory. Inventories serve as a link between production and distribution processes. Due to its major composition in current assets, the management of inventories occupies a key role in working capital management. Excessive investment affects the liquidity. Inadequate investment makes the firm to loose the business opportunities, otherwise available. Profitability would be affected with excessive or inadequate investment. So, **inventory management is essential to allow the firm to avail the opportunities to improve profitability and at the same time does not impair its liquidity, with excessive or unproductive investment.** A firm, which neglects the inventory management, jeopardizes its long-term profitability. So, it is absolutely imperative to control and manage inventory holding, both efficiently and effectively, to avoid unnecessary investment.

20.2 MEANING AND NATURE OF INVENTORY

Inventory means only stock of finished gods, in accounting language. However, it includes raw materials, work-in-process, finished goods and stores in a manufacturing organisation.

Raw Materials: Raw materials are the basic inputs, which are converted into finished products in the manufacturing process. They are needed to carry out the production, smoothly, uninterrupted. **Holding period of raw materials depends on the length of conversion cycle and time needed to replenish them.**

Work-in-progress: Work-in-progress is the semi-finished products. To become finished products, still, they are to undergo further process. They are in the intervening stage, between raw materials and finished products. The quantum of work-in-progress depends upon time that is needed for completing the manufacturing process. **Longer the manufacturing process, more amount would be blocked in the form of work-in-progress.**

Finished Goods: Finished goods are those, which are completely manufactured and ready for sale. When a firm manufactures, on receipt of order only, to suit the individual specific needs of the buyer, there will be no finished stock. Firms, which produce goods, without waiting for any formal order, have to maintain the finished goods. **Finished goods are a buffer between production and market.** Adequate stock, with full range, is necessary for marketing.

Stocks of raw materials and work-in-progress are necessary for the smooth production, while finished stocks are important for marketing operations.

Nature of Business: The levels of the above inventories depend upon the nature of business. If the activity is manufacturing, large quantity is always blocked up in raw materials, finished goods and work-in-process. If the business is retail or wholesale, the inventory holding lies only in the form of finished goods only.

Supplies: Stores and spares are called as 'supplies', the last category of inventories. They do not enter into production, but are necessary for the purpose of production. Examples are brooms, soap, oil, fuel, light bulbs etc. The consumption pattern of spares is different from the normal consumption pattern of raw materials, work-in-progress and finished goods. They do not require, normally, any sophisticated system of inventory control technique for maintaining them, unless the spares are highly expensive.

20.3 BENEFITS OF HOLDING INVENTORIES

Holding of inventories is expensive in the form of storage costs, interest charges, deterioration of quality in holding stocks, theft and pilferage. Firms hold inventories, basically, for the following reasons:

Transaction Motive: Sufficient stocks of raw materials are to be maintained to facilitate uninterrupted production. There is always a time lag between the date of placing the order and its actual receipt. There could be delays due to strikes, lock out and transport problems. Transaction motive takes care of these contingencies.

Precautionary Motive: Holding of inventories is necessary to safeguard the unforeseen changes in demand and supply forces and other factors, which cannot be anticipated. Production is dependent on demand of the finished product. If there is more demand for the product, more raw materials would be consumed. Consumption of raw materials cannot be forecast, with absolute accuracy. Sufficient stocks are to be maintained to suit the fluctuations in demand. Similarly, problems in supply may arise. Here, stocks are to be kept to guard against the changes in demand and supply, which are not foreseen. **Forces, which could be foreseen, are taken care by the transaction motive, while forces that cannot be foreseen are guarded by precautionary motive.**

Speculative Motive: When the firm anticipates increase in prices of raw materials, in future, it stocks to take the advantage. Firm takes suitable decisions to change the stock holding pattern depending on the increase or decrease in prices. Bulk order discounts may be offered to attract higher purchases. Reordering costs may be another factor in holding more quantity of inventories, than needed.

20.4 RISK AND COST OF HOLDING INVENTORIES

The following are the risks and costs associated in holding inventories:

(A) **Capital Costs:** Holding inventories involves funds. Funds may be used from own sources or borrowings. If own sources are not blocked up in inventories, they can be used elsewhere, profitably. This is the opportunity cost, the firm has incurred. If funds have been borrowed, interest has to be paid. So, in both the cases, firm incurs cost. In case of own funds, it is opportunity cost and in case of borrowings, it is interest cost.

(B) **Recurring Costs:** Firm incurs recurring costs, in the form of storage and insurance charges. Storage costs can be rent for the godown or warehousing charges, if stored in outsiders' godowns.

(C) **Risk of Deterioration:** Stocks may deteriorate in quality, due to long storage. Once goods loose their quality, they may not be in saleable condition.

(D) **Risk of Obsolescence:** Goods may cease to be useful, due to technological changes, changes in requirements and tastes etc. Now, we do not see floppy drive in the new computers coming into the market, as floppy drive has given place to CD drive.

20.5 OBJECTIVES OF INVENTORY MANAGEMENT

The primary objective of inventory management is to maintain the right quantity of stocks, in right location, at right time to ensure the uninterrupted production and, at the same time, minimize the investment in stock holding. Every firm is faced with two conflicting issues:

- Maximise investment, by maintaing excessive quantity so that production is not affected and business opportunities are not lost, for want of stocks.
- Minimise investment in inventories as they involve costs and affect profitability, adversely.

Optimum Stock Holding

Both the issues- excessive and inadequate stocks-are conflicting. Both are undesirable. Excessive stocks result in additional costs due to storage charges, interest cost, and deterioration loss and obsolescence risk. Above all, funds are tied up in inventories and this creates liquidity problem. Inadequate stocks result in stock-out situations and cause loss in profits. In other words, excessive and inadequate stocks move in opposite directions. Both the extreme situations are unacceptable. Firm has to maintain that much stock, just enough to meet the production needs so that there is no interruption in production and no customer goes back disappointed for lack of stocks. This situation can be achieved by maintaining optimum stock level, which is in between the excessive stocks and inadequate stocks. So, every firm tries to achieve that optimum stock holding. The level of optimum stock holding is not static. The optimum level changes due to changes in demand and problems of supply. Demand for the product varies and supply constraints crop up, which are not anticipated. The finance manager has to ensure the optimum stock holding to achieve the conflicting objectives of profitability and liquidity, at the same time.

To sum up, the objectives of inventory management can be summarized:

- Maintain continuous supply of raw materials so that production is not affected,
- Minimise the carrying costs and lead-time in supplies,
- Maintain sufficient stocks of finished goods for smooth sales operations and business opportunities are not lost,
- Ensure perpetual inventory control so that physical stocks are always in agreement, with stocks shown in records and
- Facilitate furnishing of data for short-term and long-term planning and inventory control.

20.6 TOOLS AND TECHNIQUES OF INVENTORY MANAGEMENT

Efficient inventory management requires effective control system. A proper inventory control system helps the enterprise in solving the problems of liquidity, eliminating excessive stocks and achieving increased profits, with substantial reduction in working capital.

The following are the techniques of inventory management and control:

(A) Determination of stock levels

(B) Determination of Economic Order Quantity

(C) A.B.C Analysis

(D) V E D Analysis

(E) Perpetual Inventory System

(F) JIT Control System

(G) Inventory Turnover Ratios

20.7 DETERMINATION OF STOCK LEVELS

Carrying too much stock and too little stocks, both are detrimental to the firm. If stock is too little, frequent stock-out situations firm faces. Due to inadequacy of stocks, firm misses business opportunities. If it is too high, profitability will be affected due to increased cost of stock holding. In this context, it is relevant to discuss various types of stock levels.

(a) Minimum Level: This is the minimum quantity that must be maintained, at all times. If the stock holding falls below this level, production stops, due to shortage of materials. This level is fixed, considering the following factors:

Lead-time: After placing the requisition for materials, some time is needed to process and place the order. After receipt of the order, supplier too takes some time to execute the order. So, raw material holding is needed, during the process time and execution time, so that production does not suffer, which is called 'Lead Time.

Rate of Consumption: It is the average rate of consumption of raw materials in a factory. This rate of consumption can be calculated based on the earlier period's consumption rate, past experience and future plans. If the capacity of the factory enhances to match the increased production plans, the consumption rate also enhances.

Nature of Materials: The nature of materials affects the minimum level. If the firm produces, soon after the receipt of the order, no minimum stock is needed.

The formula for computation of minimum stock is as under:

Minimum Stock Level = Re-ordering level - (Normal Consumption × Maximum Re - Order Period)

(b) Re- ordering Level: When the stock level reaches the re-ordering level, the order is placed for replenishment of stocks. This level is fixed in between the maximum stock and minimum stock. This level is decided after consideration of the following factors, such as maximum consumption per day and maximum number of days required to supply the stocks. It is difficult to foresee the consumption pattern, with full accuracy. Days that may be required to get the supply of stocks may vary depending on the unforeseen problems of transportation, bottlenecks and other factors. To be on safe side, maximum consideration is given for both the factors. Supply of materials would be received when the stock position reaches the minimum level; even when materials are consumed at the maximum requirement.

The formula for calculation is

Re-ordering Stock Level : Maximum Consumption per day × Maximum Re - order period

Maximum Level: It is the level, beyond which the stock level should not exceed. If this level is exceeded, there would be blockage of working capital, loss due to wastages, risk of obsolescence and more rent for storage space etc.

The formula is as under:

Maximum Stock Level = Re-Ordering Level + Re-ordering Quantity - (Minimum Consumption × Minimum Re-ordering Perod)

Average Stock Level: The formula for calculating average stock is as under:

Average Stock Level = Minimum Stock Level + ½ of re-order Quantity

Safety Stock: Consumption of raw materials depends upon production level. Production changes on the demand for the finished products. The demand for the finished product is not always constant due to varying conditions. So, consumption of raw materials is not, always, constant. There should be safety stock to take care of fluctuations in consumption pattern of raw materials. The time taken for getting replenishment of stocks may also vary, due to unforeseen problems of strikes or lockouts. So, every firm has to maintain certain amount of stock as safety stock to take care of unforeseen consumption pattern as well as time for procurement of materials. Basically, safety stock is to meet unforeseen contingencies.

Danger Level: This is the absolute minimum level, below which the stocks should not fall. When the stock reaches this level, stock would be issued only to the emergency requirements and just to maintain the machinery working, to avoid dry out situation.

The formula for calculating danger level is as under:

Danger Level = Average Consumption × Maximum re-order Period for Emergency Purchases

Illustration No. 1

In a firm, two types of materials 'A' and 'B' are used. Per week usage is as under:

	"A"	**"B"**
Normal Usage	500 units	300 units
Maximum Usage	750 units	400 units
Minimum Usage	250 units	100 units
Re-order quantity	A-3000 units and B- 5000 units for both A and B	
Re-order period	A-4 to 6 weeks	
	B- 2 to 4 weeks	

From the above information calculate:

(i) Re-order level

(ii) Minimum stock level

(iii) Maximum stock level

(iv) Average stock level

Solution:

(i) Re-ordering Level: Maximum Consumption per week × Maximum Re-order Period

A = 750 × 6 = 4,500

B = 400 × 4 = 1,600

(ii) Minimum Stock Level = Re-ordering level – (Normal Consumption × Normal Re-Order Period)

A = 4,500 – (500 × 4) = 4,500 – 2,000 = 2,500 units

B = 1,600 – (300 × 2) = 1,600 – 600 = 1,000 units

(iii) Maximum Stock Level = Re-ordering Level + Re-ordering Quantity – (Minimum Consumption × Minimum Re-ordering Period)

A = 4,500 + 3,000 – (250 × 4) = 4,500 + 3,000 – 1,000 = 6,500 units

B = 1,600 + 5,000 – (100 × 2) = 1,600 + 5,000 – 200 = 6,400 units

(iv) Average Stock Level = Minimum Stock Level + ½ of re-order Quantity

A = 2,500 + ½ × 3,000 = 2,500 + 1,500 = 4,000 units

B = 1,000 + ½ × 5,000 = 1,000 + 2,500 = 3,500 units

20.8 DETERMINATION OF ECONOMIC ORDER QUANTITY

For effective inventory management, it is necessary to determine what should be the quantity of stock that has to be ordered for replenishment, periodically. The stock that is ordered should be neither more nor less. To avoid accumulation of stocks, if frequent ordering of stock is made, more handling costs ordering costs would be incurred. On the other hand, lesser number of stock orders results in accumulation of stocks, which result in higher carrying costs.

Ordering Costs: The costs that are associated with purchasing and placing an order is called ordering costs. These are also known as buying costs as they are incurred, at the time of purchase only.

Carrying Costs: These are the costs for holding inventories. Higher the stock holding, larger would be carrying costs and they would be lower if the stocks are lower. Inventory may be high sometimes and low other times. So, the carrying cost is calculated on the average inventory.

The components of costs for both the categories are as under:

Components of Ordering Costs and Carrying Costs	
Ordering Costs	**Carrying Costs**
• Requisitioning costs (Indent for Materials)	• Interest on cost of capital, invested in inventories
• Processing & placing order	• Rent for storing
• Transportation of goods	• Handling costs
• Receiving and inspecting costs for incoming materials	• Clerical and staff costs for recording receipts and issues
• Cost of stationery, typing, postage and telephone etc.	• Insurance
	• Deterioration and obsolescence loss
• Clerical and staff costs for rendering the above services	• Cost of spoilage, in handling materials

Ordering costs and carrying costs constitute the total cost of stock holding. Ordering costs and carrying costs behave in an opposite direction. In other words, they have an inverse relationship.

Determination of economic order is important, from the viewpoint of achieving a compromise between handling costs and carrying costs. To avoid stock-outs, frequent re-orders have to be made. More orders result in more ordering costs. By holding lesser stocks than required, enterprise misses business opportunities and, in consequence, profitability is affected. To avoid frequent orders, the other alternative is to maintain higher size of stock holding. A higher size of stocks involves loss of liquidity, as more funds would be tied up. More so, too much stocks result in more carrying costs. Carrying costs are incurred for maintaining a given level of inventory. Carrying costs vary with the size of the inventory. If the size of inventory holding is more, more costs will be incurred. So, a higher level of stocks mean liquidity problem and also cause reduced profitability too. This is also not an acceptable situation. In other words, if ordering costs are to be reduced, carrying costs become more. If carrying costs are to be reduced, ordering costs become more. **The economic order size of inventory brings a trade off between carrying costs and ordering costs.**

The formula for determining Economic Order Quantity is:

$$\text{EOQ} = \sqrt{\frac{2AO}{C}}$$

Where A = Annual consumption of unit, in rupees

O = Cost of Placing an order

C = Inventory Carrying costs, per one unit

Assumptions: While calculating EOQ, the following assumptions are made:

(A) The total usage of a particular material is known and the usage is even through out the year,

(B) Material is readily available and there is no time lag between placing an order and receiving the supplies,

(C) Cost of carrying inventory is also fixed and uniform though out the period,

(D) There are only two costs associated with the cost of holding, i.e. cost of ordering and cost of carrying and

(E) The prices of the goods are stable.

Graphical Presentation: The EOQ model can be presented graphically. The size of order is presented on the horizontal axis. The costs – carrying, ordering and total costs - are shown on the vertical axis. The picture show that the ordering cost decreases, with the increase in the size of the order. To explain, let us take a small example. If annual consumption of an item is 1,000 pices and order is placed for 200 pices, each time, orders have to be placed five times in a year. If we increase the size of the order form 200 to 500 pices, the number of orders has to be reduced from 5 to 2. The ordering costs would be lower for two orders, compared to five orders. In other words, with the increase in size of the order, total ordering cost would reduce.

As the size of the order increases, the total number of orders for a particular item decreases, resulting in decrease in the total order costs. Due to increase in size of order, more stocks are purchased and more money is tied up in inventory, which results in increase of carrying cost. To reduce carrying cost, the firm stats cutting the size of the order. Then, the carrying cost starts falling.

Now, let us see the reaction of the total cost, in the entire process. The behaviour of the total cost is interesting. The total cost is an aggregate of ordering cost and carrying cost. The declines, initially, due to reduction in the orering cost on account of the bigger size of the order. But, later, the total cost starts increasing, due to higher carrying cost as the size of the order has gone up. The total cost starts increasing when the increase in the carrying cost is more than the decrease in ordering cost. At this level, the decrease in ordering cost is more than offset by the increase in carrying cost.

The order size, at this particular level, is designated as economic order quantity. If the firm places the order for that item at that economic order quantity, then the annual cost of inventory of that item will be minimized.

To sum up, **in inventory Management, Economic Order Quantity is** achieved, when the total cost is at its minimum for the enterprise.

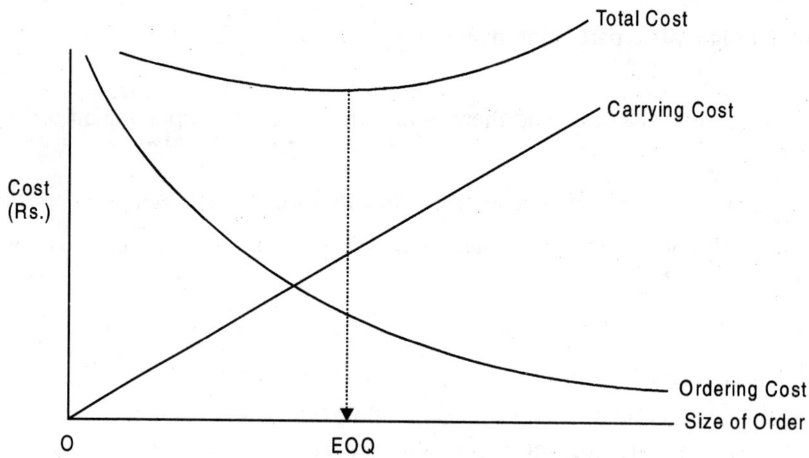

Graphical presentation of the EOQ Model

Illustration No. 2

The following information is available in respect of an enterprise:

Annual consumption of a raw material = 20,000 units

Ordering cost per order = Rs. 1,875

Carrying cost = Rs. 3 per unit / per annum

Find out the Economic Order Quantity of the raw material, number of orders to be placed in a year. Please verify the results, assuming any increased quantity and lower quantity.

Solution:

The formula for determining Economic Order Quantity is:

$$EOQ = \sqrt{\frac{2AO}{C}}$$

Where A = Annual consumption of unit, in rupees
O = Cost of Placing an order
C = Inventory Carrying costs, per one unit

$$= \left[\frac{2 \times 20{,}000 \times 1{,}875}{3}\right]^{1/2}$$

= 5, 000 units

The total consumption in a year is 20, 000 units and economic order quantity is 5,000. It means the number of orders in a year is 4 (20,000/5,000).

(A) If 5,000 units are the EOQ, let us check what the total cost is:

Total order cost = 1,875 × 4 = Rs. 7,500

Average inventory = 2,500 (5,000/2)

Total carrying cost = Average inventory × Carrying cost per unit

= 2,500 × 3 = 7,500

Total cost of inventory = Total order cost + Total carrying cost

= 7,500 + 7,500

= Rs. 15,000

(B) Let us check, what is the total cost for 2,000 units

The total number of orders would be 10 (20,000/2,000)

Total order cost = 1,875 × 10 = Rs. 18,750

Average inventory = 1,000 (2,000/2)

Total carrying cost = Average inventory × Carrying cost per unit

= 1,000 × 3 = 3,000

Total cost of inventory = Total order cost + Total carrying cost

= 18,750 + 3,000

= Rs. 21,750

(C) Let us check, what is the total cost for 10,000 units

The total number of orders would be 2 (20,000/10,000)

Total order cost = 1,875 × 2 = Rs. 3,750

Average inventory = 5,000 (10,000/2)

Total carrying cost = Average inventory × Carrying cost per unit

= 5,000 × 3 = 15,000

Total cost of inventory = Total order cost + Total carrying cost

= 3,750 + 15,000

= Rs. 18,750

Conclusion: It may be noted, the total cost of inventory is the lowest at the Economic Order Quantity. If the quantity per order is increased, the total cost increases. Similarly, if the quantity per order is reduced, even then, the total cost increases. This only establishes that the total cost is the lowest, only at the economic order quantity.

20.9 A.B.C ANALYSIS

A.B.C Analysis is concerned with selective control of inventory management. An analytical survey of the composition of inventory in most of the manufacturing organisations has revealed that 10% of the materials contribute for 70% of the cost of materials, while 70% of the materials constitute 10% of the total cost. The first category is classified as 'A' category while the later is 'C' category. In between falls the 'B' category, this contains 20% of cost as well as materials. If same importance is given in respect of control for all materials, equally, result would not be effective. **The essence of selective control of inventory management is to allocate the importance of control to goods based on the cost composition.** So, organization has to give more concentration for 'A' category of items due to higher cost composition in the total inventory cost. As concentration is on the fewer items, result would be effective.

The ABC analysis is based on the following presumptions:

(i) Managerial time and effort is scare and limited and

(ii) Some items of inventory are more important than others

Under ABC analysis, the item is allocated to the group, depending on the amount of attention it deserves. "A" group requires the maximum concentration of the finance manger. This group constitutes a higher % in terms of value, while it occupies lesser significance, in terms of number of units. "B" group requires lesser attention, compared to "A" group. The last group "C" has to be given the least attention, as it constitutes less value in the total annual consumption.

In other words, the procedure is to divide the total inventory into three groups, based on the total cost of each group. The first group should cover 70% of the total cost of inventory, where closer concentration has to be given to achieve better control on a selective basis. The second group should cover 20% while the last group falls into the category of 10% cost.

Method of Preparation: The method of preparation is as under:

(A) Calculate the annual consumption of each item in the year.

(B) Arrange the annual consumption of the different items of materials, in the descending order i.e. highest value first and the next like that.

(C) Calculate consumption of each item, as a per cent of total consumption of all materials.

(D) Calculate the cumulative consumption, in terms of per cent.

(E) When the total touches around 70%, the first group where concentration is needed, is arrived at.

(F) The following groups are to be calculated for 20% and 10%, accordingly.

An illustration explains the concept, better.

Illustration No. 3

The following is the consumption of Dimpy & Co for different items of inventory. Calculate the items as per ABC analysis and advise the group, where concentration is required most.

Item No.	Annual consumption (in terms of units)	Rate (per unit) (Rs.)	Total Value of Consumption (Rs.)
1.	6,000	100	6,00,000
2.	10,000	65	6,50,000
3.	5,000	50	2,50,000
4.	25,000	2	50,000
5.	4,000	25	1,00,000
6.	15,000	10	1,50,000
7	25,000	6	1,50,000
8	10,000	5	50,000
Total	1,00,000		20,00,000

Solution:

Priority order	Item No.	% each item in total No. of units	Total Value of Consumption (Rs.)	% of each item in total value	Cumulative %
1	2	10%	6,50,000	33%	33%
2	1	6%	6,00,000	30%	63%
3	3	5%	2,50,000	12%	75%
4	6	15%	1,50,000	8%	83%
5	7	25%	1,50,000	8%	91%
6	5	4%	1,00,000	5%	96%
7	4	25%	50,000	2%	98%
8	8	10%	50,000	2%	100%
Total		100%	20,00,000		

Group	Item No.	% Items (in units)	% Items (in value)
A	2,1,3	21%	75%
B	6,7	40%	16%
C	5,4,8	39%	9%

Conclusion

This exercise shows, where concentration is needed.

Group 'A' = This group requires maximum monitoring by the finance manager. By concentrating on three items, out of eight items, around 75% of materials, in terms of value, is monitored, though the materials in number constitutes only 21%. This proves how a lesser amount of concentration can yield better results.

Group 'B' = This is the next group, where concentration is needed. Concentration of two products gives result for controlling 16 % in terms of value, while in number of materials the group constitutes 40%.

Group 'C' = Items 5,4 and 8 requires least concentration as their value is only 9%.

20.10 VED ANALYSIS

The V E D Analysis is used for control of spare parts. A-B-C analysis is concerned with materials and is not totally and properly suitable for spares. So, the spares are divided into three categories, **Vital, Desirable and Essential.** Here, the cost is not of importance but its necessity for the smooth production assumes importance. If the spares are vital, a must for the smooth running, they are to be stored in adequate quantity. Highest importance is to be accorded for this category of spares. If the vital spares, required for uninterrupted production, are not available there would be havoc in production. **The classification has to be done by the technical staff depending on the necessity of spares for smooth running of the production. It is important that no interference is to be made with the classification, made by the technical department.** Vital items have to be kept in high quantity, while essential items are to be kept, in reasonable limits. If the desirable items are readily available on placing the order, no need to keep those items, except a small quantity just to fill in the occasional need.

20.11 PERPETUAL INVENTORY SYSTEM

Normally, stocktaking is done at the end of the year. In perpetual inventory system, the stock taking may be done either regularly or continuously.

The procedure is as under:

(A) Stock taking team selects the storeroom, where stock taking is to be done, on a random basis.

(B) All the bins in that storeroom are checked.

(C) The physical balance in the bin is counted or measured, dependent on the type of the material.

(D) The actual stock is recorded in the sheets provided for this purpose.

(E) There is no prior intimation to the stores department to maintain surprise element.

(F) All the stores are checked, at least, three or four times in a year, on a rotation basis.

(G) There is a surprise element to the stores personnel so that shortages cannot be accommodated from other sources as intimation is given on the day of checking only.

(H) If there is discrepancy between stock ledgers, bin card with physical stocks, they are investigated, immediately, as there could be posting mistakes in stores ledger.

(I) Only after verification and obtaining proper approval, shortages and excesses, if any, are recorded in the bin cards and stores ledger, as physical stocks rule the actual position.

Advantages: These are the following advantages:

1. **Stock records are always updated:** As the inventory taking programme is not known, in advance, all the stores departments keep their bin records and stores ledgers, up dated, always.
2. **Quick calculation of closing stock:** Stocktaking need not be done, separately, at the end of the year. So, closing stock can be valued at the end of the year, without delay, and financial statements like profit and loss account and balance sheet are prepared, well in time.
3. **Check on the Stores personnel, due to surprise element:** Due to the surprise element, there is a regular check on the stores personnel. Stores personnel keep their records, updated. If advance intimation is given, there is a possibility for the stores personnel to accommodate the shortages, from some other sources, for a temporary period. Above all, there would be greater control on theft and pilferage.
4. **Errors and Shortages easily detected:** Due to continuous verification, the mistakes and irregularities come to light, early, for proper control. There would be fear that the defalcations would be detected early. Laxity in control is avoided.
5. **Reconciliation between stores ledger, bin card and physical stocks:** Reconciliation between Stores ledger, bin card and physical stocks occurs, periodically, which otherwise is not done in stock taking, except at the end of the year.
6. **Helping in Formulating purchase policies:** The system is helpful in formulating the purchase policies. Stores personnel know when the materials are needed, which material is more needed by production department. They can provide the information relating to quantity, time and quality of the materials, which helps the management in formulating suitable policies.
7. **Investment in inventory, under check:** The system helps in fixing minimum and maximum quantity so that stock-out situation is avoided, while controlling the excessive maintenance of stocks. This helps in controlling the investment in inventories.
8. **Increases the overall efficiency of organisation:** The system tones up the performance of the organisation on all fronts, resulting in the overall improvement in liquidity as well as profitability.

20.12 JUST IN TIME (JIT) INVENTORY CONTROL SYSTEM

The basic philosophy of JIT is to keep only enough quantity of stock on hand to meet the immediate production requirements. **This concept relies on the suppliers to furnish 'stock' 'just in time', as and when needed.**

Just In Time (JIT) inventory control system aims at eliminating wastages, from every aspect of manufacturing. This was first introduced in Japan in 1950s. Toyota was the first company to practice this technique. Broadly, there are two aspects, (i) Just in time purchasing and (ii) Just in time production. JIT wants to avoid materials for storing and they should be available, only when they are needed to meet the requirements.

Goal of JIT: The conventional inventory control system is totally in contrast to this concept. The traditional system is based on maintaining a healthy level of safety stock to protect against the uncertainties in production. The traditional system has worked well, so long as the interest costs and storage costs have been low. When the carrying cost has gone up, due to high interest rate and other associated costs, the goal of JIT- maintain only essential stocks–is highly relevant, in the current context of competitive environment. **The focus of JIT is to maintain relationship building with suppliers to enable them to purchase right quantities, at right time.** The major thrust is to purchase or produce in response to need, rather than as per plan and forecasts.

Objectives of JIT

(A) Minimum/Zero inventory and associated costs.

(B) Zero breakdown and continuous production.

(C) Manufacturing the right quantity, at right time.

(D) Ensure timely delivery of inputs as well as outputs.

Major Advantages of JIT:

(A) Right quantities are purchased and produced, in right time.

(B) Wastages are eliminated, totally.

(C) Investment in inventory is controlled.

(D) Carrying cost is reduced.

20.13 INVENTORY TURNOVER RATIOS

Inventory turnover ratios indicate the efficiency in using the inventory. Inventory turnover ratio indicates the number of times the stock has turned, over a period of one year. More the number of times, more efficient the organisation is. The inventory conversion period shows the number of days the stock is blocked. A detailed coverage has, already, been made in the chapter dealing with ratio analysis.

Review Questions

1. What is the importance of inventory management? Describe the objectives of inventory management? **(20.1, 20.2 and 20.5)**
2. "There are two dangerous situations that management should avoid in controlling the inventories". Elaborate? **(20.1 and 20.5)**

3. Explain the nature, meaning and benefits of holding inventory? **(20.1, 20.2 and 20.3)**
4. Describe the risk and cost of holding inventories? **(20.4)**
5. Define the economic order quantity? How it is computed? **(20.1 and 20.8)**
6. "The management of inventories must meet two opposing needs". What are they? How a balance is brought between the opposing needs? **(20.1, 20.5 and 20.8)**
7. Define the term inventory control? What are the inventory control systems? **(20.6 to 20.13)**
8. Explain the various tools and techniques used for inventory management? **(20.6 to 20.13)**
9. What is meant by 'Economic order quantity'? What are the various costs, which affect economic order quantity? **(20.8)**
10. What is a selective control of inventory? Why is it needed? **(20.9)**
11. "In inventory management, economic order quantity is achieved, when the total cost is at its minimum for the enterprise". Explain the concept, with suitable pictorial presentation? **(20.8)**
12. Write short notes on the following:
    (A) A.B.C. Analysis **(20.9)**
    (B) Perpetual inventory system **(20.11)**
    (C) V E D Analysis **(20.10)**
    (D) JIT **(20.12)**

Check your Understanding

State whether the following Statements are True or False

1. Inventories serve as a link between production and distribution processes.
2. Stocks of raw materials and work-in-progress are necessary for marketing operations while finished stocks are important for the smooth production.
3. Holding period of raw materials depends on the length of conversion cycle and time needed to replenish them.
4. The primary objective of inventory management is to maintain the right quantity of stocks, at right location and right time to ensure the production uninterrupted and minimise the investment in stock holding.
5. The economic order size of inventory brings a trade off between carrying cost and ordering cost.
6. The costs that are associated with purchasing and placing an order is called carrying costs.
7. Higher the stock holding, larger would be carrying costs and they would be lower if the stocks are lower.
8. The time required to process and execute an order is called lead-time.
9. The total cost is not an aggregate of order cost and carrying cost.
10. ABC analysis is used to manage spare parts, etc.
11. Ordering costs is also known as buying costs.

12. The level when total cost starts increasing, the decrease in average of the order cost is more than offset by the increase in carrying cost, is designated as economic order quantity.

Answers

1. True	2. False	3. True	4. True	5. True
6. False	7. True	8. True	9. False	10. False
11. True	12. True			

21

INTERNAL FINANCING

21.1 INTRODUCTION

A new company can raise finances from external sources, public issue of shares, debentures, term loans and public deposits. It has no other alternative, other than raising funds from external sources. However, an existing company can raise finances from the internal sources, additionally. The internal sources of financing are depreciation and retained earnings.

22.2 DEPRECIATION AS A SOURCE OF FINANCE

Meaning: Depreciation means decrease in the value of the asset due to wear and tear, lapse of time, obsolescence, exhaustion and accident. Even if a new asset is not used, still, the value of the asset decreases. Depreciation may be regarded as the capital cost of the asset, spread over the life of the asset. The typical example is a brand new vehicle. After purchase, if the new car is kept in a garage, even though not used, the value of the asset goes down, significantly. Here, the reason for providing for depreciation is for lapse of time.

Depreciation is a simple book entry. While computing the net profits, depreciation is provided. In fact, company cannot declare profits, without providing for depreciation, as per the provisions of Companies Act. Depreciation reduces the value of the asset and profit of the current year. Depreciation is an operating cost, but there is no outflow of cash. While calculating funds from operations, depreciation is added back to the profits.

Source of Finance: Is depreciation a source of finance? **There cannot be definite 'yes' or 'no'. There is difference of opinion about depreciation as a source of finance.** Operating profits are a source of finance. If depreciation were really a source of finance by itself, any enterprise could have improved its position, at will, simply by increasing the provision for depreciation. Depreciation is a non-cash item of expense. Provision of depreciation does not affect the working capital. Working capital is neither increased nor decreased with depreciation. Working capital remains the same, before and after providing for depreciation. So, it is argued that depreciation is not a source of finance.

Depreciation is a source of finance, under the following circumstances:

Valuation of closing stock: Depreciation finds its way in the valuation of closing stock. Stock is valued at cost or market price, whichever is lower. As depreciation is an overhead, it is included as an element of cost. As closing stock is a part of current assets, working capital, indirectly, increases.

Saving of Funds: In the absence of the asset, it is hired and rent is paid, which is a charge to profit and loss account. Once the asset is purchased for use, there is no rent. **Depreciation does not generate funds, but it definitely saves outflow of funds.**

Reduces Tax Liability: Depreciation reduces taxable profits. So, tax liability is reduced, with the provision of depreciation. To the extent of reduction of tax liability, depreciation saves out flow of funds. However, when the firm is in loss, there is no tax liability. In such a situation, the provision of depreciation does not result in saving of funds.

To sump it up, depreciation is not a direct source of funds, but it can be taken as a source of funds, in a limited sense.

This will be clear through this example.

Illustration No. 1

Income before depreciation is Rs. 1,00,000. Depreciation provided is

Rs. 20,000. Tax rate is 50%. Establish depreciation creates internal source of financing.

Solution:

	Case A	Case B
Income before depreciation	1,00,000	1,00,000
Depreciation provided (A)	---------	20,000
Taxable Income	1,00,000	80,000
Income tax @ 50%	50,000	40,000
Net income after tax (B)	50,000	40,000
Net flow of funds after tax (A+ B)	50,000	60,000

In Case 'A', depreciation has not been provided, while in Case 'B', depreciation has been provided to explain the impact of depreciation on flow of funds. In case of 'B', the net flow of funds is more than by Rs. 10,000. This is due to provision of depreciation, which has been claimed as an expense while computing the taxable profits. On account of this, tax liability has been reduced by Rs. 10,000.

So, depreciation is a source of financing, when the firm makes taxable profits.

22.3 RETAINED PROFITS OR PLOUGHING BACK OF PROFITS

A company can retain a portion of the profits it has earned, without distributing the total profits. This is known as "Retained Profits". It is, strictly, not a method of raising finance but refers to accumulation of profits. **The process of retaining the profits, year after year, and their utilisation in the business is also known as 'Ploughing back Profits'.** Ploughing back of profits is called as 'self-financing'.

According to the latest provisions of the Companies Act, a certain percentage, as prescribed by the central government (not exceeding 10%) of the net profits, after tax, has to be transferred, every financial year, to reserves, before declaring dividend for the year. These profits are transferred to General Reserves, Reserve Fund or Replacement Fund Account.

Need: The need for ploughing back the profits is to meet the following purposes:

1. Replacement of old assets, which have become obsolete.
2. Expansion and growth of business.
3. Purchase of fixed assets as well as meeting the requirements of working capital.
4. Making the company self-dependent and avoiding outside financing. Existing borrowing for working capital requirements may no longer be necessary.
5. Redemption of loans and debentures.

22.4 FACTORS THAT INFLUENCE RETAINED EARNINGS

A number of factors influence the ploughing back of the profits in an organisation:

1. Earning Capacity: Earning capacity plays a key role in deciding the quantum of retained earnings. If the earning capacity of the firm is high, retained earnings also can be high. If a firm does not have adequate earning capacity, there is no possibility for retained earnings.

2. Desire and Type of Shareholders: The policy in respect of retained earnings is largely influenced by the desire and type of the shareholders the company has. If majority of the shareholders are retired people, widows and who look for the dividend as a regular source of income, the shareholders always prefer to have higher amount of dividend. A company having that category of shareholders cannot afford to retain more amounts in the form of retained earnings. A company that has wealthy shareholders may not mind if the company followes the policy of retained earnings.

3. Future financial requirements: The future financial requirements of the company affect the policy of retained profits. If the firm has more expansion plans, the requirement of funds is more. So, company prefers to retain profits rather than distribute higher dividends.

4. Dividend Policy: A company that wants to declare more dividends cannot afford to retain more profits. The dividend policy has a reciprocal relationship with the retention policy. **More profits retained, lesser is the amount of profit available for distribution and vice versa.**

5. Taxation Policy: A high taxation policy of the government leaves lower amount in the hands of the company towards retention of profits. On the other hand, a liberal policy of the government allows more profits to retain as tax liability is less.

22.5 MERITS OF PLOUGHING BACK OF PROFITS

Ploughing back profits has several advantages to the company, shareholders and society.

(i) **Advantages to Company**

(A) **Cushion to Absorb shocks:** Ploughing Back of Profits acts as a cushion to the company. Trade cycles are not uncommon. During the period of depression- time when profits fall- the company with accumulated profits can withstand the shocks, with more preparedness and comfort.

(B) **Economical method of Financing:** Company need not depend upon outsiders for meeting the requirements of expansion and growth. Profits accumulated would be adequate to meet the requirements for expansion.

(C) **Stable Dividend Policy:** Stable dividend policy refers to the regularity in payment of dividends. A company can pay regular dividends, even if the company has not made adequate profits in the lean years.

(D) **Adds to Creditworthiness:** Retained profits help the firm to repay borrowings. Firm can declare itself "No Borrowing Company". This adds to its image in the minds of investors. When the company is not doing well, no financial institution comes forward to lend. Outsiders are just like fair weather friends. In case of need, they may not come to your rescue. A company with accumulated reserves does not require outsiders' assistance for the purpose of borrowing.

(E) **Increased Needs of Inflation:** The economy, presently, is passing through increase in prices. Machinery that has been purchased ten years back for Rs. 1,00,000 is not available for the same price, today. The amount provided towards depreciation is not adequate for the increased cost of the asset. The deficiency in the amount of depreciation can be met out of the retained earnings.

(F) **Redemption of Long-Term liabilities:** With the creation of accumulated profits, firm can redeem the long-term liabilities such as debentures and can reduce the interest burden, which is a fixed commitment.

(ii) **Advantages to Shareholders:**

(A) **Enhances Value of Shares:** Ploughing back of profits enables the company to adopt stable dividend policy. With stable dividend policy, shareholders get dividend, regularly. This increases the market price of the share as investors gain confidence in the company to invest. Shareholders can sell their holding at an increased price in the market and enjoy higher earnings. Additionally, they can offer their higher valued holding as collateral security for any borrowing that is needed, in case of need.

(B) **Safety of Investments:** Investors prefer to invest in those companies that can withstand any shocks the economy gives. Economy is never stable, fluctuations are common. The shares of those companies are treated as safe investments.

(C) **Earning Capacity Enhanced:** With the increased investment opportunities, the company uses the retained earnings and, in consequence, the earnings of the company increase. In turn, the earning per share increases as there is no change in the number of shareholders.

(D) **No Loss of Control:** With retained profits, there would be no need for the company to issue new shares for meeting the additional financial requirements. If the company happens to issue new shares, the existing shareholders have to acquire the new shares to keep the same amount of control. In case, they do not have the funds to invest, there is a threat in respect of loss of control. With retained profits, this danger does not arise, as there would be no need to issue new shares to meet the needs of expansion.

(iii) **Advantages to the Society or Economy**

(A) **Capital Formation:** Retained earnings help the economy as capital formation is made at a higher rate. It is beneficial to the society as well as economy.

(B) **Accelerated Industrialisation:** The capital formation stimulates accelerated industrialization of the economy and nation.

(C) **Higher Standard of Living:** As the economy progresses, productivity increases, which results in reduced prices, better quality of goods and increased employment opportunities. The society, as a whole, would be benefited with higher standard of living.

22.6 LIMITATIONS OR DANGERS OF PLOUGHING BACK PROFITS

Financing through retained earnings is not free from evils or misuse. The demerits can be summarised as follows:

(A) **Manipulation in value of Shares:** Certain managements, having vested interests, may use the concerned companies to their personal advantage. They may skip the dividend to plough back profits. Once the share price falls, with the skipping of dividend, they buy the shares of those companies, at reduced price. They can use the retained earnings to cover their inefficiencies in managing the affairs of the company, by declaring the same amount of dividend. Shareholders may remain under illusion about the continued satisfactory performance of the company as many do not go through the financial statements, but observe the rate of dividend declared by the company. At times, the management can manipulate the value of the shares in the stock exchange, with the retained earnings.

(B) **Creation of Monopolies:** Creation of retained earnings for a long period may create a possibility for the organization to grow into monopoly, with all the evils. The company may expand to such levels that it may become uncontrollable.

(C) **Harmful to Society:** Retained earnings facilitate the organisation to invest in the way it wishes. As retained earnings do not allow the shareholders to have dividends, the shareholders are not allowed to invest in those businesses, which may be beneficial to the interests of the society.

(D) **Dissatisfaction to Small Shareholders:** Excessive retention of profits creates dissatisfaction amongst small shareholders. When the shareholders fall in low-income groups, they get dissatisfied with the retained profits. They are prevented from having dividends to the extent of the retained earnings.

In nutshell, the quantum of retained profits is influenced by the dividend policy pursued by the firm. **The higher the dividend rate, lower is the amount of retained earnings and vice versa.**

Review Questions

1. What is meant by Internal Financing? Discuss the different methods of internal financing? **(22.1, 22.2 and 22.3)**
2. "Depreciation is not a direct source of funds, but can be taken as a source of funds in a limited sense". Explain? **(22.1 and 22.2)**
3. Discuss the role of retained earnings for the development of company, shareholders and society? **(22.3 and 22.5)**
4. What is meant by 'retained earnings'? Discuss the factors that influence retained earnings alongwith their merits and demerits? **(22.3, 22.4 and 22.5)**

Check your Understanding

State whether the following Statements are True or False

1. Depreciation is a non-cash item of expense.
2. Whether the depreciation is a source of finance or not, there is difference of opinion on this important point.
3. Earning capacity plays a key role in deciding the quantum of retained earnings.
4. Ploughing back profits is the same as self-financing.
5. Management of earnings has nothing to do with ploughing back of profits.
6. Capital reserves are built out of revenue profits.
7. As the retained earnings have a distinct merit to the company, the company should not distribute any dividend to its shareholders.
8. There is no gain to the shareholders, if the company adopts the policy of retained earnings.

9. Excessive retention of profits creates dissatisfaction amongst small shareholders.
10. Retention of profits may lead certain companies to become monopolistic.
11. Depreciation reduces taxable profits.

Answers

1. True	2. True	3. True	4. True	5. False
6. False	7. False	8. False	9. True	10. True
11. True				

22

DIVIDEND POLICY

22.1 INTRODUCTION

Dividend is a part of the profits earned by the company, distributed amongst its shareholders. The company distributes only a part of profits, while the balance is retained. The retained portion is known as 'retained earnings'. Payment of dividend is necessary from the viewpoint of the shareholders, as dividend constitutes the current earnings on the shares held by them. Dividend is to be paid to satisfy the expectations of the shareholders. Company cannot afford to ignore the expectations of the shareholders, totally, as the aim of the company is to maximise the value of the shares held by them and, equally satisfy them.

22.2 DIVIDEND POLICY

The term 'Dividend policy' refers to the policy concerning quantum of profits to be distributed as dividend. A company's dividend policy influences the division of its net earnings into two parts: retained earnings and dividend. **What amount is to be retained and how much to be distributed is the essence of the dividend policy.**

Role of dividend in Wealth Maximisation: The dividend policy is of crucial importance to the finance manager since it determines the amount to be distributed to the shareholders and the amount of profit to be retained as earnings for financing its long-term growth. There is a reciprocal relationship between the dividends and retained earnings. If dividend distributed is more, lesser would be the amount of retained earnings. Less dividend payment results in larger retained earnings. **The finance manager takes into account the effect of the dividend decision on the maximisation of the shareholders' wealth, the main objective of the company.** In case, payment of dividend helps in achieving that objective, it is desirable to distribute dividend. In case, dividend payment does not help in achieving the objective, it is desirable to retain the profits for financing investment programme. Thus, the dividend decision is, largely, based on the impact of dividend policy on the value of the firm. The value of the firm is reflected through the share price in the stock market.

Financing Decision: Dividend decision may be treated as financing decision. External equity, raising funds by issue of shares or debentures, could be used for investment purposes. The alternative way is to use profits, company has earned, for investment purposes. In such a case, company distributes the profit only when it does not have the investment opportunity to invest. In other words, company is retaining all the profits for the purpose of investment. **Instead of raising long-term funds, the company is totally using all the profits for the purpose of investment, without distributing any part of profits, in the form of dividend.** Reason may be that the external fund rising is more expensive. The idea behind in using retained profits is to avoid floatation costs, costs incurred at the time of raising capital. Approach of using retained funds for meeling investment needs is adopted when the firms anticipate their growth would be faster. With this approach, dividend decision is viewed as 'residual decision'.

Shareholders' Needs: Shareholders expect return when they invest, in the shares of a company. Dividend received is their current earnings. When a firm opts not to distribute dividend and use the total profits, for expansion, the shareholders can get future dividend and capital gain, when they sell the shares, later. Wealthy shareholders, who are in high tax bracket, may be happy to receive the capital gain rather than the current dividend, if dividend is taxable. But, majority shareholders want current dividend. As and when company enhances the dividend rate, the market price increases. When the company skips the payment of dividend, for one reason or other, the market price would dip with the announcement of the company. **It is necessary to pay a certain portion of profits in the form of dividend to keep the majority of shareholders satisfied.**

Balanced Approach: The management of a company has to strike a balance between the above two conflicting approaches. When the firm increases the retained portion, lesser amount is available for distribution. Firm can use the amount for expansion or other investment opportunities. The use of retained earnings increases the future earnings of the firm. On the other hand, when the dividend is declared, shareholders' current income increases. In consequence, the firm has to avoid some of the investment decisions, immediately. The dividend policy is greatly influenced by the investment opportunities, the firm has. **Every firm has to evolve an optimum way that increases the wealth of the shareholders, which would satisfy the expectations of the shareholders as well as meeting its investment ideas.**

22.3 FACTORS OR DETERMINANTS OF DIVIDEND POLICY

The payment of dividend involves a certain amount of legal and financial considerations. It is difficult to establish a common dividend policy to all the companies, at different periods of time. Dividend policy depends on a case to case basis, depending upon the circumstances of each company concerned. Some of the factors, which influence the dividend policy of the firm are:

(A) Legal Restrictions: A company can declare dividend out of the current profits or past profits only. **Before payment of dividend, provision of depreciation for the current year as well as arrears of depreciation, is necessary.** The other alternative way to pay dividend is out of the monies provided by the government, when there is a government guarantee for payment. Dividend can be paid in cash or by issuing fully paid bonus shares, capitalising the profits. A company cannot pay dividend, which may result into the reduction of share capital.

(B) Shareholders' expectations: The board of directors recommends the payment of dividend. Finally, the shareholders have to approve, as they are the owners of the company. Shareholders can reduce the rate of dividend, in the interests of the company, recommended by the Board. However, **shareholders do not have a right to increase the rate of dividend.** beyond the sate recommended by Board of directions. Shareholders' preference for dividend or capital gains depends on their economic status. If they are wealthy, tax considerations prevail. When the shareholders are people of small means or belong to retired category, they prefer dividend as majority consider it as a supplementary source of earning.

(C) Financial needs of the company: The financial needs of the company may go in conflict with the desires of the shareholders. Firms want to retain while majority shareholders prefer to receive dividends. **It is not wise to retain 100% of profits for investment or distribute the whole profits as dividend.** A mature company can afford to distribute major amount of profits as dividend, while retaining a small part for a few investment opportunities. A growing company prefers to retain a higher part of profits for the expansion. The firm chooses to retain profits, rather than distribute the dividdend to shareholders, looking to the better investment opportunities, it has. However, it is not prudent to the company to retain profits, if its investment opportunities are infrequent. As the investment opportunities are not immediate, the firm invests the retained profits in short-term securities, yielding nominal return. For sometime, the funds may remain idle even. This action will have an adverse impact on reducing the welth of shareholders. It is prudent to the company to retain a part of profits, whether it has investment opportunities or not, to maintain the company a sound and solvent enterprise.

(D) **Liquidity constraints:** The payment of dividend involves cash outgo. Company might have made the profits, but its cash or liquidity position may not be comfortable to make the payment. It is, therefore, necessary for the company to take into consideration the cash and liquid position, both before and after the payment of dividend. If the liquidity problem persists, despite profits, it is desirable for the company to declare stock dividend i.e. issue of bonus shares to the existing shareholders. **The issue of bonus shares also satisfies the existing shareholders, without affecting their liquid resources.**

(E) **Financial Condition and Borrowing capacity:** If a company is already overburdened with debt and is having high degree of financial leverage, it would be vulnerable to the changes in earnings. Financial leverage is a double-edged sword and it affects adversely, when the earnings decrease. It may experience difficulty to pay interest charges, if funds are raised, further, by way of borrowings. It becomes difficult for such a company to raise funds, externally. **A highly leveraged company is, therefore, required to retain the earnings to strengthen its equity to reduce the leverage.**

(F) **Access to Capital Market:** Easy accessibility provides the flexibility to the company to raise the funds required for expansion or growth and distribute dividend from the profits. **If the ability of the firm were greater to raise funds in the market, greater would be the ability to distribute dividends.**

(G) **Restrictions in Loan Agreements: Lenders may put restrictions for payment of dividends, at the time of lending.** This is the case, normally, when the profitability or liquidity position of the firm is not comfortable. At the time of sanction, lenders may put a condition that the company cannot declare dividend so long as the debt-equity ratio of the company is more than 1.5 or the current ratio is less than 2. Once such conditions are incorporated in the contract, companies cannot declare dividend, unless the stipulated conditions are complied with.

(H) **Control:** When additional shares are issued, the existing group may loose control if they do not have the funds to acquire the new shares. They may be afraid that their control may be diluted. To avoid rising of funds by issue of shares, the company may resort to accumulation of profits, by not distributing dividend. In such an event, they may not distribute the dividend and use the profits for fresh investment opportunities, alternatively issue bonus shares. **When bonus shares are issued, every shareholder gets additional shares, so control is not lost.**

(I) **General State of Economy:** The general state of economy influences the firm to distribute dividend or retain profits more. **If the economy is passing through the boom, investment opportunities would be more and so company wants to retain more funds, even though the firm has made more profits.** It is also easy for the company to raise funds during the boom period. During the period of depression, firms retain profits to absorb the future shocks, the economy may give.

(J) **Nature of Earnings: A company having stable earnings can afford to have higher dividend pay out ratio and declare higher dividend.** A company, which faces more competition with unstable earnings cannot declare higher dividend.

22.4 STABILITY OF DIVIDENDS

The term 'Stability' means consistency or lack of variability in the stream of dividend payments. Generally, shareholders prefer stable dividends to the fluctuating ones.

The stability of dividend can take any one of the following forms:

(i) **Constant dividend per share:** According to this policy, the **shareholder is paid a fixed amount per share in the form of dividend.** For example, a company may declare Rs. 2 per equity share having a face value of Rs. 10. Whether the company makes more or less profits, the company declares Rs. 2 per share. In this case, there is no uncertainty about the payment of dividend. People who look for regular returns invest in such companies. As the company does not alter the pay out ratio, irrespective of the level of earnings, the investors look upon this dividend as their regular source of income.

(ii) **Constant percentage or Pay out: Companies pay regularly a fixed portion of their earnings as dividend.** If the earnings increase, the amount of dividend gets increased or vice versa. Suppose, a company fixes a proportion of 25% as dividend, then, the amount would be calculated accordingly and distributed amongst the number of equity shares outstanding. If there is no change in capital, the dividend payable per share is linked, directly, to the increase or decrease in earnings. In case, the share capital increases and the profits do not increase in the same proportion, the dividend payable to each share goes down.

(iii) **Stable dividend plus extra earning per share:** In this policy, the firm maintains stable dividend rate. So, shareholders are assured of the minimum amount of return on their investment. In case, the firm makes abnormal profits, the company shares a part of the increased profits to the shareholders. The extra dividend is made available so long as the exceptional profits continue. Once the abnormal profits disappear, the regular dividend only continues.

Out of the above three policies, constant dividend per share is preferred by the shareholders. Some companies prefer the second method of making payment, constant percentage, as the dividend is correlated to the earnings they make. If their earnings increase, equally, the shareholders would be benefited in the same proportion. In case the earnings fall, the return of the shareholders also falls. But, the shareholders do not prefer this type of payment as there is uncertainty of dividend payment. In case, the firm does not make any profits, there would be no dividend, at all. In the case of stable dividend plus extra earning per share too, there is uncertainty about the amount of dividend receivable. One thing is clear, all shareholders expect dividend, regularly. So, firms try to adopt stable dividend policy to satisfy the shareholders, always.

22.5 SIGNIFICANCE OF STABILITY OF DIVIDENDS

A stable dividend policy is advantageous for the following reasons:

(A) **Desire for Current Income:** There are many investors, such as retired persons or widows who look for regular income to meet their living expenses. To them, a constant or fixed amount of dividend would be supplementing their other resources to meet the expenses, comfortably. Such persons invest in those companies who declare regular and fixed dividends rather than the companies that declare a fluctuating dividend.

(B) **Perception of Stability:** When the company declares regular dividend, investors consider the declaration as a continuation of normal operations. **When the company declares a reduced dividend rate, it looks as signal of dismal future.** Immediately, without the checking the reasons for the reduction in dividend, investors sell the shares of that company in the market. A massive decision of majority selling creates ripples in the market and results in a drastic fall in market price. Such a situation can be avoided by following a consistent dividend payment.

(C) **Requirements of Institutional Investors:** Generally, the public purchases shares of the companies. where the dividend sate is stable. Of late, even educational and social institutions and unit trusts have started investing heavily in private sector companies to improve their earnings. They find the investment as a good avenue to enlarge their earnings, more so, when they are flush with funds. In India, institutional investors like IDBI, IFCI, UTI, LIC and other mutual trusts are the biggest investors. Every company wants to have the institutional investors as their shareholders as it indicates the image, reputation and strength of the company. More so, the investment of the institutional investors is more or less committed. In other words, they look for the long-term growth, not to the immediate short-term gains. **Institutional investors do not, normally, prefer a company that has an erratic track record of paying dividend.** So, a company prefers to follow a stable dividend policy to attract and retain the institutional investors.

(D) **Raising additional finances:** Stable dividend policy paves the easier way for raising the finances. Investors' value consistent dividend paying companies for investment. They recognize the share of such company as quality investment rather than a speculation. Their loyalty and goodwill will be sustained. As and when those companies issue new shares for raising finances, the existing shareholders would be more receptive to invest. Stable dividend policy serves as a way to spread ownership amongst many investors and, in consequence, chance of loss of control is reduced.

22.6 DANGER OF STABILITY OF DIVIDENDS

The greatest danger lies when a company, following stable dividend policy, skips to pay the dividend. Stable dividend paying companies create a 'clientele of shareholders' who depend on them for regular income for living and operating expenses. They consider a 'cut in dividend' as a 'cut in salary'. At times, directors of the company declare even when it is not prudent, not to depress the investors. Consequently, it is desirable to have a fixed rate of dividend on a lower side and declare additional dividend, as and when the companies can afford with the increased earnings.

22.7 FORMS OF DIVIDENDS

Dividend can be classified into three categories depending upon the form in which they are paid. The various forms of dividend are as follows:

(A) **Cash Dividend:** Dividend has to be paid in cash only. In addition to cash dividend, some companies may issue bonus shares also. **As and when dividend is paid, there is outflow of cash.** So, companies should plan for the payment of cash, at the time when dividend is due for payment. Regular dividend paying companies should prepare cash budget to plan for the payment of dividends. If the company does not have enough cash, the company should plan to arrange borrowing to meet the needs. This type of planning is possible with the companies, which have a consistent dividend declaring policy. However, this planning is not possible with companies, which do not have stable dividend declaring policy as they may or may not declare dividend.

Effect on Market Price: After the payment of dividend, there would be reduction both in current assets and balance in profit and loss account or reserves, representing accumulated profits. As a result, the net worth of the company goes down. Due to reduction in net worth, there may be fall in the market price of the equity share. However, the fall in the market price depends on several factors, in particular, the perception of the investors about the future of the company. In share market, the likely future events relating to the company influence the share price in the market, more than the past results. So, it is difficult to state, with certainty that the fall in market price is due to reduction in net worth of the company. This could be one of the factors.

(B) **Bonus shares (Stock Dividend): When the company does not have adequate cash resources, the other alternative to satisfy its equity shareholders is by way of issue of bonus shares.** Issue of bonus shares, in lieu of dividend is not allowed, according to the section 205 of the Companies Act. 1956 Issue of bonus shares represents distribution of shares to the existing equity shareholders. Bonus shares are issued, proportionately, to the shareholders. Bonus shares can be in lieu or addition to the cash dividend. Bonus shares are known as stock dividend, in U.S.A.

Bonus issue can be made out of the profits of the company, alone. Capital Reserves are created by the revaluation of the assets. Such capital reserves cannot be utilised for issue of bonus shares.

When share premium is available in share premium account, that balance is first utiilised towards the share premium on bonus shares. When there is no balance in the share premium account, then the balance in the profit and loss account or reserves is used for the premium on bonus shares.

Impact on company: In what way, issue of bonus shares affects the earnings of the company? After issuance of bonus shares, earning per share gets diluted.

Let us explain with a simple example. An individual has 1,000 shares in a company, while the total number of shares outstanding in the company is 10,000. The company has issued bonus shares in the ratio of 1:1. The individual would get 1,000 shares extra as present holding of one share entitles another share, as bonus share. The earnings of the company are Rs. 50,000. Before issue of bonus shares, earnings per share are Rs. 5(50,000/10,000). The individual would get Rs. 5,000 as dividend. If there is no change in the amount of earnings of the company, the same earnings of Rs.50, 000 have to be distributed by the increased number of shares i.e. 20,000. Now, the earning per share is Rs.2.50 (50,000/20,000). Now, the individual gets Rs. 5,000 as dividend, now (Rs. 2.50 earning per share × 2,000 shares).

Accounting Treatment: When bonus shares are issued, profits are transferred from Profit and Loss account/reserves to equity share capital account. In other words, there is a reduction in the aggregate profits and similar increase in equity share capital account. **Issue of bonus shares does not result in any change in the net worth of the company.** Due to increase in share capital, the number of equity share outstanding gets increased. As there is no change in the investment opportunities to the company, if the same trend of profits continues, there would be no change in the profits. The same amount of profit or earnings has to be distributed by the increased number of equity shares. More so, the ownership in the company does not change. Earlier, the individual has 10% control in the company (1,000/10,000) and even after issue of bonus shares; still, he has only 10% control (2,000/20,000)

Capitalisation of Profits: Issue of bonus shares does not affect the capital structure of the company. In other words, there would be no change in the net worth of the company. Issue of bonus shares results in the conversion of company's profits into equity share capital. This is known as capitalisation of company's profits.

Illustration No.1

The following is the capital structure of Dotty & Ltd.

	Rs.
Equity share capital Ltd. (Rs. 10 face value)	2,00,000
Share Premium	2,50,000
Reserves and Surplus	3,50,000
Total Net worth	8,00, 000

The company issues bonus shares to the existing shareholders in the ratio of 1:10 at the market price Rs. 15 per share.

You are required to show:

(i) the new capitalisation of the company,

(ii) earning per share both before and after the bonus issue, presuming the net earnings as Rs. 80,000 and

(iii) Cherry is holding 100 shares in the above company. What would be the market value of his total holding, before and after the issue of bonus shares?

Solution

Dotty & Ltd. is issuing bonus shares in the ratio of 1:10. It means a shareholder who is having 10 shares, presently, would get one additional share, free of cost.

The share capital is Rs. 2,00,000 and its face value per share is Rs.10. The number of shares in the company is 20,000 (2,00,000/10). As the allotment of bonus shares is 1:10, number of bonus shares issued are 2,000. Bonus shares are issued at the market rate of Rs. 15 (Face value Rs. 10 and premium Rs. 5).

Bonus issue = Number of existing shares 2,000 × 15 = Rs. 30,000

Composition of Bonus Issue

Transfer from reserves to equity share capital 2,000 × 10 = 20,000

Transfer from share premium to share premium 2,000 × 5 = 10,000

(i) The **new capitalisation** of the company will be as follows:

Equity share capital	2,20,000
(22,000 shares of Rs.10 each)	
Share Premium (2,50, 000 – 10,000 + 10,000)	2,50,000
Reserves & Surplus (3,50,000 – 20, 000)	3,30,00
Total Net Worth	8,00, 000

This establishes that there would be no change in the net worth, after the issuance of bonus shares, as the net worth, earlier, too was Rs.8,00,000.

(ii) **Earning per share before bonus issue**

Net Earnings	80,000
Number of Equity Shares	20,000
Earning per share	4

Earning per share after bonus issue

Net Earnings	80,000
Number of Equity Shares	22,000
Earning per share	3.64

It will be seen that as a result of bonus issue, the EPS has decreased from 4 to 3.64. However the total earning of Cherry remains unchanged. Before bonus issue, his earning has been Rs. 400 (100×4). After bonus issue, his earning is Rs. 400 (110×3.64).

(iii) The issue of bonus shares will have no impact on the wealth of Cherry.

The market value of the equity share drops from Rs.15 to Rs. 13.65

(15×3.64 /4) on account of the increase in number of shares. However, the total wealth does not under go any change.

Market Value of Cherry's holding (Before Bonus issue):

Market value of 100 shares = 100×15 = 1,500

Market Value of Cherry's holding (After Bonus issue):

Market value of 110 shares = 110×13.65 = 1,501.50 say = 1,500

22.7 ADVANTAGES OF ISSUE OF BONUS SHARES

Issue of bonus shares is advantageous to the company as well as shareholders.

Advantages to the Company

(A) **Conservation of cash:** Issue of bonus shares helps the company to retain the liquid or cash resources to finance the profitable opportunities for the purpose of investment. The Board of Directors must consider the financial needs of the company and also satisfy the needs of the shareholders. These two objectives are often in conflict, with the payment of dividend. Dividend payment results in satisfaction to shareholders, but leaves reduced balance of liquid resources for investment. Retained profit helps the company to go for investment, but does not give dividend to the shareholders. Receipt of bonus shares satisfies the shareholders, psychologically. So, **issue of bonus shares is a compromise to satisfy these conflicting objectives of the firm.** The company can retain the earnings as well as satisfy the expectations of the shareholders, with the issue of bonus shares.

(B) **Keeps EPS at Reasonable Level:** The company, having a high EPS, may have to face problems from the consumers as well as its employees. Consumers may feel that the company is charging higher price on its products and its EPS, at high level, is a proof to support their thinking. The employees may feel that the company has been earning well, by not passing on the due salaries to them.

By issue of bonus shares, the EPS decreases, due to increased number of equity shares. As the number of shares increases, EPS is reduced to a reasonable level.

(C) **Only means to pay dividend under financial difficulties and contractual restrictions:** When firm experiences liquidity crunch, the only option to replace cash dividend and satisfy the shareholders is by issuance of bonus shares.

Lenders may impose restrictions on the payment of dividend, at the time of sanction of the loan. In such circumstances, company can issue bonus shares, which satisfies the expectations of the shareholders, without violating the terms of the covenant entered into with the lender.

(D) **Wider Marketability of company' shares:** With the increased business, the established companies become highly profitable and so the market price of the shares of those companies would be high. The market price may not be within the range of the ordinary investors.

Once bonus shares are issued, while the wealth of the existing shareholders does not change, the market price decreases and become within the reach of the ordinary investors to buy. The reasonable price of the share provides wider marketability to company's shares. Here, the bonus issue is used as a means to keep the market price of the share, within a desired trading range.

Advantages to the Investors

(A) **High Psychological Value:** News about the issue of bonus share, normally, is well received in the market, unless the market has been expecting more favourable bonus issue, than the one declared. After, the issue of bonus shares, the price has to fall as there would be no change in the earnings, immediately, and the number of shares that claim a share in the earnings increase. However, price of the share may not fall or even increase, when the market expects that the future earnings of the company increase. It is always to be remembered that the market price of a share is influenced by several factors, not one alone, at any time.

(B) **Increase in Future Dividends:** Some companies may maintain a dividend policy of declaring a fixed amount of dividend, per share. When bonus shares are issued, the number of shares held increases. If the company continues the same policy of declaring a fixed amount of dividend per share, the shareholders would be benefited, by larger dividend. If the company has issued 1:2 bonus shares, the shareholder, holding 100 shares, gets 50 bonus shares, increasing the total holding to 150. If the company has been declaring a dividend of Rs. 5 per share, the shareholder, now, gets a dividend of Rs. 750, in place of the earlier dividend of Rs. 500.

(C) **Indication of higher Future Profits:** Normally, companies issue bonus shares, when they expect their future profits would increase. If the future profit does not increase, the earning per share gets diluted, which is not desirable.

(D) **Tax Benefits:** When dividend is taxable, the dividend is included in his ordinary income and tax is calculated. This tax rate, normally, is higher than the rate applicable to capital gains. The incidence of tax on capital gain, profit made on sale of share, is always lower than the normal tax rate. So, the shareholder can sell the share, book the profit and pay a reduced tax. Still, the total holding of number of shares would not decrease if sale is made to the extent of bonus shares received. Shareholder would have the benefit of capital gain, while retaining the same number of shares, held by him, before issue of bonus shares. This situation arises, when the dividend is not tax-exempt.

Presently, dividend income is not taxable. It is not certain, how long the exemption would continue.

(E) **Booking Profit:** Psychologically, some investors do not want to sell their original shares, considering it as their principal. However, they do not mind selling the bonus shares, as they consider bonus shares as windfall gain and not a part of the principal.

Disadvantages of Bonus Issue

Bonus issue has the following limitations

(A) **Shareholders' Wealth remains unaffected:** Bonus shares are considered valuable by a majority of shareholders. But, **factually, there is no change in the wealth of the shareholders, in real terms.** It is simply a division of the existing corporate pie into a larger number of pieces. Shareholders' proportional ownership and control does not change. But, it has a psychological impact on the shareholders.

(B) **Costly to Administer:** Company has to print more share certificates and post them to thousands of shareholders. With the increase in capital, more shareholders may come into existence as the existing shareholders may sell some of the shares. With the introduction of D mat, cost of administration has reduced. However, by and large, in all, the cost of administration increases.

22.8 SHARE SPLITS

A share split is a method to increase the number of shares outstanding, with proportional reduction in the par value of the shares. Suppose the par value of the share is Rs. 10 and the outstanding shares are 10,000, resulting in a capital structure of Rs. 1,00, 000. When the par value share is divided into two, the par value becomes Rs. 5 and the number of outstanding shares increase to 20,000. There is no change in the share capital amount of Rs. 1,00,000.

Reasons for Share Split

The following are the reasons for the split of shares

(A) **To make shares Attractive:** When the price of the share is too high, only wealthy can afford to invest in a company. When the share is split, the market price is divided into the number the share is split into. If the par value of a share is Rs. 10 and its market value of a share is Rs. 10,000, when the share is split into ten parts, the par value becomes Rs. 1 and the market price becomes Rs. 1,000. This price level would be within the range of many to buy.

(B) **Indication of Higher Future Profits:** The share splits are used by the management of the company to communicate to investors that the company is expected to earn higher profits, in future.

Bonus Share Vs Split Share

The features of comparison between bonus share and split share are as under:

1. Issue of bonus share increases the share capital amount while split share does not increase.
2. In case of bonus share, the balance in the profit and loss account, reserves decreases, with a similar increase in the share capital account. Split share does not affect the balance in the profit and loss account, reserves and even share capital amount.

Review Questions

1. Explain the concept "Dividend Policy" and its role in the wealth maximization? **(22.1 and 22.2)**
2. If retained earnings and dividend are conflicting with each other in "Dividend Policy", what approach is to be adopted? **(22.1 and 22.2)**
3. What is meant by 'Dividend Policy' and indicate the factors that a company should consider while formulating the dividend policy? **(22.2 and 22.3)**
4. 'The primary purpose for which a firm exists is the payment of dividend. Therefore, irrespective of the firm's needs and the desires of the shareholders, a firm should follow very high dividend payout'. Explain your reasoning? **(22.1 and 22.2)**
5. What are the factors, which influence the management to pay a certain amount in the form of dividend, every year? **(22.1 and 22.3)**
6. What is the significance of stable dividends? **(22.5)**
7. What are the different payout methods? How the shareholders react to these methods? **(22.7 and 22.8)**
8. What is a bonus issue or stock dividend? Evaluate its advantages with disadvantages? **(22.8 and 22.8.1)**
9. What is a stock split? Why is it used? How does it differ from issue of bonus shares? **(22.9)**

Check your Understanding

State whether the following Statements are True or False

1. The term 'Dividend policy' refers to the policy concerning quantum of profits to be distributed as dividend.
2. Company can ignore the expectations of the shareholders while formulating dividend policy.
3. The essence of the dividend policy is what amount is to be retained and how much amount is to be distributed to the shareholders.
4. Issue of bonus shares results in the conversion of company's profits into equity share capital, which is known as capitalisation of profits.
5. Once bonus shares are issued, there would be change in the net worth of the company.
6. A share split is a method to increase the number of shares outstanding, with proportional reduction in the par value of the shares.
7. Once bonus issue is made, face value of the share capital amount is transferred from the amount of accumulated profits and reserves to equity share capital account.
8. Payment of dividend does not involve any legal considerations.
9. A company should follow an ad-hoc dividend policy.
10. Bonus issue of 1:2 means, two additional shares are issued to the shareholder who holds one share.

11. Issue of bonus shares is a compromise to satisfy the conflicting objectives of the firm as the company can retain the earnings as well as satisfy the expectations of the shareholders.
12. Balance in capital reserves can be utilised for issue of bonus shares.

Answers

1. True	2. False	3. True	4. True	5. False
6. True	7. True	8. False	9. False	10. False
11. True	12. False			

23

FINANCIAL MODELING

- *Introduction*
- *Purpose*
- *Factors affecting financial modelling*
  - *Identifying the Steps needed to reach a Decision*
  - *Relevant data concepts: Future Oriented Revenues and Costs*
  - *Probability and Expected Value*
- *Objective Question*
- *Check Your Understanding*

23.1 INTRODUCTION

Financial modeling is integral to the financial management function. The finance manager, often, is required to evaluate the business wisdom of different alternatives. Through the use of financial models, the finance manager is able to predict outcomes for various alternatives. Different assumptions are to be made for the variables included in the model.

23.2 PURPOSE

In an uncertain environment, many a time, decisions are to be taken. Financial modeling facilitates to predict the outcome based on the presumptions made. It involves consideration of numerous elements including gathering of relevant costs and revenues, with application of probability analysis. **Financial modeling is the foundation for decision-making.**

23.3 FACTORS AFFECTING FINANCIAL MODELING

The different factors that affect financial modeling are:

Identifying the steps needed to reach a decision

Steps commonly recognised to reach a decision include

(A) Obtaining information,

(B) Identifying alternative courses of action,

(C) Making predictions about future costs and revenues,

(D) Choosing an alternative,

(E) Implementing a decision and

(F) Evaluating performance to provide feedback.

Steps necessary to make decisions are generally evaluated, within the context of a decision - making process.

(A) **Determine the strategic issues:** Managers begin the decision–making process by identifying problems and focusing on strategic rather than short-term issues associated with those problems. In other words, strategic issues influence the decision-making process.

(B) **Specify criteria and identify alternative courses of action:** Managers identify multiple criteria, associated with the decision.

1. Short – term Quantifiable Criteria: Managers may initially focus on short – term operational issues that produce quantifiable criteria such as reduced cost, increased profitability, improved return on investment, etc.

2. Non – quantifiable Criteria: Managers must also often focus on non-quantifiable criteria such as shareholder value requirements, required by owners, and quality requirements imposed by customers, etc.

(C) **Perform analysis of relevant costs and strategic costs**

1. Obtain Information

Managers must identify and collect information relevant to the decision criteria.

2. Make Predictions about Future Costs and Revenues Managers must predict the future values of relevant costs and revenues.

3. Consider Strategic Issues

Managers must consider the degree to which quantifiable and non-quantifiable data address the issues associated with the multiple objectives.

(D) **Choose an alternative**

Selection and implementation of the best course of action is the concluding step in the decision–making process. Managers select a course of action that best addresses the strategic objectives identified in the first step, and they then implement the decision.

(E) **Evaluate performance to provide feedback**

The final phase of the decision – making process is to evaluate the effectiveness of the decision in accomplishing strategic objectives as a means of identifying and refining future decisions.

Example:

Select and implement the best course of action: Management decides on outsourcing various functions of Human Resources (including staff training and development and recruiting) as a means of stabilizing the costs of these functions. As a means of maintaining its nurturing objectives, however, management elects NOT to outsource employee relations or performance evaluations.

Evaluate performance: Compare Human Resource costs before and after implementation of the outsourcing. Compare results of employee satisfaction surveys before and after implementation of the outsourcing initiative.

Relevant data concepts: Future oriented revenues and costs: Future revenues and costs are only deemed to be relevant if they change as a result of selecting different alternatives. Those costs and revenues that change as a result of a decision are deemed to be relevant to that decision. Costs that do not change as a result of course of action are not relevant because they do not impact the total costs that result from the decision.

Relevant costs can be, either fixed or variable. Variable costs are more likely to be relevant because they change with production, volume and output,

23.4 PROBABILITY AND EXPECTED VALUE

Probability is the chance that an event will occur. Probabilities are assigned values between zero (0) and one (1). A zero (0) probability indicates that there is no chance the event will ever occur (i.e. an impossibility). A probability of one (1) indicates that the event will always occur (i.e., a certainty).

A. Types of probability

1. Objective Probability

a. Objective probability is based on past outcomes.

b. The objective probability of an event is equal to the number of times that an event will occur divided by the total number of possible outcomes.

Example: The chances of selecting the letter "a" from the 26 letters in the alphabet are 1 in 26 or 1/ 26.

2. Subjective Probability

Subjective probability is based on an individual's belief about the likelihood that a given event will occur. It is estimated based on judgment and past experience of the likelihood of future events.

B. Expected value

Expected value is the weighted-average of the probable outcomes of a variable where the weights are the probability of an outcome occurring.

Calculation of Expected Value

Multiplying the probability of each outcome by its payoff and summing the results find expected value.

Problem: The expected value of profits (E [X]) can be found by multiplying the different possible profit levels by the associated probabilities and summing the results. (e.g., a 5% chance of earning Rs.0 profit, a 10% chance of earning Rs. 100 profit, etc.).

E [X] = (Rs. 0 × .05) + (Rs. 100 × .10) + (Rs. 200 × .35) + (Rs. 300 × .20) + (Rs. 400 × .20) + (Rs. 500 × .10)

E [X] = Rs. 0 + Rs. 10 + Rs. 70 + Rs. 60 + Rs. 80 + Rs. 50 = Rs. 270

Thus, given the possible profit outcomes and their associated probabilities, expected profits are Rs. 270.

Financial modeling is useful in capital decisions. The investment alternatives are many. Cash flows associated with investment alternatives are discounted to the net present value. After comparing them, the choice of investment decision is made.

Illustration:

Gokul Dairy plans to increase the sales and profitability. In its efforts in that direction, it plans to open a depot in an unexplored territory. Each milk packet costs Rs.6 and it sells at Rs.8. The company's policy is to send 100 packets per day to each depot. Any milk packets that are not sold in the depot to the consumers, directly, are sold to the hotels at Rs.5 before the expiry date of sale.

The company assigns the following probabilities of selling the milk packets direct to consumers in the new territory:

Option No.	Number of packets	Probability
1.	60	0.6
2.	100	0.4

Calculate the expected amount of profit?

Solution:

Option No. 1

Only 60 milk packets can be sold to the consumers.

Amount of profit is 60*2 = 120 as the selling price is 8 and cost is 6. However, the remaining packets 40 are to be sold to the hotel at a loss of one rupee per each packet, incurring a loss of rupees 40.

So, total profit gets reduced to Rs.80.

Option No 2

Amount of profit is 100*2 = 200

The expected value of outcome or profit is computed by multiplying the probability of each outcome by its value of profit.

80*0.6 = 48

200*0.4 = 80

Total amount of profit is 48 + 80 = Rs.128

Objective Question

1. What does financial modeling mean? Describe the factors that affect financial modeling?

Check Your Understanding

(A) State whether the following statements are TRUE or FALSE

1. Financial modeling helps the finance manager to evaluate decisions in uncertain environment.
2. Probability theory is used in financial modeling.
3. Financial modeling is not applied in capital decision-making.
4. Costs that do not change are not relevant in financial modeling.
5. Financial modeling is the foundation for decision-making.

Answers

1. True 2. True 3. False 4. True 5. True.

(B) Pick up the right answer

1. In statistical analysis, a weighted-average using probabilities as weights is the

A. Standard Deviation

B. Expected Value

C. Coefficient of Variation

D. Objective Function

2. Assume that Kishore Corp. is considering investing in a project with the following possible outcomes and related probabilities.

Outcome (present value of future cash flows)	Probability of outcome
2,00,000	0.4
3,00,000	0.3
4,00,000	0.3

Calculate the expected return of the investment

A. 2,90,000

B. 9,00,000

C. 5,00,000

D. 2,50,000

Answers

1. (B)

Amongst the four alternatives, only expected value uses probabilities as weights in determining the probability of outcome. Each possible outcome is multiplied by an appropriate weight (probability).

These are then summed to determine the expected value.

2 (A)

24

TEST PAPER-OBJECTIVE QUESTIONS

AIMS AND FUNCTIONS OF FINANCE

State whether the following statements are TRUE or FALSE

1. Financial resources are unlimited and investment opportunities are limited.
2. Issue of bonus shares results in cash outgo from the company.
3. Conversion of profits into equity shares is called capitalisation of profits.
4. Even if the company declares a higher rate of dividend than the previous year, market price of a share may fall, if market expectations are not fulfilled.
5. Unlimited liability is an important feature of a joint stock company.
6. Cash management is an important task of the finance manager.
7. Wealth created by a company is reflected through the market value of company's equity shares.
8. It is the function of finance manager to bring trade-off between risk and return in financial decisions.
9. Finance function is concerned with obtaining funds, in the best mix, and allocating them to specific assets for obtaining maximum market value for the firm's shares.
10. Efficient management of every business is closely linked with efficient management of its finances.
11. The finance manager need not maintain balance between liquidity and profitability.
12. Finance is not in anyway related to other business functions.
13. Financial planning is also a function of finance.
14. Risk and return always go together, hand in hand, however, liquidity and profitability are conflicting decisions.

Answers

1. False	2. False	3. True	4. True	5. False
6. True	7. True	8. True	9. True	10. True
11. False	12. False	13. True	14. True	

OBJECTIVES OF FINANCIAL MANAGEMENT

State whether the following statements are True or False

1. Traditional objective of financial management does not recognise rupee received today is more valuable than a rupee, received later.
2. Profit maximisation, at the cost of social or moral obligations, is a short sighted policy
3. Equity shareholder's wealth maximisation is the final goal of financial management.
4. In the objective of profit maximisation, accounting profits are considered, while cash flows are measured in shareholders wealth maximisation.
5. A finance manager's role is to maintain profitability rather than liquidity.
6. Any financial action which creates wealth or which has a net present worth, above zero, is desirable one and should be undertaken.
7. If two desirable courses of action are mutually exclusive, then the decision should be to do that action, which shows the lowest amount of net present worth.
8. Treasurer is concerned with the planning and budgetary control.
9. Provision of funds, both long-term and short-term, is the main function of treasurer.
10. Treasurer and Controller are designated as Accounts Manager and Finance Manager, respectively, in Indian corporate structure.
11. Accounting and preparation of annual report is a function of controller.
12. Internal audit constitutes the functional area of finance.
13. Financial management applies only to big companies and does not apply to small organisations.
14. Financial management handles merely routine day-to-day matters.
15. Financial management is a profit – extracting device.
16. Knowledge of economics facilitates better understanding of the financial environment.

Answers

1. True	2. True	3. True	4. True	5. False
6. True	7. False	8. False	9. True	10. False
11. True	12. True	13. False	14. False	15. False
16. True				

FINANCIAL RATIO ANALYSIS

(A) Pick the Right Answer

Q.1 Quality of debtors depends upon.

a) Amount of debtors
b) Age of debtors
c) Opening Balance of debtors
d) Average debtors
e) Closing Balance of debtors

Ans. b.

Q.2 A high gross profit Margin, compared to industry, indicates the firm is able to produce at:

a) High Cost
b) Low Cost
c) No indication
d) Same Cost

Ans. b.

Q.3 Calculate return on Capital Employed from the following information.

Net Worth: 6,000; Long Term Liabilities: 4,000; Net Fixed Assets: 7,000; Net Current Assets: 3,000; EBIT: 1,000:

a) 16.5%
b) 10%
c) 33 1/3%
d) 25%
e) 15%

Ans. b.

Q.4 Efficiency of credit division in the firm is judged from:

a) Shorter collection period.
b) Amount of closing debtors
c) Amount of Sales.
d) Amount of cost of sales.
e) Average debtors.

Ans. a.

Q.5 Calculate return on Investment from the following:

Net Fixed Assets: 2,000

Current Assets: 8,000

EBIT: 4,000

Current Liabilities: 5,000

Net Worth: 3,000

a) 200%
b) 25%
c) 20%
d) 33 1/3%
e) 80%

Ans. e.

Q.6 Commercial Bank is basically concerned with while sanctioning working capital limit for a period of one year:

a) Borrower's Profitability
b) Long Term Solvency
c) Short Term Solvency
d) Future Profitability

Ans. c.

Q 7. Calculate collection period in terms of days.

Opening debtors Rs.10, 000
Closing debtors Rs.20, 000

Cost of sales Rs.32, 400
Gross Profit 10%

a) 150
b) 100
c) 20
d) 15
e) 10

Ans. a (Sales are to be arrived at Gross Profit is 1/9 of cost of sales).

(B) Fill up the Blanks

Q 1. ________ outstanding period allowed compared to credit period, shows organisation's efficiency in collection of debtors.

a) Long
b) Short
c) Same
d) None of the factors

Ans. b.

Q 2. Average collection period should be compared with ——— to ensure that the credit policy is neither more liberal nor restrictive.

a) Firm's policy
b) Industry's Average period
c) Past collection period
d) Collection period requested by customers.

Ans. b

Q 3. Net Assets means ——— .

a) Net fixed assets
b) Total of net fixed assets + current assets
c) Total of fixed assets – current liabilities
d) Total of fixed assets + net current assets.
e) Current assets + current liabilities

Ans. d

Q 4. Net Assets equals to ——— .

a) Capital employed
b) Net worth
c) Net fixed assets
d) Net current assets.
e) Long term loans

Ans. a

Q 5. As taxes are not controllable, a better way to calculate profitability is to take — .

a) Profit after tax
b) Profit before tax
c) Operating profit
d) EBDIT
e) Gross profit

Ans. b.

Q.6. Operating profit is equivalent to ——— when it does not have non-operating income.

a) Earnings after interest and taxes
b) Earnings before interest and taxes
c) Gross profit
d) Net profit.

Ans. b.

Q.7. If earnings per share is 15 and dividend per share is 5, Dividend Payout Ratio is ———

a) 15%
b) 5%
c) $33^{1/3\%}$
d) 20%
e) 10%

Ans. c

(C) Choose the Right Answer

Q 1. Calculate operating income from the following

Gross Profit: 20,000; Selling and Administrative expenses: 2,000;
Other income: 1,000;
Interest: 5,000;
Income Tax: 2,000;

a) 18,000
b) 16,000
c) 17,000
d) 12,000
e) 19,000

Ans. a.

Q 2. Calculate EBIT from the following

Gross Profit: 20,000;
Selling and Administrative expenses: 2,000;
Other income: 1,000;
Interest :5,000;
Income Tax: 2,000;

a) 18,000
b) 16,000
c) 17,000
d) 12,000
e) 19,000

Ans. e.

(D) State whether the following statements are TRUE or FALSE

Q 1. In calculating debt–equity ratio, long-term borrowing is included in debt.

Ans. True.

Q 2. Debt–Equity ratio of 2:1 is normally acceptable.

Ans. True.

Q 3. Interest coverage ratio is used to test firm's debt–servicing capacity.

Ans. True.

Q 4. Interest coverage is calculated dividing EBIT by interest.

Ans. True.

Q 5. Activity Ratio indicates firm's efficiency in utilising its assets.

Ans. True.

Q 6. Protecting short-term creditors' interest is long-term solvency of firm.

Ans. False.

Q 7. A highly burdened debt firm often experiences difficulty in raising funds by debt or equity.

Ans. True.

Q 8. If risk is high, return would also be, normally, high.

Ans. True.

Q 9. Debt is always more risky from the firm's viewpoint as interest is to be paid whether there are profits or not.

Ans. True.

Q 10. If the firm's collection period of debtors is high, quality of debtors is low.

Ans. True.

Q 11. A firm need not manage its assets more efficiently to generate more sales.

Ans. False.

Q 12. Net Assets Turnover is also called Capital Employed turnover.

Ans. True.

Q 13. Management, creditors and owners are interested in the profitability of a firm.

Ans. True.

Q 14. Earnings before interest and taxes show direct earnings from operations.

Ans. False. (other income is included in EBIT)

Q 15. Gross profit to sales indicates Gross Profit Margin.

Ans. True.

Q 16. Investment in plant and machinery results in High Profit Margin.

Ans. False.

Q 17. It is the duty of finance manager to initiate action as and when low profit margin, compared to industry, is noticed.

Ans. True.

Q 18. A firm having low net profit margin can withstand better in the face of falling selling prices or rising cost of production.

Ans. False.

Q 19. A high gross profit margin not followed by the high net profit margin indicates falling operating expenses.

Ans. False.

Q 20. Current Ratios do not help in forming a qualitative judgment about the liquidity in organisation.

Ans. True.

Q 21. Total wealth of a shareholder remains the same before or after bonus issue.

Ans. True

(D) Pick up the correct answer

a. Current assets include

a. Trade investments.

b. Machinery.

c. Sundry debtors.

Ans. c

b. Which of the following is a non-current asset

a. Goodwill.

b. Cash balance.

c. Bills receivables.

Ans. a

c. State which of the following is a non-current liability?

a. Mortgage loan.

b. Bank balance.

c. Outstanding salary.

Ans. a

d. Ratio of 'Net Sales' to 'Net Working Capital' is a

a. Working Capital Turnover Ratio

b. Profitability Ratio

c. Liquidity Ratio.

Ans. a

e. Observing changes in the financial variables across the years is

a. Vertical Analysis

b. Horizontal Analysis

c. Inter-firm Comparison.

Ans. b

f. Ratio of Net Profit before Interest and Tax to Sales is

a. Operating Profit Ratio

b. Capital Gearing

c. Solvency Ratio.

Ans. a

g. The statistical yardstick that provides a measure of the relationship between two accounting figures are

a. Current Ratio

b. Accounting Ratio

c. Input Output Ratio.

Ans. b

h. Debt Equity Ratio is a

a. Liquidity Ratio

b. Solvency Ratio

c. Profitability Ratio.

Ans. b

i. The Turnover Ratio helps management in

a. Managing Resources

b. Managing a debt

c. Evaluating performance of assets.

Ans. c

j. Long–term solvency is indicated by

a. Current Ratio

b. Debt/ Equity Ratio

c. Net Profit Ratio.

Ans. b

k. With a share capital of Rs. 1,00,000 (F.V. Rs. 10 per each share), company's profit after tax is Rs. 70,000. After issue of additional share capital of Rs. 5,00,000, proceeds were invested in 10 % govt. securities. What is the revised EPS?

a. 3 b. 5.5 c. 4 d. 2 e. 1

Ans. d

(E). Fill up the blanks

8. Liquid ratio is also known as .... ratio.
9. The liabilities payable in a ....are called current liabilities.
10. Rule of thumb for a current ratio is ....
11. Debt – equity ratio is the relationship between outsiders' funds and ....
12. Operating ratio ....

Ans. (1) Acid-test; (2) Year; (3) 2:1; (4) Shareholders' funds; (5) $\frac{\text{Operating cost}}{\text{Net Sales}} \times 100$;

(F). Identification of Symptoms - Match the following

1. Inability to pay interest.	A. Finished Goods Turnover Ratio
2. Liquidity crisis.	B. Average Collection Period Ratio and age of debtors schedule.

3.	Low capacity utilisation.	C.	Current Ratio and Quick Ratio
4.	Falling demand for the product in the market.	D.	Debtors' Turnover Ratio
5.	Longer period of credit period and overdue debtors.	E.	Return on Equity and Return on Capital Employed Ratios
6.	Return on shareholders' funds being much higher than the overall return on investment	F.	Interest Coverage Ratio
7.	Inefficient collection of debtors.	G.	Inventory Turnover Ratio
8.	Large inventory accumulation in anticipation of price rise in future	H.	Debt Equity Ratio
9.	Inability to pay dues to financial institutions.	I.	Fixed Assets Turnover

Ans.

1– F; 2–C; 3– I; 4– A; 5– B; 6– E; 7– D; 8– G; 9– H

SOURCES AND APPLICATION OF FUNDS

(A) State whether the following statements are True or False

1. Discount on issue of debenture is non-operating charge.
2. Decrease in working capital is source of funds.
3. Flow of funds will not take place, if both the accounts of transaction belong to non-current category.
4. Redemption of debentures is application of funds.
5. Preliminary expenses are operating expenses.
6. Depreciation is a direct source of funds.
7. A company's funds flow may become inadequate because of unsuccessful operations.
8. Basic financial statements (Profit and Loss account and Balance sheet) fail to show the movement and causes of changes in assets and liabilities during the year.

Answer

1. True 2. True. 3. True 4. True. 5. False.
6. False 7. True 8. True

(B). What effect do the following transactions have on net working capital

1. Declaration of dividend Rs.30,000.

2. Payment of dividend Rs. 50,00 that was declared last year.
3. Insurance of 1,000 debentures of Rs. 100 each for Rs. 1,10,000.
4 Payment of Rs. 500 made-on the current debt.

Answers

1. Decrease net working capital by Rs. 30,000;
2. No effect on working capital as provision has been made during last year.
3. Increase net working capital by Rs.1,10,000;
4. No effect on working capital

(C) Pick up the right answer

1. Calculate increase of net working capital if machinery costing Rs. 60,000, which has the book value of Rs. 30,000, is sold for cash of Rs. 45,000:

   A) Rs. 60,000

   B) Rs. 30,000

   C) Rs. 45,000

   D) Rs. 15,000

2. A building stands in the last year's balance sheet at Rs. 30 lakhs has been revalued at Rs.35 lakhs in the current year balance sheet and the gain on revaluation has been credited to Capital Reserve Account. The revaluation gain has to be shown in

   A) Schedule of Changes in Working Capital

   B) Funds Flow Statement

   C) Both in A and B

   D) None of the above statements

3. Debentures of Rs.10 lakhs have been redeemed totally by issue of equity shares at a premium. This transaction of redemption and issue of shares in exchange is to be shown in:

   A) Schedule of Changes in Working Capital

   B) Funds Flow Statement

   C) Both in A and B

   D) None of the above statements

4. Which of the following will result into application of funds?

   (A) Sale of plant

   (B) Issue of share capital

   (C) Payment of Creditors

   (D) Purchase of land

Answers

1. (C) 2. (D) 3. (D) 4. (D)

D. Fill up the Blanks

1. Liabilities are ——— of funds.
2. Assets are ——— of funds.
3. Depreciation is an indirect ——— of funds if the firm makes profits due to reduction of tax payment.
4. A "Where got and where gone statement" shows changes in ——— and ——— between ——— dates.
5. Increase in working capital indicates the ——— of funds and decrease in working capital ——— of funds

Answers

1. Sources 2. Uses 3. Source 4. Assets; Liabilities; Two 5. Uses; Sources

CASH FLOW STATEMENTS

A) Check your statements whether True or False

1. It is mandatory to prepare and enclose cash flow statement in the prescribed format under indirect method for every listed company alongwith the financial statements.
2. Cash flows are classified under two main categories.
3. Cash flow statement is a substitute of a Cash Account.
4. A sound cash position and a sound funds position mean the same.
5. An income statement takes into account both cash as well as non-cash items.
6. Net cash flow means net income of business.
7. Cash flows resulting from the sale of fixed assets are classified as cash flows from financing activities.
8. Net increase or decrease in the long-term funds will not be reflected on the working capital of the firm.
9. In the context of comparison of Cash Flow Statement with Funds Flow Statement, "inflow of cash" results in "inflow of funds" but inflow of funds may not necessarily result in inflow of cash.
10. Cash flow statement is useful for short–term financial analysis.
11. A company should keep large balances of cash in hand so that it can meet all contingencies.
12. Conversion of cash into cash equivalents and vice versa does not constitute cash flows because they are not part of operating, financing and investing activities.
13. Only when Cash Flow Statement is prepared, the real situation about the adequacy of funds, in the sense of cash, is known.

Answers

1. True	2. False	3. False	4. False	5. True
6. False	7. False	8. False	9. True	10. True
11. False	12. True.	13. True.		

(B) Fill in the blanks

1. Cash comprises cash on hand and .... deposits with banks.
2. Decrease in creditors is .... of cash.

Answers

1. Demand 2. Outflow

(C) Choose the right answers

1. While preparing cash flow statement, decrease in the amount of bills receivable results in:
   (a) Increase in cash; (b) Decrease in cash; (c) No change in cash
2. While preparing cash flow statement, increase in the amount of debtors has to be shown as:
   (a) Decrease in cash; (b) Increase in cash; (c) No change in cash

Answers

1. (a) 2. (a)

COST-VOLUME PROFIT ANALYSIS

A) State whether the following statements are True or False

1. Contribution covers total fixed costs and profit.
2. In break-even analysis, unit fixed cost decreases as and when the volume of production decreases.
3. In break-even analysis, fixed costs are assumed to be constant.
4. Break-even analysis and CVP analysis are one and the same.
5. CVP analysis studies the relationship of cost-volume-profit at different levels of output.
6. Profit at various levels of output cannot be determined by break-even analysis.
7. Sales beyond break-even point represents margin of safety.
8. Margin of safety is an important indicator of the strength of business.
9. The break-even analysis is a useful device of profit planning.
10. In cash break-even analysis, depreciation is eliminated from fixed costs and variable costs.
11. The effect of a price reduction is always to reduce P/V Ratio that raises break-even point and shortens margin of safety.

Answers

1. True	2. False	3. True	4. False	5. True
6. False	7. True	8. True	9. True.	10. True
11. True				

(B) From the following choose the most appropriate answer

1. When fixed cost is Rs.20,000 and P/V Ratio is 50%, the break-even point is
   A) 40,000 B) 20,000 C) 10,000
2. Contribution Margin is also known as
   A) Gross Profit B) Marginal Income C) Net Income
3. When the Profit-Volume Ratio is 30% and sales value is Rs.20,000, the contribution is
   A) 14,000 B) 6,000 C) 20,000 D) None of these
4. When sales are Rs. 1,00,000, fixed cost Rs.10,000, P/V Ratio 40%, the amount of profit is
   A) 40,000 B) 30,000 C) 10,000
5. When the margin of safety is 60% and P/V Ratio is 20%, profit is
   A) 12% B) 40% C) 80% D) None of these

Answers

1. (A) 2. (B) 3. (A) 4. (B) 5. (A)

Formula is

$$\text{Margin of Safety} = \frac{\text{Net Profit}}{\text{P/V Ratio}}$$

Net Profit = Margin of Safety × P/V Ratio

LEVERAGES

A) Check whether the following statements are True or False

1. There would be no operating leverage, if there is no fixed cost to a firm.
2. Financial leverage is the use of fixed return securities only.
3. If a firm is able to earn on borrowed funds more than the interest it pays, the return to owners will be magnified.
4. Operating Leverage refers to the use of fixed costs in the operation of a firm.
5. A management would be considered too cautious if both operating and financial leverage are kept at a high level.
6. It is risky to have a high operating leverage as even a slight fall in sales results in a disproportionately large fall in profits.
7. Dividend on preference share capital is ignored while calculating financial leverage.
8. Composite leverage explains change in taxable income on account of change in sales.
9. High operating leverage with high financial leverage constitutes a large risky situation.

10. Every firm must make all possible efforts to combine the operating and financial leverage to suit its risk-bearing capacity.
11. A totally equity financed firm does not have financial risk.
12. Combined leverage is the sum of operating leverage and financial leverage.

Answers

1. True	2. False	3. True	4. True	5. False
6. True	7. False	8. True	9. True	10. True
11. True	12. False.			

B) Pick up the right answer

1. Fixed-return securities include equity share capital

   A) Yes B) No C) Not relevant

2. Preference shares always form part of debt while calculating financial leverage.

   A) Yes B) No C) Not relevant

3. Net equity returns are measured on the basis of net earnings after interest and taxes.

   A) Yes B) No C) Not relevant

4. The objective of 'Trading on equity' is to give ... ..rate of return to the equity shareholders ..... the general rate of earning on capital employed in the company to compensate them for the risk they bear.

   A) equal, similar to B) high, above C) low, below

5. The combined effect of operating leverage and financial leverage can be seen by .... of the two, which becomes combined leverage.

   A) Addition B) Subtraction C) Multiplication

Answers

1. (B) 2. (B) 3. (A) 4. (B) 5. (C)

C) Fill in the blanks

1. It is risky to have both operating leverage and ......leverage at a high level.
2. An ideal situation would be to keep .... leverage high and .... leverage low.
3. Trading on equity implies having a .... debt-equity ratio.
4. Financial Leverage ________.

Answers

1. Financial 2. Financial, operating 3. High 4. $\frac{\text{Precentage Change in EPS}}{\text{Percentage Change in EBIT}}$

TIME VALUE OF MONEY

(A) State whether the following statements are True or False

1. Annuity tables can be used for calculating present value and future value of all types of cash flows.
2. Total amount of interest will be one and the same when compounding of interest is made quarterly, half yearly or annually.
3. While calculating simple or compound interest, the basic amount on which interest is calculated remains one and the same.
4. With infinitely increasing time periods and interest rates, annuity discount factor does not increase proportionately.
5. Annuity is a series of equal payments lasting for a specified duration.
6. If cash flows occur at the beginning of the year, the annuity is called annuity due.
7. In the compounding technique, the interest earned on the initial principal becomes a part of principal, at the end of the compounding period.
8. Compounding technique and discounting technique are one and the same.
9. The present value approach is based on the concept that money has opportunity cost for money lying idle.
10. Annuity can be a receipt or payment, which should be fixed.
11. Present value of series of cash flows and future value of series of cash flows is same.

Answers

1. False	2. False	3. False	4. False.	5. True
6. True	7. True	8. False	9. True	10. True
11. False				

(B) Select the most appropriate one

1. Multiple compounding means
   (A) calculating interest in different methods
   (B) interest is compounded more than once in an year
   (C) Comparing simple interest and compound interest
2. Time preference for money is relevant because
   (A) money has value for time
   (B) money is preferred for every purchase
   (C) money is needed for every necessity
3. Rule of 72 is useful to calculate period required for ..... principal amount, if interest rate is known.
   (A) doubling (B) multiplying (C) dividing

4. The time preference for money is generally expressed by ....
   (A) interest rate (B) discount rate (C) compound rate
5. Interest rate covers
   (A) Risk-free rate (B) Risk premium (C) Risk-free rate + Risk premium
6. Composition of funds is important to increase ....while minimising risk of the firm.
   (A) profitability (B) liquidity (C) liquidity and profitability
7. Financial structure refers to ....
   (A) short-term resources (B) all the financial resources (C) long-term resources

Answers

1. (B) 2. (A) 3. (A) 4.(A) 5. (C) 6. (A) 7. (B)

INVESTMENT AND CAPITAL STRUCTURE

State whether the following statements are True or False

1. Capital structure refers to the break up of the securities raised by the company.
2. Dividend paid on equity is allowed for income tax.
3. The optimum capital structure is defined as that relationship of debt and equity which maximises the value of the company's equity share in the stock exchange.
4. It is desirable to have similar capital gearing during the periods of inflation and depression.
5. The capital structure decision is a continuous process and has to be taken as and when firm needs additional finances.
6. If preference share capital and other fixed interest bearing loans are less than equity share capital and free reserves, the company is said to be highly geared.
7. Capital gearing ratio analyses the capital structure of the company.
8. Cost of preference share capital is less than the cost of long-term debt.
9. The capital gearing in the financial structure of a business is compared with the gears of an automobile.
10. A high-geared firm is desirable during the period of depression.
11. Increased use of debt increases the financial risk of equity shareholders.
12. The term 'capital structure' also includes the financial structure.

Answers

1. True	2. False	3. True	4. False	5. True
6. False	7. True	8. False	9. True	
10. False	11. True	12. False		

INSTRUMENTS OF LONG -TERM FINANCE

State whether the following are True or False

1. If the company has made sufficient profits, the equity shareholders can, legally, compel the company to declare, at least, some dividend.
2. As and when a public limited company wants to issue fresh equity shares, they can be offered as per the choice of the management.
3. Equity shareholders cannot increase the rate of dividend but they can reduce the dividend, recommended by Board of Directors, in the interests of the company.
4. Non-payment of preference dividend does not compel the company to go into liquidation and dividend is also not tax deductible.
5. Debentures do not carry any voting rights.
6. An alternative form of debenture is Bond, in India.
7. Long term financing is made through term loans for expansion, modernisation and diversification, which is also called project financing.
8. While sanctioning term loans, during moratorium period, payment of interest as well as installment is not suspended.
9. A company negotiates term loan for project finance with the term lending institution, directly, which is called Private placement.
10. The new name for ordinary shares is Equity shares.
11. There are two types of corporate securities - ownership securities and creditorship securities.

Answers

1. False	2. False	3. True	4. True	5. True
6. True	7. True	8. False	9. True	10. True
11. True				

COST OF DIFFERENT SOURCES OF RAISING CAPITAL

State whether your statements are True or False

1. Cost of capital is the minimum rate of return, which will maintain the market value of the shares, at its present level.
2. Cost of capital helps the management in taking decisions about the choice of capital expenditure projects in capital budgeting.
3. Cost of capital is not cost to the firm, in fact, it is the minimum rate of return that the investors require.
4. Cost of capital is the maximum rate of return expected by its investors.

5. The opportunity cost is the rate of return foregone on the next best alternative investment opportunity of comparable risk.
6. Cost of capital is a cut-off or discount rate for evaluating investment projects.
7. When the debenture is issued at par and to be redeemed at par, the cost of debt, simply, is the contractual rate of interest.
8. The cost of equity capital is a function of the expected return by its investors.
9. Cost of capital is a compensation for time and risk.
10. Cost of capital serves as cut-off rate for capital investment decision.
11. Preference shares carry fixed dividend but the dividend is subordinated to interest on debentures.
12. Effective cost of debt for a loss making firm and profit making firm is same.
13. Cost of retained earnings is the return foregone by the investors on the amount of profit not distributed to them and kept in the business.

Answers

1. True	2. True	3. True	4. False	5. True
6. True	7. True	8. True	9. True	10. True
11. True	12. False	13. True		

WEIGHTED AVERAGE COST OF CAPITAL

State whether your statements are True or False

1. Overall cost of capital is used as the discount rate or cut-off rate in evaluating the capital budgeting proposals.
2. The cost of each source of capital is known as specific cost of capital.
3. In common parlance, capitalisation refers to the par value of securities i.e. shares and debentures plus any other reserves kept to meet the long-term and permanent needs of the company.
4. According to Earnings theory of capitalisation, the capitalisation of a company depends upon its earnings and the expected fair rate of return on its capital invested.

Answers

1. True	2. True	3. True	4. True

VALUATION AND RATES OF RETURN

State whether the following statements are True or False

1. Interest rate is also called coupon rate.
2. Dividend capitalisation model is a basic valuation model for equity shares valuation.

3. Securities like equity shares, preference shares and debentures are real assets.
4. The fundamental concepts of risk and return determine the value of real assets as well as financial assets.
5. To arrive at the book value per share, the net worth is to be divided by the number of equity shares outstanding.
6. Value is what an asset is worth as on date, in terms of potential benefits.
7. In times of inflation, replacement value is always lower than the book value of the asset that is already depreciated.
8. When the business is a going concern, the values of the assets that can be realised are, normally, lower than the liquidation value.
9. What the market considers more important is about the potentialities of the share, in future, rather than the condition of business today.
10. Government sector companies or public sector companies, normally, issue bonds while private sector companies issue debentures.
11. In respect of bonds, interest is always paid at the time of redemption.
12. The risk in holding a government bond and debenture issued by a company is one and the same.

Answers

1. True	2. True	3. False	4. True	5. True
6. True	7. False	8. False	9. True	10. True
11. False	12. False			

BUDGETING AND BUDGETARY CONTROL

State whether the following Statements are True or False

1. Budgetary control is not one time action, but a continuous process.
2. Budget acts as a barometer of a business as it measures the success from time to time, against the standard set for achievement.
3. A budget centre is that part of organisation for which the budget is prepared.
4. Every one in the enterprise is aware of long-term budgets the enterprise prepares.
5. Budgets can be classified on the basis of time, function and flexibility.
6. The master or Final Budget is a summary budget, which incorporates all functional budgets, in a summarised form.
7. Fixed budget is prepared on the basis of fixed level of activity.
8. Flexible budgets are prepared when the level of activity can be estimated with accuracy.
9. The term 'Zero Base Budgeting' means starting from the scratch.
10. A flexible budget is appropriate if the demand of the products is stable.

11. Budget centres are necessary for the purpose of ascertaining cost, performance and its control.
12. ZBB has scope in flexible budgeting.

Answers

1. True	2. True	3. True	4. False	5. True
6. True	7. True	8. False	9. True	10. False
11. True	12. False			

METHODS OF CAPITAL BUDGETING

State whether the following Statements are True or False

1. Pay back period method is the simplest Capital budgeting technique.
2. Internal rate of return method recognises the principle of shareholders' wealth maximisation.
3. The net present value technique does not recognises the time value of money.
4. The NPV method cannot be used to select between mutually exclusive projects.
5. The virtue of the IRR rule is that it does not require the computation of the required rate of return.
6. In order to take a decision about the acceptance or rejection of the project, the IRR is to be compared with the required rate of return, which is also known as cut-off rate or hurdle rate.
7. For calculating proper IRR rate on a trail and error method, if the calculated present value of the discounted inflows is higher than the present value of the outflows, a lower discount rate should be tried.
8. NPV is a discounted technique while IRR is not a discounted technique in evaluating capital budgeting decisions.
9. On account of simplicity, many firms follow pay back method as an Accept or Reject criterion as well as a method for ranking projects.
10. Capital expenditure decision like replacement and modernisation reduces costs and increases profitability.
11. Independent investments do not compete with each other and serve different purposes.
12. The essential property of a sound investment evaluation criterion is that it should maximise the shareholders' wealth.
13. In contingent investments, the choice of one investment necessitates undertaking more than one or more investments.
14. Payback method is not useful when the cash flows are equal or unequal.

Answers

1. True	2. True	3. False	4. False	5. True
6. True	7. False	8. False	9. True	10. True
11. True	12. True	13. True	14. False	

SHORT-TERM FINANCING AND INVESTMENTS

State whether the following are true or false

1. Accrued expenses represent spontaneous and interest-free source of financing.
2. Cash credit is not the common form of financing for meeting working capital requirements.
3. The greatest convenient feature of the advance against bills of exchange is its self-liquidating character.
4. Issue of commercial paper is not governed by Reserve Bank of India.
5. Company has the option to raise short-term finance through cash credit and issue of commercial paper but the aggregate can not exceed the total of permissible bank finance.
6. Low-risk securities always earn lower return.
7. Commercial papers are secured securities issued by highly creditworthy companies.
8. The govt. companies also accept public deposits.
9. Interest on public deposits is exempted from income-tax.
10. There is no ceiling on the amount a company can accept in the form of public deposits.

Answers

1. True	2. False	3. True	4. False	5. True
6. True	7. False	8. True	9. False	10. False

MANAGEMENT OF WORKING CAPITAL

State whether the following Statements are True or False

1. In a broader sense, working capital refers to gross working capital and in narrower sense, it is net working capital.
2. The basic objective of working capital management is to manage firm's current assets and current liabilities in such a way that a satisfactory level of working capital is maintained in the firm.
3. A company can afford to have inadequate working capital.
4. The terms "permanent working capital" and "core current assets" have the same meaning.
5. The cash inflows and cash outflows can be synchronized with absolute matching.
6. The need for working capital does not vary with changes in the volume of production or sales.

7. Longer the process period of manufacture, larger is the amount of working capital needed.
8. The rate of return on investments increases with the shortage of working capital.
9. Net working capital is the excess of current liabilities over current assets.
10. Depreciation is to be excluded from the expenses in computing cash operating cycle.
11. Efficiency of working capital management is evaluated in terms of actual days, against the original operating cycle planned or anticipated.

Answers

1. True	2. True	3. False	4. True	5. False
6. False	7. True	8. False	9. False	10. True
11. True				

RECEIVABLES MANAGEMENT

State whether the following statements are True or False

1. Receivables are liabilities.
2. It is not better to accept minimum bad debts and maximise profits.
3. Credit terms include period of credit and cash discount granted to the customers for early payment.
4. In practice, firms follow credit policies ranging between stringent and lenient policies.
5. If goods are perishable, longer payment period is a desirable receivable management policy.
6. Trade off between profitability and liquidity is important for achieving optimum amount of receivables.
7. When the firm sells 2/30, net 60, it means 2% cash discount would be allowed, if payment is made within 60 days.
8. The objective of receivables management is to make a sound investment in debtors till such a point where the cost of investment is less than the return on investment.

Answers

1. False	2. False	3. True	4. True	5. False
6. True	7. False	8. True		

INVENTORY MANAGEMENT

State whether the following Statements are True or False

1. Minimum stock level is the quantity of materials, which must be kept in stock, at all times.
2. In inventory Management, Economic Order Quantity is achieved, when the total cost is at its minimum for the enterprise.
3. The essence of selective control of inventory management is to allocate the importance of control to goods based on the cost composition.

4. In A.B.C. analysis, the cost is not of importance but its necessity for the smooth production assumes importance.
5. Ved analysis is concerned with the control of spares.
6. In perpetual inventory system, the stock taking is done at the end of the year.
7. Efficient inventory management requires ineffective control system.
8. A proper inventory control system helps the enterprise in solving the problems of liquidity, eliminating excessive stocks, and achieving increased profits, with substantial reduction in working capital.
9. The basic philosophy of JIT is to keep only enough quantity of stock on hand to meet the immediate production requirements.
10. Inventory management is essential to every organization because investments in stocks are high.

Answers

1. True	2. True	3. True	4. False	5. True
6. False	7. False	8. True	9. True	10. True

DIVIDEND POLICY

State whether the following Statements are True or False

1 Dividend has to be paid in cash only.
2. Issue of bonus shares affects the capital structure of the company.
3. Stock dividend affects liquidity position of the company.
4. The issue of bonus shares amounts to a corresponding increase in the paid up capital of the company.
5. The part of profits distributed among the shareholders of a company is known as dividend.
6. Premium received in cash can be used for issue of bonus shares.
7. The bonus issue is allowed out of free reserves of the company.
8. Bonus issue is made to reduce the market value of the shares of the company so that the price of the share becomes within the range of the ordinary investor to invest.
9. As and when company enhances the dividend rate, normally, the market price increases.
10. A company cannot pay dividend, which may result into the reduction of share capital.
11. Issue of bonus shares results in loss of control to the existing group.
12. Normally, after issue of bonus shares, market price of the company's share falls.

Answers

1. True	2. False	3. False	4. True	5. True
6. True	7. True	8. True	9. True	10. True
11. False	12. True			

INTERNAL FINANCING

State whether the following Statements are True or False

1. A new company can finance its assets by ploughing back of profit.
2. Retained earnings provide a cushion to the company to absorb the shocks, the economy may create.
3. Ploughing back of profits results in dilution of control, which is not beneficial to the existing shareholders.
4. Ploughing back of profits is a tool to the company to adopt stable dividend policy.
5. Excessive ploughing back of profits, without distributing any dividend, does not create any dissatisfaction to the existing shareholders.
6. Ploughing back of profits helps to improve the earning per share.
7. Ploughing back of profits is also known as retention of profits.
8. Ploughing back of profits enhances value of shares.
9. Provision of depreciation reduces taxable profits and becomes a source of funds, in a limited sense.

Answers

1. False	2. True	3. False	4. True	5. False
6. True	7. True	8. True	9. True	